ARTIFICIAL INTELLIGENCE
AND
COGNITIVE SCIENCES

Proceedings in nonlinear science

Published in association with the Centre for Nonlinear Studies, The University, Leeds LS2 9NQ, UK

Series co-ordinator: Arun V. Holden

Also in this series:

Structure, coherence and chaos in dynamical systems

Editors: Peter L. Christiansen and Robert D. Parmentier

Other volumes are in preparation

05/07

UNIVERSITY OF
WOLVERHAMPTON

Harrison Learning Centre
City Campus
University of Wolverhampton
St Peter's Square
Wolverhampton WV1 1RH
Telephone: 0845 408 1631

2 5 NOV 2013

Telephone Renewals: 01902 321333 or 0845 408 1631
Please RETURN this item on or before the last date shown above.
Fines will be charged if items are returned late.
See tariff of fines displayed at the Counter.   (L2)

ARTIFICIAL INTELLIGENCE
AND
COGNITIVE SCIENCES

Edited by

J. Demongeot, T. Hervé, V. Rialle *and* C. Roche

Manchester University Press
Manchester and New York

distributed exclusively in the USA and Canada
by St. Martin's Press

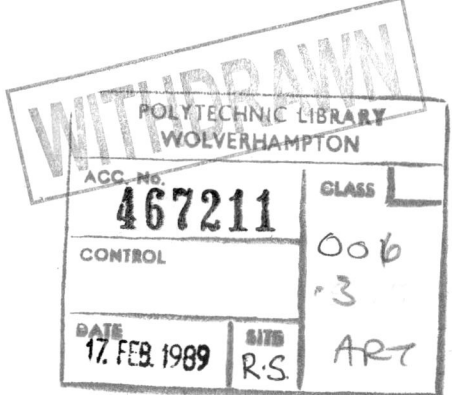

Published by
Manchester University Press
Oxford Road, Manchester M13 9PL, UK
and Room 400, 175 Fifth Avenue, New York, NY 10010, USA

Distributed exclusively in the USA and Canada
by St. Martin's Press Inc.,
175 Fifth Avenue, New York, NY 10010, USA

British Library cataloguing in publication data
Artificial intelligence and cognitive
   sciences. – (Proceedings in nonlinear
   science).
   1. Artificial intelligence
   I. Demongeot, J. (Jaques) II. Series
   006.3

Library of Congress cataloging in publication data applied for

ISBN 0-7190-2679-2 *hardback*

Printed in Great Britain
by Biddles Ltd, Guildford and King's Lynn

Contents

Preface

In medical decision-making, as in many other fields of application of artificial intelligence (A.I.), we face the double problem of finding :
- the appropriate representation of knowledge
- the optimal decision mechanism.

On the one hand, specialists of A.I. are defining object-oriented representations of knowledge and object-oriented languages. On the other hand, experts of neurosciences are intensively studying sensory representation, memorization and pattern matching processes. Our aim in this volume is to gather together these different communities in order to present the state of the art, to facilitate exchange of experience and to compare A.I. tools created in computer science to natural intelligence (N.I.) homologous mechanisms discovered in neurosciences.

The volume contains most of the lectures given at the Conference "A.I. and Cognitive Sciences" held in Grenoble from the 18th to the 20th February 1987. This meeting was sponsored by :
- the Centre Mondial Informatique Ressource Humaine (Paris)
  (Former President : Pr. Funck Brentano)
- Pôle Rhône-alpin de Génie Biologique et Médical (Lyon) (President : Pr. Collombel)
- Société Française de Biologie Théorique (President : Pr.Thom)
- Institut de la Machine Intelligente (Directeur : Pr. Della Dora).

The proceedings have been divided into three parts. The first part is devoted to the object-oriented representations and languages; the second part comprises those contributions which deal with the representation of neural information and pattern matching in neurosciences; the last part groups papers about medical decision making and expert systems in biomedicine. Each author has made an effort to be understandable by other communities who assisted the meeting and we hope that the final result will serve biomedical as well as computer science readers.

Special thanks are due to C. Benchetrit for the typing and to R. Coleman and Y.E. Yarker for the careful reading of the manuscripts.

Grenoble, March 1988.

J. Demongeot
T. Hervé
V. Rialle
C. Roche

Contributors

Abdi, H.
Laboratoire de Psychologie
Ancienne Faculté
36, rue Chabot-Charny
21000 Dijon
France

Albert, P.
ILOG
2, avenue Galliéni
34250 Gentilly
France

Aubas, P.
Département de l'Information Médicale
Hôpital Lapeyronie
CHRU de Montpellier
34059 Montpellier
France

Axelrad, H.
Laboratoire de Physiologie
CHU Pitié-Salpêtrière
91, Bd de l'Hôpital
75634 Paris Cédex 13
France

Berrut, C.
Laboratoire IMAG de 'Génie
Informatique'
BP 68
38402 Saint Martin d'Hères
France

Beuscart, R.
CERIM - MCU
Faculté de Médecine de Lille III
Place de Verdun
59045 Lille Cédex
France

Beuscart-Zéphir, M.C.
CERIM - MCU
Faculté de Médecine de Lille III
Place de Verdun
59045 Lille Cédex
France

Borst, F.
Hôpital Cantonal de Genève
Division Informatique
CH - 1211 Genève 4
Switzerland

Caelen, J.
Laboratoire ICP
Institut National Polytechnique de
Grenoble
46, avenue Félix Viallet
38031 Grenoble Cédex
France

Carré, B.
LIFL - CNRS UA 369
Université des Sciences et Techniques de
Lille - Flandres - Artois
Cité Scientifique - Bât. M3
59655 Villeneuve d'Ascq, Cédex
France

Cervantes, O.
Laboratoire ICP
Institut National Polytechnique de
Grenoble
46, avenue Félix Viallet
38031 Grenoble Cédex
France

Chauvet, J.M.
Neuron Data Incorporation
29, rue Dareau, 75014 Paris
France

Chein, M.
Centre de Recherches en Informatique de
Montpellier
860, rue de Saint Priest
34000 Montpellier
France

Chiaramella, Y.
Laboratoire IMAG de 'Génie
Informatique'
BP 68
38402 Saint Martin d'Hères
France

Cinquin, P.
Département de Mathématiques,
Statistiques et Informatique Médicale and
TIM3-IMAG
Faculté de Médecine
38700 La Tronche
France

Cogis, O.
Centre de Recherches en Informatique
de Montpellier
860, rue de Saint Priest
34000 Montpellier
France

Comby, S.
Laboratoire de Biométrie
Université Claude Bernard
43, Bd du 11 Novembre 1918
69622 Villeurbanne Cédex
France

Comyn, G.
IUT Département Informatique, BP 179
59655 Villeneuve d'Ascq Cédex
France

Dang, W.
Laboratoire de Recherches en
Informatique
490, Université de Paris-Sud
91405 Orsay Cédex
France

Demongeot, J.
Département de Mathématiques,
Statistiques et Informatique Médicale
and TIM3-IMAG
Faculté de Médecine
38700 La Tronche
France

Duhamel, A.
CERIM
Faculté de Médecine de Lille III
Place de Verdun
59045 Lille Cédex
France

Dujols, P.
Centre de Recherches en Informatique
de Montpellier
860, rue de Saint Priest
34000 Montpellier
France

Ferber, J.
LAFORIA
Université de Paris IV, T 45-46
4, place Jussieu
75252 Paris Cédex 05
France

Fernandez, Y.
Laboratoire de la Communication Parlée
INPG
46, avenue Félix Viallet
38031 Grenoble Cédex, France

Flandrois, J.P.
Laboratoire de Bactériologie
Faculté de Médecine de Lyon Sud
CHLS
69310 Pierre-Bénite
France

Froment, J.C.
Service de Radiologie
Hôpital Neurologique et Neurochirurgical
BP Lyon Montchat
69334 Lyon Cédex 3
France

Garbay, C.
Laboratoire TIM3
BP 68
38402 Saint Martin d'Hères
France

Guérin, A.
Laboratoire de traitement d'image et de
reconnaissance des formes
INPG
46, avenue Félix Viallet
38031 Grenoble Cédex
France

Hérault, J.
Laboratoire de traitement d'image
et de reconnaissance des formes
INPG
46, avenue Félix Viallet
38031 Grenoble Cédex
France

Hervé, T.
Laboratoire de la Communication Parlée
INPG, 46, avenue Félix Viallet
38031 Grenoble Cédex
France

Jung, S.
CRIN, Campus Universitaire, BP 239
54506 Vandœuvre les Nancy
France

Jutten, C.
Laboratoire de traitement d'image
et de reconnaissance des formes
INPG
46, avenue Félix Viallet
38031 Grenoble cédex
France

Masson, V.
Laboratoire IRISA / INRIA
Avenue de Général Leclerc
35042 Rennes Cédex
France

Mohr, R.
CRIN, Campus Universitaire,
BP 239
54506 Vandœuvre les Nancy
France

Napoli, A.
CRIN, Campus universitaire,
BP 239
54506 Vandœuvre les Nancy
France

and

Laboratoire MIAS
Université Louis Pasteur
4, rue Blaise Pascal
67008 Strasbourg
France

Noussi, R.
Laboratoire IRISA / INRIA
Campus de Beaulieu
Avenue du Général Leclerc
35042 Rennes Cédex
France

Pavé, A.
Laboratoire de Biométrie
Université Claude Bernard
43, Bd du 11 Novembre 1918
69622 Villeurbanne Cédex
France

Pesty, S.
Laboratoire TIM3, BP 68
38402 Saint Martin d'Hères
France

Quiniou, R.
Laboratoire IRISA / INRIA
Campus de Beaulieu
Avenue du Général Leclerc
35042 Rennes Cédex
France

Rechenmann, F.
Laboratoire IMAG B, BP 68
38402 Saint Martin d'Hères
France

Rialle, V.
Département de Mathématiques,
Statistiques et Informatique Médicale and
TIM3-IMAG, Faculté de Médecine
38700 La Tronche, France

Robert, C.
IRMA and TIM3-IMAG, BP 68
38402 Saint Martin d'Hères
France

Roche, C.
Laboratoire d'Intelligence Artificielle
Université de Chambéry
BP 1104
73011 Chambéry Cédex
France

Romanczuk, A.
CRIL
12 bis, rue Jean Jaurès
92800 Puteaux France

and

LIFL - CNRS UA 239
Université de Lille - Flandres - Artois
Cité Scientifique - Bât. M3
59655 Villeneuve d'Ascq Cédex
France

Rousseau, B.
Laboratoire IMAG B
BP 68
38402 Saint Martin d'Hères
France

Scherrer, J.R.
Hôpital Cantonal de Genève
Division Informatique
CH - 1211 Genève 4
Switzerland

Schneider, F.
Institut de Mathématiques
et d'Informatique, Université de
Neuchâtel, Chemin de Chantemerle 20
CH - 2000 Neuchâtel
Switzerland

Sérignat, J.F.
Laboratoire de la Communication Parlée
INPG
46, avenue Félix Viallet
38031 Grenoble Cédex
France

Tiberghien, G.
UER de Psychologie et Sciences de
l'Education, BP 47 X
38040 Grenoble Cédex
France

Unterreiner, R.
Laboratoire du Traitement du Signal
INSA - Bât. 502
20, avenue Albert Einstein
69621 Villeurbanne Cédex
France

Vila, A.
Service d'Electromyographie
Hôpital A. Michallon
38700 La Tronche
France

PART 1

OBJECT ORIENTED LANGUAGES AND OBJECT ORIENTED REPRESENTATIONS OF KNOWLEDGE

Even though the neurosciences and artificial intelligence have many common aims, specifically the study of knowledge, its representation and its uses, there are very few contacts between these two domains.

Combining artificial intelligence and the neurosciences seems all the more interesting, and even indispensable since, for example, the concept of 'object' is widely used in artificial intelligence at the moment. Let us remember that the frame concept (object) has its origin in psychology .

Part 1 of this book aims to present one of the most important concepts in artificial intelligence and in classical programming today: the concept of 'object'. This section covers three topics more or less tackled according to the different chapters.

The first one is to present what an object is. Indeed the notion of 'object' in data-processing refers to a number of different concepts. Therefore it is necessary to begin with a synthesis of these different concepts and their advantages when developing artificial intelligence systems and, more specifically, expert systems. Some examples of objects systems, or realizations of such systems in Smalltalk, for example, illustrate this part.

At the present time, most expert systems use the production rule formalism to represent expert knowledge. So, many projects try to combine the production rule approach with the object one. This is the second topic.

The third topic is devoted to object-based realizations. This includes object-expert systems and more classical applications based on this approach showing us how useful the object concept is.

From a synthesis of the concept of object, to their integration to the more traditional production rule formalism, through expert systems and classical realizations, Part 1 gives the reader a broad presentation of what the object approach is.

1 *C. Roche*

OBJECT IN EXPERT SYSTEMS

1.1 **Introduction**

I assume the structure of expert systems is familiar to the reader (Hayes-Roth *et al.*
1983). However without going into details concerning this structure, let me remind you
that expert systems are among the commonness of Artificial Intelligence systems and also
that they represent a programming technique.

Data-processing systems developed with this technique are usually organized in three
parts.

- A KNOWLEDGE BASE

This again is made up of two parts

The first one contains all the descriptive and factual knowledge about
the world in which the system works.

The second part includes the deductible knowledge, usually called
expert knowledge.

This kind of knowledge uses a declarative representation,
for example : frames for the former ; production rules for the latter.

- AN INFERENCE ENGINE

As it is obvious from the name, its aim is to make inferences by
applying deductive knowledge to descriptive knowledge.

- A CONTROL

The aim of this control part is to "control" the inferences (the parsing of the research space) in order to reach the solution as fast as possible.

The representation of this control knowledge might be either procedural (included in the inference engine), or declarative with a meta-rule base, for example.

The figure 1.1 sums up this presentation.

Developing an expert system brings about a certain amount of problems, among which two are encountered most frequently, namely programming problems and knowledge representation problems.

1.1.1 *Programming problems*
An inference engine is actually a program which might become very large. We are faced with classical software engineering problems : modularity, debugging, protection, updating /maintenance..

For all these problems, the object approach of Object Oriented Programming provides interesting solutions.

We will examine this family of languages in chapter 1.2 Object Oriented Programming.

1.1.2 *Knowledge representation problems*
The problem of knowledge representation, i.e. the choice of the most suitable formalism to be used is of course one of the main problems when writing an expert system. This issue is so important that it has become a real part of Artificial Intelligence. At the moment the most popular formalism is the object (frames). It is the basis of Object oriented Representations of knowledge. Chapter "1. 3 Object Oriented Representation" presents those systems.

1.1.3 *Hybrid Systems*
As we have seen, different object concepts are used for writing the inference engine and for representing the knowledge base. It is tempting, therefore, even though their aims are different, to try to unify these different object concepts in a single language. Such are hybrid languages. We will study an example of this sort of languages in chapter "1.5 Hybrid languages".

The figure 1.2 sums up these two kinds of problem and the hybrid systems approach.

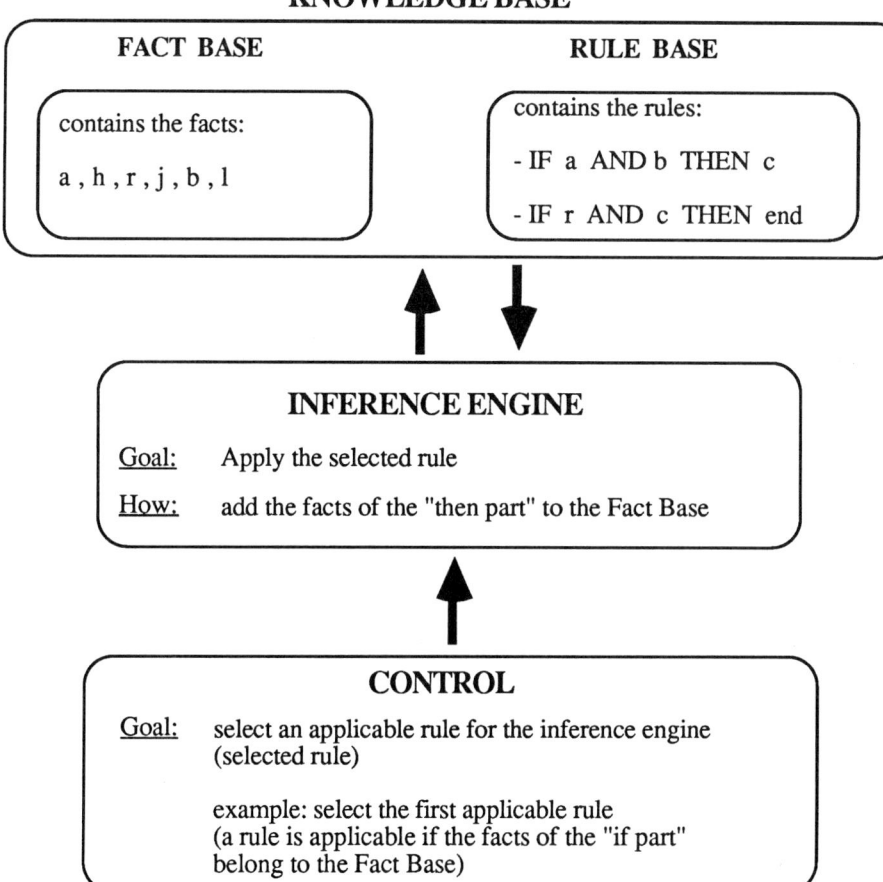

Figure 1.1.

1.1.4 *Actor Languages*

A third object concept called actor is meeting with increasing interest because of distributed Artificial Intelligence essentially because these languages deal with the resolution by a society of actors, ie no longer centralized in one entity.

We will examine this actor approach in chapter 1.4

1.1.5 *A new approach to expert systems*

The concept of objects is interesting not only for programming engine and knowledge representation, but it also introduces a new and different approach to expert systems :

everything is an object, including the inference engine itself which can be manipulated like any other object, and this makes cooperation between engines much easier. The state of the research space generated by the engine during the resolution is also an object. This declarative representation of the resolution makes it easier to implement modules that reason "about reasoning", explanations or sophisticated backtracking.

1.2 Object oriented languages

1.2.1 *Origins*
Object Oriented Languages stem from classical Software engineering problems. These problems are usually met when writing and using large software : debugging and maintenance modularity, protection, reusability....

These Languages provide a real programming approach which is very different from classical programming, where we encounter two different types of entities that are physically distinct although there is non semantic separation between them : The data and the programs. This is not the case with object oriented programming. There we have only one type of entity : the object.

1.2.2 *Basic Concepts*
The basic concepts of Object Oriented Languages may vary from one language to another, but most of them are based on the four following concepts :

> - object
> - sending messages
> - class
> - the hierarchy between classes and inheritance of properties.

Objects :
Objects are the only entity used in 0bject Oriented Languages. The data that define its structure and the procedures that make use of these data are embodied in this single concept. Thus objects allow the packing of data (see figure 1.3.).

For example in Smalltalk-80 (Goldberg and co, 1985), data are called instance variables, and procedures are known as methods.

A production rule can be defined for example by two instance variables : its condition part and its action part ; and three methods : the first one will evaluate the rule, it will call two other methods, one will evaluate the condition part and the other the action part. (see figure 1.4.).

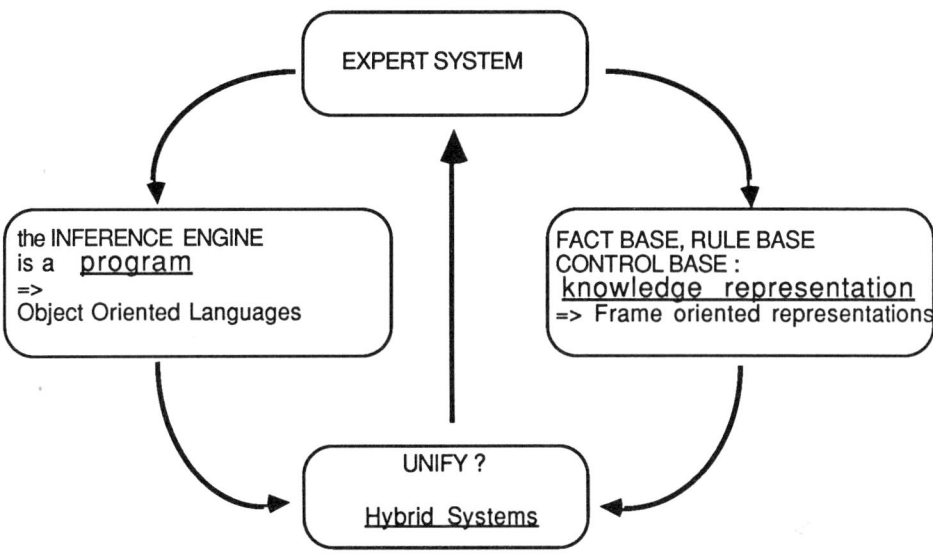

Figure 1.2.

OBJECT = (DATA + PROCEDURES)

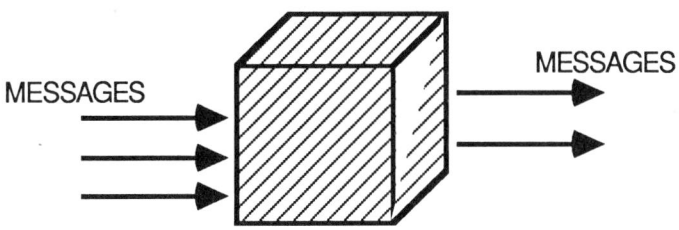

Figure 1.3. Object = (DATA + PROCEDURES)

Message sending :

The only way to manipulate objects is to send them messages. (to access the instance variable for example). These messages will execute the methods associated with the object. (methods and messages associated with the object bear the same name).

The syntax of message sending is fairly simple. It can look like this : "receiving-object message". Thus the evaluation of rule 15 will be hired by the message :

        rule-number-15 eval-rule.

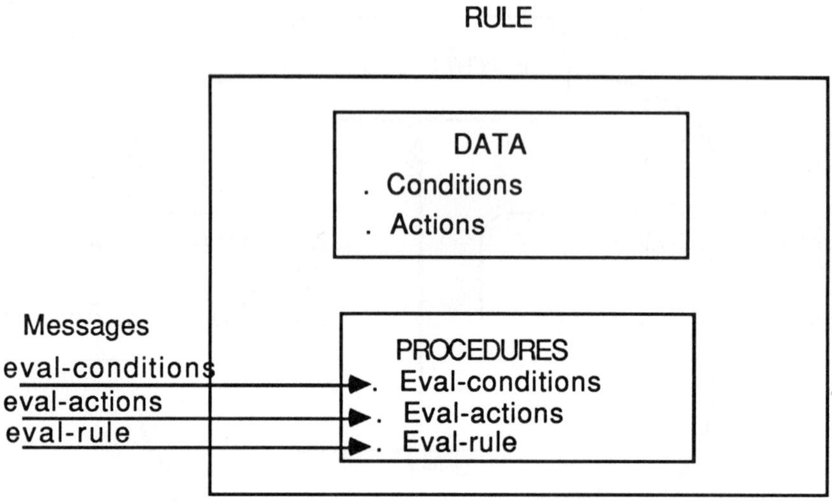

RULE

Figure 1.4

Classes

Classes are made up of objects which have a similar description and behaviour. Thus the rule class describes the set of objects that are able to answer evaluation requests, and have a condition part and an action part. Each object has its own instance variables. They are duplicated when an object is created from the class ; but methods are created at class level. Objects of one class are also called instances of this class.

Class hierarchy and associated inheritance.

Separating, reusing and specializing information are operations one would like to do when developing an application. Object Oriented Programming provides such possibilities, because classes can be organized in a hierarchy. A class can be defined from one or several existing classes (multiple inheritance). In this case, the newly created class inherits information from its super-class, and of course it is still possible to redefine inherited informations and/or add new information. For example we can define the weighted rule class as a subclass of the rule class (see figure 1.5.).

1.2.3 *Examples*

The first Object Oriented Programming Simula 67 (Dahl and co, 1966)] was created in 1967. It is a very universal programming language, and simulation is just one of its possible applications.

But it was really Smalltalk 80 that popularized the concept of objects for programming.

The first version of this language appeared in 1972 at Xerox Palo Alto Research Center.

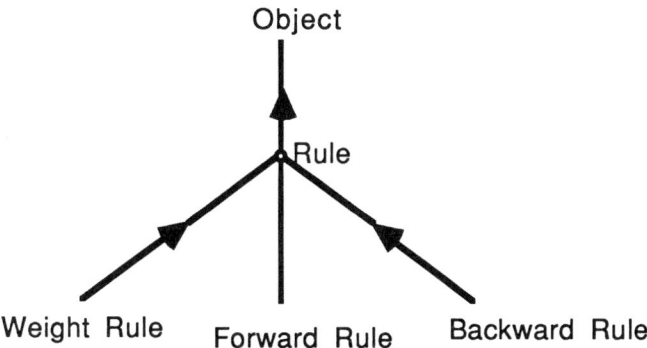

Figure 1.5.

Though Smalltalk 80 is a direct heir of Simula 67, it differs from it on several points. Let us notice for example the possibility of sending messages in Smalltalk 80 which replaces the pointed notation in Simula 67, and also the fact that every entity in Smalltalk 80 is an object, which means that classes are also objects.

Let us return to our initial problem of writing expert systems, and see how to create a production rule class with Smalltalk 80.

The class "rule" is defined by sending the adequate message to the root class "object".
Object subclass : Rule
              instanceVariableNames : 'conditions actions'.

A production rule knows how to answer three kinds of messages :
              "eval-conditions", "eval-actions" and "eval-rules".

They can be defined very easily as follows :

        eval-conditions :
              "returns the evaluation of the conditions,
              Compiler evaluate : conditions

        eval-rule :
              "evaluates the action part of the rule if the rule can be applied."
              (self eval-conditions)
              ifTrue : [^ self eval-actions]

1.3.1 *Origins*

Object Oriented Representations of Knowledge were developed as a result of knowledge representation problems encountered by Artificial Intelligence and Psychology. Basically, we can sum up those problems with these two remarks :

  - "chunks" of knowledge have to be grouped and structured.
  - Human behaviour when facing a given problem is not always inferential.

1.3.2 *Basic concepts*

It is possible to sum up the different concepts of 0bject Oriented Representation in one generic concept : the Frame concept (Minsky 1975).

A frame is linked to other frames by relations, which may include semantic inheritance. (For example a relation from class to instance) (Wright *et al.*, 1983).

The Frame concept was first introduced by Minsky in his notorious article (Minsky 1975) : "A framework for representing knowledge" published in "The Psychology of Computer Vision". The following sentence is from this article.

"Here is the essence of the theory : When on encounters a new situation, one selects from memory a substantial structure called a frame. This is a remenbered framework to be adapted to fit reality by changing details as necessary".

A frame is a set of slot-value couples. These couples define the frame structure. Each slot is itself described by a set of attached facets. There are specific facets to define authorized values of slots, the default value of a slot... Noted the existence of special facets called "procedural attachments", The value of these facets is a procedure which will be triggered at each time the slot is accessed.

Frames allow the use of procedures, as Object Oriented Programming does, but the activation mode is dual. Here one does not explicitly ask for a procedure to be applied, contrary to what happens when a message is sent. Here the procedure is triggered by the need to access the data - we call this the **Data Driven Programming.**

Finally let us make a special reference to the specific role some slots have when they represent relations, as is the case for predefined slots such as "is-a" and "instance-of".

Figure 1.6 shows the structure of a frame applied to a planning problem.

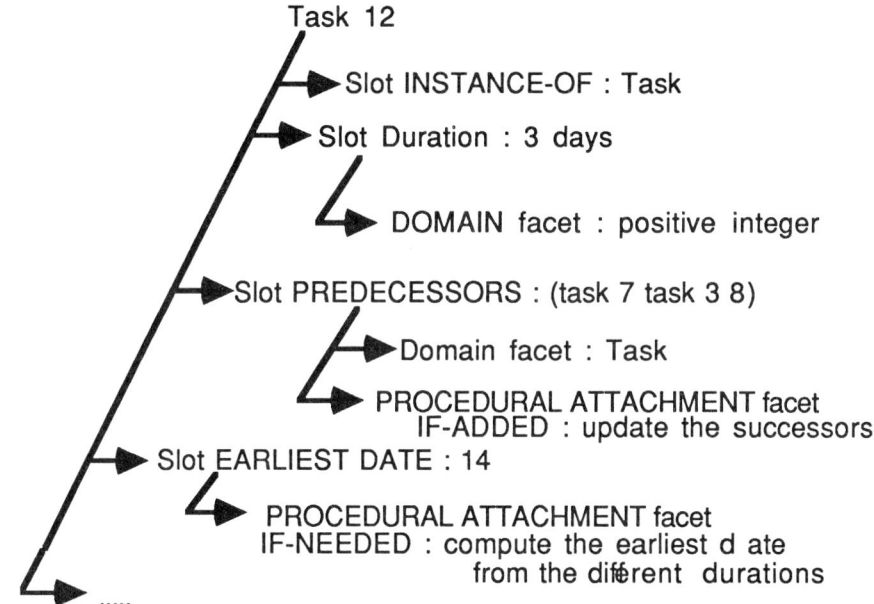

Task 12
- Slot INSTANCE-OF : Task
- Slot Duration : 3 days
  - DOMAIN facet : positive integer
- Slot PREDECESSORS : (task 7 task 3 8)
  - Domain facet : Task
  - PROCEDURAL ATTACHMENT facet
    IF-ADDED : update the successors
- Slot EARLIEST DATE : 14
  - PROCEDURAL ATTACHMENT facet
    IF-NEEDED : compute the earliest d ate
    from the different durations
- .....

Figure 1.6.

1.3.3 *Examples*

A number of frame based systems actually exist. One of the first ones, FRL, remains interesting. Written in LISP, the system combines the advantages of being simple and yet powerful.

It does not include the notion of class, but it provides a predefined slot which describes the relation between frames ; the "ako" slot which includes an inheritance semantics.

Let us conclude with SRL (Wright *et al.*, 1983) , or more precisely CRL the knowledge representation language of knowledge Craft (Carnegie Group, 1985) which is one of the most powerful systems. In this model everything is represented as a frame ; attached procedures and even relations to which the user can attach his own inheritance semantics.

1.4 **Actor languages**

1.4.1 *Origins*

The idea of Actor Languages stems from two points that can be made when considering Artificial Intelligence and data-processing.

At the moment, parallel machines are becoming a reality ; but most languages are global state-oriented languages, and do not allow the use of parallelism. Therefore it seems necessary to define a new model of computation which would make it possible to get the most of parallelism.

The second point has to do with problem solving. Until now we have tended to consider mainly problem solving by a single person, where as interesting solutions could probably be provided if we used a set of actors. Such solutions would involve division of the problem, distributed type application domain, optimal use of parallelism.

1.4.2 *Basic concepts*
The basic concept is the actor (Lieberman 1981, Theriault 1983).
This object concept differs from the ones we have just analyzed, for parallelism implies several new characteristics :

- All the actors are independent from one another, and have all the knowledge necessary for their execution.

- Message sending is asynchronous, which allows the sending actor to deal with other requests. The synchronization will be made either with the help of other actors (called continuations) or with the help of serialized actors.

Information is no longer shared through the mechanism of inheritance but through the rerouting to another actor of a message that has not been recognized by the receiving actor.

1.4.3 *Examples*
Actor Languages mainly stems from the work of the "message passing" laboratory at M.I.T. The first version was PLASMA, then came ACT1. Finally the aim of ACT2 is to combine ACT1, the OMEGA actor description language, the apiary parallel machine of M.I.T. and the ETHER resolution system which is based on the cooperation of sprites.

1.5 Hybrid systems

As we mentioned in the introduction some systems now try to combine the different object concepts which we have examined, eventhough aims and concepts are sometimes different. (The black box concept of Object Oriented Languages which can be compared to the packing of data, is different from the glass box concept of frames, just as method and attached procedure activation differs according to the system considered).

LRO2 (Roche 1986) is a language which belongs to this category of systems. It originates from problems encountered when writing expert systems which I described in the introduction. (LRO2 is commercialized by CRIL, a Paris based company under the name of KEOPS). An LRO2 object is made of a set of property-value couples. As with frames, it is possible to attach procedure to the property. These procedures will be activated when the property is accessed.

But above all LRO2 is an Object Oriented Language. Each object belongs to a class, and is able to answer messages. This message answering capacity of object is the characteristic of LRO2, which makes it different from other languages. Messages can be sent in four different manners according to the way they are processed (in a synchronous or asynchronous way), and according to the type of receiver which can be either an explicitly described object, an unknown object, or a set of objects characterized by properties...

There is another category of messages in LRO2 which allows for a different programming approach. This approach is declarative and consists in having message sending controlled by events.

The message sending controlled by events is made up of two parts :

- The first part consist in sending a message according to one of the four types we have just described.

- The second part is a pattern which determines whether the message shall be considered or not.

Those message sending controlled by events are considered as soon as events that can be implied with the pattern associated to the message appears in LRO2.

A pattern is a triplet describing the sender object, the action requested, and the receiver object. Thus it is possible to make the activity of a set of objects dependent on the activity of another set of objects, without interferring with objects "spied on".

References

Carnegie Group. (1985). *Knowledge Craft 3.0., reference manual.* **1, 2.** Carnegie Groupe Inc, Pittsburgh, Pennsylvania , U.S.A.

Dahl & Jordan, O. (1966). Simula, an algol based simulation language. *ACM communication,* **9**, 671-81.

Golberg, A. & Robson, D. (1985). Smalltalk 80 the language and its implementation.*Addison Weslay Publishing Company*

Hayes-Roth, Waterman, D.A. & Lenat, D.B. (1983). Builing Expert Systems. *Addison Weslay*

Lieberman, H. (1981). A preview of Act 1. *A.I. memo,* n° **625**, MIT (June 1981)

Minsky, M. (1975). A framework for representing knowledge. In:*The psychology for computer vision.* Eds Winston & Mc Graw Hill

Roche, C. & Laurent, J.P. (1986). Artificial Intelligence & Object Oriented Languages : LRO2, IFIP'86, Dublin, september 1986

Wright, J.M. & Fox, M.S. (1983). SRL, I.S. user manual. Draft of 1 december 1983. Intelligent Systems Laboratory, Carnegie Mellon University

KOOL : MERGING OBJECT FRAMES AND RULES

2.1 Bits of History

Kool, which stands for Knowledge representation Object Oriented Language is a long term project. The first design occurred in 1983 and intended to merge Frames, Objects and Production rules. At that time the idea was still new and challenging. The system was implemented in MacLisp on a Multics and then rewritten in Mulisp on a PC/XT. After some experiments in computer configuration and diagnosis applications, the Bull group decided to turn the prototype into a product. This process that took more than a year had as a first output a review of the object model, in order to take into account the experiments and better understanding of both the problems to be solved and the solutions to be used. The product is now being sold. It is implemented in Le-Lisp, and runs on the Bull workstations.

2.2 The principles

The basic idea of Kool is to integrate at low level an object based representation, and a rule based style of programming. This idea came from practical experiments, and from an in depth study of EMycin [Van Melle, 1979] , OPS-V [Forgy, 1981] , KRL [Bobrow, 1977] and Loops [Bobrow, 1981]. Each of these systems have their own interest, but each of them is limited in the expressive power or in the quality of the multi-paradigm integration. We then decided to set up the following objectives

- Frame based knowledge representation
- Instantiation and message passing
- Extensibility of the object model
- Availability of rule based programming
- Deep connection between objects and rules.

2.3 The Object model

The objects handled in Kool are based upon the Class/Instance paradigm. An object is an instance of one class. The classes are linked together by a specialization relation introducing a tree structure. Methods can be defined on both classes or instances, defining the behaviour of a collection of object (using defClassMethod) or of an individual object (using defInstanceMethod). A class defines the structure of its instances through a "schema" that introduces a set of attributes and their properties. The structure of an instance is defined by the merge of all the schemas defined in the classes it inherits from.

2.3.1 *MetaClasses*
The Kool Classes are "first class" objects. They are themselves instances of the Class *MetaClass*. The name *MetaClass* stands for "a class whose instances are also classes". The class *Class* is an instance of MetaClass whose instances are basic classes. The model could be defined with only one class, but we found that it was more easy to explain and learn using this distinction. A class owns attributes and methods which applies to itself, it owns too a schema that describes its future instances. If the schema is a Class schema, the instances will be classes. If the schema is not linked to a class schema, the instances will not be classes. Based on this simple model, we can have an infinite number of instantiation links. In practice however, no one application has used more than four levels of instantiation.

2.3.2 *Inheritance*
Kool is based on a simple inheritance mechanism. We choose this simple model because of its conceptual clarity. All of the multiple inheritance based systems only offer a pragmatic solution to the known problems of naming conflicts. We decided then to go along a more pure (thought more restrictive) way, while designing a clean model based on perspectives, before enhancing the inheritance scheme.

2.3.3 *Attribute classes*
The description of the attributes is one of the most original features of Kool. It allows the knowledge engineer to use the objects as frames. The attribute classes describe the attributes as standard objects. The facets of the attribute are described as attributes of the schema of the attribute class. This attributes (or facet) are in turn described by instances of classes named DescriptorClasses (which are classes of facets). Using this model, the attributes and facets are fully integrated with the object description language. The extension at the set of the predefined attribute classes is done in the same manner as the extension of the set of predefined classes (which is the kernel of the description of an application). The attribute classes build a hierarchy. At the root is the class *Attribute*, that introduces the descriptors *Type, WhenFilled, WhenRemoved, Inheritance* and

valued attributes (class *Mono*), the second one describes the multi-valued attributes (class *Multi*). The mono-valued attributes are then specialized by the special case classe *YesNo*, that represents the attributes that can take their values in the set [*yes, no*].

For example, the class *YesNo* is described as :

```
{AttributeClass : YesNo          ; an attribute class
    Super : Mono                 ; more specific than Mono
    < -- Type : [yes, no]        ; possible values are yes or no.
        -- Default : no          ; if no value is found, assume no.
        -- Determine : determineYesNo >     ; a function that computes the
value.
    }
```

This attribute class is defined exactly in the same way as one defines, for example, the class *Man* as a specialization of the class *Human* :

```
{Class : Man                     ; a class
    Super : Human                ; more specific than Human
    Author : P.Albert            ; author of the class
    CreationDate : nil           ; should have been filled
    < -- age : nil               ; the age of a man
        Mode : Mono
        Default   : 0
        Type : [0 .. 150]
        -- Old : nil             ; a Man may be old (or not).
        Mode : YesNo
        -- Sex : Male >          ; ...
    }
```

In this class the attribute *Old* is used as a *YesNo* attribute. It inherits then the information defined in the attribute class *YesNo*. The possible values are *yes* or *no*, and the default values is *no*. One can notice then that exactly the same principles, and the same syntax are used to extend the language itself (the set of predefined attribute classes), and to describe the classes involved in the application.

As seen above, the class of an attribute is referenced through the special descriptor *Mode* that links an attribute to an AttributeClass. This descriptor cannot be modified in a specialization of the attribute found lower in the class hierarchy. This is guaranteed by the value of the descriptor *Inheritance* which is set to *strict* in the schema of the class *Attribute*. This descriptor defines the way the value of an attribute -- or descriptor -- is the new value is refused. If the Inheritance is set to default, the new value overrides the values found above in the hierarchy (as those birds that don't fly). If the value of Inheritance is set to union, the new value is merged to the previous one. This feature allows the knowledge engineer to define precisely the semantic of the values inherited from the classes.

The attribute and descriptor classes may also be used to define specific facets needed for the full description of the application. The following example illustrates the introduction of attributes that represents measures :

{**MonoDescriptor** : Unit   ; a new descriptor (or facet)
    -- Type : [second, meter, volts]   ; possible values}

{**AttributeClass** : Measure   ; an attribute class
    Super : Mono   ; more specific than Mono
    < -- Type : Number   ; possible values are numbers.
        -- Default : 0   ; if no value is found, assume *no*.
        -- Unit : nil   ; introduction of the *unit* facet
            Default : meter >   ; by default, *meter* is the unit.}

{**AttributeClass** : Distance   ; an attribute class
    Super : *Measure*   ; more specific than Measure
    <   -- Unit : meter>   ; *meter* is the unit.}

{**Class** : Jump   ; a class
    Super : Action
    <   -- Actor : nil
            Type : Sportive
        -- Lengh : nil
            Mode : *Distance* > }

{Jump   : ?   ; a specific Jump
    -- Actor : Louis
    -- *Lengh* : 8}

These descriptions have created the descriptor *Unit*, which is used to define the attribute class *Measure*, which is in turn refined by the attribute class *Distance*. The class *Distance* can then be used as the *Mode* of any attribute of any object, in the same way that the predefined classes are used. The attribute *Length* of the class Jump is defined as a *Distance*, and finally the *Length* of a distance is defined as being 8 Meters (*Meters* are inherited from the attribute class *Distance*).

Distance, and finally the *Length* of a distance is defined as being 8 Meters (*Meters* are inherited from the attribute class *Distance*).

2.3.4 *Instantiation*

The instantiation process is the basis of the Class/Instance model. It consists in the introduction of a new object in the knowledge base. This object must have a known class and may have values for its attributes. The meta-class AbstractClass is used to create classes that must not be explicitly instantiated (for examples numbers, strings, or application specific classes).

Once an object has been added to the Knowledge Base, one can send messages to the classes asking for their instances. Depending on the classes, the instances may be computed or retrieved in an attribute of the class. The tuning of this aspect of the class implementation relies on the skill of the knowledge engineer.

Once linked to a class at creation time, an object can move along the hierarchy of the classes. The message *Isa* can be used to refine the class of an instance. For example, a forward rule can decide that if the sex of a HumanBeing is male, then he is a Man.

This traversal of the hierarchy takes in account the demons and forward rules that may react on values asserted at the class level.

2.4 **The rule system**

2.4.1 *Introduction*

The objects defined in the object based part of Kool may be used in the rule system. The rules which are instances of the class *Rule* are closely integrated to the object model. They test or modify the objects and their attributes through the use of typed variables. The names of the types are the names of the classes in the class hierarchy. The typed variables understand the specialization relation of the class hierarchy, in the sense that a variable of type *Human* can be substituted by instances of the class *Man* , as well as by instances of the class *Woman*. The rules that bear on instances of a high level class are thus inherited by the low level classes.

2.4.2 *Syntax*

A rule has a name, a priority , a premise and a conclusion part. It may too have an *external* part that describes in a free syntax the precise meaning of the rule. As rules are standard objects, one can add new attributes to a new class of rule that refines the predefined class *Rule*. A rule has also a mode which indicates if the rule is to be used in forward chaining, in backward chaining or in both modes.

denoted the sister of Louis. The references can be nested, as in Louis^sister^telephoneNumber which denotes the telephone number of the sister of Louis.

The multi-valued attributes may be referenced in two ways. The standard notation lets the user reference the whole set of values (i.e. *the parents* of Louis). Another construction enables the reference of any of the values (i.e. *a parent* of Louis, or *one of the parents* of Louis). This special construct allows one to use an undeterministic reference (as in Prolog) to a value of an attribute. This style of reference is very useful to map on values on a slot.

Examples :

```
{Rule : Rule112
        interest : 100
        If *Human:friends = *1Human
            *Human^sister^look =pretty
        Then (phoneTo *Human *1Human)}


{Rule : myRule
        If *Car^body^color = red
        Then *Car^color = red}
```

2.4.3 *Semantics*

The rules may be used forward or backward. At read time, the rule is compiled into several lisp functions that interpret the different triggers of the rule. When a rule is used forward, all the references to the attributes found in the premises, are used to generate lisp demons. These demons are added to the *WhenFilled* facet of the attributes. At run-time, they bind internal variables to the object and the new slot value, and call the lisp function that is specialized in this interpretation of the rule. As a result, as soon as a new value is added or set to an attribute, this specific value is tested in the rule and the facts are added or removed as needed.

A backward rule is compiled into one lisp function that evaluates the premises, following the order of the definition. Optimization is made to cut paths when an attribute that is needed by a backward rule is deduced by a forward one. The control of the backchaining search is based on the class of the attribute. For a mono-valued attribute, the search may be stopped when one value is found. For a multi-valued attribute, the search, by default, tries to determine all the values of the slot. The knowledge engineer has access to a more specific control of the search within the facet *Determine* that contains a lisp function used to determine the unknown value of an attribute. For example, he/she search, by default, tries to determine all the values of the slot. The knowledge engineer has access to a more specific control of the search within the facet *Determine* that contains a lisp function used to determine the unknown value of an attribute. For example, he/she may which to store or not the deduced values, or to control the search more precisely, using the *Cardinality* facet of an attribute.

2.5 Conclusions

We have described the main ideas involved in the design and implementation of Kool. The system is now in use in more than twenty sites. The rule system though limited in functionalities (no ATMS, nor multiple viewpoints) is robust and efficient. The attribute class model has also proved to be useful in the implementation of a tight connection of Kool to relational databases.

The main enhancement of the model is to allow the notion of attribute classes to be fully recursive. This enhancement would allow one to set or access the values of attributes of attributes of ... of an object. This work is motivated by a research point of view, but it is also needed form the application point of view. For example, the knowledge engineer would like to state conditionally (using rules) that an attribute is, or not, askable. This simple need, if it is not implemented by a "hook" needs such an extension of the model.

References

Albert, P. (1983), Kool : *représentation des connaissances*, Bigre 10-1983.

Albert, P. (1987), *Kool reference manual* (Bull).

Bobrow, D.G. & Stefik, M. (1982). *The LOOPS Manual.*, Memo KB-VLSI-81-13, Knowledge Systems Area, Xerox Palo Alto Research Center, Ca.

Bobrow, D.G. & Winograd, T. (1977). *An overview of KRL*, Cognitive Science, **1**, 3-46.

Forgy, C. (1981)*The OPS5 users's manual.* Technical Report. CMU-CS-81-135, Computer Science Department, Carnegie-Mellon University, Pittsburgh, Pa.

Van Melle, W. (1979). *A domain independant production tule system for consultation program,* IJCAI 6, 923-25.

3 *J. Caelen, O. Cervantes, J.F. Sérignat and Y. Fernandez*

DATA AND KNOWLEDGE FOR SPEECH PROCESSING

3.1 Introduction

In Automatic Speech Processing (ASP) not only speech sounds but articulatory parameters (face images, physiological signals), phonetic and linguistic symbols are treated. The nature of these entities is largely varied since they emerge from multiple knowledge sources: acoustic, articulatory, perceptive, phonetic, lexical, syntactic, semantic, etc. This multiple source origin renders the recognition and synthesis tasks difficult. Two main schools are prevalent in Automatic Speech Recognition (ASR):

PR which relies on Pattern Recognition (PR) (as structural and stochastic methods),

AI which relies on Artificial Intelligence (AI), through the use of multiple cooperation knowledge sources in single-or-multi-expert systems.

Recognition systems are mostly oriented to the problem of Acoustic-Phonetic Decoding (APD), an operation which allows the correspondence between the speech signal and the abstract phonetic units. This stage of processing constitutes a bottleneck because of the rate of information reduction to be attained. It poses a fundamental theoretical problem: the superposed correspondence between a phonetic-phonologic model and the sound signal. This is the reason for the present existence of two schools, PR and AI, oriented towards solving the problem:

PR makes use of automatic learning methods and pattern matching kinds of reasoning, such as DTW (Dynamic Time Warping) or HMM (Hidden Markov Models), thus trying to circumvent the problem of obtained knowledge,

AI makes use of knowledge-based methods and logic type reasoning.

In this paper we place ourselves under the second perspective.

Among the most important APD problems we find the availability of "good" knowledge: knowledge which allows the pertinent and minimal description of the phonetic facts, independently of speakers and vocabulary. One of the main difficulties is that the great quantity of information and variabilities involved (due to speaker, environment, etc.) make it impossible to find a single expert with complete knowledge of the area. One may try then to acquire this knowledge in several ways: (a) from the knowledge of many experts, (b) by automatic learning, (c) by mixed methods of types (a) and (b). It is this last alternative that seems the richest to us since it is controllable by the expert - as opposed to (b) - and since it is feasible to complete the knowledge (derived in type (a) from experience only) with methods similar to learning. From this perspective, a system embodying knowledge acquisition (Caelen *et al*, 1986) would provide the expert with tools to assess his knowledge, to quantify certain parameters that he currently uses and to allow him to search for new knowledge more systematically.

Such a system should be able to:

manage pertinent speech data (recorded sounds, articulatory parameters, acoustic spectra, etc.),

produce knowledge from these data as well as from the knowledge of experts,

manage the obtained knowledge.

There is really no true frontier between data and knowledge (also called "information"). They may be managed by a single formalism: the object-based representation (Cervantes & Serignat, 1987) . In contrast, knowledge production arises from reasoning (Halpern, 1986) over the facts extracted from the data. The reasoning mechanisms extend the strict framework of basic knowledge management. We propose then an interactive system adapted to the speech domain, the SIDOCParole --*Système Intégré de Données et de connaissances pour la Parole (Data and Knowledge Integrated Sytem for Speech)*.

The system has three main components:

1. a speech data and knowledge base, BDCParole (Base de Données et de Connaissances Parole=Data and Knowledge Speech Base); the base is conceptually defined upon an object oriented data/knowledge model and administered by a management system.

2. an extensive specialized toolbox for speech processing, developed for a preciously proposed system, ARCANE (Acquisition et Recherche de Connaissances Acoustico-phonétiques dans un Noyau Evolutif=Knowledge Acquisition and Research into Nucleus Evolving) (Caelen *et al*, 1986). ARCANE, intended for validation of new acoustic-phonetic knowledge, is a working component that is now being adapted into the SIDOCParole system.

3. the SIDOCParole reasoning mechanisms control the advanced knowledge processing (deductions, learning) and assure the interfacing of all the other system components (Fig. 3.2).

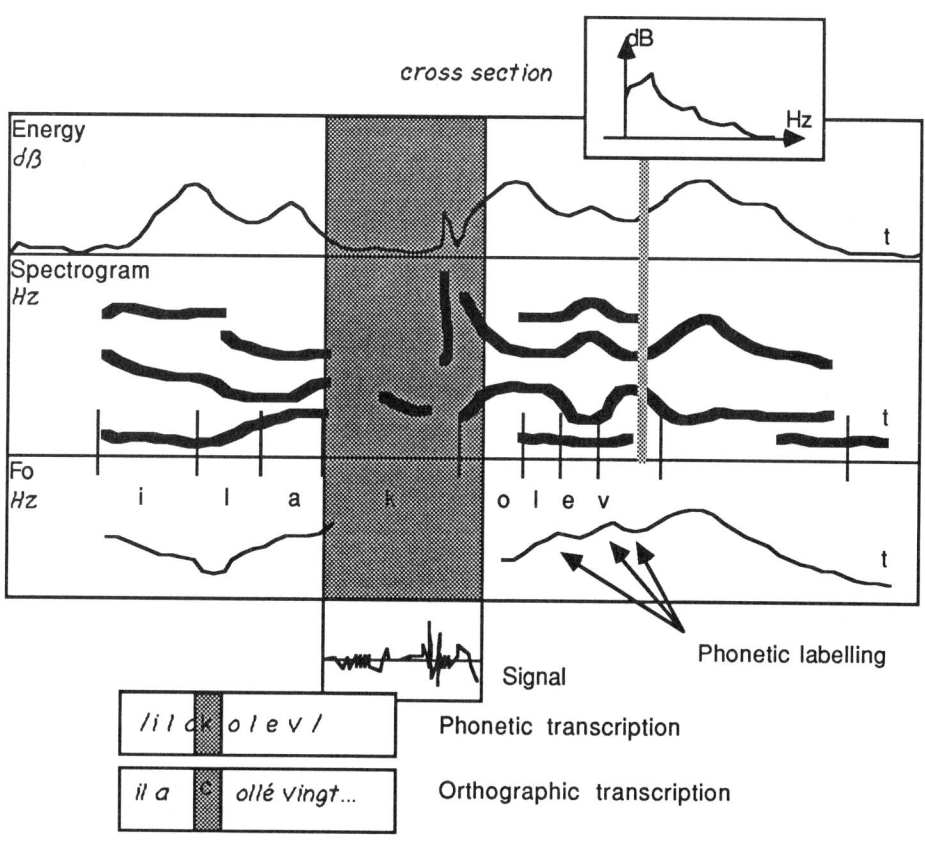

Figure 3.1. Some objects managed in speech processing: sound signal, spectrogram, phonetic and orthographic transcriptions, labels, bursts, energy and pitch curves. Links must be established among these objects to be able, for instance, to select a portion of the spectrogram (shaded) and to obtain the corresponding signal as well as the phonetic and orthographic transcriptions.

Each component makes a specific contribution:

The management system of the BDCParole administers the base containing:
data
    articulatory data,
    french language recorded sounds,
    acoustic data (spectra, formants, pitch, intensity, phones, etc.) obtained from analysis,
    phonetic data (labels, transcriptions, etc.),
    linguistic data (prosodic, syntactic, semantic) obtained or not from experience;
    knowledge
    derived from the experiences of experts,

inferred with the aid of learning mechanisms,

case histories of the experimentation plans carried out by the experts.

The BDCParole manager is an extended capability knowledge and data base management system (Wiederhold, 1984). Among its tasks are the following:

management of data and knowledge,

coherence control of generic operations such as the creation and deletion of objects, reading and writing of attribute values,

production of observations obtained by querying complex informations stored in an experience base,

management of experimentation sessions and their associated history.

A special sub-module of the BDCParole manager is the user-query interface, which accepts, interprets and processes all queries.

The ARCANE toolbox provides the fundamental tools on which the acquisition and search of knowledge from data relies. It encodes an important part of knowledge of the speech domain:

interpretation of the experimentation plans (seen as objects throughout)

linking with resolution mechanisms (inference engine),

linking with numeric and symbolic learning processes by providing the examples and counter-examples.

The SIDOCParole reasoning mechanisms contain the rules to conduct the usage of knowledge. It consists of the different inference engines that will allow deductions and inductions (from inheritance and other relationships among the speech objects) in the universe. It also contains the knowledge that will coordinate all reasonings. The mechanisms are defined in an evolutive fashion, from basic to advanced capabilities.

Thus SIDOCParole is conceived as an integrated knowledge/data based system which through its different modules, allows management capabilities for speech data and knowledge.

Most of the concepts existing in BDCParole are the objects formally described by the model's description language. The toolbox concepts are mostly object related re-write or production rules. This double formalism benefits from the advantages of these two modes of representation (Fernandez, 1987, Narat & Lachet, 1987 ; Hayes-Roth, 1985).

(a) for the objects:

data structuring and organization,

storage of past experience,

possibility of reasoning over incomplete information (default values),

inferences derived from property inheritance.

(b) for rules:

modularity,
relatively natural representation for the expert,
possibility of introduction of heuristics,
easy and flexible logic formalization.

3.2 Object oriented representation

An object based representation seems best adapted for applications such as speech processing, which is subject to the constraints of real-time processing (Gevarter, 1987). It permits grouping under an entity, the object, the data structure and the treatment procedures. Earlier studies (Cervantes & Serignat, 1987) have shown that the relational data base model is insufficient for treating the complex speech objects enumerated in the introduction.

BDCParole contains many objects of different nature. Fig. 3.3 shows the complexity of their structuring and their great variety: sounds, images, linguistic units, physiological parameters, etc. The notion of multiple inheritance is then indispensible here, because certain objects have a dual existence. The phone, for example, is an acoustic segment of concrete nature and a portion of a phone, of abstract nature: it shares the properties associated with these two aspects. In contrast, the links induced by inheritance are not sufficient by themselves to completely describe the speech universe: semantic links must be added (in object oriented languages these links can be taken care of through procedural attachment.

3.2.1 *Semantic linkse,*

In speech recognition one generally proceeds by stages to obtain the characteristic parameters: the spectrum and the acoustic cues are computed from the speech signal, the signal is segmented and the segments are merged to obtain the phonetic units. It then becomes necessary to establish relations between objects to use them for ordering their manipulations and to follow their evolution.

For this purpose two categories of links are introduced, aside from the links induced by the inheritance mechanism:

(a) composition links,

(b) equivalence links.

Composition links materialize the prerequisites (ordering) to the creation of an object. There are two such links:

(1) direct composition links, $CD_{i,j}$ between object i and object j, which indicate that object j has attributes that depend on those of object i.

(2) the expertise composition links, $CE_{i,j}$ between object i and object j, of the same nature as the $CD_{i,j}$ links. The difference is that the expert participates in the construction

of object j from object i.

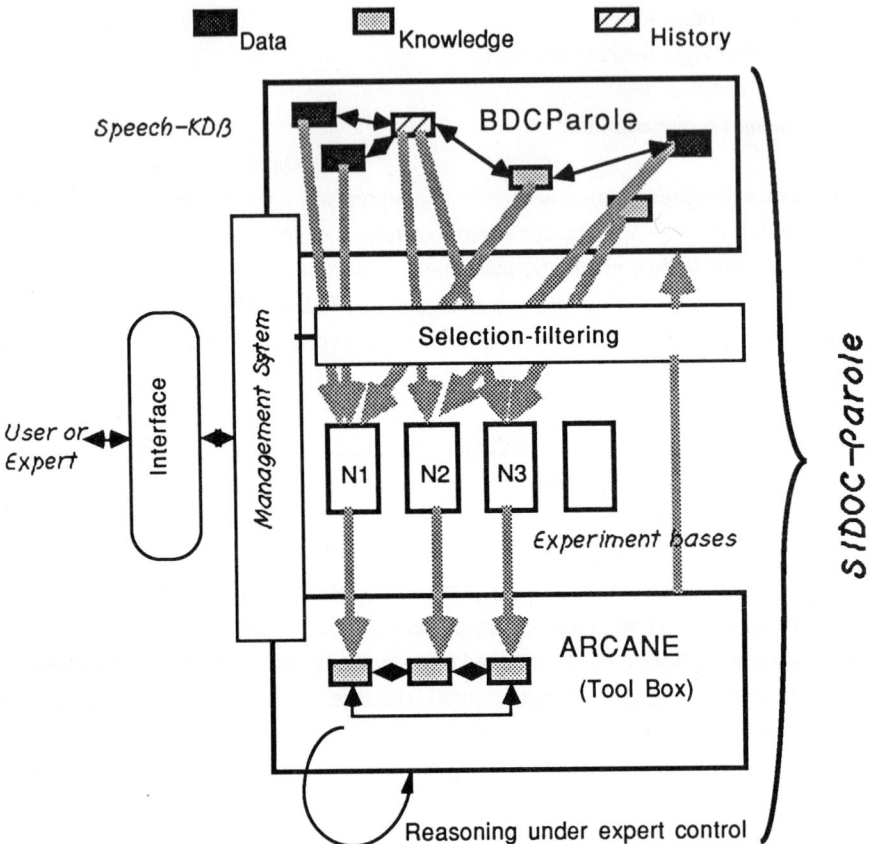

Figure 3.2. General proposed structure of the SIDOCParole system. Every expert-user creates his own experience base (data and knowledge extracted from the BDCParole) over which he performs his reasonings aided by specific tools. The results are selected by a data base administrator and are incrementally incorporated to the BDCParole.

Equivalence links $E_{i,j}$ connect the different aspects i and j of a same concept: for example, the signal and its phonetic transcription, its temporal representation and its spectrogram, the phoneme and the acoustic features, etc. (fig. 3.4).

3.2.2 The views of an object
Speech studies are multidisciplinary, each object is seen differently by experts of these disciplines: a phonetician interprets the vocal signal while a signal processing scientist applies mathematical treatments to this signal. For a phonetician, the signal is not only a mathematical object.

We will simply call these views different ways to see an object. Among these views there effectively exist concrete views, also called graphical representation such as: 1D graphs (frequency-time, amplitude-time, amplitude-frequency, histogram), 2D graphs (spectrogram, clusters, trajectory), IPA code (International Phonetic Alphabet), orthographic code, etc.

This notion of (view) allows one to group into classes the attributes of an object. It also allows one to consider the aggregation of attributes as objects. There exists implicit equivalence links among the views of an object that differ from the preceding one ($E_{i,j}$). Since they are implicit they are not materialized in the object base.

3.2.3. *Structuring of speech objects*
From the preceding paragraphs we can conclude that the notions of inheritance, semantic links (with implicit equivalence links) and view affect a double structuring of the speech objects:

(a) external --through the organization of objects by classes,
(b) internal --through the specification of views within an object.

To this structuring must be added the one induced by the other semantic links (implicit composition and equivalence). Property inheritance is accomplished amongst the objects and within the same view ; the inheritance graph is a superior semi-trellis. The equivalence links relate together those objects which have at least an identical view and that belong to different families (Fig. 3.5). The composition graph is an inferior semi-trellis.

3.2.4 *Examples of speech objects:*
The schema of an object is separated in views under these conventions as follows:
   the definition takes here the form of an explanatory comment on the nature of the object, the content of a view assemble the properties of the object related to this view, described herein in a general fashion.
   In the following paragraphs we present an example of different views of some common speech objects.

Speech-signal:
   Definition: sound wave carrying a "sense"
   View [Mathematical, acoustical, formal, perceptive, articulatory, structural, phonetical, concrete]
   Mathematical set of properties of monodimensional signals: stationary, ergodic, stochastic or not, periodic, etc.
   Acoustical: properties obtained from an analysis: spectra, formants, cues, etc.

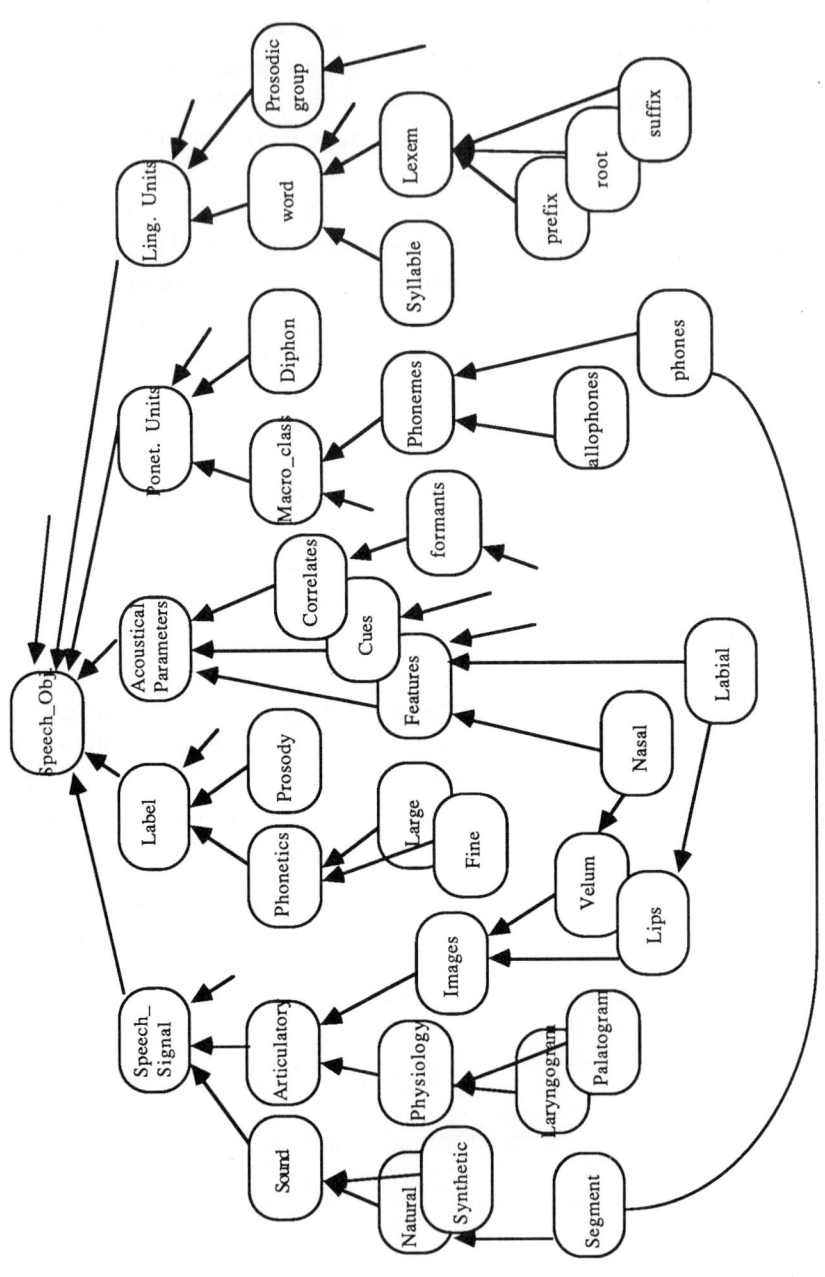

Figure 3.3   Inheritance graph for some objects.

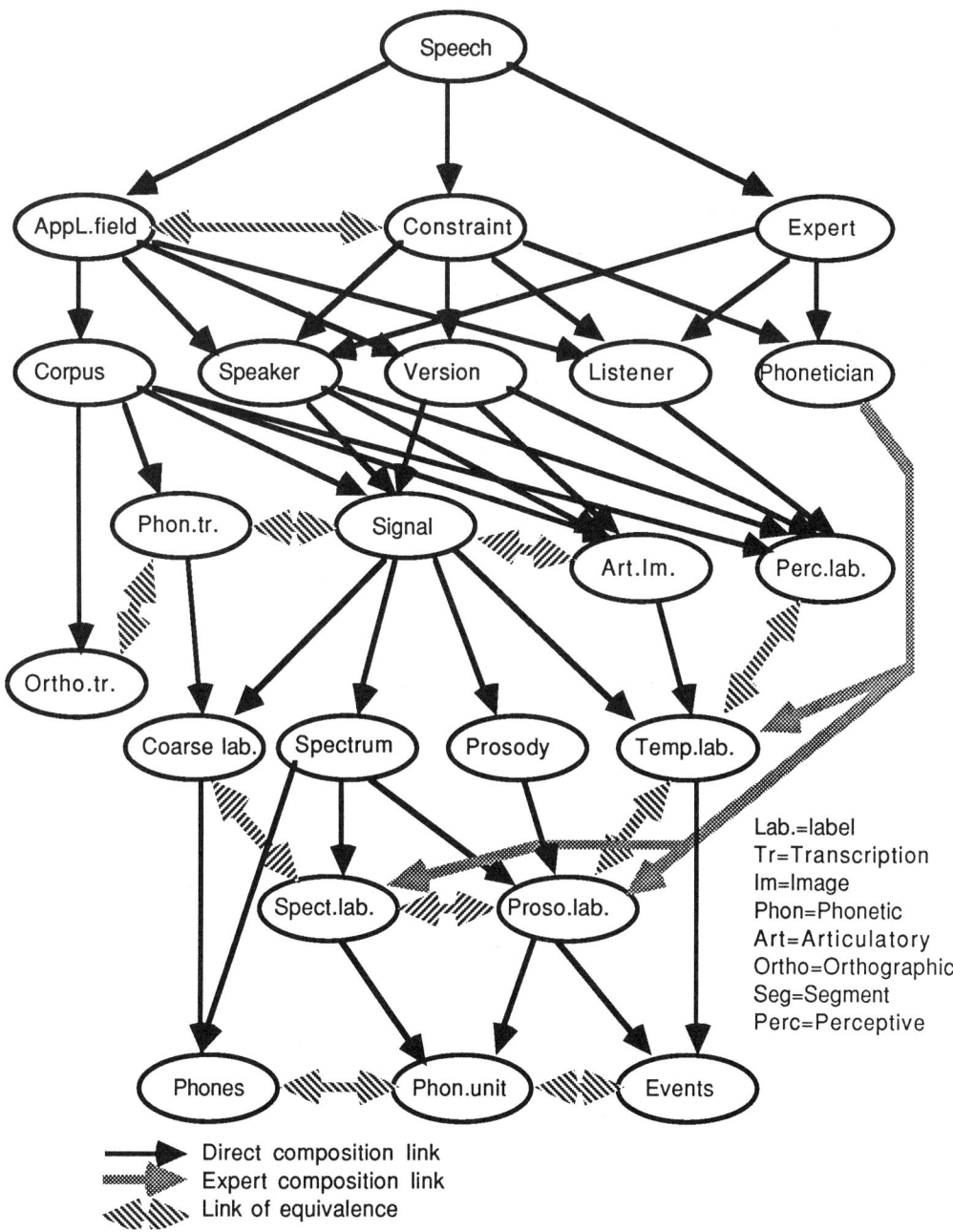

Lab.=label
Tr=Transcription
Im=Image
Phon=Phonetic
Art=Articulatory
Ortho=Orthographic
Seg=Segment
Perc=Perceptive

→ Direct composition link
⇒ Expert composition link
⇒ Link of equivalence

Figure 3.4. Composition and equivalence links among certain speech-objects.

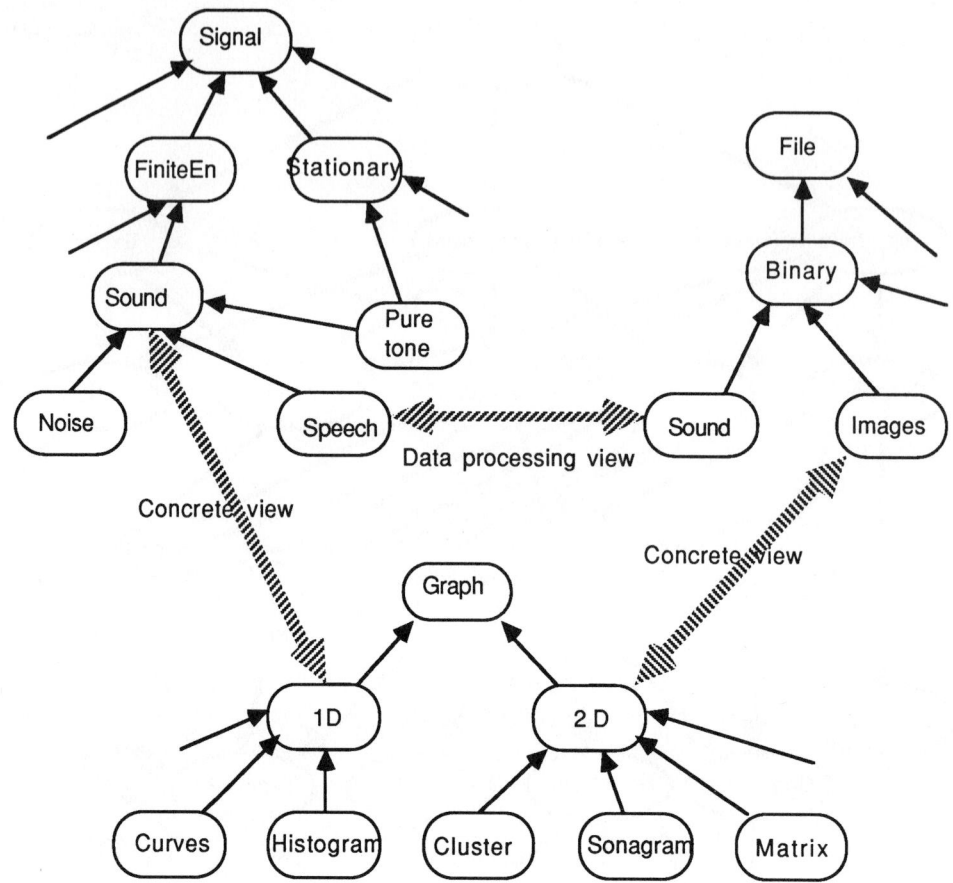

Figure 3.5. This graph represents certain objects with inheritance and equivalence relations (same conventions as for the preceding figures). Speech in this graph is a "sonorant-finite-energy-signal" (thus sonorant in particular) that can be represented --following the equivalence link-- as a "1D-graph" (curve or histogram). The "speech" object is thus linked with the "graph" object through a link internal to the attribute "concrete-view". Similarly through the "computer science-view" the "speech" object is linked with the "binary-sound-file" (or more simply: the speech is stored in a binary sound file).

Formal: series of bounded values (samples) arranged in a file,

Perceptive: audition deducted properties: intelligible or not, speech rate, etc.

Articulatory: articulatory properties related with the acoustics: closure, velum movements, etc.

Structural: properties which are deducted from the signal pattern description: continuity, temporal organization, etc.

Phonetical: properties related to segmentation into phonetic units: archiphonems, acoustic features, phonemes, etc.

Representation: 1D

Phone:

Definition: minimal acoustic unit of phonetic articulation
Views: [mathematical, acoustical, structural, phonetical, concrete]
Mathematical matrix or trajectory in R^n space,
Acoustical: properties derived from segmentation: homogeneous, stationary, transitory, etc.
Structural: temporal segment or event organization in a phonetic model,
Phonetical: properties related to phoneme,
Representation: 1D.

Acoustic cue:

Definition: characteristical acoustic value of phones
Views: [mathematical, acoustical, structural, phonetical, concrete]
Mathematical probability or plausibility coefficient,
Acoustical: properties derived from signal description organized as paradigms such as: closed/open, compact/diffuse, etc.
Structural: organization as patterns: bursts, vocalic transitions, etc.
Phonetical: clustering and modality effects properties related to phonetic model,
Representation: 1D.

Pattern:

Definition: mono- or multidimensional prototype
Views: [mathematical, formal,concrete]
Mathematical geometric figure: peak, valley, slope, singular point, etc.
Formal: procedure,
Representation: 1D, 2D.

Acoustic feature:

Definition: distinctive acoustic property of a phoneme
Views: [mathematical, acoustical, structural, phonetical, phonological, concrete]
Mathematical boolean value or predicate,
Acoustical: properties derived from acoustic cues,
Structural: syntagmatic combinatory,
Phonetical: phonemes properties on feature matrix,
Phonological: transformation rules as: deletions, insertions in context,
Representation:binary code.

Phoneme:

Definition: elementary (abstract) unit of a language sound

Views:[acoustical,formal, structural, phonetical,phonological, concrete]
Acoustical: rules on cues, features, etc.
Formal: symbolic values: labels, codebook, etc.
Structural: substance-form coupling or numeric-symbolic correspondence,
Phonetical: structuring of phones and features into phonemes,
Phonological: context description, joints between words, etc.
Representation: IPA code.

File:
Definition: collection of data
Views: [formal, concrete]
Formal: data structure, access, descriptors,
Representation: coding, size, etc.

Graph:
Definition: geometric representation
Views: [mathematical, concrete]
Mathematical geometrical properties
Concrete: histogram, pie, curve, 3D-projection, etc.
Representation: 1D, 2D.

The SHIRKA language (Rechenman, 1987) is well adapted to the expression and manipulation of these objects. "SHIRKA is an object-centred knowledge base management system. It uses a knowledge representation model inspired in 'frames' in which knowledge is organized in independent units. A representation unit is called a schema. A schema represents either a class of objects or a particular object . A class and its representatives, called instances, possess attributes. An attribute is described in turn by a list of valued slots (facets); the values are either schemas or references to schemas. The classes are organized in a structured trellis in which a class inherits attributes from dominant classes.

Example 1: the phoneme object and some of its attributes in the SHIRKA language (see inheritances in fig.3):
sorte - de=kind-of, est - un=is-a, etc. are key-words of SHIRKA language. '$' preceeds facets key-words

```
{ phoneme
  sorte_de = macro-class;
  acoustic-view   $un acoustic-parameter
        $com "cues, formants, prosodic-parameters";
  formal-view     $un phoneme-label
```

```
        $com "computer code closed to IPA code";
    structural-view      $un acoustic-phase
        $com "onset, steady-state, release";
    phonetical-view      $un acoustic-feature;
    phonological-view  $un coarticulatory;
    representation  $un strin
        $domaine IPA-code
        $com "IPA = International Phonetic Alphabet";
    composition-link     $com "none"
    equivalence-link     $liste_de transcription
        $com "orthographic, multilingual" }


{ acoustical-parameter
   sorte_de = speech-object;
   formant   $liste-de formant;
   cue         $liste-de cue;
   intensity $un real
        $com "dB unit"
        $intervalle [0 100];
   duration            $un real
        $com "ms unit"
        $intervalle [0 150];
   Fo          $un real
        $com "pitch in Hz"
        $intervalle [50 400] }


{ formant
   sorte_de = correlate;
   vocalic-formant      $un vocalic-formant;
   nasal-formant        $un nasal-formant;
   noise-formant  $un noise-formant }


{ vocalic-formant
   sorte_de = correlate;
   F1   $com "1st formant"
     $un real
     $intervalle [200 800];
   F2   $com "2d formant"
     $un real
     $intervalle [700 2000]
     $à-vérifier { greater-than
```

```
      x  $var <- F2;
      y  $var <- F1 }
  F3   $com "3rd formant"
      $un réel
      $intervalle [1800 3200]
      $à-vérifier { greater-than
          x  $var <- F3;
          y  $var <- F2 }}


{ greater-than
   sorte-de = predicate;
   function-name        $valeur sup
      x  $un real;
      y  $un real;
          $com "sup  is a Lisp function, true if x>y" }
etc.
```

Example 2: an allophone of phoneme /i/ (instance of the class "phoneme"):

```
{ phoneme-/i/
   est_un = phoneme,
   acoustic-view =
      { est-un = acoustic-parameter
         { est-un = formant
             { est-un = vocalic-formant
                   F1 = 260;
                   F2 = 2150;
                   F3 = 3100 }}

   { est-un = cue;
        acute-grave = 0.2;
        closed-open = 0.2;
        flat-sharp = 0.3;
        compact-diffuse = 0.75;
        mat-strident = 0.6 }
      intensity = 64;
      duration = 80;
      Fo = 146 }
   formal-view = etc. }
```

3.3 **Expertise and reasoning: the problem**

The latter part of this paper is concerned with knowledge manipulation by the expert (acquisition and researching). His role in the SIDOCParole system is situated at several levels: (L1) querying the information, data and/or knowledge contained in the base, and (L2) production of new knowledge and its integration in the base. The first level (L1) is a "classic" in the area of data and knowledge base fields. For the second level (L2) it is possible to separate the processes into tasks (T1-T4) as following:

(T1) The user extracts information from the base according to a certain experience plan: he builds an experience base (EB). This base can be considered as a personalized and structured working memory that permits non-centralized application of treatments.

(T2) In this EB he can eventually introduce weighted information (as probability coefficients, notes, etc.) or qualify them with symbols.

(T3) He can also introduce his own knowledge as facts (quantitative information) or as rules (symbolic informations) in this EB.

(T4) He may specify the reasoning mode of the system:

- problem solving mode, when he wants to assess his knowledge. In this case the system tries to prove this knowledge from the data. Reasoning is of a backward chaining type since what is known are the goals (conclusions),

- learning mode, when he wants to introduce a new piece of knowledge. The expert separates the observations into two groups; examples and counter-examples, and the system tries to produce knowledge by learning over these two sets of information. Thoise reasoning is of the forward chaining type since one cannot know the goals a priori but only the premises,

(T5) At the end of his experimentation, he can ask for the filing of his results. The BDCParole management system must organize the different experiences and control their coherence to allow further consultations.

The role that knowledge acquisition plays in KBS (Knowledge Based Systems) development is also given by Breuker, 1987): "Experts do not express their knowledge and know-how in a rule or frame like formalism, nor as verbal data easily mapped upon such formalisms. Strategies and inference methods can only be abstracted if such categories as goals, premises, facts, etc. can be read from the data. For knowledge acquisition some special purpose formalism at an intermediate level is required... Brachman, 1979) identifies primitives at five different levels of representation of static knowledge. These levels are: linguistic, conceptual, epistemological, logical and implementational. These levels can be extended to the analysis of verbal data on expertise."

3.3.1 *Formalization of experience bases*

The different interventions of the expert (tasks T1 to T3) amount first to the assembling of facts (observations selected from the general base) and then to inserting this knowledge into the base. (fig 3.6). For this the expert selects the necessary data for his experimentation, eventually weights them aided by modulators (symbols, coefficients, notes, etc.) and adds premises (properties that initialize the research of new knowledge) or conclusions (properties to be proven). The system is in charge of the production of knowledge and of the generation of a history of the experience.

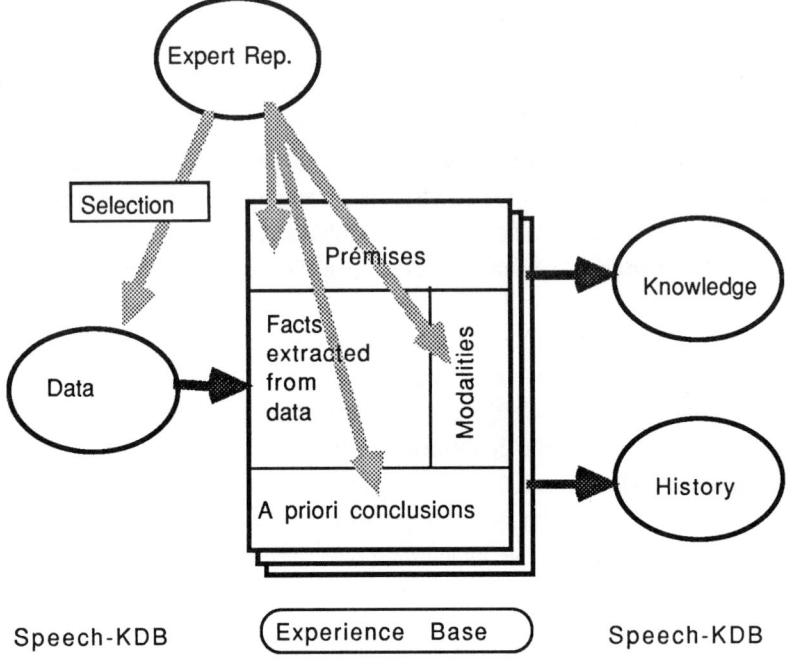

Figure 3.6. Structuring of an experiment base after selection of facts by the expert. The expert adds modulators (or modalities) to the extracted data, premises and/or conclusions (logical rules, re-write rules). The system initiates the inferencing process from this set of informations to infer new knowledge or to validate an a priori piece of knowledge. In the case of a concluding experiment, the experience history is saved in the base.

The premises, observations and conclusions of an experience can all be expressed under a re-write rule formalism where the left hand is a symbol and the right hand is a data structure (scalar or vector or matrix or list or tree):

$$S_{di}/H_{di} \dashrightarrow S_{oi}/H_{oi} \bmod \pi_i, \quad \text{for } i = 1,n$$

$$S_{dk}/H_{dk} \dashrightarrow S_{ek}/H_{ek} \bmod \pi_k, \quad \text{for } k = 1,m$$

where: S_d is a symbolic entity (class, name, etc.) defined in the H_d history,

S_o is the observed entity associated to S_d in the H_o history,

S_e is the entity hypothesized by the expert in the H_e history,

H_d, H_o, H_e are history containing the context and conditions in which the corresponding entities are obtained,

mod π is a modulator set by the expert on data selected (probability or plausibility coefficients, etc.).

History are objects which correspond nearly to the syntax defined for objects (cf.above).

3.3.2 *Example of experimentation problem*
Study of the acute feature for the /i/ vowel. We know that this feature is defined from acoustic functions and properties through the mutual opposition of phonemes. Facts scooping over the corpus /i/ and /other vowels/ must first be assembled to create opposition clusters. For this, two individual/variable statistics matrices are built, where the individuals are the means of the spectra vectors. The modulators are for example all taken equal to 1 (equiprobable). In the $BE_{/i,V/}$ we would have:

/i/ --> I_m [individual/variable matrix],

/other vowels/ --> V_m [individual/variable matrix],

modulators --> I   unit vector (here equiprobability),

$H_{d/i}$ are history for /i/ and /other vowels/ selection (as: name of corpus, speaker name, linguistic context, etc.),

$H_{o/mat/}$ is history for variable and computing mode definition (here they are the spectrum channel and cues).

In this stage of the experience, the expert can choose the mode of reasoning to be applied to the data: problem solving or learning.

(a) problem solving mode:

We suppose in this case that the property "acute-feature(phoneme /i/)=+acute" is to be proved: the problem is then to validate this knowledge over the data. By convention, the expert places this assertion in the "conclusion" part and selects from the function table the computing mode for acute-feature from the spectrum, for example by F'2 method. He sets acute-feature=F'2. If the feature always takes the value "+acute" over the $EB_{/i,V/}$ (relative to a limit Σ, to be specified, for example such that F'2>Σ where Σ is expressed in Hz), then the predicate can be considered to be locally true and the property is declared to be proven. Otherwise the system would provide the counter-examples such as to suggest a new experiment to the expert. In the case of a success, the system stores the knowledge "acute-feature(phoneme /i/)=+acute" with the history H_e=(), which would imply adding the facet \$à-vérifier (=check) and the calculation mode "F2" for the "acute-feature" attribute of the phoneme object /i/ in the BDCParole at the time of saving the experience.

(b) learning mode:

This is the inverse situation: supposing the predicate to be true (it is placed by convention as premise) the problem is to explain what being "+acute" means for data in the $BE_{/i,V/}$. The expert now selects the learning method: for example, an optimal discrimination alternative, that is, He=linear discriminator. Under these conditions the problem is to find those variables permitting the best separation of /i/ from other vowels; or, worded differently, does there exist a hyperplan that separates the cluster element, that is, a list of coefficients of the orthogonal direction of this hyperplan, if it exists. In SHIRKA this would result in the association (through the \$sib-filter facet) of the calculating method of the hyperplan with the acute-feature slot of phoneme /i/.

3.3.3 *Reasoning*

The SIDOCParole system can eventually offer a diverse reasoning mechanism from AI and PR fields according to the types of problem to be treated. Taking the term "reasoning" in its wider sense, the following types of reasoning could be handled in the system:

from IA:

logical reasoning (deduction)

reasoning by analogy

non-monotone reasoning

reasoning by generalization (induction)

from PR:

clustering reasoning

discrimination reasoning

like hood reasoning

This last group makes heavy use of data analysis and optimization techniques, which are kinds of learning.

In the PR domain we find a large variety of pattern matching and data clustering methods, as well as stochastic learning methods (Markov models, for example). Descriptive or explicative multidimensional data analysis also offers an optimization framework within which it is possible to find knowledge spanning across large data tables. These are numeric methods. We can switch to syntactic vector quantization methods (VQ) of numerical entries and find ourselves in a symbolic domain, the concern of AI. This is the way structural coupling methods (Ganascia, 1987; Guizol, 1985) have been used in ASP (Automatic Speech Processing).

3.4 **Knowledge manipulation**

By knowledge manipulation we understand:
- knowledge acquisition,
- search of knowledge in the base,
- reasoning which permits oneto obtain new knowledge.

In our system these manipulations are maintained under the control of the expert. Appropriate software must be offered to him which adequately manages his experiences. As mentioned above, this software includes a tool-box with procedures such as data analysis, logic inference and query interpreter modules allowing the chaining of the requested actions.

We distinguish two levels of queries:

(a) the selection query level which permit on to pick up an object from the base (data or knowledge) and to evaluate one or more attributes. Note here that the access path to the objects may be particularly complicated when an accumulation of conditions over corpus types, speakers, repetition number, linguistic context, etc. occur.

(b) the logical query level, involving reasoning over data and/or knowledge and that is generally preceded by a series of selection queries.

3.4.1 *The first level: SELECTION*

By SELECTION we mean only those queries that call for intervention of procedural calculations and location mechanisms of requested information in the base. Thois informations retrieves data and/or knowledge.

The following examples are illustrative of those queries posed by a user. For these queries the keywords may sometimes call for an explicit definition, since not all of them will be taken care of explicitly in the base. A dialog module would be available through the user interface. Two dialog cases are distinguished according to the objects involved: they are either already defined or demand an explicit definition (they are not present in the BDCParole). In the examples no explicit distinction is made between the base questioning queries and those that permit the gathering of facts in the EB. (These last though, would involve an active verb such as "produce" instead of "what is").

Example 1: What is the value of the first formant of sample 12 ?

After formulation of such a query the system may demand further specification of the keywords: (a) their definition or relation to other definitions --we do not treat recursive definitions here-- (b) the procedures involved during the instantiation of variables, (c) the unambiguous definition, (d) the deviation towards another formulation (the dialog can take place along the following lines with Q=system question and R=user's response):

Q1=value ? R1=numeric instantiation=assignment
Q2=1st formant ? R2=shown on spectrum
      (or R2=call predefined procedure
      or R2=? Q3=procedure ? R3=LPC + peak detection)
Q3=sample 12 ? R3=spectrum index 12
   This query searches for data and is to be distinguished from:
"What is the value of the 1st formant of /i/?" which constitutes a knowledge search in the phoneme /i/ object (the answer would be "250 Hz" following example in §2.4).

Example 2: Is there a peak on the intensity curve of /p/ phoneme at the end of words ?

   This query implies locating information aided by the form "peak". It can be located either from "knowledge" if it can be deduced from attributes of the phoneme /p/ objects, or from the intensity curves data for all the instances of the /p/ phoneme occurring at the end of words. In this case the dialog would be:

Q1=peak ? R1=pattern predefined
  (or R1=? then Q2=pattern ? R2=triangular)
Q2=intensity curve ? R2=object=prosodic-correlate, attribute=intensity
Q3= phoneme /p/ ? R3=object delimited by 'P' label
Q4= end of word ? R4=local_definition=followed_by_pausepause = 'X' label

   These two examples show this selection problem as a classic one:
   - in data base domain, through the search of data (even though some queries might be particularly complex),
   - in knowledge base domain, through the search of knowledge from object oriented representations.
   They show also that a decision between data and knowledge must be taken by the query interpreter of the system. We also notice that it is through these type of requests that the expert constructs his experiment base EB (see 3.2.1).

3.4.2 *The second level: DEDUCTION and INDUCTION*
With the second level of queries we enter into the domain of the logic. In a general way we call DEDUCTION any new information deduced from those contained in the base. We call INDUCTION any new information obtain by generalization from particular cases.

3.4.2.1 Deduction
As before, some examples will illustrate the most important points.

Example 3: Knowing that /a/ has a 1st formant about 600 Hz, is sample 12 an /a/ ?

First order logic permits a formalization of this problem. Let: $P = (F1 < 600+ \quad \& \quad F1 > 600-)$, given
and Q=(phoneme=/a/),
the problem can be solved by:
knowing that P => Q, if P then Q
which amounts to verifying P for sample 12 --we could alternatively use fuzzy logic as variants for validation of P. The predicate is already present in object /a/ as the value of attribute "F1". If $F1(600-, \quad 600+)$ is a default value for object /a/, then the query reduces to: "Is sample 12 an /a/ ?", which in turn becomes simply an automatic speech recognition problem.

Example 4: Are there any compact /i/'s ?

Let P(x)=(phoneme /x/ is compact)
the problem can be solved by:
$x ? tq P(x) \& (x=i)$
Which allows reasoning by contradiction since the expert knows that he must not find compact /i/'s in the phonological sense of the term.

Example 5: Knowing that sample 1 is an /a/, is sample 12 an /a/ ?

Here, in contrast with example 3, nothing says why sample 1 is an /a/. The analog operator ◊ would be defined. The problem can thus be formulated using first order logic:
Knowing P ◊ Q, if P then Q
The analog operator can be, for example, a likehood measure between two spectra (euclidian cepstral difference function, etc.).

Along this same line of thought, one could also use modal logic to weight the knowledge of experts amongst themselves. An epistemic modality could be introduced when phonetically labelling the sounds (association of a phonetical qualifier to portions of the sound signal being examined by the phonetician). This presupposes a phonetic modelisation that is necessarily shared by other experts: "expert X believes that P" denoted CX(P) and "X knows P" denoted SX(P), where additionally P is true with plausibility $\pi(X)$ attached by the same X (denoted P mod $\pi(X)$). This justifies a posteriori the notion of modulator coefficients introduced in §3.1.

3.4.2.2 Induction and learning
Induction and learning meet through methods founded on examples and counter-examples (Michalski, 1983). There are several ways to apply them:

either in their general sense, using the coupling mechanism,

or in a dichotomic fashion, using counter-examples only to validate the results obtained over the examples. This last manner is really a case of "learning from examples" plus a deductive trace over the counter-examples. These mechanisms are known in AI (Artificial Intelligence domain). We are only interested in two induction cases involving pattern recognition (PR) techniques.

a Backward chaining induction

Example 6: Is the FO cue of vowels correlated with the aperture ?

This is an induction case, since the aim is to generalize a property of the FO cue (Open/closed cue) for the vowels: we desire to know if the acoustic cue is correlated with the aperture parameter (openness of the lips). The correlation never gives a firm answer (results between -1 and +1). Therefore for this type of query there must be a supplementary decision criterium to answer it. This decision criterium also depends on the type of data, expert, etc.

The elements of the dialog are:

Item definition of the query:

Q1=FO cue? R1=object=Cue (attribute=FO)

Q2=vowel ? R2= 'V' label

Q3=correlated ? R3=predefined procedure=object

Q4=aperture ? R4=object=Correlate (attribute=articulatory)

Fact selection:

Q5= Examples ? R5=1st middle of corpus CVC

Q6= Counter-examples ? R6=2nd middle of corpus CVC

Q7= Premises ? R7=none

Q8= Conclusions ? R8=Correlation_function(Cue_FO,aperture)

Q9= Modulators ? R9=equiprobability

Choice of reasoning type:

Q10= Method ? R10=object=Data_analysis (Attribute=correlation_function)

Q11= Decision ? R11=greater_than (variable=threshold)

(b) Forward chaining induction

Example 7: How is an FO cue to be defined for the vowels so that it is correlated with the aperture ?

This case differs from the preceding one since the proposition "the FO cue is correlated with the aperture" is now a premise. The generalization to be achieved is over the FO cue which is considered as a function that one tries to define through one of its properties. This involves inverting answers R7 and R8 in the dialog and modifying the answers R1=linear_function(spectrum_channels) et R10=object=Data_analysis, Attribute= linear_regression. The result will be the linear function of the channels, named FO cue, which best explains the variable aperture.

This series of examples (1to 7) show that the general scheme (experience plan) of a query's interpretation and execution demands the following:

(a) assembling the facts by selecting data from the base and modulating them if necessary,

(b) separating them in statistical clusters (examples, counter-examples, or other),

(c) applying a series of reasoning procedures (AI and PR procedures) under control of the expert (he selects the modulatores, the clusters, etc.),

(d) confronting the results over several sets of experiments,

(e) concluding according to a decision criterium,

(f) filtering the conclusions and storing the historials. This last part is performed by the expert with the aid of the system tools (such as consultation tools, updating tools, etc.).

3.5 Conclusion

The reflexions contained in this paper, still ahead of the implementation, have emerged to answer important needs of automatic speech processing: to obtain the necessary knowledge within the framework of pattern recognition, knowing that (a) this knowledge is scattered among the many experts and (b) that it must be completed by systematic studies over data extracted from a large population. It is evident that this research should be guided by an "intelligent" usage of a comprehensive data and knowledge speech base, aiming at the accumulation of knowledge under the control of many experts. In the system proposed here (SIDOC-Parole), knowledge is obtained incrementally as the experiments of the experts are performed. Each of them disposes of a personalized experience base over which he can a priori validate his knowledge or perform guided learning. The results thus obtained by each expert are organized to be available for others.

We have arrived at a conceptual modularization of the SIDOC-Parole system into three parts:

(i) the data and knowledge speech base BDC-Parole administered by its managing system ,

(ii) a pattern recognition and data analysis tool-box ,

(iii) and the reasoning control mechanisms .

The formalism for data and knowledge that has appeared to us as the most adequate is based on object centered representation.

A language like SHIRKA is an interesting tool that has already allowed us to clarify the inheritance mechanisms in our application. The fact that there is still no interface with a data base management system (which would allow the easier management of the instances) obliges us to develop specific tools. SHIRKA includes inference mechanisms that permit the solution of part of the problems related to the execution of certain queries, especially of deduction. In this case we witness that available AI tools are not always well adapted to the problem of pattern recognition. For this we have developed data analysis procedures and related tools for related speech recognition. In this last case, the re-write rule formalism and the use of predicates are better adapted.

Our experience allows us to pose the fundamental problem of the practical integration between data base systems and knowledge base systems, as well as the harmonization of the AI and PR types of reasoning. It is actually difficult to conceive homogeneous systems with the existing tools and languages.

References

Brachman, R. (1979).On the Epistemological Status of Semantic Networks. In: *Associative Networks*, Ed. N.V. Findler , Academic Press, New York.

Breuker, J. (1987). *Model-Driven Knowledge Acquisition*, ESPRIT project 1098, Deliverable A1, University of Amsterdam and STL.

Caelen, J., Caelen-Haumont, G., Vigouroux, N., Barrera, C. & Malet, J. (1986). ARCANE: Acquisition et Recherche de Connaissances Acoustico-phonétiques dans un Noyau Evolutif. *Proc. of 15èmes JEP,* Aix-en-Provence, 207-11.

Cervantes, O. & Sérignat, J.F. (1987). Représentation objet dans BDCParole (Base de Données et de Connaissances pour la Parole). *Proc. of 16èmes JEP,* Hammamet.

Fernandez, Y. & Cervantes, O. (1988). Elément pour le gestionnaire de connaissance du sidoc-parole, to appear in : *Bulletin de l'Institut de la Pommunication Parlée, 2.*

Ganascia J.G. (1987). Agapé: de l'appariement structurel à l'apprentissage. *Intellectica,* **1**, N°2/3, 6-27.

Gascuel, O. (1987). Plage: un outil pour construire des systèmes d'apprentissage. *Intellectica,* **1**, N°2/3, 28-47.

Gervarter, W.B. (1987). The nature and evaluation of commercial Expert System Building Tools. *Computer,* **6**, 24-41.

Guizol, J. (1986). Apprentissage inductif de règles pour le décodage acoustico-phonétique. *Proc. of 15èmes JEP,* Aix-en-Provence, 227-30.

Halpern, J.Y. (1986). Reasoning about knowledge: An overview. *IBM Research Report* RJ5001.

Hayes-Roth, F. (1985). Rule Based System. *Communication of the A.C.M.,* **28**.
Hayes-Roth, F. & Mc Dermott, J. (1978). An Interference Matching Technique for Inducing Abstractions. *Communication of the A.C.M.,* **21**, n° 5, 401-10.

Michalski, R.S. (1980). Inductive Learning as Rule-Guided Generalization and Conceptual Simplification of Symbolic Descriptions. *Workshop on Current Developments in Machine Learning,* CMU Pittsburgh.

Michalski, R.S. (1983). A Theory and Methodology of inductive learning. *Artificial Intelligence,* **20**, 11-161.

Narat, V. & Lochet, P.Y. (1987). Les différentes techniques de représentation de connaissances utilisées en Intelligence Artificielle. *MDB,* **6**, 26-36.

Rechenman, F. (1987). SHIRKA, manuel de présentation. *Institut National de Recherches en Informatique et Automatique.*

Roulle, A. & Quinqueton, J. (1987). Dialogue pour l'apprentissage. *Intellectica,* **1**, N°2/3, 178-94.

Wiederhold, G. (1984). Knowledge and Data Base Management. *IEEE Software.*

Wielinga, B.& Breuker, J. (1986). Models of Expertise. Proceedings of ECAI, Brighton.

ON MULTIPLE CLASSIFICATION, POINTS OF VIEW AND OBJECT EVOLUTION

4.1 Introduction

Over the past few years, we have seen the development of several knowledge representation models. Ferber in (Ferber,1983) presents the two fundamental and opposite formalisms, which are relational and object oriented paradigms. The principal quality of a knowledge representation language is its declarative power. This one is based on the adequation criterion by which the artificial representation must be as close as possible to the natural expert 's representation. Many languages have implemented the object oriented paradigm like *Smalltalk* (Goldberg and Robson, 1983), Loops (Bobrow and Stefik, 1981), *Flavors* (Moon, 1986), *Mering* (Ferber, 1983) , *Kee* (Fikes and Kehler, 1985) ...Basic concepts of object oriented languages can be found in (Stekik and Bobrow, 1985), (Nygaard, 1986) or for a minimal, general and uniform definition in Objvlisp (Briot and Cointe, 1986).

We are interested here in one of the most declarative concepts which is classification expressiveness. It will be shown that this feature is constrained by the instantiation feature, particularly for multiple classification, points of view and object evolution. Then we will present the *Rome* language and its multiple and evolutive representation principle, as a simple and uniform solution to the previous problem.

4.2 Object oriented representation

4.2.1 *Preliminary*

In an object oriented approach one describes its problem (knowledge) as a set of interrelated objects. Each object has its own *characterization* . Conventionally the characterization is a set of characteristics of fundamentally two types. *Factual characteristics* are data owned by the object, they describe its local state, its attributes (instance variables, fields, attributes, slots ...). *Behavioral characteristics* are actions the object can realize (methods, procedures ...). The characterization is owned by the object, we say encapsulated, ie, the object is responsible for its local knowledge. The only way to activate an object is by a sending message: one does not manipulate an object but must communicate with it. This is summarised by the two well known citations "actors are potentially active chunks of knowledge which communicate by exchanging polite messages" (Hewitt and Smith, 1975) where actors can be replaced by objects and "knowledge should be organized around conceptual entities with associated descriptions and procedures" (Bobrow and Winograd, 1977).

One of the major controversies in the object oriented community is how to specify object characterization and particularly object similarities. There are essentially two answers to this question which we can qualify as prototype oriented and class oriented object oriented languages (poool and coool !). We will not dwell on this controversy since our paper is only concerned with the class oriented approach and because *Rome* is very class oriented, see (Lieberman, 1986b) for a good discussion on this and (Lieberman, 1986a) for a presentation of prototype oriented approach.The declarative way to specify objects characterization in the class oriented model is *classification*.

4.2.2 *Classification*

Classification includes both class notion and class-subclass relation. Some objects have similar characteristics and the expert naturally groups them around a general and abstract concept of class according to some abstraction process (Lalonde and Pugh, 1985; Wegner, 1986). The class notion has two fundamental interpretations. First, the *set interpretation* of a class associates to it the set of all the similar objects it generalizes. According to this, objects are considered as members of classes. This interpretation is intuitive and is at the root of algebraic models of object oriented languages such as in Bruce and Wegner, (1986).Secondly, by the *schematic interpretation* a class defines a general and abstract characterization or scheme for all its members.

Objects are more or less similar, which induces on the set of classes a class-subclass relation with respectively two interpretations. Associated to the set interpretation of a class is the *inclusion interpretation* of this relation, by which the set of all the objects members of a subclass is included in that of each of its superclasses.So the subclass is a restriction of one of its superclass. Associated to the schematic interpretation of a class is the *specialization interpretation* of the previous relation, by which the characterization defined by a subclass is a specialization or a refinement of that of each of its superclasses (inversely a generalization, an abstraction).

This constructs a classes lattice, assuming that a class can be subclass on more than one class, on which runs the fundamental inference mechanism which is inheritance (Ducourneau and Habib, 1987, Snyder, 1986 ; Briot, 1985).

4.2.3 *Instantiation*

It will be shown now that classification expressiveness is constrained by instantiation. Conventionally a class has two tied functionalities which are *abstraction* and *instantiation.* The abstraction functionality refer to the previous interpretations of a class. A class generalizes a set of similar objects and define their characterization. So in a uniform manner a class is also an object with its own characteristics which are the attributes "attributes" and "methods" by which it can define an objects scheme and the attribute "superclasses" which contains the list of its superclasses (assuming the multiple inheritance feature). The instantiation functionality is the potentiality for a class to create, generate objects, so called its instances, according to the scheme inferred from it by the inheritance mechanism.These objects are consequently members of this class, so called their instantiation class, and of all of its superclasses.

But instantiation is also the only way to declare objects membership, which hard-wires the object to its instantiation class by the instantiation link ("is-a" attribute) at creation time.This is what we call U.R.C for *Unique Representation Constraint* by which an object only exists as instance of its unique instantiation class. So it cannot be member of other classes unless they were superclasses of its instantiation class. As regards schematic interpretation of a class, an object is so completely and definitively characterized at creation time. Consequently an object cannot be directly characterized by more than one class and its characterization cannot simply evolve. Let us show in the following sections two consequences on knowledge object oriented representation.

4.2.4 *Multiple classification and points of view*

We have seen earlier that classification is one of the most declarative aspects of object oriented languages for knowledge representation and particularly to specify taxonomies.Though a problem arises when there are multiple classification of the same objects. Each classification consider distincts criteria from different points of view or perspectives (Goldstein and Bobrow, 1980; Bobrow and Stefik, 1981). This is particularly important in knowledge representation where the classification is rarely unique, notably in multi-expertise. As for example (Carré and Comyn, 1987ab) in electronic design one can consider a component from functional, technological and spatial points of view. In nutrition proteins can be classified from biochemist's point of view in the four classes "basic protein" n-cyclic protein" "neutal protein" acid protein" and from nutritionist's point of view in "essential protein" or "non-essential protein".

Let us take the following simple example about multiple classification of persons from the professional, leisure and social points of view. The respective classes hierarchies are:

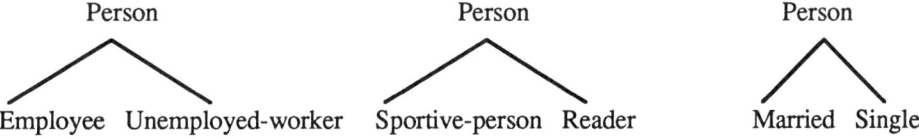

How can one declare that a person, say John, is unemployed, sportive and single or in an object oriented representation how to declare that the object representing John is member of the classes Employee sportsman and Single? Because of U.R.C the classical answer is to create a product subclass of these three classes and also all the other potential combinations over these three hierarchies, which leads to a product lattice using multiple inheritance:

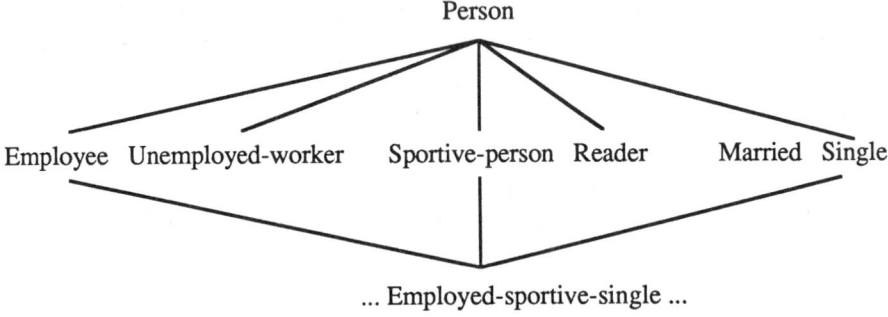

... Employed-sportive-single ...

With this solution John is created as an instance of Unemployed-sportive-single.It is easy to see how the lattice would be artificially complicated when the number of classes would grow. As mentioned in (Lang and Pearlmutter, 1986) "above a certain level of complexity, finding a type with certain known characteristics can become difficult" and the management of this "plethora of possible combinations of *mixing* " become a thorny problem. Of course facilities can be implemented to manage them by some additional mechanism like the mixin_manager of Oaklisp, presented in the above paper.

Since our discuss is concerned with the classification expressiveness, our solutions are intentionally designed with a classification or inheritance oriented approach as opposed to some *aggregation* oriented approach. Briefly aggregation (Madsen, 1986) refer to the "is-part-of" relation according to another abstraction mechanism which is based on decomposition/ aggregation as opposed to the "is-a" and "is-kind-of" relations supported by the classification and inheritance features of object oriented languages. With such an approach the previous expert's classification is translated into the flat lattice of only the class Person, much more complicated. This class must define the three attributes "professional-aspect", "leisure-aspect" and "social-aspect" which will contain references to respective instances of classes "Professional-aspect" ... as parts of an instance of Person. Since these objects are encapsulated in this latter object, their management must be programmed in the Person class, assuming the respect of block structure or encapsulation rules (Madsen, 1986; Snyder, 1986). Here again facilities can be implemented to manage such structures like the notion of composite objects in *Loops*. This language and also *Pie* (Goldstein and Bobrow, 1980) offer a generalization of this aggregation oriented approach with the notion of *perspective*. They define the class Node whose members are characterized by a list of perspectives (instances of the class Perspective) and methods for managing this internal objects such as "AddPersp"

"DeletePersp" "GetPersp" to respectively add, delete and get a perspective.We will not divell on this controversy since, as mentioned above, they do not use classification/inheritance expressiveness. This controversy is discussed in (Carré and Comyn, 1987c).

Another solution is announced in (Hendler, 1986) where mixins could be added directly to instances by an *enhancement* technique. Mixins are viewed as "packets of functionality that can be added to entities of a given type". So with such an approach one can define the "packets" Employee ... Sportsman ... Single as independent mixins and add the wanted ones to some instance of Person. Such packets ("enhancement categories") are separate from the classes hierarchy so that you must choose whether Employee is a proper subclass of Person or only an independent packet, which can be potentially added to entities of some type.

We will see in the 4.3 section that in *Rome* U.R.C is denied so that it is possible to make an object direct member of subclasses of its instantiation class which is viewed as its minimal class. This is called "multiple representation". So, intuitively on the previous example, the classification is strictly preserved. John is created as an instance of Person, its instantiation class, and will be dynamically member of Employee, Sportsman and Single. This problem is solved in a uniform manner with the following evolution problem.

4.2.5 *Object evolution*

This problem arises when one wants to make class membership of an object and consequently its characterization evolve. This evolution capability could be useful in design, diagnosis, identification processes or more generally during a decision process. In (Carré and Comyn, 1987b) we show the evolution necessity of an electronic component during a design process from the theoretical phase to the technological phase. We have seen earlier that U.R.C stands in the way of this evolution because the object is hard-wired to its instantiation class by its fixed instantiation link at creation time. So an object cannot simply evolve inside the classes hierarchy and one cannot use the generalization/refinement relation to make evolve the object characterization itself evolve.

Let us come back to the previous example about the classification of persons, and suppose we want to specify that John is now unemployed, ie, the corresponding object is now member of Unemployed-worker. This can be decided by the application of some expert rule like "if a person works in a company and this company goes bankrupt then this person becomes unemployed". A basic solution would be to create another object, instance of Unemployed-Sportive-single, to copy the common instantiated characteristics from the old version to this new one and to destroy the old version. It would be the same problem if John get married ... Of course this can be done by programmed methods similar to *coercion* operations as in *Oaklisp* but it is shown in (Hendler, 1986) that it is not a suited solution notably because of complexity (coercion of an Employed-sportive-single object in an Unemployed-sportive-single one ...). Another solution for this management would be something like an additional mechanism similar to *virtual copy* (Mittal, Bobrow and Kahn, 1986) "at the boundary between classes and instances" or rather between class oriented approach and prototype oriented approach (see 4.2.1).The idea would be to consider the old version of John as a prototype of the new version, or inversely the new version as an *extension* of the old one, using the prototype oriented jargon (Lieberman, 1986ab). In such a solution the extension can share by *delegation* all the characteristics of its prototype it wants to, and have its "personal" characterization. Notably it can inhibit the characteristics it does no longer have such as Employee's ones for the new John.

Here again an *aggregation* oriented design could "solve" this problem as mentioned in Carré and Comyn, (1987c). One can define methods which manipulate the previous "professional-aspect" "leisure-aspect" and "social-aspect" attributes in the very general class Person. The dynamical aspect of the perspectives in *Loops* or *Pie* (because they are managed by the above methods AddPersp ...) would be also a solution in such an aggregation oriented approach.

It seems that the announced *enhancement* technique (Hendler, 1986) will result in a more simple solution since one can dynamically add (and delete ?) mixins to instances and implicitly use the new added functionalities which satisfy characterization evolution.

In *Rome* this problem is solved by the *evolutive representation* principle or the evolutive membership of an object to subclasses of its instantiation class. Intuitively John, who was member of the classes Employee, Sportive-person and Single at the end of the previous section, will be no longer member of Employee but become member of Unemployed-worker.The uniform *multiple and evolutive representation* solution will be explained in the next section.

4.3 Rome

4.3.1 *Preliminary*
Rome is an experimental object oriented language which implements original features such as those introduced here, multiple and evolutive representation (*Rome* as Evolutive an Multiple Object Representation). It is a *lisp*-based metacircular language which definition will be briefly exposed (see (Carré and Comyn 1987c) for a detailed presentation) , and which implementation was made in *Le_lisp* (Chailloux, 1984).

4.3.2 *Basic notions*
It is always difficult to present a metacircular kernel since "it is almost as though the reader must know everything before knowing anything" (preface of the *Smalltalk* book (Goldberg and Robson, 1983)). So we will present at first place the central object notion, then the class notion, knowing that objects are defined by classes and classes are objects.

A *Rome object* has a three-parts characterization, *attributess, methods* and *selectors*. Attributes and methods define its internal and encapsulated characterization. Attributes are classical fields or instances variables. Methods are *lisp* lambda-expressions which can be applied only by the object with the primitive application *(applymeth method-name arguments)*. Selectors define its external characterization. Each selector has an associated method, as defined above. Message sending is the only way to communicate with an object from outside by the primitive *(send an-object selector-name arguments)*. The object reaction is to apply ("to applymeth") its local method associated to the selector-name, if they both exist. This selector/method or external/internal distinction is a proper feature of *Rome* that we will no longer discuss, since it is not the goal of this paper. Each object is created as an instance of a unique instantiation class at which it is linked by the *iclass* attribute and become member of this class by the *rclasses* attribute. This basic object notion is described in the more general class *OBJECT* which defines the latter attributes and methods such as <- ? bprint error ...for respectively writing reading an attribute printing its characterization returning an error ... Some of this methods are associated to selectors like (print bprint). Particularly <- and ? are only internal methods, as defined earlier, with no associated selectors and so encapsulated in the object and only applyable by itself (applymeth), which is a guarantee of encapsulation.

Rome classes are defined by two classes ("metaclasses") *R-CLASS* and *I-CLASS*. R-CLASS is the more general class of all the classes, so called at this level representation classes. It is a subclass of OBJECT, that is why classes are objects. It defines the basic abstraction functionality (see 4.2.3) by which a class generalizes a set of similar objects and defines their characterization. So R-CLASS defines the attributes *attributes methods* and *selectors* by which its members, among them itself OBJECT and I-CLASS, can characterize objects. It also defines the *surcl* multivalued attribute which will contain the list of the superclasses for multiple inheritance. I-CLASS is a subclass of R-CLASS and defines the instantiation functionality by which its members, so called instantiation classes and among them itself R-CLASS and OBJECT, can create objects, their instances. So I-CLASS essentially defines the method *basicnew* and the associated selector *new* for the instantiation mechanism. Notice that the distinction abstraction/instantiation functionalities and consequently R-CLASS/I-CLASS is also a proper feature of Rome. The fact that I-CLASS is only a subclass of R-CLASS and not merged with it must be interpreted as followed: all the classes have basically the abstraction functionality as members of R-CLASS and only some of them , members of I-CLASS, have the added instantiation functionality. Consequently abstract classes and mixins (only inheritable classes) can be created in Rome as instances of R-CLASS, they will not be instantiated. The inheritance mechanism runs for an object on the rclasses attribute and then on the classes lattice implemented by the surcl attribute. It will be explained in the special 4.3.4 section, since it is an original feature of Rome.

To sum up OBJECT R-CLASS and I-CLASS are arranged according to the following metacircular scheme:

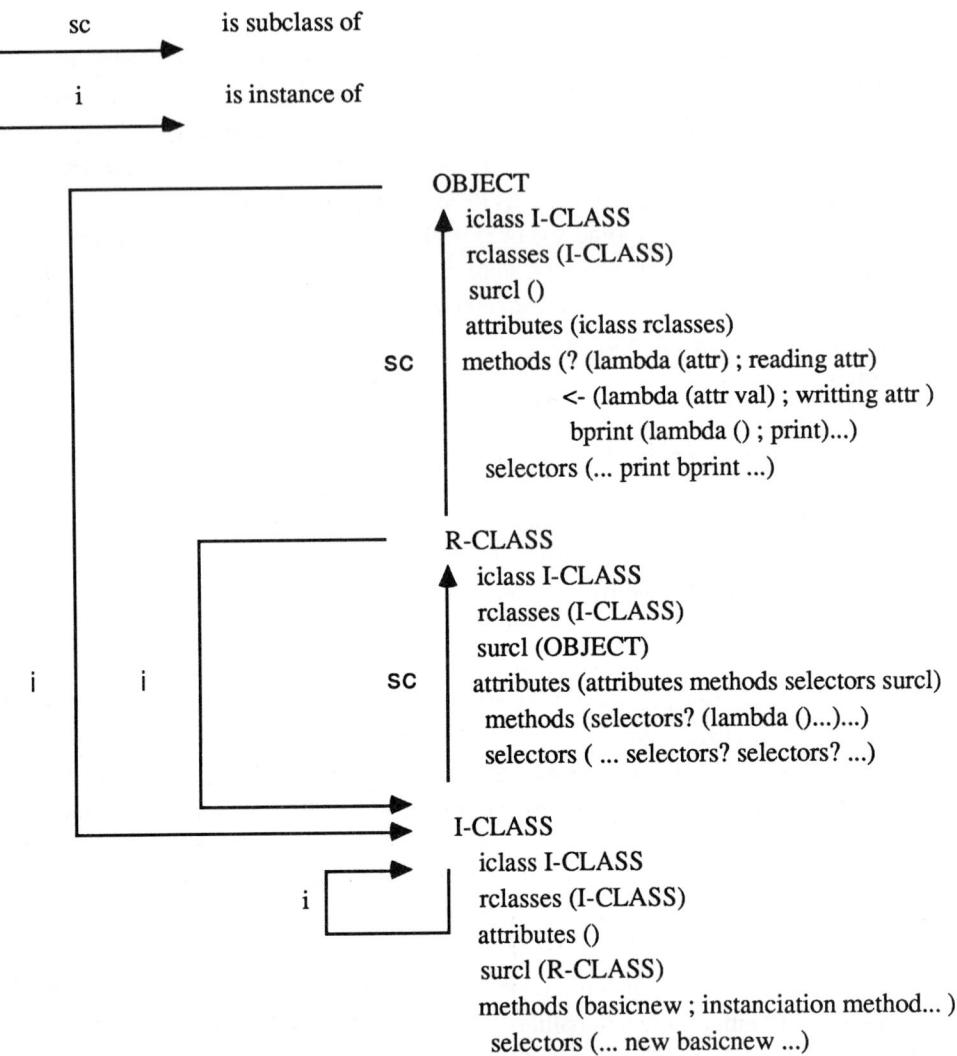

Notice that at this level the object notion, defined by OBJECT, is quite classical, since it is instance of one unique instantiation class (iclass attribute) and direct member of only this one (rclasses attribute is initialized at instantiation time). Evolutive and multiple representation is described in the following R-OBJECT subclass of OBJECT so that only objects members of this subclass have the inherent potentialities. Consequently at this stage *Rome* remains similar to most of the existing object oriented languages.

4.3.3 *Evolutive and multiple representation*
The basic idea is the definition of a subclass of OBJECT, called R-OBJECT, whose members can dynamically manipulate their rclasses attribute. This is done by the methods *basicr+* and *basicr-* parameterized by a class, let C. By the application of the first method

the object become member of C, if it was not yet. By the application of the second method the object is no longer member of C (and of course of all its subclasses), if it was, but remains member of the superclasses of this one. Since basicr+ and basicr- are associated to the respective selectors *r+* and *r-* these applications can be made by message sending.The C parameter is constrained by what is called *R.C* for *Representation Constraint* which specifies that potential dynamic representation classes of an r-object must be subclasses of its instantiation class. Intuitively R.C can be interpreted as the fact that an r-object can only evolve under its instantiation class. So this one is considered as its minimal and irrevocable representation class.

Let us consider the initial multiple classification of persons. First of all the persons are all members of the very general and minimal class Person, which is their instantiation class (Person is instance of I-CLASS). Persons can be viewed from professional, leisure and social points of view which result in the respective subclasses Prof-person, Leisure-person and Social-person. Persons from professional point of view can be subclassified in Student, Employee and Unemployed-worker, from leisure point of view in Sportive-person and Reader, and from social point of view in Married-person and Single. This leads to the following hierarchy:

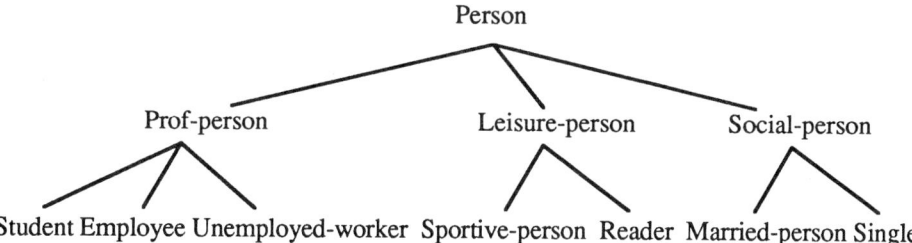

Person is subclass of R-OBJECT so that its members can have the multiple and evolutive representation potentialities. Since the subclasses of Person are only potential representation classes for its instances they are instances of R-CLASS. We will not show all the instantiation and subclass links.

John is a person, so the corresponding object is instance of Person by the message (send 'Person 'new 'john). He is unemployed, sportive and single by the respective messages (send 'john 'r+ 'Unemployed-worker), (send 'john 'r+ 'Sportive-person) and (send 'john 'r+ 'Single). After all that, the status of its rclasses attribute is (Single Sportive-person Unemployed-worker) and that of its iclass attribute is (and will remain) Person. Now consider that John is no more unemployed by the message (send 'john 'r- 'Unemployed-worker). Then he can become an Employee by the message (send 'john 'r+ 'Employee).The value of its rclasses attribute is now (Employee Single Sportive-person). Notice that John will be always a person unless the object is detroyed, the message (send 'john 'r- 'Person) will provok an error because the class person does not respect the R.C constraint. It will be the same error for the application of r- on all the superclasses of Person.

4.3.4 *Inheritance*

The multiple inheritance mechanism determines the characteristics of an object from its rclasses attribute, ie, from all its direct representation classes and then over the consequent classes sublattice of all their superclasses built on the surcl attribute. The set of the attributes of an object is computed at creation time and updated each time the rclasses attribute is modified for an r-object. On the other hand the lookup of methods and selectors is dynamic. This inference mechanism is based on two principles which make no difference between the three types of characteristics.

First of all, let the following definition of *independent classes* : two classes are independent if one is not subclass or superclass of the other one, ie, there is no inheritance way between these two classes, and particularly no generalization/refinement relation between them. Then the *V-principle* (V as Vertical) or *refinement principle* specifies that characteristic search is ascendant over the classes lattice and stops at the first definition encountered, so that it is the most specific one which is always considered. The *H-principle* (H as horizontal) or *independence principle* specifies that there is no conflict of same-named characteristics defined in independent classes. These conflicts classically appear for multiple inheritance (Ducourneau and Habib, 1987; Snyder, 1987) when a characteristic has the same name in more than one independent superclasses of a class. There are two types of strategies for dealing with multiple inheritance. Linear strategies take care of the order of the list of the superclasses (surcl attribute) so that the class-subclass partial order is translated in a total order and the inheritance graph is changed in a linear chain.With such strategies only one conflicting characteristic is inherited. They are based on a depth first search as in *Flavors* or *Loops* or on a breadth first search as in *Mering*. Graph oriented strategies run directly on the inheritance graph so that a class can specify a path to inherit a characteristic such as prefixing its name by a class. This solution is used in extended *Smalltalk* (Borning and Ingalls, 1982) with the compound selectors.

In *Rome* this problem is still more crucial because of the multiple representation feature.With multiple representation an object can be a direct member of more than one class, and these classes are independent , ie, the representation classes appearing in the rclasses attribute are independent. Moreover, because of evolutive representation, a characteristic can be dynamically redefined for an object from one representation state to another. So, as regards the V-principle, an object will always behave according to its most specific characterization and the H-principle ensures that there will be no multiple representation conflicts. This problem is solved in a uniform manner for multiple inheritance among classes and multiple representation of objects.

The solution is based on the "as a-class" parameter which can be associated to a characteristic. Intuitively this parameterization corresponds to a point of view on the object, "a-characteristic as a-class" can be interpreted as "a-characteristic from the point of view of a-class". Technically, let the representation lattice of an object be the sublattice of all its representation classes (that is its direct representation classes, contained in its rclasses attribute, and all their superclasses). Then "a-characteristic as a-class" for an object, where a-class must be of course one of its representation class , makes a virtual projection of its representation lattice which results in the sublattice of all the superclasses and the subclasses of a-class.Then a breadth first search, which always respects the V-principle, runs on this projection to find a-characteristic. Notice that the specified class may not be necessarily this one where the characteristic will be found, since the search is not made directly in this class but over the projection of all its related classes. This respects the V-principle (a characteristic can be refined by one of the suclasses of the specified class). That is why this solution is different from simple renaming the characteristics by prefixing it with the class name. This notion adds the *point of view interpretation* to the class notion by which each representation class of an object can be considered as a point of view on it.This parameterization can be associated to an attribute in the ? and <- methods applications, (applymeth '? '(an-attribute as a-class)) or (applymeth '<- '(an-attribute as a-class) val), to a method in the application primitive (applymeth '(a-method as a-class) arguments) and finally to a selector in the message sending primitive (send an-object '(a-selector as a-class) arguments). On the previous example, assume that both Student and Sportive-person define the attribute card-number the method (cn<- (lambda (val) (applymeth '<- 'card-number val)) for writing this attribute and the associated selector card-number=. The object john is instance of Person and member of the subclasses Student and Sportive-person. Then the following messages (send 'john '(card-number= as Student) "E12") (send 'john '(card-number= as Sportive-person) "S12") will have the wanted behavior, that is respectively affecting the card-number attributes as defined in Student and in Sportive-person.The following messages would have the same effect (send 'john '(card-number= as Prof-person) "E12") (send 'john '(card-number= as Leisure-person) "S12) because of the projection principle. Consider now that the class Sportive-person has two subclasses Tennis playor and Baseball-player which redefined the method cn<- to verify that the val parameter begins respectively by a "t" and a "b". John is now member of the subclass Tennis playor then the message (send 'john '(card-number= as Leisure-person) "t12") will result in the projection (Tennis playor Sportive-person Leisure-person R-OBJECT OBJECT) on which the inheritance mechanism retrieves the cn<- method in Tennis playor, which is correct. The fact that one can specify a high level class in this parameterization is well suited for the point of view notion. Indeed with such a solution the user does not have to know exactly the object representation under a point of view class. This is shown in the previous messages where Leisure-person and Prof-person are typically independent and high level points of view on a person.

4.4 Conclusion

In this paper we have shown that the instantiation feature stands in the way of classification expressiveness which is one of the most declarative aspect of object oriented languages based on the class notion for knowledge representation. Particularly some problems raise for multiple classification of objects from independent points of view and for object evolution inside the classes hierarchy. Classical solutions were discussed and we have introduced the *Rome* solution based on the multiple and evolutive object representation principle. We hope that this approach extends the declarative power of the object oriented model and the interest of its fundamental inference mechanism , which is inheritance.

References

Bobrow, D.G. & Stefik, M.S. (1981). *The Loops manual*. Memo KB-VLSI-81-13, Xerox Parc.

Bobrow, D.G. & Winograd, T. (1977). An overview of KRL a Knowledge Representation Language, **1**. *Cognitive Science*.

Borning, A.H. & Ingalls, D.H. (1982). Multiple inheritance in Smalltalk-80. *Proceedings of the AAAI 82*, Pittsburgh.

Briot, J.P. (1983). *Instanciation et heritage dans les langages objets. Thèse*, LITP, Paris.

Briot, J.P. & Cointe, P. (1986). The Objvlisp model: definition of a uniform, reflexive and extensible object oriented language. Rapport n° 1, CMI, Paris.

Bruce, K.B. & Wegner, P. (1986). An algebraic model of subtypes in object oriented languages. *Sigplan Notices*, **21**, n° 10.

Carré, B. & Comyn, G. (1987 a). *Instanciation et representation*. Rapport n° 94, LIFL, Lille.

Carré, B. & Comyn, G. (1987 b). Contraintes liées à une representation par objets. Rapport n° 95, LIFL, Lille.

Carré, B. & Comyn, G. (1987 c). Etude et specification d'un noyau orienté objet pour la réalisation d'un outil de développement de systèmes experts. Rapport n° 96, LIFL, Lille.

Chailloux, J. (1984). *Le_Lisp, manuel de référence*. INRIA, Paris

Ducourneau, R. & Habib, M. (1987). La multiplicité de l'héritage dans les langages orientés objet. Rapport n° 1/87, LIB, Brest.

Ferber, J. (1983). Mering: un langage d'acteurs pour la representation et la manipulation des connaissances. *Thèse*, Paris VI.

Fikes, R. & Kehler, T. (1985). The role of frame-based representation in reasoning. *Communications of the ACM*, **28**, n° 9.

Goldstein, I.P. and Bobrow, D.G. (1980). Extending object oriented programming in Smalltalk. *Conference record of the 1980 Lisp conference*, Stanford.

Goldberg, A. & Robson, D. (1983). *Smalltalk-80, the language and its implementation*. Addison-Wesley.

Hendler, J. (1986). Enhancement for multiple inheritance. *Sigplan Notices*, **21**, n°10.

Hewitt, C.E. & Smith, B. (1975). A Plasma primer. MIT Artificial Intelligence Laboratory.

Lalonde, W.R. & Pugh, J.R. (1985). Specialization, generalization and inheritance, teaching objectives beyond data structures and data types. *Sigplan Notices*, **20**, n° 8.

Lang, K.J. & Pearlmutter, B.A. (1986). Oaklisp: an object oriented scheme with first class types. *Proceedings of the OOPSLA' 86 conference*, Portland, Oregon.

Lieberman, H. (1986 a). Delegation and inheritance: two mechanisms for sharing knowledge in object oriented systems. *Actes des journées langages orientés objet*, Bigre + Globule n° **48**, Afcet-informatique, Paris.

Lieberman, H. (1986 b). Using prototypical objects to implement shared behavior in object oriented systems. *Proceedings of the OOPSLA' 86 conference*, Portland, Oregon.

Madsen, O.L. (1986). Block structure and object oriented languages. *Sigplan Notices*, **21**, n° 10.

Mittal, S., Bobrow, D.G. and Kahn, K.M. (1986). Virtual copies: at the boundary between classes and instances. *Proceedings of the OOOPSLA' 86 conference*, Portland, Oregon.

Nygaard, K. (1986). Basic concepts in object oriented programming. *Sigplan Notices*, **21**, n° 10.

Snyder, A. (1986). Encapsulation and inheritance in object oriented programming languages. *Proceedings of the OOPSLA' 86 conference*, Portland, Oregon.

Stefik, M.S. and Bobrow, D.G. (1985). Object oriented programming: themes and variations. *The A.I magazine*, 40-62.

Wegner, P. (1986). Classification in object oriented systems. *Sigplan Notices*, **21**, n° 10.

5 W. Dang

MODELLING COMPLEX HUMAN-COMPUTER DIALOGS IN OBJECT ORIENTED LANGUAGES

5.1 Introduction

With the growing progress of computing technology, the end users of computer systems have shifted from professional to nearly everybody, so have human factors become so important that they must be considered in the early design of a computer system (Shackel, 1987). Further more, human - computer interaction has dramatically changed in the area of graphics . Instead of typing simply on the keyboard, users can use a pointing device to manipulate the graphic object, select a choice in a menu, and draw pictures on the screen. The introduction of graphics ha lend to the construction of the user friendly interface, but it has made software development very time consuming. The objective of human - computer interaction modelling is twofold: to study the human factors in computer systems and to facilitat the construction of a user - machine interface .

In an interactive computer system, the user inputs and the computer processing are interleaved, the system would take the actions and produce the outputs at any point of an input stream, resulting in a dialog. The software engineering suggests separating the user interface part and the functionality part of an interactive system, so a generic system called a User Interface Management System (UIMS) can be constructed independently of the application program. The dialog model is the central issue of n UIMS and it determines the architecture of the UIMS. Models of human - computer interaction fall into two categories. The first one is the linguistic model which views user - computer interaction dialog as a language (Reisner, 1981), so different grammatical phrases can be used to formally specify the interaction. The second one is the spatial model which understands the interaction as events and event processing (Green, 1985). Although the linguistic model provides a formal method that separates the semantic, syntactic and lexical levels of a dialog, it has limitations when used for specifying complex cases such as multiple dialog management. Based on the general idea of the event and event processing, we describe in this paper how complex dialogs can be modelled in object oriented paradigm, how some artificial intelligence techniques facilitat modelling and how this model can help us in constructing a complicated user - computer interface. Section 2 gives the general architecture of dialog modelling. Complex dialog modelling is the main topic of this paper; problems such as form based communication, interruption of a dialog and multiple dialog management will be studied in section 3. Finally, implementation considerations will be discussed.

5.2 Dialog modelling and object oriented paradigm

An interactive computer system is characterized by frequent user - computer interactions: the user types on the keyboard to enter a text string, clicks the mouse button to choose an entry of a menu, or uses a mouse or light pen to draw pictures on the screen. All these actions are called 'user events' or simply 'events'. An event is composed of its type (string, menu choice, etc.) and a list of parameters. We find here there are two problems : one is how to capture and construct the user events, another is how to specify the legal user event stream and the computer actions in response to these events. The former is referred to as event capture and the latter event control. We propose a four stage architecture to model the dialog in object oriented paradigm (Figure 5.1). The first stage is the event capture, which interacts with the users and constructs the events for the next one. The second stage is the dialog management for complex dialog control. The event stream is handled by the third stage to constitute a dialog, and the event processing is carried out by the fourth one. The second stage will be discussed in the next section, and the others will be presented in the following sections.

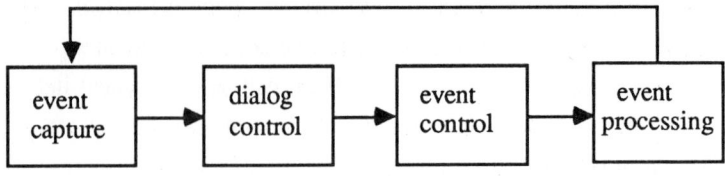

Figure 5.1. Four stage architecture of dialog modelling.

5.2.1 *User event capture*

An interactive system always has an infinite user event capture loop that waits for a user event, transmits it to the dialog control module, and then waits for the next event. The user event capture is to describe, at a point of a dialog, how a program prompts on the screen the possible permitted user actions and, when the user acts, how the user event can be constituted.

In a graphic system or a window manager system, many types of user inputs are defined. For example, "CursorMoveIntoWindow", "CursorMoveOutofWindow", "PushButtonInWindow", "PushButtonInMenu" and "KeyBoardType" are the typical inputs. What type of input will be available depends on with which graphic system or window manager an object oriented language would be bound. Here we suppose that the above listed input types are possible. We can assume that the user inputs come from one object which is graphic system dependent.

The user input messages often contain a lot of information of no interest in dialog controls. The "event_constructor" object could be defined in order to build the events from these inputs. Another function of this stage is, at a given point, to limit the event types. The non-interesing events will be ignored, and only specified events will be transmitted to the next stage. A hierarchy of classes could be defined for event construction and the first level control. The method names correspond to the message types that an object can receive. For example, in a logging session, first only a string such as a login name and password are accepting. After receiving the correct password, the system will display the screen as in the figure 2a; the user can get help by pushing the mouse button, or type the security level using the keyboard. The class hierarchy presented in Figure 2b is used to construct the user events. The "stringonly" object accepts only a string, but the "string" object can receive both a string and the "PushButtonInMenu". When receiving a message, the event_constructor does some processing and then sends the event to the next stage.

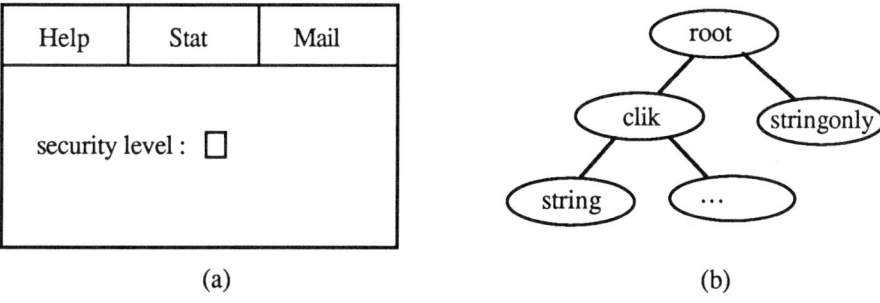

(a) (b)

Figure 5.2. A screen and a class hierarchy for the purpose of user event capture purpose.

5.2.2 *Event control*

Once we know how to construct the user events, the problem is how to specify legal user event sequences, and how to process them, i.e. how to associate the computer actions with respect to a user event stream. An object "event-handler" is an object that is used to accept the user events and dispatch them to the appropriate objects which process the events. These, inturn, are called "event-processors". The event-handlers and the event-processors are at the third and the fourth stages, and constitute the basic dialog.

The role of an event-handler is to receive from the event capture stage the user events and transmit them to the appropriate event-processors by sending messages. In each event-processor, the messages it can accept represents the legal events at this point of a dialog. Each event corresponds to a method declaration in the object. The operations taken in this method represent the computer's actions to process the event. At the end of processing, the event-processor object sends a message to the event-handler indicating the next event-processor. The legal user event stream is controlled by an event-processor chain via an event-handler.

Example : A logging session. The system prints first "enter login name".The user enters a login name, then password and security level. The system checks if the login name has been recorded in the system and if the security level is less than the authorized level. If so, it continues and if not, it prints "reenter user name" or "security level too high" and repeats the lecture actions. If the password is incorrect, the system will print "password incorrect" and return to the initial point (Figure 5.3).

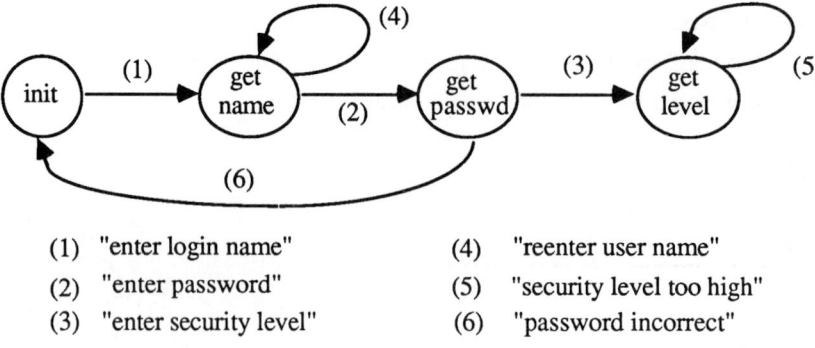

(1)	"enter login name"	(4) "reenter user name"
(2)	"enter password"	(5) "security level too high"
(3)	"enter security level"	(6) "password incorrect"

Figure 5.3. A logging session diagram. The nodes represent the system waiting for user events. The arcs represent the system's outputs.

This example could be modelled by one event-handler and four event-processors: we use a pseudo *smalltalk* syntax to specify these objects.

Object Event-handler
  NextEventProcessor: Name
    NextEP <- Name
  Event: EventName Parameters
    NextEP EventName Parameters

Object init
  start
    print "enter logging name"
    Event-handler NextEventProcessor get-name

Object get-name
  string: name
    if exist name
    then {print "enter password", Event-handler NextEventProcessor get-passwd}
    else {print "reenter logging name", Event-handler NextEventProcessor get-name}
    ... ...

This modelling is equivalent to the traditional specification technique using a state transition diagram. This equivalence allows us to use a graphic specification via state transition diagram and then translate it directly into an object oriented language. This means that the dialog control programs could be generated by manipulating the graphic objects, leading to a visual programming. The detailed discussion of this issue is out of the scope of this paper.

5.3 Complex dialog modelling

The human - computer interaction is a complicated process since there are many unpredictable user behaviours during a dialog. The help demands, undo operations and faulty actions are some examples. In this section, we present first the model for the form based communication. Then by introducing the dialog-manager as the basic component of the second stage, interruption and multiple dialog management will be studied.

5.3.1 *Form based communication*

Suppose we want to fill in a form, and the order in which we fill the different entries is of no significance. The basic model we used in the previous section will become complex for this type of communication. One way to resolve this problem is to make use of the frame based programming mechanism incorporated in many object oriented programming languages. Here we propose the use of procedural attachment on object as a trigger to program the form based communication.

The procedural attachment is a mechanism of trigger a computation by condition, not by message receiving. A form to fill in can be represented by one object. The different entries are declared as different methods. Instead of transferring the processing to another object after treating one event, several successive events are dealt with in the same object. The condition flag is established in each method access, when the condition is satisfed, the procedure attached to the condition will be triggered. The control is delivered to the next event-processor by an attached procedure.

Example : Filling in a form of employment, the fields are name, sex, salary etc.
Oject FormToFill
    Name: String
        name <- string
        flagname <- true
        Event_handler NextEventProcessor FormToFill
    Sex: string
        sex <- string
        flagsex <- true
        Event-handler NextEventProcessor FormToFill
    Salary: number
        salary <- number
        flagsalary <- true
        Event-handler NextEventProcessor FormToFill
    Condition flagname &flagsex & flagsalary
        Event-handler NextEventProcessor xx

5.3.2 *Interruption*

A dialog could be interrupted either by the system in order to ask the user for a special reaction (this is often the case in a real time system), or by the user for help, for retrieving a document, etc. The interruption is considered as an exception. For this purpose, we introduce "dialog-manager", a class used to program the Event-handler. The objects of this class act as message filters which pass the messages other than the interruption. A stack could be used to manage the interrupted dialog. When an interruption message arrives, the current dialog will be stacked and a new dialog will be started to treat the interruption message. The stacked dialog could be restored when the interruption processing is finished.

Example : Interruption management.
Object Dialog_manager
  interruption: dialog_to_start
    stack push current_dialog
    current_dialog <- dialog_to_start
    dialog_to_start start
  finish
    current_dialog <- stack pop
  Default: parameters
    current_dialog parameters

5.3.3 *Multiple dialog management*

When one wants to run several dialogs concurrently, instead of managing the dialogs in a stack, a dialog table could be established . As in the previous case in treating an interruption, there is always one active dialog. The current active dialog could be determinted by special user actions (explicit choice, for example), or by mouse position on the screen like many window managers (X, Suntool, for example) do. In the latter case, the "CursorMoveIntoWindow" event would signify that the window in which the cursor presents is the dialog that is chosen by the user as the current active dialog. The "CursorMoveOutofWindow" event makes the dialog inactive.

5.4 **Implementation consideration**

To construct a good user interface, we want both a set of tools for dialog control and a set of powerful graphic primitives. A standard graphic system like GKS (GKS 1983), or a window manager like X window manager (Gettys, 1987) could be chosen. An interface between one of these systems and an object oriented language is necessary to make the graphic primitives available in the language. Because of the general acceptance of the object oriented paradigm, several graphic systems have been proposed based on the object oriented philosophy, this makes the language - graphic binding easier.

The dialog control model proposed in this paper is not particular by difficult to implement. Some frame based operations used in this paper have been available in many object oriented languages, for instance LOOPS (Bobrow, 1983). The default method is very helpful for implementing this model. The multi-message transfer paths, like the "bus" notion in LRO2 (Roche, 1986), and the event controlled programming style could facilit at the construction.

5.5 Conclusion

We have proposed the use of the object oriented paradigm for modelling human - computer interaction. This model shows its powerful expressibility in modelling some complex dialogs. The implementation of the model is under consideration. The visual programming in object oriented languages for constructing user interfaces will also be carried out and the human factors study in object oriented interactive systems is envisaged. Another interesting theme is the use of concurrent object oriented languages (Dang 86) for modelling human - computer interaction, since the concurrence could give a very natural operational semantics for dialogs and dialog control.

5.6 Acknowledgement

The work presented here has benefitted a lot from discussion with Annya Romanczuk and Jean-Marc Goetz; their remarks were very helpful. Special thanks are due to Christophe Roche who encouraged the author to write this paper.

References

Bobrow, D. (1983). *The LOOPS manual.*, December 1983.

Dang, W. (1986). Concurrent programming in object oriented programming languages., *Proceedings of 3th workshop on object oriented programming languages*, Paris, 149-55, (in french).

Gettys, J et al. (1987). Xlib - C language X interface protocol version 11., *MIT project Athena.*

GKS (1983). Graphical kernel system (GKS) - functional description., *International Organization for Standardization*, ISO/DIS 7942.

Green, M. (1985). The University of Alberta user interface management system, *SIGGRAPH 85 Conference proceedings*, 205-13.

Reisner, P. (1981). Formal grammar and human factors design of an interactive graphics system., *IEEE transactions on software engineering*, **SE-7**, No.2.

Roche, C. & Laurent, J.P.(1986) LRO2 - Artificial intelligence and object oriented languages., *IFIP 86*, 797-902.

Shackel, B. (1987). Human factors for usability engineering., *ESPRIT'87, Achievements and Impact*, 1019-40, North-Holland.

COREFERENTIALITY: THE KEY TO AN INTENTIONAL THEORY OF OBJECT ORIENTED KNOWLEDGE REPRESENTATION

6.1 Introduction

Knowledge representation uses a great deal of classes and objects, frames, actors, scripts, etc... for representing knowledge. But these notions seems to result from an empirist approach without real theoretical foundations, and for many logicians or theorists, objects and frames are just an implementation tool, a way for structuring representations in order to improve systems performance.

Moreover, hybrid systems where knowledge can be represented with rules and objects reduce the strength for establishing a real epistemological status of object oriented knowledge representations.

This paper is a step towards a real theory about knowledge representation with objects, using an intentional point of view. Few attempts have been done in this field, except works on semantic networks, and especially those of Woods [Woods, 1975] and Brachman [Brachman, 1979]. More recently Steels [Steels, 1987] has defined a description calculus, founded on the same epistemological point of view. Other related works are the OMEGA description language by Attardi and Simi [Attardi, 1981], the subsumption calculus described by Aït-Kaci [Aït Kaci, 1985], the theory behind the LORE language [Caseau, 1987] and some of the practical approaches in RLL languages [Haas, 1984].

The main difference with our theory is the emphasis we put on the notion of coreference, and the fact that objects are implementation of various viewpoints that denote things. Therefore our theory is able to cope with problems such as the modification of objects whereas others remains in a monotonic world. For instance, Omega treats non-monotonic updating of the world by introducing a viewpoints mechanism which allow the user to build hypothesis on other possible worlds. However, there is no possibility for updating the current world consistently.

6.2 General principles

6.2.1 *Predication and reification*
Objects are reified concepts, i.e. they serve as implementation of concepts. and denote real things, whereas sentences that assert propositions by using predication refer to truth values. Predication and reification are dual processes, related though distincts, as the two faces of the same issue: the production of meaning.

Predication postulates that, taking a predicate and a set of arguments, one can construct a proposition which will assert something about the world. From a realistic point of view, this proposition will relate to the world as a truth condition given an interpretation function which maps syntactic components to "real" things. Such a proposition is then true of false if it is satisfied or not, i.e. if the elements of the logical expression are really in the relation stated by predicates and connectives.

The other process, called reification, is very close to nominalization in natural languages. It consists in transforming a thing, an idea, a being, a situation, an event, ... in an abstract entity, a concept which one can manipulate as an object, by virtue of a computational process (whether this process lies in a computer program or a human mind). Such a process postulates that there is a third realm of entities on top of expressions and referents. These entities are called *intentions* from the work of Frege. Many logical theories have defined an intention as a function from the set of possible worlds to referents, such as, given a world, it is possible to compute the referent of an expression. Our approach will be somehow different in that an object is the implementation of a mental concept related to an individual. Thus, all references are relative to a subject's environment and not to a possible world environment.

Predication and reification are two related process. Usually, it is possible to transform a predicative sentence into a reified concept, or vice versa. For instance, the sentence, *the car is starting* is made of a predicate IS-STARTING and an argument THE CAR, which will be true (relative to an interpretation context) if the car really starts, and false otherwise. The dual sentence is the noun phrase: *the starting of the car*. In this case, the reification process will produce the object STARTING-1, a kind of EVENT, where one of the arguments is the object CAR-1, representation of the starting car. To say that a sentence is true or false has no meaning any more. STARTING-1 is the object of which the event is the referent. Then we will talk only of object adequation, i.e. the fact that the object is operationally analogical to the reified event or thing.

6.2.2 *Usage of the reification process*

Knowledge representation can be seen as an internal structure which constitutes, for a computational process, an adequate model of an external entity, i.e. one which is such that any model transformations are in close relation with real world transformations.

The object oriented approach in knowledge representation postulates that all external entities (things, events, situations, people, etc..) can be mapped into computational structures defined as a set of slots and operations, the so called "objects" or "frames" structures.

The process of reification is then to establish an object oriented representation of an external entity which denotes that entity. The following figure shows how this reification process can be applied to real and abstract entities.

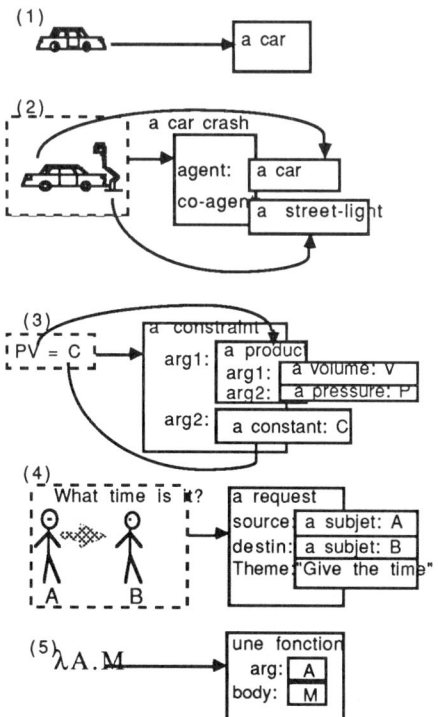

Figure 6.1.

In the first example a car is mapped unto an internal object which represents that car. The second one shows the representation of a car accident: participants are the car and the street lamp the car has crashed into. In the third example, it is neither a real object or a situation but a physical law. Here again, this law can be reified into an internal object. Instances of related operations are the evaluation and transformation into an equivalent law (ex: $U = RI$ can be transformed into $I = U/R$). The fourth example is a dialog where one person is asking a question to another. The last one shows that mathematical or computational notions can be represented in the same way.

6.3 A conceptual theory of objects

Our approach for definining a theory of structured knowledge representation is intentional by nature:

- objects are implementations of concepts, and denote real (or imaginary) entity of the external world.
- two objects denoting the same entity are said to be coreferential, and are linked by a coreference relation.
- it is possible to define an order on general concepts, such that it constrains the set of possible values of concept attributes.

6.3.1 *Concepts, referents and coreferentiality*
What is a concept? **a concept is a point of view, an intention, that denotes a real** (or imaginary) **entity, relative to a specific context** (individual, social group, location, time, etc...). The main point of our theory is that we cannot talk about "real" properties of "real" entities, but only of structured images of those things, the so-called concepts. Concepts makes things understandable and easy to handle, but in the same time hide their essence.

By working only on concepts, we cannot postulate anything on the nature of real world entities: the latter are only referents of the former. Outside referents will be noted by characters in relief. For instance, the individual John will be noted John. This should neither be confounded with the name "John", which designates him for particular people in specific contexts, nor will the different points of view that describe John.

For instance, one can consider John as a person, as a student, or as a tennis player. All concepts are related to specific roles, characteristic informations and prototypical situations in which John behaves as a student, a tennis player or simply as a person.

The denotation function, π is a function which maps elements from the set of concepts $\mathbb{C}$ to the set of referents $\mathbb{R}$. We will define below the structure of $\mathbb{C}$, by defining a special kind of data structure which capture and implement concepts. Asserting that John can be seen from all three point of views, can be done by the three equations:

$\pi(\text{PERSON-JOHN}) = \text{John}$
$\pi(\text{STUDENT-JOHN}) = \text{John}$
$\pi(\text{TENNIS-PLAYER-JOHN}) = \text{John}$

Definition: *two individual concepts a and b are said to be coreferential (notation a == b), if $\pi(a) = \pi(b)$.*

Coreferentiality is a fundamental part of an intentional theory about knowledge representation. Woods (1975) said that "in the appropriate internal representation, there must be two mental entities (concepts, nodes, or whatever) corresponding to the different intentions, morning star and evening star. Then there is an assertion about these two intentional entities that they denote one and the same external object (extension)".

Thus in our theory, the famous Fregean sentence about morning star and evening star can be asserted in the following way:

$\pi(\text{EVENINGSTAR}) = \pi(\text{MORNINGSTAR})$

and then

$\text{EveningStar} \quad = \quad \text{MorningStar}$

which can be written:

$\text{EVENINGSTAR} == \text{MORNINGSTAR}$

6.3.2 *General Concepts*

Many individuals play tennis and can be considered as tennis players. For instance, Fred, a friend of John, plays tennis too. Thus the following equations holds:

$\pi(\text{PERSON-FRED}) = \text{Fred}$
$\pi(\text{TENNIS-PLAYER-FRED}) = \text{Fred}$

In order to describe such similarities, it is important to provide special kind of concepts that represent sets of individuals having common properties, and we will call them **general concepts**.

Definition: a general concept is an intentional representation of a set of individual concepts, which is defined as a function from referents to individual concepts.

We will describe a concept as a conceptualization function, i.e. as a one place function which takes a referent and returns an individual concept which denotes that referent.

For instance, the general concept TENNIS-PLAYER, is defined as a function which takes a person, John for instance, and returns a tennis player concept that denotes John.

TENNIS-PLAYER : Referents $\rightarrow$ {TENNIS-PLAYER-JOHN, TENNIS-PLAYER-FRED ..}
with
TENNIS-PLAYER (John) = TENNIS-PLAYER-JOHN.

Thus the set of all general concepts, is defined as follows:

GeneralConcepts = { f | f : Referents $\rightarrow$ IndivConcepts such as $\pi(f(x)) = x$}

Furthermore, an individual concept is related to its general concept via an instantiation relation, traditionally called ISA:

TENNIS-PLAYER-JOHN   ISA TENNIS-PLAYER

In order to complete our definition, we will assume that there is a null concept (noted NULL) that refers to the "real" nothing (noted NULL) such as:

$$\pi(\text{NULL}) = \text{NULL}.$$

Let us introduce the notion of concept validity which will play an important part in the definition of an inference mechanism that preserves concept validity.

Definition: A concept is said to be valid if it does not refer to NULL, i.e. if it is not coreferencial to the NULL concept:

$$\text{Valid}(c) \text{ iff } \pi(c) \neq \pi(\text{NULL})$$

We will define the extension of a general concept A, noted Ext(A), as the set of all the individual concepts that are related to the general concept via an ISA relation:

$$\text{Ext}(A) = \{ x \mid x \in \text{IndivConcepts, and } x \text{ ISA } A \}$$

The referent function on general concepts, noted Π, maps general concepts into classes of referents:

$$\Pi : \mathrm{GeneralConcepts} \to \mathbb{P}_\mathbb{R}$$
$$\text{such as } \Pi(A) = \{\pi(a_i) \mid a_i \in Ext(A)\}$$

General concepts can also be coreferential, and we will see below that this ability is central to our theory: representing knowledge will consists in describing general concepts related by coreferential links.

6.3.3 Conceptual Entailment

General concepts are related to each other. For instance to say that *all humans are mortal* can be seen as a way to state that the general concept HUMAN entails the general concept MORTAL, because all real individuals described as humans are also the denotation of individual concepts belonging to the general concept MORTAL.

Definition: *let A and B two general concepts, we say that A is less general that B (or that A conceptually entails B), noted $A \leq_c B$, iff $\forall a_i \in A$, $\exists b_i \in B$ such that $\pi(x) = \pi(y)$, or in other word that $\Pi(B) \supseteq \Pi A$).*

For instance, the meaning of HUMAN $\leq_c$ MORTAL, is that the set of the referents of HUMAN is included into the set of the referents of MORTAL. The relation $\leq_c$ is reflexive and transitive (by reflexivity and transitivity of $\supseteq$). But this is not a partial order relation: from $A \leq_c B$ and $B \leq_c A$ it does not follow that $A = B$, but only that $\Pi(A) = \Pi(B)$.

Conceptual entailment is a set theoretic property, defined by inclusion of sets of referents. This point is very important because it will allow us to define notions such as generalization and specialization in terms of set inclusions.

The following diagram shows the different links between general concepts, individual concepts and referents in the case of John (see Figure 6.2)

From conceptual entailment, we can induce the notion of coreferential general concepts. Two general concepts are said to be coreferential if they mutually entail.

Definition: *let A and B two general concepts, A is said to be coreferential to B, noted $A == B$ iff $A \leq B$ and $B \leq A$, i.e. if $\Pi(A) = \Pi(B)$.*

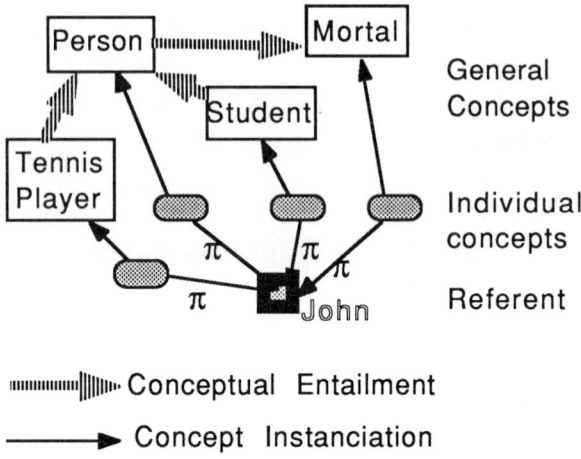

Figure 6.2.

6.3.4 μ-terms

We have now seen the basic part of our intentional theory of representation based on coreferentiality and conceptual entailment. But so far we have said nothing about the structural part of concepts: the properties to describe them and the various relations which links them to other concepts. We have said that objects are implementation of concepts, thus we need a special kind of data structure to handle aspects of concepts we have seen above. One of the most classical interpretation regards objects as records [Cardelli]. But, in order to deal with the referent part of concepts, we need to introduce a new kind of data structure called μ-**term** which extend the notion of record by giving it a referent tag.

A basic μ-term is defined as a tuple

<r, a1 : v1, .. ,an : vn>

where r is the referent constant, a1,..an are labels (i.e.) attributes names and v1,..vn are values, possibly other μ-terms. In other words, basic μ-terms are elements of the recursive domain $\mathbb{M}_0$ whose definition is given as a solution of the following domain equation:

$$\mathbb{M}_0 = \mathbb{R} \times [\mathbb{Id} \rightarrow [\mathbb{M}_0 + \mathbb{B}]]$$

Where $\mathbb{R}$ is the set of referent constants, $\mathbb{Id}$ is the set of identifiers, and $\mathbb{B}$, the domain of basic values (numbers, booleans, symbols, lists, etc..). We will call NULL the null μ-term, i.e. the bottom of the domain.

6.3.5 *Relations on μ-terms*

6.3.5.1 Basic comparisons

μ-terms can be compared. Two basic μ-terms are said to be equal if they represent the same thing, and if their structure is similar (the order of components does not count). Thus,

$$\langle r, \ ..., \ a_i{:}v_i, \ .. \ a_j{:}v_j \ ...\rangle = \langle r, \ .., \ a_j{:}v_j, \ ... \ , \ a_i{:}v_i \ ...\rangle$$

We will introduce an ordering relation on basic μ-terms with the following rules:

(1) $m1 = m2 \Rightarrow m1 \leq_{b\mu} m2$

(2) $\langle r, a_1{:}v_1, .. , a_n : v_n\rangle \leq_{b\mu} \langle r, a_1{:}v'_1, .. , a_n : v'_n\rangle$ if $v_i \leq_{b\mu} v'_i$ for all $1 \leq i \leq n$

(3) $\langle r, a_1{:}v_1, .. , a_n : v_n, a_{n+1}{:} v_{n+1}\rangle \leq_{b\mu} \langle r, a_1{:}v_1, .. , a_n : v_n\rangle$

For instance:

$$\langle John, age : 32, job: Programer, sex: male\rangle \leq_{b\mu} \langle John, sex:male, age:32\rangle$$

For our purpose we will define a type as an abstract μ-term, obtained by making the referent a variable. Thus, if $\langle r, ..a_i{:}v_i ..\rangle$ is a μ-term, $\lambda(x).\langle x, .. a_i{:}v_i ..\rangle$ is a type such that

$$(\lambda(x).\langle x, ..a_i{:}v_i ..\rangle \ r) = \langle r, .. a_i{:}v_i ..\rangle$$

From our definition, a type is a function from referents to μ-terms. For instance the type RR expressing the "roundness" and "redness" of something can be abstracted from the μ-term m = $\langle$Ball-1, color: red, form: round$\rangle$ which is a simple point of view on the ball "ball-1", by simply stating that

$$RR = \lambda(x).\langle x, color: red, form: round\rangle$$

leading to:

$$(RR \ Ball\text{-}1) = m$$

A μ-term is valid if it is not the NULL μ-term. We say that a conceptualization is valid if the application of a type to a referent does not yield a NULL μ-term.

Definition: *a μ-term is either a basic μ-term or a type.*

Therefore, the set of μ-terms, noted $\mathbb{M}$ is equal to the union of $\mathbb{M}_b$ and $\mathbb{M}_t$, the set of types.

We will note m.a, the selection operation, which returns the value associated to the label 'a' in the μ-term m if it exists and NULL otherwise.

We can see that μ-terms capture our intuition of a concept as defined above. Basic μ-terms represent individual concepts whereas types implement general concepts. We will now see that properties of concepts, like conceptual entailment, can be obtained by concept subsumption on one side and formulas on the other side.

6.3.5.2 Subsumption

The set of μ-terms can be organized along a partial order called subsumption, which capture our intuition of subtyping with that of pattern matching.

We say that a μ-term m1 is subsumed by a μ-term m2, noted m1 ~ m2, if and only if one of the following conditions occurs:

(1) NULL ~ m forall m $\in$ $\mathbb{M}$

(2) m1 and m2 $\in$ $\mathbb{M}_b$ and m1 $\leq_{b\mu}$ m2

(3) m1 $\in$ $\mathbb{M}_b$ and m2 $\in$ $\mathbb{M}_t$ and m1 $\leq_{b\mu}$ (m2 π(m1))

(4) m1 and m2 $\in$ $\mathbb{M}_t$ and m1 = m2

(5) m1 and m2 $\in$ $\mathbb{M}_t$ with m1 = λ(r).<r, a_1:v_1, .., a_n:v_n,>,
    and forall $1 \leq i \leq n$ v_i ~ m2.a_i

Examples:

```
<ball-1, color:red, form:round, play:football>
    ~ λ(x).<color:red, form:round>

λ(y).<y, color:red, form:round, play:football>
    ~ λ(x).<y, color: red, form:round>
```

The Ext function is defined as a function from μ-terms to basic μ-terms which returns the set of subsumed basic μ-terms, thus implementing the intuitive notion of the extension of a concept:

Ext : $\mathbb{M} \to \mathbb{M}_b$, with Ext(m) = {x $\in$ $\mathbb{M}_b$ I x ~ m}

6.3.7 Descriptions and concepts

With descriptions, we introduce the third aspect to this theory of knowledge representation. Descriptions are elements of syntactic domains, which are used to describe things, events and situations.

Because of our intentional approach, these descriptions refer both to concepts and to real things. In addition to the the π function which maps concepts (implemented as μ-terms) to referents, two other semantic functions are provided in order to map descriptions to implementation of concepts on one side (function Θ), and descriptions to referents on the other side (function Φ). Thus the resulting semantic schema is given by the following commutative diagram, in which (by hypothesis) $\Phi = \pi \circ \Theta$.

In order to express the Θ function, we need a language for descriptions. This will be the subject of the next section.

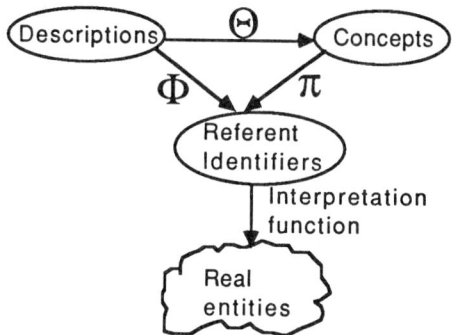

6.4 A language for coreferential reasoning

We will now introduce a very simple language whose purpose is to implement the above ideas into a general framework. It is a subset of the MERING III language [Ferber, a,b,c] which integrates functional programming and object oriented knowledge representation. This is an applicative language supporting side-effects only on objects (i.e. on μ-terms), while remaining purely functional on every other aspects.

The syntax of the language is derived from SCHEME [Abelson] except on a few notations:
- lists are noted by brackets: ['a 'b] denotes a list containing two symbols 'a and 'b.
- symbols are noted 'a, and are never dereferenced like in 3-LISP [Smith].
- (the <id> of <expr>) is used to refer to the value of the attribute <id> of the μ-term resulting from the evaluation of <expr>. Access to attributes can be

cascaded, and the expression (the x of the y of a) is syntactically transformed
into (the x of (the y of a)).

6.4.1 *Using concepts and descriptions*

The syntax of description bears some similarities with the Omega syntax, for easy
reading. A description is either an identifier which refers to another description, or an
expression which begins by the keyword $a (or $an), followed by an identifier and a
referent identifier or a variable, and a list of unordered attributes starting with the
keyword WITH. Here is the grammar:

```
<Description> ::= <GeneralDescription> | <IndividualDescription>
<IndividualDescription> ::= ($a <Identifier><RefId>{<Attribution>})
<GeneralDescription> ::= ($a <Identifier> <Var> {<Attributions>})
<Attributions> ::=   (with <Attribution>+)
<Attribution> ::= (<Label>{<TypeDescription>}{<ValueDescription>})
<TypeDescription> ::=   ~ <GeneralDescription>
<ValueDescription> ::=  <Comp> <Description>
<Comp> ::=   = | ≠ | < | > | ≤ | ≥
```

There is a distinction between identifiers and labels, because identifiers can be bound to
concepts (using an interpretation function), whereas labels are used only to index an
attribute. Variables are prefixed by the character '?' and referents are prefixed by
characters '#$'.

For example, the following descriptions are correct:

```
1 - ($a person #$John (with (age = 35)))
2 - ($an event ?x
            (with (agent = ($a person $John))))
3 - ($a person ?x
          (with girlfriend =
            ($a person $Mary
                  (with (age = 25)
                        (profession = ($a Job $Journalist))))))
5 - ($a professor ?x)
4 - ($a professor ?x
            (with (students ~
                          ($a person ?y (with age > 18)))))
6 - ($a professor #$Peter
            (with (students = ($a person ?y)))))
```

The first one is an individual description which designates an individual concept whose referent is John. The second is a general description which designates a general concept representing the set of events whose agent is John. The third is a general description of a person whose girlfriend is a journalist and is 25 years old. The fourth designates the general concept of a professor (whose extension is the set of professors). The fifth designates the concept of 'professor for adults' and the sixth is a description of the students of Peter.

Descriptions can be used for different purposes: building types and individual concepts, checking out if an individual concept is subsumed by a description, and, as we will see later, for relating general concepts by conceptual entailment.

Creation of concepts, either types or instances, is done automatically by evaluating a description. For instance, the concept of a Person can be described by the following type description:

```
(define Person
    ($a Something ?-
            (with
                (sex ~ ($or 'male 'female))
                (age ~ Number)
                (father ~
                    ($a person ?- (with (sex = 'male))))
                (mother ~
                    ($a person ?- (with (sex = 'female))))
                (job ~ Profession))))
```

Person is defined as an essential type, i.e. a type with no values attached to attributes. But the concept of "adulthood" is a specialization of Person, whose age is greater than 18 (at least in some countries).

```
(define Adult
    ($a Person ?- (with (age > 18))))
```

Then the word Adult now stands for "a person whose age is greater than 18", and whenever 'Adult' is used in a description, it is equivalent to the above definition: for instance the two following descriptions are equal:

```
($a Professor ?x
    (with (students ~ Adult)))
```

```
($a Professor ?x
    (with (students ~ ($a Person ?y (with (age > 18)))))))
```

Instance creation is done in the same way by evaluating an individual description:

```
(define John
    ($a person #$John
        (with
            (age = 35)
            (sex = 'male)
            (mother = ($a person #$Susan))
            (father = ($a person #$Peter)))))
```

will create an individual concept, noted #<a person #$John> such that:

```
(describes ($a person ?x) John)
→ #t
```

It means that #$John (the referent identifier which stands for the real individual that we call John, given a interpretation function) can now be seen as a person, an adult and a son of Mary:

```
(Person #$John)
→ #<a person #$John>

(Adult #$John)
→ #<a person #$John>

;; we can use the longer definition of adult
    (($a Person ?- (with (age > 18))) #$John)
    → #<a person #$John>

;; John is also a son of Mary
    (($a Person ?-
        (with (mother = ($a person #$Mary))))
    #$John)
    → #<a person #$John>
```

But other descriptions of John are not valid:

```
(($a person ?- (with (age < 15))) #$John)
→ #null
```

John can also be described as a professor for children:

```
(define John-Prof
    ($a Professor #$John
        (with (students ~ ($a Person (with age < 12)))))))
→ #<a Professor #$John>
```

Moreover, all individual concepts described by a type description can be found using the FINDALL function:

```
;; finding all persons
    (FindAll ?x ($a Person ?x))
    -> {#<a person #$John> #<a person #$Peter> ... }


;; finding all the students whose age is less than 15
    (FindAll ?x ($a Professor ?-
                    (with (students ~ ($a Person ?x
                                        (with (age < 15)))))))
    -> {#<a person #$Bob> #<a person #$Pam> #<a person #$Liz>...}
```

The descriptive function Θ maps descriptions into concepts in a given environment. Its definition is bound to the semantic function Eval which express the meaning of all expressions in the language. We will give only the semantics equations of Eval in the case of descriptions.

Semantics equations of the two functions are given using the following notation: Identifiers will be denoted by upper case letters, A, B, P, .. attribute names (labels) by the lower case letters a, b or c, variables by x, y, or z, μ-terms by letters m or m', descriptions by the greek letters α, β, δ, environments by the greek letter ρ, and referents by letters r or r'. All letters can be followed by an indicia.

Θ : Descriptions $\rightarrow$ Env $\rightarrow$ M where Env = [Id $\rightarrow$ B + M]

Eval : Expression $\rightarrow$ Env $\rightarrow$ B + M

$\Theta[\delta]\rho = \{m \in M_b \mid m \sim Eval[\delta]\rho\}$

$Eval[A]\rho = \rho(A)$

$Eval[(\$a\ P\ r\ (with\ (a_1 = \alpha_1)... (a_n = \alpha_n))]\rho =$
             $Eval[P]\rho\ <=0=\ <r, a_1:Eval[\alpha_1], ..., a_n:Eval[\alpha_n]>$

$Eval[(\$a\ P\ x\ (with\ (a_1 = \alpha_1)... (a_n = \alpha_n))]\rho =$
             $Eval[P]\rho\ <=0=\ \lambda(x)<x, a_1:Eval[\alpha_1], ..., a_n:Eval[\alpha_n]>$

Where the operator $<=0=$ is an overloading operator which implements single inheritance by copying all informations that are not redefined. This operator is defined on μ-terms in the following way:

$<=0=:\ M\ X\ M \rightarrow M$

NULL $<=0=$ m = m

m $<=0=$ NULL = m

$<r, .. a_i:v_i ..> <=0= <r' .. a_j:v_j .. > = $ NULL if $r \neq r'$

$<r, .. a_i:v_i ..> <=0= <r, .. a_j:v_j .. > = <r, .. a_i:v_i ,.., a_j:v_j .. >$ if $i \neq j$

$<r, .. a_i:v_i ..> <=0= <r, .. a_j:v'_i .. > = <r, .. a_i:v'_i ..>$

$\lambda(x)<x, .. a_i:v_i ..> <=0= \lambda(y)<y, .. a_j:v_j .. > = \lambda(z)<z, .. a_i:v_i ,.., a_j:v_j .. >$ if $i \neq j$

$\lambda(x)<x, .. a_i:v_i ..> <=0= \lambda(y)<y, .. a_i:v'_i .. > = \lambda(z)<z, .. a_i:v'_i ..>$

It can be seen that values from the right part replace values of the left part when they belong to identical attributes. Thus, the resulting μ-terms is equal to the right μ-term plus informations inherited from the left μ-term.

6.4.2 *The coreferential reasoning process*

We have seen so far how to describe things and how to relate them to the universe of discourse. We are now ready to introduce a reasoning system using the theory of conceptual entailment as its hard core. Informally the point is to provide ways of defining how a concept is related to another one, or how it is modified when some state of a concept is reached.

In order to define such relations, new types of expressions, called **formulae**, will be introduced. Syntactically, formulae are given in two forms: implication formulae, written $\delta_1 \Rightarrow \delta_2$, and equivalence formulae, written $\delta_1 \Leftrightarrow \delta_2$, where δ_1 and δ_2 are (usually general) descriptions. These formulae are used for describing coreference between concepts, and are satisfied if valid concepts described by the left and right part of the formulas follow the relation.

We will first describe the case of implication and equivalence between general descriptions. In this case, an implication is interpreted as a conceptual entailment between concepts, and an equivalence is interpreted as a coreference between general concepts. Let δ_1 and δ_2 be two general descriptions:

> **S1:** $/= (\delta_1 \Rightarrow \delta_2)$ *iff* $\Theta[\delta_1] \rightarrow \Theta[\delta_2]$, *i.e.* $\forall c \in Ext(\Theta[\delta_1]), \exists c' \in Ext(\Theta[\delta_2])$, *such that* $\pi(c) = \pi(c')$.

> **S2:** $/= (\delta_1 \Leftrightarrow \delta_2)$ *iff* $\Theta[\delta_1] \leftrightarrow \Theta[\delta_2]$, *i.e.* $\pi(\Theta[\delta_1]) = \pi(\Theta[\delta_2])$.

Naturally, equivalence is expressed as a reciprocal implication:

> **S3:** $/= (\delta_1 \Leftrightarrow \delta_2)$ *iff* $/= (\delta_1 \Rightarrow \delta_2)$ *and* $/= (\delta_2 \Rightarrow \delta_1)$

The case of individual descriptions is even simpler, because there is no difference between implication and equivalence, and both are interpreted as a coreference between individual concepts.

Let δ_1 and δ_2 be individual descriptions:
> **S4:** $/= (\delta_1 \Rightarrow \delta_2)$ *iff* $\pi(\Theta[\delta_1]) = \pi(\Theta[\delta_2])$.
> **S5:** $/= (\delta_1 \Leftrightarrow \delta_2)$ *iff* $\pi(\Theta[\delta_1]) = \pi(\Theta[\delta_2])$.

But formulae can also be used to generate new concepts related in a precise way to old ones. For instance, the formula:

```
($a P ?x (with a = ?z)) ⇒ ($a Q ?y (with b = ?z))
```

when applied to an individual concept described by:

```
($a P r (with a = v))
```

having no coreferential concept derived from the type Q, will generate a new individual concept described by

```
($a Q r (with b = v))
```

and coreferential to the first one. Moreover, any modification in the attribute 'a' of the former concept, will cause a similar modification in the attribute 'b' of the latter. For instance, a vector can be seen from two different viewpoints, using polar or cartesian coordinates. It is always the same vector, and modifying some of its values (for instance by applying a geometric transformation) in one point of view should cause a corresponding modification in every other points of view. This can be asserted by using two implication formulas: one from polar to cartesian coordinate, and the other from polar to cartesian coordinate.

```
($a PolarVector ?v
      (with
           (rho = ?n)
           (theta = ?a)))
  ⇒
($a CartesianVector ?v
      (with
           (x-axis =   (* ?n (cos ?a)))
           (y-axis = (* ?n (sin ?a)))))

($a CartesianVector ?v
      (with
           (x-axis = ?x))
           (y-axis = ?y))))
  ⇒
(a PolarVector ?v
      (with
           (rho = (sqrt (sqr ?x)(sqr ?y)))
           (theta = (atan ?x ?y))))
```

Let us define two coreferential definition of the same vector. First the vector defined by its cartesian coordinates:

```
(define c-v1 ($a cartesian-vector #$v1
                   (with
                        (x-axis = 10)
                        (y-axis = 10)))))
```

second, the definition of the same vector using the polar coordinates:

```
(define p-v1 ($a polar-vector #$v1))
```

we can get the list of values of this polar vector, implicitly using the above formulae:

```
[(the rho of p-v1)(the theta of p-v1)]
→ [14.14  0.78]
```

if we modify the values of c-v1, changes are automatically propagated to the corresponding values of p-v1:

```
(update c-v1 (with (x-axis = 20)(y-axis = 0)))

[(the rho of p-v1)(the theta of p-v1)]
→ [20.0 0.00]
```

but due to the second formula, the converse is also true, and it is possible to compute the values of c-v1 from those of p-v1:

```
(update p-v1 (with (rho = 10 ) (theta = 20)))

[(the x-axis of c-v1)(the y-axis of c-v1)]
→ [4.08 9.13]
```

Thus we have seen that it is possible to relate two different viewpoints of the same thing by using formulae as constraints over the possible set of values, and that all changes are automatically propagated to all coreferential concepts. We will now be concerned by giving some more formal definition of this process by providing a set of inference rules which can be used as a basis for any implementation of coreferential reasoning.

6.4.3 Axiomatisation of coreferential reasoning

In this section, the relations between concepts are shown by defining an axiomatisation of coreferential reasoning based on a set of inference rules which preserve the validity of concepts related to formulae.

6.4.3.1 Inference Rules

The first two rules are very close to the *modus ponens* and *modus tollens* rules used in logic, but the third one shows how attribute values are constrained via variables in formulas:

R1 Rule of existence: every valid entity described by the left part of an implication formula is coreferential to an entity described by its right part.

$$if (\delta_1 \Rightarrow \delta_2) \ and \ c = \Theta[\delta_1] \ and \ valid(c)$$
$$then \ \exists c' \in \Theta[\delta_2] \ such \ that \ valid(c') \ and \ \pi(c) = \pi(c')$$

R2 Rule of inexistence: if a description of the right part of an implication formula does not describe any valid entity, then the left part of the formula does not describe any valid entity either.

$$if (\delta_1 \Rightarrow \delta_2) \ and \ Ext(\Theta[\delta_1]) = \emptyset \ then \ Ext(\Theta[\delta_2]) = \emptyset$$

R3 Rule of constraint: this rule states that two coreferential individual concepts are constrained by formulae associated to their general concepts. Variables in descriptions are denoted by greek letters.

$$if (\delta_1 \Rightarrow \delta_2)$$
$$and \ \Theta[\delta_1] = \mu(\alpha).<\alpha, ... \ a_i : \sigma, ...>$$
$$and \ \Theta[\delta_2] = \mu(\beta).< ...b_j : F(\sigma)) ...>$$
$$and \ c = <r, ... \ a_i : v_i, ...> \ such \ that \ c \sim \Theta[\delta_1]$$
$$and \ \exists c' \sim \Theta[\delta_2] \ such \ as \ \pi(c) = \pi(c')$$
$$then$$
$$c' = <r , ... \ b_j : F(v_i), ...>$$

6.5 Conclusion

We have developed the basic points of our theory of object oriented knowledge representation based on an intentional point of view. We have seen that the introduction of referents into data structure allows us to reason across different conceptualization of the same thing. This allows for a new kind of reasoning called coreferential reasoning which is a generalization of classification. Furthermore, due to the presence of referents, it is possible to derive a mechanism that preserves validity of the deduced objects by considering formulae as constraints over the set of attribute values.

This theory should be completed on two different points:
• Introduce the subject, i.e. the concept holder, into the theory in order to partition sets of concepts into different worlds. Then a concept is in adequation to an external world if the result of concept transformations is identical to the result of a reified transformation on this external world.

• The other point concerns the soundness and consistency of the theory, i.e. the relation between descriptions and concepts on one side, and concepts and referents on the other side. Our assumption is of course that this theory is complete in terms of description and concepts validity, but moreover that it is consistent with the notion of concept adequation. Obviously this hypothesis remains to be proved.

References

Abelson, H. et al. (1986).The revised[3] report on the alorithmic language Scheme SIGPLAN, *Notices V21*, n°**12**

Aït Kaci, H. (1985). Login: A logic programming language with built-in inheritance, *MCC Technical Report* , Number AI-068-85

Attardi, G. & Simi, M. (1981).Semantics of inheritance and attributions in the description system Omega, *M.I.T. AI Memo 642*

Brachman, R. (1979). On the epistemological status of Semantic Networks. In: *Associative Networks*, N.Findler Ed., Academic Press

Cardelli, L. (1984). A semantics of multiple inheritance. In: *Semantics of Data Types*, LNCS 173. Springer Verlag

Caseau, Y. (1987). *Etude et réalisation d'un langage objet: LORE* , PhD, Université Paris 11 - Orsay
Cointe, P. (1985) *Implémentation et interprétation des langages orientés objets: application aux langages Smalltalk, Objvlisp et Formes* Thèse d'état, Paris 6

Ferber, J. (1986) Towards a reflective actor language , *Proceedings of the ECAI 86*

Ferber, J. (1987) Conceptual reflection and actor language. In: *Meta level architectures and Reflexion*, Eds P.Maes & D.Nardi, North Holland

Ferber, J. (1987) Des objets aux agents: une architecture stratifiée, *Proceedings of the 6th AFCET conference on "Reconnaissance des Formes et Intelligence Artificielle"*

Haas, K. (1984). ARLO: the implementation of language for describing representation languages, *MSc. M.I.T*

Smith, B.C. (1982).*Reflection and semantics in a procedural language*. PhD Thesis, M.I.T

Steels, L. (1987). The explicit representation of meaning. In: *Meta level architectures and Reflexion,* Eds. P.Maes & D.Nardi, North Holland

Woods, W.A. (1975). What's in a link: foundation for semantic networks. In: *Representation and understanding* , Eds. D.G.Bobrow & A.Collins, Academic Press

7 *S. Jung, R. Mohr and A. Napoli*

ORPHEE, A 0++ SYSTEM

7.1 Introduction

In this paper, we present ORPHEE (for "Objets et Règles de Productions Hiérachisées pour l'Expression de l'Expertise"), a both object and rule oriented knowledge system.

Knowledge about a domain must be considered with different points of view and described with different kinds of representation. Vocabulary definitions, stereotypes, domain's entities descriptions and behaviour are better expressed with objects. On the other hand, contextual knowledge like decision rules, heuristics and constraints is easier represented by production rules (Fikes *et al.*,1985). Meta-knowledge can be modelled by means of meta-rules and procedures attached to objects variables.

In ORPHEE, like in any object oriented language, the basic notion is the class of objects, being described by variables and associated methods. The classes are organized in a tree hierarchy, the root of the tree is the most general class, the nodes describe generic objects, the leaves are specific objects, instances of higher classes.The system is written in CEYX, an object oriented level on the Le_Lisp language from INRIA (Chailloux,1986), (Hullot,1984). Actually, CEYX is an object oriented language, member of the SMALLTALK family (Goldberg *et al.*,1983), and does not allow frame based language facilities for knowledge representation as facets or procedural attachment (Bobrow *et al.*,1977), (Colnet *et al.*,1986), (Ferber,1983).

Thus, we have implemented an original kind of procedural attachment, which is one of major features of ORPHEE. So, the system allows procedural, object oriented, rule oriented and data driven programming like in LOOPS (Bobrow *et al.*,1982), (Stefik *et al.*,1983), KEE (Fikes *et al.*,1985) and YAFOOL (Ducournau *et al.*,1986).

Knowledge can be expressed in both a declarative and procedural form, so the reasoning ability of the system can be achieved in several ways. The inferences are made either by computation, using objects methods and procedural attachment, or by inheritance, using specific features of object oriented programming like defaults values (Rechenmann,1985).

ORPHEE is considered to work with 0++ logic, in between propositional logic and predicate logic. The 0+ character is classic of a system allowing manipulation of variables which can be substituted by constants. The 0++ character indicates that the values of objects variables can be objects, which in turn, can have variables being also valuated with objects.

First, we will introduce the ideas underlying ORPHEE, as objects, rules and procedural attachment. Then, we discuss the 0++ logic concept. An application of the system to organic chemistry concludes the paper.

Examples are written in a common LISP form with eventually specific CEYX functions which are mentionned when used.

7.2 Objects and Rules in ORPHEE

7.2.1 *About Objects*
Knowledge is considered from two points of view. First, static knowledge like facts, definitions, descriptions, etc. can be considered as passive knowledge. Secondly, contextual knowledge acts on the latter, is validated under some conditions and appears like active knowledge.

The first kind of knowledge can naturally be described with objects of an object oriented language. For example, suppose we consider that the model, the builder and the supported languages are the characteristics of a computer. Then, a computer can be described by a class, with three variables as follows :

```
(deftclass COMPUTER
        Model
        Builder ~string
        SupportedLanguages '(C Le_Lisp Ceyx))
```

Figure 7.1 The Ceyx function deftclass defines the COMPUTER class. The type of a variable is optional and can be indicated as for the variable Builder with the ~ character. The list (C Le_Lisp Ceyx) is a default value, which can be redefined via message passing in each instance. Computer_1 is an instance of the COMPUTER class, created with the Ceyx primitive omake, with all variables instantiated e.g.

```
(setq Computer_1
        (omake 'COMPUTER
        Model 'Vax
        Builder "Digital"))
```

The classes and the instances are linked with isa links, classes and subclasses with ako links. CEYX inheritance mechanism is simple, so the universe of objects is a tree, specific objects inherit behaviour and description of higher classes. In the above example, there is no need to redefine the default value of the variable SupportedLanguages in the instance Computer_1 ; this variable and its value are inherited from the COMPUTER class.

7.2.2 *About Rules*
In ORPHEE, production rules are implemented as objects. A specific rule is a subclass of the general class RULE which is the root of a hierarchy where rules are linked.The class RULE is described by three variables :

- "IF" whose value is true when all rule's conditions are checked, else nil.
- "THEN" stands for conclusions or actions associated to the rule.This variable is used to save some variables values (see 2.3).
- a variable "MODE" specifies the kind of search (three are possible) the system must achieve when it is looking for values of arguments which are local variables attached to the rules. This variable looks like a control variable.

A specific rule is a subclass of RULE, and so inherits of IF, THEN and MODE variables definitions, but can owns specific variables called *arguments*. Their values refer to the sets of objects the rule acts on and are used to check the rule conditions.

Suppose we define a subclass of RULE, named RULE_PC, with two arguments, P and C respectively standing for Program and Computer :

$$({RULE}:RULE\_PC$$
$$P$$
$$C)$$

The notation {RULE}:RULE_PC indicates that the object RULE_PC is a subclass of the class RULE.

ORPHEE doesn't directly manipulate classes or subclasses, but instances. Then, defining a rule consists of creating a subclass of RULE and an instance of this subclass called *primitive instance*. When they are known, the values of the arguments are specified in the primitive instance. So, a simple access to these values gives the set of objects that can be substituted to arguments when the rule is activated.

```
(setq rule_pcl (omake 'RULE_PC
                P' (Orphee Sesame)
                C' (Vax Sm90 Dps8)))
```

Figure 7.2 rule_pc1 is the primitive instance of the rule RULE_PC, the value of the argument P refers to instances of the PROGRAM class as defined below, the value of C refers to supposed COMPUTER class instances named Vax, Sm90 and Dps8. For the completeness of the example, let us define the PROGRAM class and two instances Orphee and Sesame :

```
(deftclass PROGRAM
           Name
           Written_in)
```

```
(setq Sesame (omake 'PROGRAM (Name 'Sesame) (Written_in 'Le_lisp)))
(setq Orphee (omake 'PROGRAM (Name 'Orphee) (Written_in 'Ceyx)))
```

However, arguments values are not always known in advance. In this case, an attached procedure computes their values, as it will be explained in the next section.

Actually, the conditions and the conclusions of a rule are specified by methods attached to the subclass which defines the rule.The values of IF and THEN variables are used by a method of the class RULE called ACTIVATE, which acts like an inference engine. This method manages arguments values access and rule activation. It searches for a set of possible values for arguments through the knowledge base. Three kinds of search, appearing as values of the variable MODE, are possible :

- a rule doesn't own any arguments or arguments values are known: in this case, no search is needed and the value of the rule's MODE is "Without",
- a specific rule owns arguments, but the search must stop as soon as a value that fits conditions is found, the value of the rule's MODE is "With1",
- in the last case, the search for arguments values must be done for all values fitting conditions: the value of the rule's MODE is "WithAll".

The value of the MODE variable is a LISP function, applied on a set of arguments lists, which is respectively the *funcall, any* and *mapc* function.

Funcall is a default value for the MODE in the class RULE, but the different kinds of search are tied with rules activation strategies. If the first selected rule only needs to be activated, the MODE will be Without or With1, according to the presence of arguments values . In the other hand, when breadth first search is required, the MODE value will be WithAll (Jung,1986).

7.2.3 *Procedural Attachment in ORPHEE*

Facets and procedural attachment are major features of frame based languages. They are lacking in object oriented programming. When the goal of the language is knowledge representation, these features allow better expression of personal description and behaviour of a variable (Ferber,1983).

Therefore, knowledge representation with an object oriented language, e.g. CEYX, requires substantial modifications of the language like the redefinition of the *read* and *write* access to variables of an object .

One way is to consider each variable as an object. In this case, the attached procedures are methods of the class that define the variable (Ferber,1986).

Another way is to define procedures as methods of the object class and to differentiate their use by means of a prefix concatenated with the name of the variable to which they are attached (Jung,1986). This second solution is implemented in ORPHEE and allows a simple construction of procedural attachment using common facilities underlying any object oriented language. The construction lies on the redefinition of the variables access functions read and write, named *getval* for getting value and *putval* for putting value.

When a variable or argument value is unknown, the getval function returns the result of the activation of a method associated to the variable named "p-<variable name>". This methods acts like an *If-needed* reflex in a frame based language.

(defineMethod {RULE_PC}:p-C (rule)
    (mapcan (lambda (instance)
        (when (eq (Model instance) 'Vax)
        (list instance)))
    (Computer_1...)))

Figure 7.3 The procedure p-C, attached to the variable C of the class RULE_PC, lists the instances of the COMPUTER class whose Model value is Vax:

On the other hand, the putval function acts like *If-added* or *If-removed* demons. When the variable value is modified, a method named "d-<variable name>" achieves the writing of the value and can also execute actions.

This procedural attachment is fully used in ORPHEE for the class RULE using the method ACTIVATE which manages the variables values access. The getval function checks for the IF value of a rule. If there is no value, a p-IF procedure, when it exists, is activated to valuate the IF variable. If it succeeds, a d-THEN procedure is activated in order to achieve the conclusion of the rule.

The THEN variable is also used to collect the computed arguments values in order to avoid loops in the rules activations.

(defineMethod {RULE_PC}:p-IF (rule)
    if (member (Written_in P) (SupportedLanguages C))
    then return true)

The d-THEN demon, tied to the variable THEN of the class RULE_PC, is activated when the rule conditions are validated:

(defineMethod {RULE_PC}:d-THEN (rule)
    print "The programm" (Name P) "runs on" (Model C))

Figure 7.4 Fist, we define a p-IF procedure, attached to the variable IF of the class RULE_PC, that returns true when the value of the variable Written_in of an instance of the class PROGRAM agrees with the value of the variable SupportedLanguages of an instance of the class COMPUTER:

However, the activation of p-IF or d-THEN methods may be controlled by special methods of the RULE class called *evaluators*. An evaluator acts like a "meta-procedure", and defines an original way of activation for sets of rules (Ferber,1985).

When the conditions of a rule are checked, say the value of IF is not nil, an "e-THEN" evaluator allows two kinds of activation for the d-THEN demon. First, when the value of IF variable of the primitive instance of a rule is not nil, the activation can be immediate, the d-THEN demon is triggered. In all other cases, the p-IF procedure is activated to search for arguments values. When such a procedure fails, the system must consider another rule. When the procedure is successful, a new instance of the considered rule is dynamically created with arguments instantiated. According to a chosen strategy, the considered rule may be activated, else the new instance is pushed on an agenda. The values of the IF and MODE variables of the instance are "not nil" and "Without" respectively, no more search being required.

The agenda is managed like a stack, activation of rules whose instances belong to the agenda are differed. On other hand, when an instance is popped from the agenda, its activation is immediate, no more procedures triggering is required.

ACTIVATE algorithm

```
define ACTIVATE (Rul Mode Argument)
Value = search for Argument value in the knowledge base
if Value ≠ nil or Argument list is empty
        then 'apply Mode ; funcall, any or mapc Lisp functions)
            (lambda (Argument)
                if GETVAL IF Rule then PUTVAL THEN Rule true)
            Value)
```

For each ARGUMENT value, the rule conditions are checked with the GETVAL function. If success, the conclusion can be trigged with the PUTVAL function

> GETVAL algorithm
>> define GETVAL (Argument Instance)
>> Value = read Argument value

; if the argument values of a rule are not specified in the primitive instance, the function looks for an attached procedure named "p-<variable>" and for an evaluator with getfunction.

> if not Value
>> then   Procedure = getfunction Instance "p-" Argument
>>   Evaluator = getfunction Instance "e-" Argument
>>   if Procedure exists
>>   then activate Evaluator and Procedure
>>   else activate Procedure;
>> else Value;

> PUTVAL algorithm
>> define PUTVAL (Argument Instance Value)
>> Demon = getfunction Instance "d-" Argument
>> Evaluator = getfunction "e-" Argument
>> if Demon then
>>   if Evaluator
>>   then activate Evaluator and Demon
>>   else activate Demon;

Figure 7.5 We sketch the ACTIVATE, GETVAL and PUTVAL algorithms (Jung,1986)

7.2.4 *0++ logic*

A classic 0+ system works with variables that can be substituted by constants. Working with objects allows that the values of rules arguments can be objects. These objects can have variables whose values can also be objects.

Speaking in terms of variables depth, we say that 0+ logic allows manipulation of variables of depth 1, 0++ logic allows variables of depth 2 and even more.

Let us consider the following rule :

> If C is a Computer,
> and if P is a Program,
> and if C has supportedLanguages L,
> and if P is Written_in L,
> then print "the program" L "runs on " C.

This rule can be modelled by the class RULE_PC and its primitive instance (figure 2) associated with the p-IF and d-THEN methods (figure 4). The values of the variables of C and P are instance of objects of the classes COMPUTER and PROGRAM.

0+ calculus consists of searching for values of P and C. These values can be only constants. In our context, 0++ logic, P and C are instances of objects classes, and variables as SupportedLanguages or Written_in can be accessed.

First, ORPHEE searches for the values of variables that are involved in *isa* links as P and C. These values are instances of the PROGRAM and COMPUTER classes respectively. Then, the system selects the instances of these classes whose variables values accord with the conditions of the rule. So, the system will choose each instance of the PROGRAM class whose Written_in value agrees with the value of SupportedLanguages of an instance of the COMPUTER class. When the previous rule is activated, according to the instances previously defined (figure 2), we obtain :

> The program Sesame runs on Vax
> The program Orphee runs on Vax

The value Vax of the instance Computer_1 (figure 1) is obtained because the variable Model is referred in the method d-THEN (figure 4).

7.2.5 *About Control*

Meta-knowledge can be specified in ORPHEE with meta-rules or by means of procedural attachment. Rules whose arguments values can be rules are called meta-rules, they also are subclass of the RULE class.

Meta-rules act on rules and are used to control the system inferences. The classic inference cycle selection-conficts resolution-activation of a production rules system can be simulated. We recall that there is no inference engine in ORPHEE, but the method ACTIVATE and the evaluators act in a same way.

When there are no evaluators attached to a rule, the system first activates a chosen meta-rule. This last one in turn, can activate other rules. In this case, all activations are immediate.

When there is an evaluator associated with a set of rule, the activation may be quite different, the evaluator allows differed activation. When rules conditions are checked, the instances of the rules are pushed on an agenda. In this case, the rule activation becomes a task which will be popped and computed according to the chosen strategies. This kind of activation has been used in the chemical application, e.g. the user may put a rule activation in waiting in order to change reactional conditions or to add new products.

7.3 A Chemical Application

7.3.1 *Introducing the application*

We have used the system for describing the "Wittig-Horner" chemical reaction which leads to formation of double bonds carbon carbon e.g. C=C.

The basic object is named ATOM and is used to describe atoms, sets of atoms are molecules. Each chemical atom is described by a CEYX class containing four variables. The variable "Type" indicates the chemical atomic type of an ATOM. The number of the molecule containing an ATOM is the value of the variable "Reactive", "Groups" gives the list of chemical functional groups to which the ATOM is attached. A functional group is a group of atoms owning some chemical specificity and is located in the knowledge base. The variable "Bonds" is valuated with a list of pairs describing the bonds in which instances of ATOM are involved. The first element of the pair is the number of the neighboring ATOM, the second indicates the order of the bond, which can be 1, 2, 3 and 4 in case of aromatic cycles. The behaviour of each ATOM is described with methods. Suppose we want to describe the following molecule:

$$
\begin{array}{c}
H \\
\backslash \\
C = O \\
/ \\
H
\end{array}
$$

The internal representation is:

	Reactive Number	Groups	Bonds
({ATOM}:(carbon	1	(Carbonyl Aldehyde))	())
({ATOM}:(oxygen	1	()	((0 . 2))))
({ATOM}:(hydrogen	1	()	((0 . 1))))
({ATOM}:(hydrogen	1	()	((0 . 1))))

Figure 7.6 In a molecule, the first atom owns the number 0. Reactive Number is the number of the molecule, 1 in this example. The value ((0 . 2)) for Bonds means that the oxygen atom is linked with the atom of number 0, the carbon atom; 2 is the bond multiplicity.

Carbonyl and Aldehyde are functional groups, they are described in the knowledge base by a list as:

(Carbonyl carbon
((oxygen) . 2)) stands for the C=O group.

Chemical reactions are described with a sub-language consisting of key-words referring to LISP functions or ATOM variables. The system goal is to solve problems as the following:

Starting Reactives --- ? ---> Products

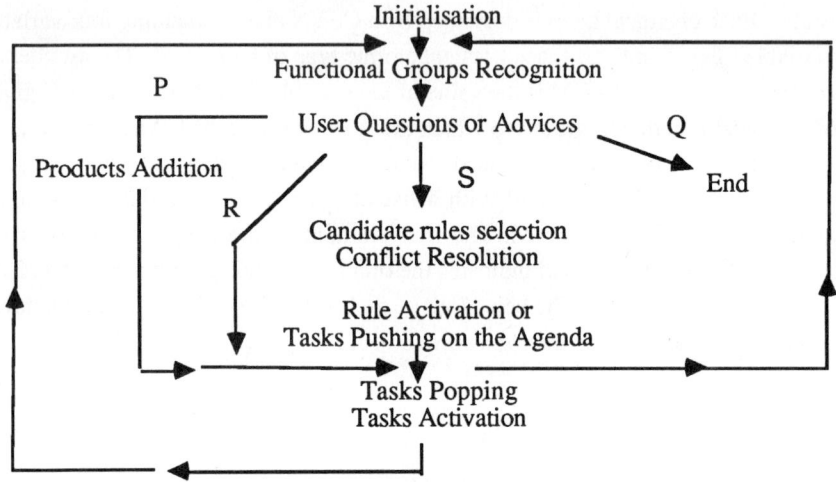

Figure 7.7 The following scheme gives the global system work

First, the system analyses the starting reactives and tries to recognize their functional groups. Then, it searches for candidate reactions under some conditions given by the user. Actually, a reaction application is a rule activation. When the system has generated new products, it tries to continue with other reactions, until it reaches a final goal given by the user.

7.3.2 *Example of Chemical Rule and Meta-rule* (Jung,1986)
The *meta-rule* 5 is used to analyse two chemical reactives, and then to select adequate rule:

(deftclass {RULE}:MR5 (C1 LC1 H1 B1 M1)

(demethod {MR5}:p-IF (rule) (C1 LC1 H1 B1 M1)
        (setq canditates ( ))   ; the set of candidate rules is empty
; Rule conditions: the first reactive must contain a carbon which is a member of a
Phosphonate group
        (is C1 (contained group phosphonate))
        (is LC1 (tied all 1 C1))   ; the groups tied to C1 must have
                                                        multiplicity 1

     (is H1 (equal type hydrogen LC1)) ; one of the group is hydrogen
; the second reactive, B1, contains a hydroxyl group, not equal to C1;
     (is B1 (contained group hydroxyl
                    (other reactive C1)))
; M1 is a metal tied to B1 by a simple bond

     (is M1 (equal type metal (tied all 1 B1))

(demethod {MR5}:d-THEN (rule) ()
     (setq canditates (append '(Rule1 Rule2))))

The rule Rule1 is controlled by the meta-rule MR5, it is defined as one of its subclass:

(deftclass {MR5}:Rule1)

(demethod {Rule1}:p-IF (rule) (LC1 M1)
  (nequal type electro-attractive LC1)   ; the group LC1 is not electro-attractive
  (comme un fort M1)   ; M1 is a strong metal
  (< temperature -30)))   ; the temperature is less than -30° Celsius

(demethod {Rule1}:d-then (rule) (C1 H1 B1 M1)
    (make C1 H1 -1)   ; break the C1-H1 bond
    (make B1 M1 -1)   ; break the B1-M1 bond
    (make C1 M1 +1)   ; make the bond C1-M1
    (make B1 H1 +1)   ; make the bond B1-H1

7.4 Conclusion

ORPHEE has been applied to a small example. The system is still limited by molecular representation problems as cycles and absence of special facets of frame based language. However, the kind of procedural attachment used in ORPHEE is easy to implement and is independent of the underlying object oriented language. The system allows data driven programming, both with rule and object oriented programming. Then, it appears like a modern knowledge representation system, able to achieve quickly an application.

References

Bobrow, D.G. & Stefik, M. (1982). *The LOOPS Manual.* Technical Report, Knowledge Systems area, Xerox Palo Alto Research Center.

Bobrow, D.G. & Winograd, T. (1977). An overview of KRL, *Cognitive Science*, **1**, 3-46.

Colnet, D., Masini, G., Napoli, A., Noiret, Y. & Tombre, K. (1986). *Les Langages Orientés Objets,* Technical Report CRIN 86-R-077, Université de Nancy, France.

Chailloux, J. (1986). *Le_Lisp de l'INRIA, Manuel de référence,* Technical Report INRIA, Rocquencourt, France.

Ducournau, R. & Quinqueton, J. (1986).*YAFOOL: Encore un langage objet à base de frames ! ,* Technical Report INRIA 72, Rocquencourt, France.

Ferber, J. (1983). *MERING: un langage d'acteur pour la représentation et la manipulation des connaissances,* Thesis, Université de Paris 6, France.

Ferber, J. (1985). Définition récursive et évaluation distribuée: Un modèle rigoureux de langage objet, *Actes 5ème congrès RFIA,* Grenoble, 1985, 715-724.

Ferber, J. (1986). Systèmes experts et approches orientées objets,*Actes des 6èmes Journées Internationales sur les Systèmes Experts et leurs Applications,* Avignon, 525-42.

Golberg, A. & Robson, D. (1983). *Smalltalk-80, the language and its implementation,* Addison-Wesley, Reading, Massachussets.

Fikes, R. & Kehler, T. (1985).The role of frame-based representation in reasonning, *Communications of the ACM,* **28**, 9, 904-20.

Hullot, J.M. (1984). *Programmer en Ceyx, version 15,* Technical Report INRIA, Rocquencourt, France.

Jung, S. (1986). *L'Ordre 0++,* Technical Report CRIN 96-R-097, Université de Nancy, France.

Rechenmann, F. (1985).SHIRKA : Mécanismes d'inférences sur une base de connaissance centrée objet,*Actes 5ème congrès RFIA,* Grenoble, 1243-1254.

Stefik, M. Bobrow, D.G., Mittal, S. & Conway, L. (1983). Knowledge programming in LOOPS: Report on an experimental course,*The AI Magazine,* **4**, 3, 3-14.

EDORA : AN OBJECT-CENTERED KNOWLEDGE-BASED APPROACH TO DYNAMIC MODELLING

8.1 Introduction

Computers have been extensively used for dynamic modelling and simulation essentially because of their increasing computational power. Numerous software products have thus been developed which allow the users to describe and then simulate or optimize their models as sets of difference or differential equations. High level mathematical languages are proposed for the declaration of variables, parameters or initial conditions as for the description of the equations. These products include libraries of numerical methods to estimate the parameters of the model working on some experimental data, to solve the equations according to their mathematical characteristics as far as they are known or to determine singular points. The trend in the field is to increase the power of these systems by continuously adding new methods and new features such as advanced graphic capabilities and to make them easier to use through the introduction of command languages and editing facilities.

8.1.1 *The insufficiencies of user assistance*

However the level of assistance to the end user does not seem to increase at the same rate. There are several good reasons for this. First of all, the user must provide a completely specified model before entering the system. Translating the model in the modelling language supported by the software can only eventually help him to detect and correct some inconsistencies. Thus the modelling activity itself is still of his responsibility. Moreover, no assistance is provided for the choice of the method adapted to a given task, such as simulation. Considering the large number of available methods and their complexity, the user generally oscillates between two opposite attitudes : either to systematically choose the more advanced method with the associated problem of selecting the appropriate values for the numerous parameters, or to restrain himself to a small subset of methods he is confident of having mastered. Finally, no means are provided to assess the quality of the results delivered by these methods. As most of them are designed for robustness, inexact results can easily be obtained, unknown to the user.

This analysis is certainly not specific of the modelling systems, and the developers of computing environments are generally aware of these problems, but the solutions they put forward are inefficient and generally limited to the task of selecting an appropriate method. These solutions fall into one of the following categories : basic on-line assistance which provides some explanation text attached to a given command or method, decision trees based on sequentially organized criteria, use of logical combination of key-words, knowledge-based techniques using decision rules. The advantages of the knowledge-based approach are well known : the knowledge base is easily extended or modified and the results or conclusions of inferences can be explained to the user. However, the common drawback of these solutions is that the final choice of the method together with the selection of its parameters values still rely on the user who has not always sufficient knowledge to understand the resulting advice. Moreover, although assistance is provided as to the choice of a method for a given task, the problem of generating a sequence of tasks in order to solve a larger problem remains untackled.

8.1.2 *The EDORA project*

Thus, it appears clearly that most of the current modelling environments lack directions for use of the methods they offer, capabilities of generating plans, knowledge about the modelling domain. In this context, the objective of the EDORA (in French : Equations Différentielles Ordinaires et Récurrentes Appliquées, Applied Ordinary Differential and Recurrent Equations) project was to specify a biological modelling environment which should include knowledge about the objects involved, such as mathematical models, equations, variables and so on, on the methods which manipulate these objects and on the modelling domain itself. The project was initiated by INRIA (Institut National de Recherche en Informatique et en Automatique). Several research laboratories joined the project latter on. A complete description of the project organization and results can be found in (EDORA, 1987).

In a first stage, the modelling domain was restrained to population dynamics, e.g. growth of populations or organisms, interactions between populations through predation for instance. To represent this knowledge, the classical rule-based model was evaluated and rejected since it tends to reduce any object as a collection of atomic facts and thus does not respect its integrity. A specific object-centered model was then specified and implemented as an operational shell, called Shirka (Rechenmann, 1985).

8.2 The object-centered knowledge representation model of Shirka

The development of EDORA and Shirka have been simultaneous. Shirka has been tailored to the needs of EDORA and some directions of work in EDORA have been decided through the use of the formal model provided by Shirka. Since then, Shirka has been used in many other applications, such as technical and financial diagnosis.

8.2.1 *Classes and instances*

Shirka makes use of an object-centered knowledge representation model based on the notion of frame (Minsky, 1975). The syntactic description unit is called a scheme. A scheme describes a class of objects or a specific object called an instance belonging to one of the existing classes. The term object is general : it can be a physical or mathematical object, a context, a situation, any entity which can be semantically defined. A class is defined by a list of slots, each slot being defined by a list of facets, each facet by a list of values. The values are themselves schemes or references to schemes. As an example, here is the definition of the *time-series* class in Shirka :

```
{ time-series
      ako        =         object ;
      nb-points  $one      integer ;
      indep      $list-of  real
                 $com      "the points in time" ;
      dep        $list-of  real
                 $com      "the values of the dependent variable "}
```

and an instance of this class :

```
{ ts#34
      is-a       = time-series ;
      nb-points  = 8 ;
      indep      = 0.0 0.5 1.0 1.5 2.0 2.5 3.0 3.5  ;
      dep        = -0.98 1.02 1.023 1.04 1.03 1.06 1.07 1.06 }
```

The slot *ako* (a-kind-of) specifies that the class *time-series* is a specialization of the predefined class *object* . The slot *is-a* indicates that *ts#34* is an instance of *time-series*. Each slot is typed with the help of the facets *$one* or *$list-of*, according to the admissible number of potential values. The type is either basic (integer, real, characters string or boolean) or complex by referencing an other class. For instance, the following class *variable* makes use of the type *interval*, which is itself defined by the homonymous class.

```
{ variable
      ako     =      operand ;
      name    $one   string ;
      range   $one   interval }
```

```
{ interval
       ako            =     object ;
       lower-bound  $one real ;
       upper-bound  $one real }
```

The instance *v#2* defines a variable whose range of admissible values is specified by the interval *int#8*.

```
{ v#2
       is-a    = variable ;
       name   = "size" ;
       range  = int#8 }

{ int#8
       is-a           = interval ;
       lower-bound  = 2.5 ;
       upper-bound  = 12.0 }
```

Shirka offers other facets to restrict the possible values of a slot : *$range* is followed by a list of intervals in which the values must fall, *$domain* is followed by the extensive list of admissible values and *$check* is followed by a list of predicates which must be true for every value of the slot.

8.2.2 *Inference of slot values*

Shirka includes an inference engine which is able to infer the unknown values of slots in instances using the knowledge attached to the corresponding classes. Thus, to use Shirka is to define classes, to create incomplete instances of these classes, where some of the slots have not received values, and to ask for these undefined slot values. To attach knowledge to slots of classes, several facets are available. *$value* fixes the value of a slot for all the potential instances of the class. *$default* assigns a default value to a slot ; this value will be retained only if other inference means have failed.

The *$if-needed* facet implements the classical procedural attachment mechanism. It is followed by a list of calls to methods. These methods are themselves described as schemes whose slots describe the various arguments of the method. In the following example, *t-mat-prod* defines a method which multiplies a real matrix *A* with its transpose, giving *B*, a real symmetrical matrix.

```
{ t-mat-prod
       ako          =       mat-method ;
       fct-name  $value   TA*A ;
       A          $one     matrix ;
       B          $one     sym-matrix }
```

The slot *fct-name* specifies the name of a Lisp function. The call to a method creates an instance of the corresponding class ; only the slots corresponding to the input arguments can receive values through inference. The incomplete resulting instance is sent to the Lisp function whose task is to compute the output parameters, that is to complete the instance, and to send it back to Shirka, where the output values are recovered. The same mechanism is used for the predicates of the *$check* facet, the result being always a single boolean value.

This mechanism presents several advantages over the classical procedural attachment, where a Lisp lambda function is directly placed in the slot description. First of all, the input parameters can be inferred as slots values, they can receive for instance default values. These values must conform with all the restrictions attached to the slot : its type, the range or domains of values, the *$check* predicates. If it is not the case, the method cannot be executed ; the reasons for this failure can be explained to the user and another method must be looked for. The results of the execution must also satisfy the constraints attached to the output slots. Conversely, the type of the results are known. For instance, the output of the *t-mat-prod* method is a matrix belonging to the class *sym-matrix*, i.e. symmetric. Then, the Lisp function has then only a computational role. Here is an harmonious way to merge descriptive and procedural knowledge.

Other inference mechanisms have been specifically designed for Shirka, such as pattern-matching and recursive classification which will be introduced latter on.

8.2.3 *Inheritance and classification*

The classes in Shirka are organized in a lattice structure, in which a class dominates several sub-classes and is itself dominated by one or several super-classes. Any class is thus a restriction of another class at least, except the *object* class at the top of the lattice, and inherits all the knowledge attached to its super-classes. The names of the super-classes appear as values of the *ako* slot. Any instance of a given class is also instance of all the super-classes, but the inverse is not always true. This lattice structure and the inheritance mechanism it supports tends to facilitate both the construction and the modification of the knowledge base. As the size of the base increases, adding a new class means essentially specializing existing classes.

As an example, the Figure 8.1 shows the hierarchy of classes of behaviour modes of one-dimension dynamic growth models. The classes are described by slots such as *monotonic* (a boolean), *number of inflexion points* (an integer), *presence of asymptotes* (a boolean) and so on. The recursive classification mechanism works on the lattice of classes. Given an instance and its class, it tries to determine to which sub-classes this instance could be attached. To do so, it requires the values of slots. In the example above, beginning with an instance of *growth* curve, values of the slots *monotonic, number of inflexion points* or *presence of asymptotes* are required. They can either be asked to the user or inferred. The result of the classification process is made up of three lists : the list of classes to which the instance cannot belong, the list of classes to which the instance can surely belong and a list of classes to which the instance could belong, the absence of some values preventing of giving a definitive answer.

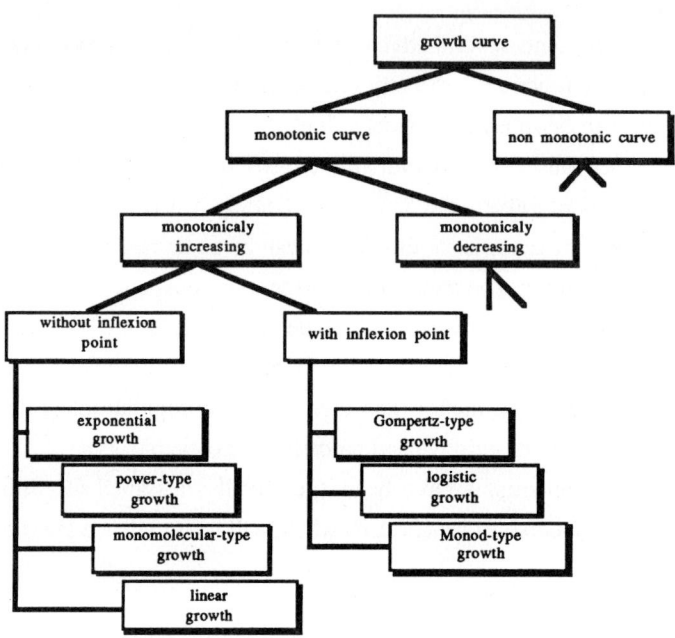

Figure 8.1. The classes of behaviour curves of one-dimension growth models are organized in a hierarchy. Any Gompertz-like curve has an inflexion point, has positive slope, is monotonic and is a growth curve.

8.3 Organization of a models base

There are several ways to assist the modelling activity. The first one is to provide a description language whose semantics maps the semantics of the application domain. The aim of this approach is to reduce the gap between the perception of the real system by the user and its mathematical formulation. The user has no longer to describe his model in terms of mathematical expressions. Various formalisms have been investigated, such as energy flow diagrams (Odum, 1983), bond graphs (Karnopp, 1975) or flow graphs (Wiitaken, 1976). In the EDORA project, chemical-like equations have been used to describe growth processes. Figure 8.2 shows the representation of the same set of differential equations with three different formalisms.

Another similar way to help a user building a model is to maintain a list of elementary sub-models together with some primitives to structure them into larger ones. A simpler way consists in building a models base and providing some associative access method to the models. The user expresses some characteristics of the process to be modelled and the related models are searched in the base. Classical data models, such as relational model, cannot be used in this context since they lack the ability to describe complex objects together with their related methods for slot values inference.

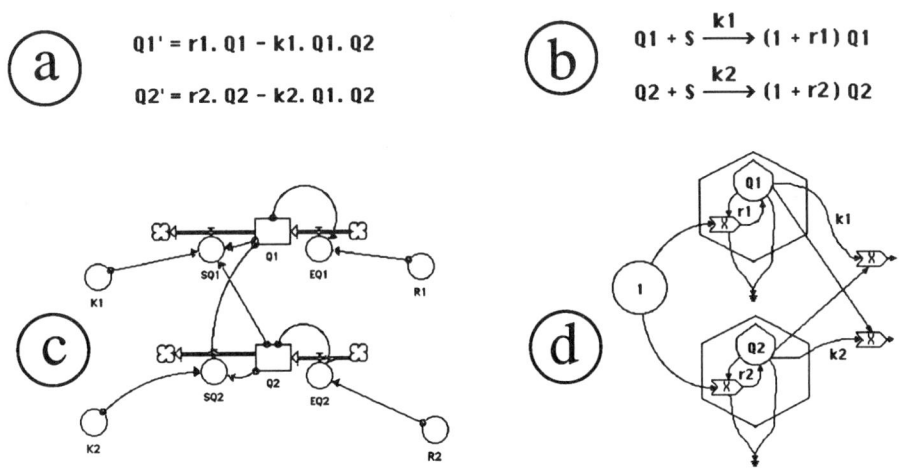

Figure 8.2. Description of a competition model between two species using several formalisms. The state variables Q1 and Q2 represent population sizes, which are assumed to depend only on natural growth and competition interaction. Figure 8.2.a : Differential formalism. Figure 8.2.b : Chemical-like formalism, introduced by (Garfinkel, 1962), and extended by (Pavé, 1980). Figure 8.2.c : Formalism used in Systems Dynamics (Forrester, 1971). Figure 8.2.d : Energy circuit language (Odum, 1983).

8.3.1 *The search for a criterion of genericity*
It seems easy to build a models base using the object-centered representation of Shirka, where models would be described by classes. The problem is to find a correct hierarchical organization. There does not seem to exist a unique acceptable criterion to decide if one model is more or less generic than another one. As an example, the very simple exponential model can be considered as a special case of the logistic growth model where the attrition parameter *b* has been set to zero.

exponential model   x' = a * x
logistic model   x' = a * x - b * x²

Conversely, the logistic model can be regarded as a specialization of the exponential model as it supports more restrictive hypotheses. A classification based on mathematical considerations, i.e. on the characteristics of the equations (linear, non linear, quadratic,...) and of the model itself (autonomous, non autonomous,...) leads to similar problems. The first conclusion of EDORA in the very beginning of the project was to accept this situation. As a matter of fact, the first version of an operational system included a hierarchy of models based only on the characteristics of its dynamic response. The dozen models contained in the base were one variable models, adapted to the description of the growth of organisms or populations.The user was helped to select a "good" model according to the description of the shape of his experimental data points. This description had to be expressed as a list of keywords, whose meanings appear in Figure 8.3.

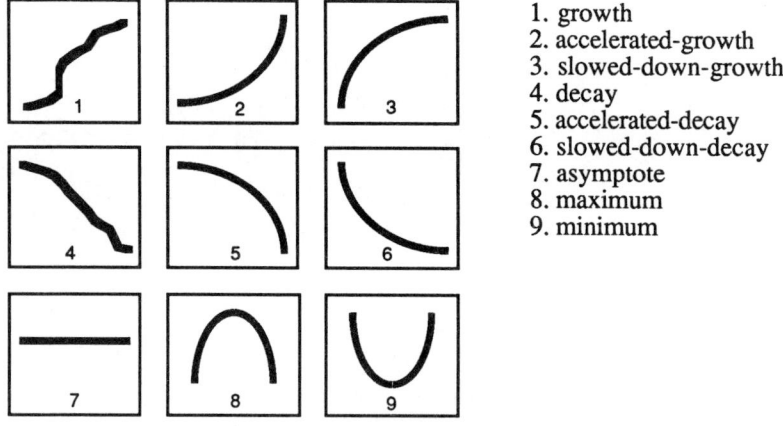

1. growth
2. accelerated-growth
3. slowed-down-growth
4. decay
5. accelerated-decay
6. slowed-down-decay
7. asymptote
8. maximum
9. minimum

Figure 8.3. For the description of the shape of experimental data points, each keyword is associated with a basic curve. The complete description is thus a list of keywords.

This first version of EDORA offered several other features. Once a model had been selected, the values of its parameters were estimated with an iterative method beginning with initial values whose computations was model-dependent. The object-centered representation has indeed the advantage to group all the knowledge which concerns an entity. In this particular case, once a class of model has been selected, all the knowledge on this class is available : adapted methods of manipulation, text of equations, mathematical properties, related models and so on.

In the successive versions of EDORA, it was decided however to take into account several different points of view on the models simultaneously.

8.2.2. *The integration of multiple points of view on models*

A dynamic biological model can be considered from at least three different points of view. The mathematical description of the equations is the first one ; it will be detailed in the next section. A second possible point of view is the behaviour mode. It has been extensively used in the first version of EDORA and requires the description of the typical evolution of the output variables. A last point of view consists in a description of the internal mechanisms of the biological process involved. It includes the description of the semantics of the various variables and parameters (population, size, density, limiting factor, threshold, growth rate, ...) together with their interactions (competition, predation, commensalism, ...). This description can be expressed in one of the non-mathematical formalisms such as chemical-like equations.

Each point of view can lead to a distinct hierarchy of classes. An example of such a hierarchy for the behaviour mode aspect has already been presented on Figure 8.1. The models base is then constituted of a collection of independent hierarchies describing the same models from the different points of views. The search mechanism must allow the user to look for a model starting with the knowledge of only one point of view such as the description of its behaviour mode or directly its mathematical expression. If several points of view are simultaneously entered, their mutual inconsistencies should eventually lead to a failure of the search process.

In the present version of EDORA, a particular class, named *situation*, has been introduced in order to store the knowledge on the different possible associations between the three points of view.

```
{ situation
      ako          =     object ;
      behaviour  $one behaviour-mode ;
      math         $one math-description ;
      bio           $one biological-process }
```

The different recognized situations are defined as specializations of the class *situation* with restrictions on the values of the three slots. Here is for instance the definition of *situation#27*, one of the situations associated with the Gompertz model.

```
{ situation#27
      ako          =          situation ;
      behaviour  $one       logistic-growth ;
      math         $one       Gompertz-model ;
               . . . . . . . . . .      }
```

These classes form a hierarchy. The search process begins with creating an instance of *situation*. This instance is then submitted to the classification algorithm which has been extended in order to skip from a hierarchy to another one when necessary. As the particular, empty situation, is processed, the values of its slots, *behaviour*, *math* and *bio*, must be inferred by classification. Each time, the control is indeed passed to the same algorithm working on the corresponding hierarchy : *behaviour-mode*, *math-description*, *biological process*. The required values of slots (such as *number of inflexion points* or *monotonic* in the hierarchy *behaviour-mode*) are this time asked to the user. The result is a classification for each point of view. The classification on the *situation* hierarchy can then be achieved, which leads to a list of sure and possible models.

8.2.3 *The mathematical description of models*

In the first version of EDORA, the mathematical models appeared only as characters strings, as information. Thus, the models could not be used directly in algorithmic manipulations such as simulation, parameters values estimation or symbolic differentiation. Moreover, it was impossible to describe the semantics attached to the various components of the model : the equations, but also the variables, parameters or initial conditions. It is indeed highly interesting to specify that a given parameter has to be considered as a growth rate or as predation rate, especially in the process-oriented point of view. Similarly, a variable is not only known by its name, but also by its unit, dimension or range of values. It seems then logical to express all these attributes as slots of schemes. As a consequence, a mathematical expression is translated into a set of schemes, a scheme describing either an operandum (variable, parameter, constant value), or an operator (addition, multiplication, derivative,...) (Pierret-Goldbreich, 1987). Thus, while manipulating an equation, any algorithm has access to the characteristics of all the entities appearing in the equation, under both the mathematical point of view and the semantic point of view since the two points of view can be merged into a unique scheme. As an example, the following instances represent the simple expression $a \cdot x - b \cdot x^2$, where the name is the unique information on the variables and parameters : the expression is only described from the mathematical point of view.

Moreover, symbolic manipulation methods can be applied on the mathematical expressions, such as differentiation, simplification, substitution or partial evaluation.

Each type of growth model (exponential, logistic, Gompertz, ...) is described as a class whose slots include for instance the lists of state variables and of parameters. One of the slots describes the mathematical expression of the model as alternative sets of prototypical equations. A prototypical equation is described by its pattern where actual names of variables and parameters are dummy. Each set of equations is associated with a typical formulation of the model. For instance, for the logistic growth model, three different formulations have been retained :

$$x' = a \cdot x^2 - b \cdot x \qquad x' = a \cdot x \cdot (x - b) \qquad x' = a \cdot x \cdot (1 - x/k)$$

It is then possible to test if a given mathematical model matches one of the possible sets of equations. If the user for instance wishes to supply its own model formulation, supplying the value of the *math* slot of the *situation* class, EDORA can check if the model appears in the base. If it is the case, the user is supplied with all the information about the model and can be assisted in the parameters estimation or simulation tasks.

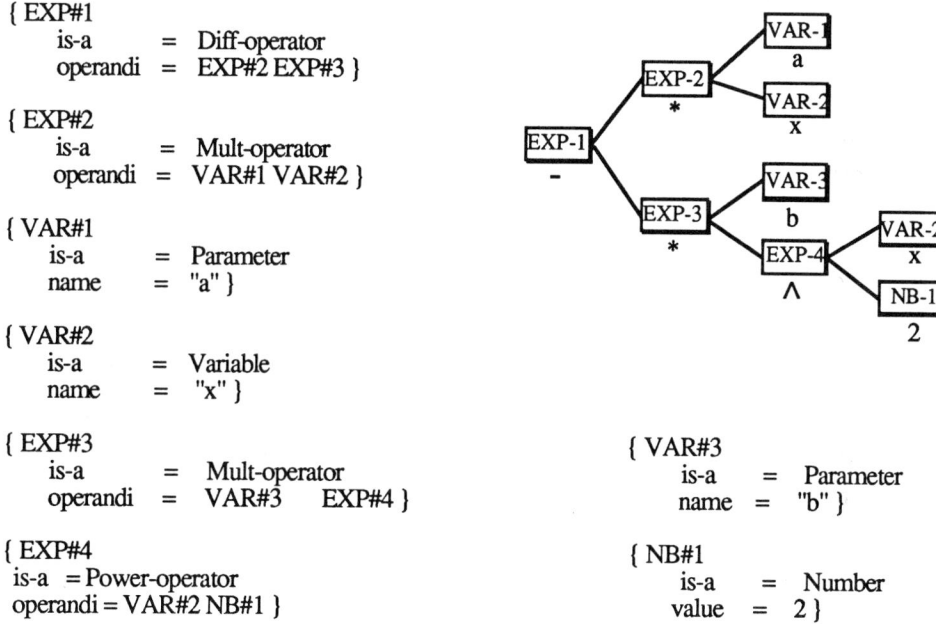

{ EXP#1
    is-a   = Diff-operator
    operandi = EXP#2 EXP#3 }

{ EXP#2
    is-a   = Mult-operator
    operandi = VAR#1 VAR#2 }

{ VAR#1
    is-a   = Parameter
    name   = "a" }

{ VAR#2
    is-a   = Variable
    name   = "x" }

{ EXP#3
    is-a   = Mult-operator
    operandi = VAR#3   EXP#4 }

{ EXP#4
is-a = Power-operator
operandi = VAR#2 NB#1 }

{ VAR#3
    is-a   = Parameter
    name   = "b" }

{ NB#1
    is-a   = Number
    value   = 2 }

Figure 8.4. The graphical representation of the mathematical expression $a \cdot x - b \cdot x^2$. The links of the tree are described by the *operandi* slot in the Shirka schemes.

8.4 Conclusion

The principles of the current state of development of the EDORA system have been presented. The present version can be easily extended by adding new models or by taking into account new points of view if necessary. The various hierarchies can be refined and extended. Here lies one of the main advantages of the knowledge-based approach.

All the results of the EDORA project have not been presented. For instance, the impact of highly interactive user interfaces has been evaluated through the development of two programs. The first one, DYNAMAC, provides the user with a complete modelling environment for studying small size differential systems. Unlike classical systems, the interaction with the user is based in a conceptual model closed to his natural work habits. The second program, called CROISSANCE, exemplifies this principle. The user can fit a theoretical growth model to a set of experimental data by interactively reshaping the curve, acting on some key points such as the position of the inflexion point or the slope at the origin. After each experiment, classical statistical tests are computed in order to evaluate the adjustment in a more precise, but less intuitive, way.

A last, but certainly not the least, impact of EDORA has been perceived on some of the research lines of the biologists involved in the project. In order to complete or refine the knowledge base, investigations in some precise directions have been decided. When the results will emerge, they will be integrated in the present knowledge base.

References

EDORA, (1987). Activity report 87. INRIA - INRA - Laboratoire de Biométrie, Université Claude Bernard, Lyon.

Forrester, J.W. (1971).*World Dynamics*,Wright-Allen Press, Cambridge, Mass.

Garfinkel, D. (1962). Digital computer simulation of an ecological system based on a modified mass action law, *Ecology*, **45**, 502-7.

Karnopp, D. & Rosenberg, R.(1975). *Systems Dynamics : a unified approach*, Wiley.

Minsky, M.A. (1975). A framework for representing knowledge,*The Psychology of Computer Vision*, Ed. Winston, P., McGraw-Hill, 211-77.

Odum, H.T. (1983). *System Ecology*, Wiley.

Pavé, A. (1980). Contribution à la théorie et à la pratique des modèles mathématiques pour l'analyse dynamique des systèmes biologiques, *Thèse Doct. ès Sciences*, Université Claude Bernard, Lyon.

Pavé, A. & Rechenmann, F. (1986). Computer-aided modelling in biology : an Artificial Intelligence approach, *Artificial Intelligence and Simulation*, Simulating Computer Society Series.

Pierret-Goldbreich, C. (1987). Object-centered knowledge representation for modelling in biology, *International Symposium on AI, Expert Systems and Language in Modelling and Simulation*, Barcelona, june 2-4 .

Rechenmann, F.(1985). SHIRKA - Mécanismes d'inférence sur une base de connaissances centrée-objet, Simulating Computer Society, *Reconnaissance des Formes et Intelligence Artificielle*, AFCET-AdI-INRIA, Grenoble.

Rousseau, B. (1988). Vers un environnement de résolution de problèmes en biométrie. Apports des systèmes à base de connaissances et de l'interaction graphique. *Thèse Doct.*, Université Claude-Bernard, Lyon.

Wiitaken, W. (1976). Modelling biological systems by means of flowgraphs, *Simulation*, **27**, 185-92.

9 *A. Romanczuk, R. Beuscart and G. Comyn*

USE OF OBJECT ORIENTED LANGUAGE "KEOPS" FOR THE CONSTRUCTION OF AN EXPERTISE IN THE FIELD OF NUTRITION

9.1 Introduction

The goal of this expert system is to plan the daily diet of a patient, integrating, on one hand, his eating habits and, on the other hand, the properties of the nutrients which make up this diet.

The knowledge which must be represented and manipulated in a system for this domain is extensive and involves a very large number of relations. So the knowledge base formalism based on production rules seems to be inappropriate. Thus, we found a formalism for the knowledge base that solves the problem posed by the manipulation and the storage of various different types of components included in production rules.

The data driven programming and the object oriented programming used in KEOPS (LRO2) constitute a simple and homogeneous way to represent this knowledge. We will illustrate these programming methods and show how to use them for processing in the field of nutrition. The advantages of the object oriented knowledge representation in KEOPS, in comparison with production rules will be clearly shown by this expert system.

To analyze clearly this expertise, we use a graphical representation which gives us an overview of an object oriented programming methodological approach. (see Appendix).

9.2 Presentation of the medical problem

9.2.1 *Aims and analysis of the problem*

The expert system aims at giving "adapted" advice in nutrition. That means planning the daily diet of a patient **without changing the type of food he eats,** thus respecting his way of life, **and intervening only to give a different distribution of absorbed nutrients.**

This adapted advice is different from the usual advice in which we balance the diet by giving a standard model meal.

In order to achieve this, a nutritional inquiry (anamnesis) will be carried out, so the doctor knows the eating habits of his patient. To determine if his diet is balanced or not, we have food composition tables which allow us to obtain the eating habits of the patient in terms of quantity of the contribution in nutrients. These contributions of nutrients will be compared to the patient's calorific needs.

The "food composition tables" include descriptions of all foodstuffs usually eaten (about 400 split up into 28 families) in terms of all nutrients (about 28).

Finally, considering that balance in the diet must be based on balance in the quantity of contribution of nutrients, we suggest, in accordance with the patient's favourite foods, a daily "diet".

9.2.2 *Example of nutritional inquiry*

IDENTIFICATION	:	Odette Duval
SEX	:	Female
AGE	:	56
HEIGHT	:	155
WEIGHT	:	104

DAILY MEAL :

**	MORNING	bread	:	2 slices
		margarine	:	2 portions
		milk	:	1 bowl
		water	:	1 glass
**	MIDDAY	pork	:	1 chop
		chips	:	1 portion
		bread	:	0.5 slices

**	EVENING	raw vegetable	:	4 soup spoons
		ham	:	1 slices
		cabbage	:	7 soup spoons
		potatoes	:	3
		bread	:	2 slices
		camembert	:	1.5 portions
		grape	:	1 bunch
**	SNACK	milk	:	2 bowls

Table 9.1 *Distribution of contribution of nutrients*

	GLUCOSE fast abs.	GLUCOSE slow abs.	LIPID unsat.	LIPID satur.	PROTEIN	ALCOHOL	CALORIES
MORNING	5.04	22.00	9.40	4.04	6.50	0.00	255.12
MIDDAY	0.00	65.50	25.35	39.41	34.75	0.00	983.84
EVENING	33.35	92.00	17.33	19.24	50.85	0.00	1033.88
SNACK	6.66	0.00	1.46	2.93	4.66	0.00	84.93
TOTAL	45.05	179.50	53.50	65.60	96.70	0.00	2357.00

9.3 Why an object oriented language ?

The goal of this chapter is to show the interest of object oriented languages for the implementation of expert systems . This question will be studied in two parts :

- In the choice of necessary treatment to represent the useful knowledge for a problem solution in a realtime and realword situation.
- In the search for useful knowledge units for a problem solution. These mechanisms are used by the inference engine.

We will look first at one of **the important** problems in expert systems, the efficiency problem, especially response time. We will show in this context the interest of object oriented languages, in data organization and in rapidity of information search.

9.3.1 *Knowledge representation and utilization*

The organization and the management of a large volume of data has not really been considered in Artificial Intelligence. The standard solution is to increase the memory space and to store all data in virtual memory. The need to store and to have access to a large volume of data outside the virtual memory, with reasonable access time, is critical, in particular in the fields of management or planning. In addition, the inheritance in object oriented languages and the search through the relations introduce some problems of data management.

Solutions might be found using notions of parallelism, data compilation or partial evaluation of data.

The expression of the structure of a large volume of data is difficult. If we consider fields of expertise where the knowledge is essentially based on a very large and well structured classification, the production rules for knowledge bases seems inappropriate **due to the number of relations defined for the expression and the manipulation of this knowledge.**

For instance, in our problem, the knowledge base must contain all the foods usually eaten, all the contributors of nutrients and all the links representing the relations between the large families of foodstuffs and their components, and in the same way, the nutrients and their components, and the relations between these foodstuffs and their contributors of nutrients.

For this problem, **the use of data driven programming and object oriented programming** would be a solution. These constitute effectively a simple and homogeneous way to represent and process large volumes of knowledge. In fact, the knowledge will be contained in the classes handled and their hierarchical structures, properties by their procedural attachments. Those classes will be organized in networks in which hierarchical links are relations (for example : SPLIT-UP-INTO/IS-A-PART-OF) which are previously defined.

This organization provides a static hierarchy between classes.

Problems in the nutritional field are essentially based on a well structured classification. (Example : foodstuffs are structured in large families that split up into different groups ...).

The interest of this static hierarchy **is the possibility to get inherited properties, and the transitivity of relations between these classes.** (Transitivity example : dairy products are one contributor of calcium and split up into milk, cheese and yoghurt, thus through the hierarchical link, milk, yoghurt and cheese will also be contributors of calcium ; Fig 9.1).

In the domain of expertise where the knowledge is well structured in information units, we will define concurrently to this natural representation of the knowledge structure, the hierarchy of classes. Thus, the hierarchy will lead to a concrete representation of the knowledge structure, as opposed to production rules where, in general, the knowledge structure is not largely evident.

Example : network of classes :

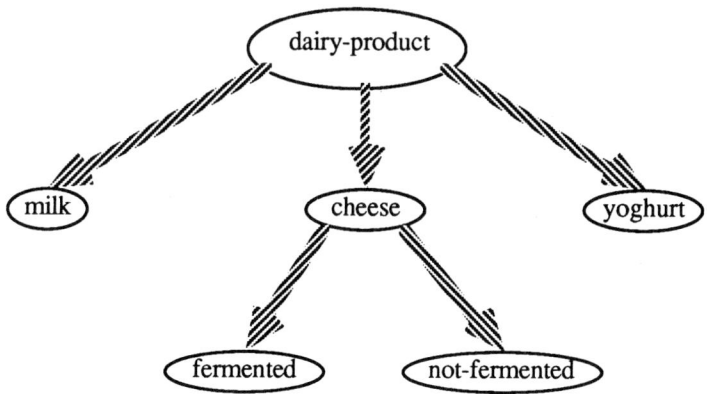

Figure 9.1 Example of a network of classes

"Prolog" production rules :

dairy-product (x) --> milk (x);
dairy-product (x) --> cheese (x);
dairy-product (x) --> yoghurt (x);
cheese (x) --> fermented-cheese (x);
cheese (x) --> not-fermented-cheese (x);

contributor-of-calcium (x) --> dairy-product (x);

Furthermore, in knowledge representation languages, the knowledge is included in the classes handled, (e.g. : dairy products are contributors of calcium), as opposed to "clauses" in a Prolog-like representation, in which properties of foodstuffs are at the same level as productions rules describing knowledge structure (see above the last rule).

9.3.2 *Search of knowledge units*

Production rules systems, in which the condition part of the rule should filter data in the working memory, could execute a lot of search processes before the completion of this filtering. In this case, the waiting time might be long.

It should be possible to compile the condition part of the rule (in order to reduce the time of the test) to determine whether this rule condition is true. Nevertheless, the problem remains if the amount of information needed in the working memory is considerable.

Knowledge representation languages or frame languages use a kind of default reasoning through inheritance. The access time for an information unit only depends upon the length of the search process which must be accomplished in the network.

Furthermore, **the processing of the class hierarchy representing knowledge may be data driven**, which allows direct access to knowledge units.

We can associate with those data an information search mechanism, ie : define plain ways to identify missing information, or what must be computed when these data are scanned.

9.3.3 *Conclusion*

According to this analysis, we see that object oriented languages among knowledge representation languages are well adapted to minimize problems when we implement expert systems in a domain where the knowledge volume is large and well structured.

Thus, object oriented languages allow knowledge organization in classes and their hierarchical links, and **allow mechanisms to adjust the knowledge treatment mechanism in all expert systems classes**. For that, it is sufficient to identify class properties, and attach to them procedures that change elements of knowledge in the knowledge used, i.e. be able to reason through this hierarchy. Thus, those classes and those procedural attachments allow a general representation of all essential knowledge for treatment, comprehension and implementation.

9.4 The specific features of KEOPS

KEOPS is an object oriented language that has specific mechanisms such as procedural attachment to objects and properties for knowledge representation and knowledge processing for artificial intelligence. Thus, the interpretation of programs implemented by those mechanisms is driven by the problem data.

Like most object oriented languages, KEOPS allows the development of programs by using most of the well known basic concepts of object oriented programming : with objects, classes of objects, class hierarchies, inheritance of properties.

In order to write artificial intelligence systems with a declarative approach, KEOPS must be used as follows :

Organizing knowledge representation into classes with a hierarchical network according to relations (For example : split-up-into/is-a-part-of, generalization/specialization, is-a/be-in).

Adjusting the knowledge treatment mechanism on several expert system classes with procedural attachments to properties, inheritance of properties and data controlled message sending.

Introducing metaknowledge into the existing expert systems with the sending of data controlled messages of KEOPS. This addition of metaknowledge will be applied without updating the inference engine of the expert system involved. In production rule systems, however introducing metaknowledge can be extremely difficult.

For KEOPS, the class notion is useful for knowledge base structuring and allows the treatment of knowledge; furthermore, it will be used for the user interface. For that, classes are used when new knowledge is acquired, and will easily allow the expansion of the knowledge base.

However, to keep the coherence of this knowledge base, some constraints will continue to be obligatory : the class must have an exact syntax, must be described with a list of properties and should not be independent of the other classes.

Thus, for KEOPS it appears that objects, as receivers or triggers of treatment, **will be used in the implementation of the inference engine, and in the realization and the use of the knowledge base in expert systems.**

(see Appendix : Definition of graphical representations of units (object, property ...) involved in a problem analysis).

9.5 Static knowledge representation

9.5.1 *Knowledge base content*
For the nutrition field, the knowledge about digestion and nutritional elements is well
structured in information units.

We will need descriptions of all foodstuffs usually eaten, all existing nutrients, and
existing relations between foodstuffs and their contributions of nutrients.

9.5.2 *Knowledge representation*
(i) Foodstuffs structuring
Together with the immediate representation of food structure, we define a hierarchy of
food classes with KEOPS.
The classes are organized in a network in which hierarchical links stand for relations :
"SPLIT-UP-INTO/IS-A-PART-OF". (Fig. 9.2)

For instance :   - Dairy products SPLIT-UP-INTO milk, cheese, yoghurt
                 - milk IS-A-PART-OF dairy products.

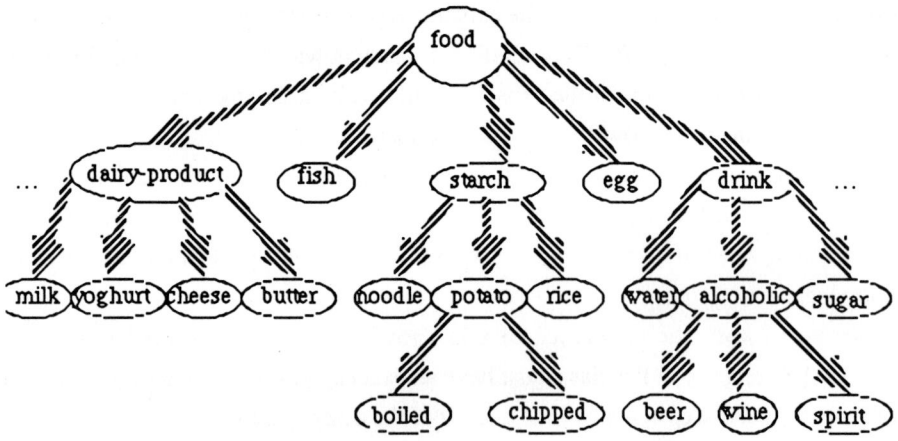

Figure 9.2 Examples of hierarchical links in foodstuffs structuring

(ii) Nutrient structuring
As for foodstuffs, nutrients may be easily structured, thus we will define together with
this structuring the hierarchy of nutrient classes (fig. 9.3).

These classes are organized in a network in which hierarchical links correspond to relations "SPLIT-UP-INTO/IS-A-PART-OF"

For instance : Lipids SPLIT-UP-INTO saturated lipids and unsaturated lipids
polyunsaturated lipids ARE-A-PART-OF unsaturated lipids.

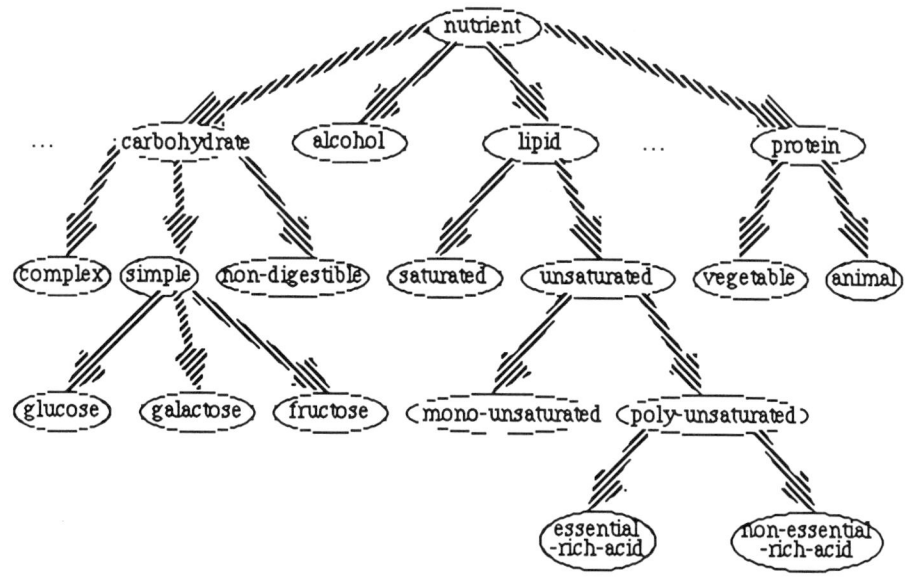

Figure 9.3 Examples of heirarchical links in nutrient structuring

(iii) Static knowledge structuring

To take into account the fact that foodstuffs are "contributors" of some nutrients, we define a class hierarchy of "contribution-of-nutrients", together with the nutrients structure. Thus, the "contribution-of-nutrients" are foodstuffs, and all <<foodstuffs>> classes are defined as subclasses of the "contribution-of-nutrients" they contain.

Such super-class links also translate a "split-up-into/is-a-part-of" relation.

Example :   Dairy products ARE-A-PART-OF contributor of calcium (Fig. 9.4).

With inheritance, the relations between food class hierarchies and contributor of nutrient class hierarchies allow "interrogation" of the foodstuff to ask them which nutrients they contain and their contribution percentage.

We "interrogate" the contributors of nutrients to know in which aliments they are contained.

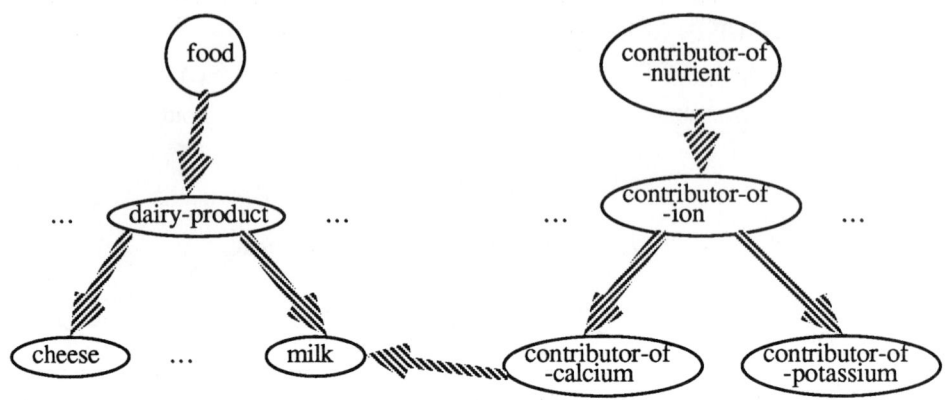

Figure 9.4 Example of static knowledge structuring

9.6 Principle of inference mechanism

The knowledge treatment mechanism is procedures attached to object properties.

9.6.1 *Search of properties attached to classes as static knowledge*
(i) Food classes network

   --> property : ***nutrient-list-for-1-food***

> The characteristics of all foodstuffs depend on the list of nutrients they contain.
>
> The property "nutrient-list-for-1-food" with its procedural attachment is declared for the food class and is <u>inherited by all these foodstuffs subclasses</u>.
>
> The procedure attached to the property consists of <u>searching the superclasses</u> of the affected food, <u>but only from the nutrient class hierarchy to the root.</u>

   --> property : ***contributor-percentage***

> Foods are also distinguished by their <u>percentage of contribution of nutrient</u> we already know (with food composition tables). There is no procedural attachment for this property.

(ii) Nutrient classes network

   --> property : ***food-list-for-1-nutrient***

> Every nutrient has a list indicating the foodstuffs containing them.

This property "food-list-for-1-nutrient" with its procedural attachment is declared for the nutrient contributor class and thus is <u>inherited by all its subclasses</u>.

The procedure attached to the property is integrated into <u>searching subclasses of contributor of nutrient classes network</u> to select components of this nutrient, and into <u>searching the subclasses of these contributors of nutrient only in the food class hierarchy</u>, down to the bottom of that hierarchy.

9.6.2 *Search of necessary properties to fire the processing*

Properties and procedural attachments are selected by reinterpreting the scenario of the problem.

The operating principle of this expertise may be divided into three phases :

(1) To get the patient's features (age, weight, waist ...)

--> From which we get :   his calorific need

his table of necessary contribution of nutrient distribution for morning, midday, evening and snack.

(2) To get his daily menu (foodstuffs list for morning, midday, evening and snack)

--> From which we get :   the distribution table of nutrient absorbed in the morning, midday, evening and for a snack.

his total absorbed calories.

(3) To propose his adapted menu

--> From which we get :   comparison of the two previous tables.

the deficiencies and the excesses of nutrients among foodstuffs the patient prefers.

a proposed menu.

From the operating principle presented above, we select the evident and necessary properties and the procedural attachments. Finally,we select the objects characterized by these properties.

A graphical representation like Fig. 9.5 is obtained after the complete operating system analysis of the expert system.

9.7 Conclusion

KEOPS, as a knowledge representation language, uses concepts close to the expressions proposed by the expert to specify both his deductive and factual knowledge. Furthermore, the system's incremental development implied by the language allows the continuous updating of the knowledge by the expert.

Data driven programming allows easy development of expert systems even if the information contained in the expertise is incomplete, because it is possible to model procedural knowledge which will be called in a context we didn't identify clearly while writing this procedure. Thanks to such demons, the updating of data allows the automatic propagation of the modification consequences, and so the guarantee that coherence is assured during expert system development.

The expert system implementation shows some desirable extensions for KEOPS. For examples,
it would be useful to be able to associate values with the links of the class network to directly model the fact that foodstuffs are contributors of nutrients with a percentage value.

There is a problem in the methodology for data driven programming : we should define programming constraints to keep, as in object oriented programming, independent objects with their own characteristics and functionalities. Thus we could, for examples define for objects, according to the context used, access rights to procedural attachments .

It is also a problem to implement expert systems with hundreds of classes or objects (for instance, our nutrition system has already 460 foodstuff classes). In order to solve the lack of memory space, we should define class groups, untriggered and triggered in groups. Generally, we think that the "knowledge base management system" support for expert system development has come to be a practical issue.

The possible extensions for this expert system are, on one hand, to add criteria other than physical characteristics of a patient (for example, some illness : such as diabetes) for the calorific need calculus, and on the other hand, the integration of this system in an overall medical treatment system.

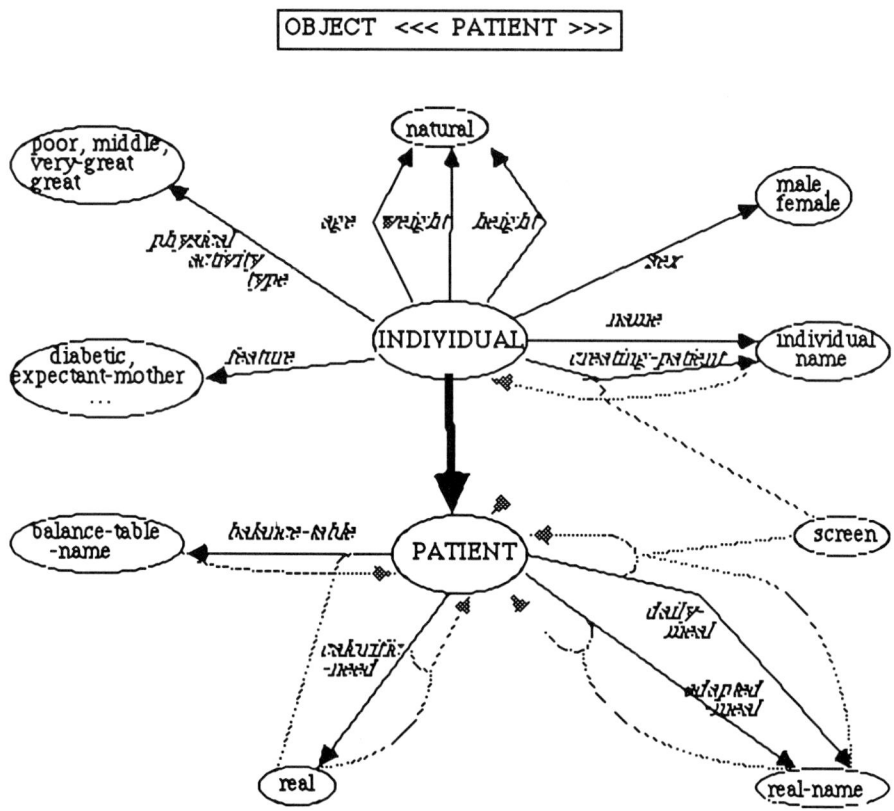

Fig 9.5 Continued overleaf

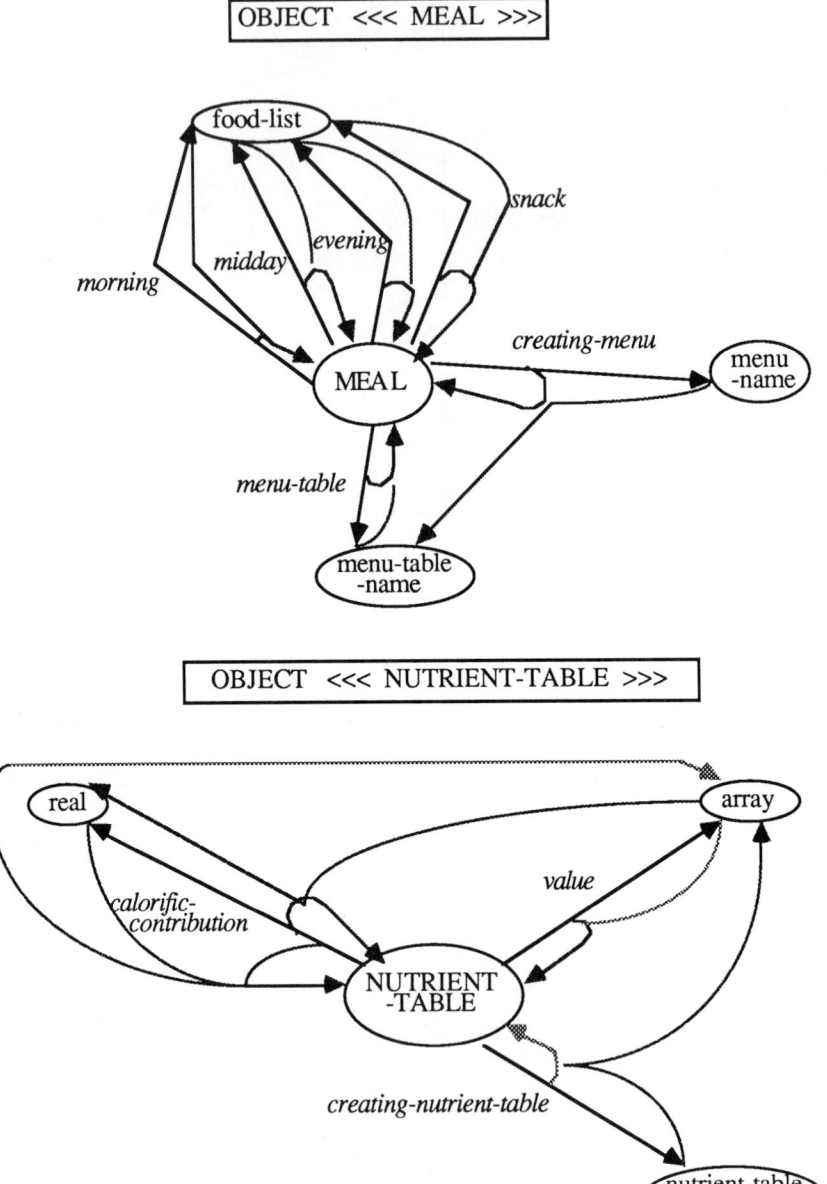

Fig. 9.5 Graphical representation obtained after the complete operating system analysis of the expert system.

Appendix : graphical representation of elements involved in the problem analysis

1.*Graphical representation of an object*

   : X is the name of an object

   : represents the set of all the possible states of the object X.

2. *Graphical representation of an object property*

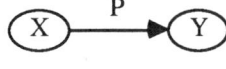
   : P is an application from the set of all the possible states of the
object X to the set of all the possible states of the object Y.

   The property P of an object X gets its value in the set of all the
possibles states of the object Y.

3. *Graphical representation of procedural attachments*

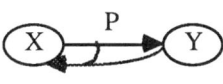

The dotted arrow represents a procedural attachment of the
property P, for which the input value is the value of this
property and links a state of the object X, to an other state of
the object X.

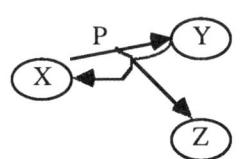

Procedural attachment of P, for which the input value of the
property P, gives as output value one element of (Z), and
links a state of the object X to an other state of the object X.

4.*Graphical representation of the hierarchical link : GENERALIZATION /
SPECIALIZATION relation.*
The arrow represents the hierarchical link of SPECIALIZATION.

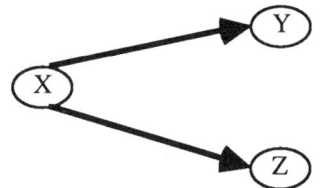

The hierarchical link "SPECIALIZATION" associates a state of the object X, with a state
of the object Y and a state of the object Z.

This graphical representation is interpreted as :

    is a "SPECIALIZATION" of   and (Z)

5. *Graphical representation of the hierarchical link associate with the SPLIT-UP-INTO/IS-A -PART-OF relation.*
The arrow represents the hierarchical link of SPLIT-UP-INTO.
The hierarchical link "SPLIT-UP-INTO" associates a state of the object X with a state of the object Y and a state of the object Z.

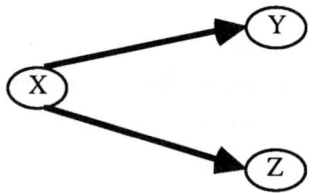

This graphical representation is interpreted as :

    "SPILT-UP-INTO"   and

References

Agha, G. (1986). *An overview of Actor languages.* SIGPLAN Notices.

Albert, P. (1983). *KOOL : représentation des connaissances.* BIGRE.

Carre, F. (1984). *ALOG : Acteurs et programmation en logique.* Thèse de docteur-ingenieur.

Farreny, H. (1985). *Les systèmes experts.* Cepadues-Editions.

Fox, M.S., Wright, J.M. (1983). *SRL : Schema Representation Language. Manuel d'utilisation.* Carnegie-Mellon University.

Fox, M.S., Wright, J.M. (1986). *The role of databases in knowledge-based systems.* Technical report - Carnegie-Mellon University.

Gœtz, J.M. (1986). *LRO2 : langage de programmation et de représentation des connaissances par objet.* Manuel d'utilisation - CRIL

Goldberg, A., Robson, D. (1983). *SMALLTALK-80 : The language and its implementation.* Addison Wesley.

Rechenmann, F. (1986). *SHIRKA : Système de gestion de bases de connaissances centrées objet.* Manuel d'utilisation - INRIA.

Roche, C. (1985). *LRO2 : Génération de systèmes experts et langages orientés objets.* Ecole d'été - AFCET.

Roche, C. (1985). *LRO2 : Intelligence Artificielle et langages orientés objets.* Cinquième congrès RFIA - Grenoble.

AN IMPLEMENTATION OF FRAMES IN SMALLTALK

10.1 Introduction

FRL (Roberts *et al.*, 1977) is the first knowledge representation system using the notion of **frames**. A frame is made of a set of **slots** that are accessed by their name. Slots are characterized by **facets**, whose most important one contains the value of the slot. FRL is interesting for its simplicity and because it implements the main features of current knowledge representation systems using frames: constraints and default values for the slots, inheritance through the AKO (A Kind Of) slot, demons that are activated when a slot is accessed. FRL has been written in Lisp. This paper describes an implementation of a similar system written in **Smalltalk** (Goldberg *et al.*, 1983) that uses the features of object oriented languages (frames, slots and their facets are instances of classes and answer messages). The main intention is to show how frames can be implemented with an object oriented language.

10.2 Structure of the system

Five new classes have been defined to implement the frames:

FrameSystem is a subclass of the predefined class IdentityDictionary. This latter implements dictionaries of objects, where each element of a dictionary is accessed by a unique key. The class FrameSystem has only one instance, that is stored in the global variable FRL and contains the dictionary of all frames. Every frame has a name that is different from the name of any other frame. This name is used as access key in the dictionary FRL.

Frame is a subclass of IdentityDictionary having two additional instance variables: name that contains the frame's name, and suffix. This latter contains a number that is used to generate new names from the frame's own name. Frames are instances of this class. They are dictionaries whose entries are the names of their slots.

Slot is a subclass of IdentityDictionary with two new instance variables: name and frame, that refers to the frame the instance of Slot belongs to. Each slot contains exactly six elements: the facets #VALUE, #DEFAULT, #REQUIRE, #IFADDED, #IFREMOVED and #IFNEEDED.

Facet is a subclass of the predefined class Set (that implements collections of objects where an object appears at most once) and has three additional instance variables: name, frame and slot, whose meaning can be easily deduced from the previous descriptions. The variable frame allows to access directly the frame the facet belongs to, instead of sending a message to the slot. Each of the six facets of a slot contains a set (maybe empty) of values.

ValueFacet is a subclass of Facet with no other instance variable. It describes particular methods for the modification of #VALUE or #DEFAULT facets, in order to check the constraints specified in the #REQUIRE facet and activate the demons defined in the facets #IFADDED or #IFREMOVED.

10.3 Creation and suppression of frames

10.3.1 *Management of frame names*
Every frame has a unique name. When an attempt is made to define a new frame having the same name as an existing frame, the message **"genName"** is sent to this latter to obtain a new name. This name is created by concatenation of the frame's name and the number stored in the instance variable suffix. This number is incremented until the resulting name is different from that of any existing frame.

```
genName              "defined in class Frame"
     I newName I
     [FRL includesKey:
                 (newName := (name , (suffix := suffix+1) printString) asSymbol)]
          whileTrue: [].
     ^newName!
```

Note that, in order to test the existence of a frame with a given name, we can simply send the message **"includesKey:name"** to FRL, the dictionary of all frames. The corresponding method has not to be written: it is inherited from the class IdentityDictionary, which uses hash tables to implement dictionaries.

10.3.2 *Elementary creation/suppression functions*
A new frame is created by sending the message **"addf:name"** to FRL. This creates a new frame containing no slot, and adds it to the dictionary FRL. Its name will be the argument of the message if no frame with the given name exists; otherwise a new name is generated

as described before. The code for the creation method is very simple, because all methods already defined to access dictionaries can be used:

```
addf: frameName              "defined in class FrameSystem"
    | newName |
    (self includesKey: frameName)
        ifTrue:    [newName := (self at: frameName) genName]
        ifFalse:   [newName := frameName].
    ^self at: newName put: (Frame new initName: newName)!
```

The message "**removef:name ifAbsent:aBlock**" sent to FRL allows the removal of the frame with the given name. If no such frame exists, the code specified in the argument "aBlock" is evaluated. The corresponding method is simply the suppression of a dictionary entry, which is already defined:

```
removef: frameName ifAbsent: aBlock         "defined in class FrameSystem"
    ^self removeKey: frameName ifAbsent: aBlock!
```

10.3.3 *The #AKO (A Kind Of) and #INSTANCE slots*

The #AKO slot is used to establish a conceptual hierarchy of frames where general information stored higher in the hierarchy is inherited by more specialized concepts defined lower in the hierarchy. The message "**instantiate:name**" sent to a frame F_1 creates a new frame F_2 that possesses only a slot #AKO with value F_1. An inverse link is maintained by adding the value F_2 to the #INSTANCE slot of F_1. This slot is created automatically if not already present in F_1. The name of the new frame is derived from the argument of the message.

```
instantiate: newName               "defined in class Frame"
    | newFrame |
    newFrame := FRL addf: newName.
    ((newFrame adds: #AKO) at: #VALUE) addv: self.
    ((self adds: #INSTANCE) at: #VALUE) addv: newFrame.
    ^newFrame!
```

"**F1 instantiate**" is equivalent to "F_1 instantiate: F_1 name", where the result returned by the message "F_1 name" is the name of the slot F_1.

10.4 **Modification of frames**

10.4.1 *Slots and facets*
The message "**adds:slotName**" sent to a frame supplies the slot named slotName, that is created if not already present. Thus, creation and access to a slot are done by the same message.

```
adds: slotName              "defined in class Frame"
     (self includesKey: slotName)
        ifTrue:    [^self  at: slotName]
        ifFalse:   [^self  at: slotName
                           put: (Slot new initName: slotName frame: self)]!
```
The six facets of a slot are created at the time of its initialization:

```
initName: aSymbol frame: aFrame                              "defined in class Slot"
     name isNil ifFalse: [^self error: 'slots can not be initialized twice'].
     self at: #VALUE put: (ValueFacet new      initName: #VALUE
                                               frame:    aFrame
                                               slot:     self).
     self at: #DEFAULT put: (ValueFacet new    initName: #DEFAULT
                                               frame:    aFrame
                                               slot:     self).
     #(REQUIRE IFNEEDED IFADDED IFREMOVED)
        do: [:i | self at: i put: (Facet new    initName: i
                                               frame:    aFrame
                                               slot:     self)].
     frame := aFrame.
     name := aSymbol
     "^self"!
```

Suppression of a slot is performed by sending to the frame the message "**removes:slotName ifAbsent:aBlock**".

Since the class Frame is a subclass of IdentityDictionary, all methods already defined for dictionaries also apply to frames. Thus, for example, it is not necessary to define a new method in order to know if a frame contains a slot named slotName: this is done by sending the message "**includesKey:slotName**" to the frame. The corresponding method is defined in class IdentityDictionary.

10.4.2 *Values*
Adjunction or suppression of values in a facet is done by sending to the facet a message with selector **addv:** or **removev:ifAbsent:**. In class Facet, the methods for these messages are those that apply to sets. We will see later that they are redefined in class ValueFacet in order to take into consideration constraints and demons.

Other methods are defined starting from those described above in order to simplify the notation of the most common operations.

For example:

> Fido at: #colour addValues: #(brown white)

is a more convenient way to express

> ((Fido adds: #colour) at: #VALUE)   addv: #brown;
>   addv: #white

10.5 Value retrieval and inheritance

Access to a facet named facetName of a slot is done by sending to the slot the message **"at:facetName"**, whose method is defined in class IdentityDictionary. As the class Facet is a subclass of Set, all operations defined for sets also apply to facets. The following paragraph will describe more elaborated methods for value retrieval, that give an inheritance semantics to the #AKO slot.

10.5.1 *Inheritance through the AKO link*

The method for the message **"inheritSlot:slotName facet:facetName"** sent to a frame goes through the hierarchical structure defined by the AKO link in order to find values for the given facet. If the frame possesses a slot named slotName whose facet named facetName contains values, the result returned by the method is this set of values. Otherwise, all frames belonging to the set of values of the #AKO slot are inspected in order to find values for the requested facet. If the #VALUE facet of the #AKO slot is empty, the frames of the #DEFAULT facet are inspected instead. Each of the AKO paths is traced, stopping at the first data encountered along each, and the set of all values thus found is returned:

```
inheritSlot: slotName facet: facetName            "defined in class Frame"
    | values slot parents |
    (slot := self at: slotName ifAbsent: []) isNil
        ifTrue:     [values := Set new]
        ifFalse:    [values := (slot at: facetName) asSet].
    values size = 0 ifFalse: [^values].
    "No value found: search along the AKO link."
    "The parents are the values or the defaults of the AKO slot."
    (slot := self at: #AKO ifAbsent: []) isNil
        ifFalse: [(parents := slot at: #VALUE) size = 0
                    ifTrue: [parents := slot at: #DEFAULT].
                parents do: [:parent |
                        values addAll: (parent  inheritSlot: slotName
                                                facet:       facetName)]].
    ^values!
```

The method corresponding to the message **"inheritAllSlot:slotName facet:facetName"** is similar to that described above, but values are retrieved along the AKO paths even if the requested facet contains values. Thus, the method provides the set of all local and inherited data.

The method for **"getSlot:slotName facet:facetName"** implements the most common inheritance mechanism. The mechanism invoked depends upon the facet:

- *inheritSlot:facet:* is used for the facets #VALUE, #DEFAULT and #IFNEEDED. Moreover, if no value has been found for the #VALUE facet, the search goes on with the #DEFAULT facet.
- The three other facets contain constraints to be satisfied by the values of the slot (that is to say the values of the #VALUE and #DEFAULT facets), or procedures to activate when these values are accessed. The inheritance mechanism used for these facets is that of *inheritAllSlot:facet:*, in order to consider that a frame bound to another by an AKO link is a specialization of this latter.

Note that these methods have to be defined at the frame level, not at the slot or facet level, because inheritance must be performed even if the frame docs not have a slot with the requested name.

10.5.2 *Procedures for value creation*

The #IFNEEDED facet is intended to contain procedures specifying how to create values for the slot. The message **"need:slotName"** sent to a frame allows to activate these procedures when new values are needed for the slot named slotName. First, this slot is added to the frame if it did not exist before. Values for the facet #IFNEEDED are then retrieved using the inheritance mechanism implemented by *getSlot:facet:*. Each of these values must be a string, representing a procedure to create a value for the slot, that will be compiled and evaluated. Compilation is performed as if the text would describe a method in class UndefinedObject. Before evaluation, the global variables FRAME and SLOT are bound to the frame and slot for which we want to create a new value. The result returned by the method for need: is the set of all results obtained by the evaluation of these procedures.

```
need: slotName              "defined in class Frame"
    | results thisSlot |
    results := Set new.
    thisSlot := self adds: slotName.
    (self getSlot: slotName facet: #IFNEEDED)
        do: [:fun | FRAME := self. SLOT := thisSlot. VALUE := nil.
                "these variables may be modified by the evaluation of fun"
            results add: (Compiler evaluate: fun)].
    ^results!
```

As for inheritance, this method is defined in class Frame, so that it can also be applied when the slot is inherited but not present in the frame.

The #IFNEEDED facet is often used in the #INSTANCE slot of generic frames, from which other frames will be created by sending the message "need:#INSTANCE". Values of such a facet could for example look like

```
|newInstance|
    newInstance := FRAME instantiate.

"creation and initialization of the new frame's slots"

^newInstance'
```

10.6 Constraints and demons

The #REQUIRE facet allows to specify constraints that have to be satisfied by the values of the slot (that is to say the values of the #VALUE and #DEFAULT facets). As for the #IFNEEDED facet, the values of the #REQUIRE facet must be strings that will be compiled and evaluated in an environment where the global variables FRAME, SLOT and VALUE are bound to the frame, slot and value to check. A constraint is considered as being satisfied when the result of the evaluation is the object true.

The message "**checkSlot:slotName value:val**" sent to a frame checks if the object val satisfies the constraints for the values of the slot named slotName. The constraints defined in the frame and those that are inherited are all evaluated, and the set of not true results is returned. The implementation of this method is similar to that of need:.

Demons are procedures that are activated when a value is added to or removed from a slot. They are defined in the #IFADDED and #IFREMOVED facets, and are represented by strings to be compiled and evaluated.

The methods for adjunction or suppression of values defined in class Facet are redefined in class ValueFacet in order to take into consideration the constraints and demons for the #VALUE and #DEFAULT facets. Thus, a new value is added only if it satisfies all constraints. The demons of the #IFADDED facet are then activated after having bound the global variables FRAME, SLOT and VALUE to the modified frame and slot, and to the added value. No test is performed, and no demon is activated if the value to add is already present.

```
addv: value          "defined in class ValueFacet"
    (self includes: value) ifTrue: [^value].
    (frame checkSlot: slot name value: value) size = 0
        ifFalse: [^self error: 'constraints not satisfied'].
    super add: value.
    (frame getSlot: slot name facet: #IFADDED)
        do: [:fun | FRAME := frame. SLOT := slot. VALUE := value.
                    "these variables may be modified by the evaluation of fun"
                Compiler evaluate: fun].
    ^value!
```

The demons of the #IFREMOVED facet are activated in a similar way when a value is removed.

10.7 Remarks

The fact that methods already defined for dictionaries and sets can be used immediately for frames is not only a precious help for the implementation of the methods described before. Above all, it allows to take advantage of a good predefined programming environment. For example, dictionary browsers can be used to display frames on windows and use the mouse to select a slot and inspect its contents, without writing any additional method for these features.

The use of an object oriented language for the implementation of frames is interesting for the realization of more complex systems where the mechanisms for inheritance, constraint propagation and activation of demons are not the same for all frames, and where some frames answer particular messages in addition to usual ones. A hierarchical organization of the different frame classes allows to share common mechanisms. This is also true when several classes of frames that have different structures, but that answer the same messages, are defined. Methods that do not depend explicitly upon the structure of the frames (for example those that access instance variables only by message sending) have not to be written for each structure.

References

Goldberg, A. & Robson, D. (1983). *Smalltalk-80: The Language and its Implementation*. Addison-Wesley Publishing Company.

Roberts, R.B. & Goldstein, I.P. (1977). The FRL Primer, *AI Memo* , **408**, MIT

PART 2

REPRESENTATION OF NEURAL INFORMATION AND PATTERN MATCHING IN NEUROSCIENCES

It is a natural temptation to try to understand how the human brain performs some cognitive tasks which are to be reproduced by some expert systems. The main relation between Artificial Intelligence (A.I.) and cognitive sciences lies in the representation of the objects processed by the systems. We define in Part 2 different approaches for describing the biological and physiological reality. This reality can be experimentally explained by either the upward or the downward approaches related to the fact that the nervous system can be represented by a succession of three levels: the first one is an interface which transforms any external stimuli in neuronal signals; this transformation is a pre-processing level which provides a very rich representation of the stimuli. The second level is the intermediary processing system realized by the intermediary neural networks of the nervous system (geniculate body, hypothalamus, etc) whose role is to spread the information over the third cognitive level (cortex).

The upward approach consists thus of recording or simulating the neural activity of a biological system belonging to the first and second levels; it is close to the experimental electrophysiology and brings, according to us, the proof that any cognitive level is efficient only on a properly pre-processed object. The downward approach based on experimental psychology brings information about real cognitive mechanisms ; in both cases of face recognition or natural memory for instance, the experimental psychology leads to face the concept of feature extraction.

The classical approaches in A.I. consider that a collection of objects may represent the knowledge which is to be processed; those objects are generally obtained from the external representation of the studied phenomena; one deals for instance with physical parameters or observed symptoms. With such rough representations of a phenomenon, one has to build an expert system whose complexity quickly increases (i.e. contains very large number of rules) in order to take into account every specific behaviour of the phenomenon.

The contribution of the cognitive sciences is to show some examples of the efficiency provided by a good internal representation of the information inside the biological systems. This representation is generally based on the concept of networks which appears to be the right paradigm in A.I. too. The dialogue between those two communities becomes therefore more and more real.

A GENERALIZED APPROACH FOR CONNECTIONIST AUTO-ASSOCIATIVE MEMORIES: INTERPRETATION, IMPLICATION AND ILLUSTRATION FOR FACE PROCESSING

11.1. Introduction

Recent years have seen an increasing number of papers in psychology that attempt to model cognitive and perceptual processes using associative memory models (e.g. Hinton & Anderson, 1981; Kohonen, 1984; Rumelhart & McClelland, 1986). Basically, these models use large sets of neuron-like units. The units are linked by connections of modifiable intensity (e.g. synapses). Learning or information storage occurs by modification of the connections. The major advantages of associative models over more traditional information processing and artificial intelligence models are that they make use of computations that are potentially completely parallel and that they employ distributed rather than localized storage of data. Parallel computations are simply those that may in principle be done simultaneously and therefore do not depend upon the outcome of the other computations. Distributed storage refers to that fact that discrete locations of memory do not code for individual pieces of data, but rather form parts of the coding of many stimuli.

The workings of both of these features have provided useful insights into some psychological and computational issues in cognition and perception that have proven quite difficult to model with logic-based information processing models.

Along with the psychological studies that have appeared recently, there have been many papers that have attempted to analyze the various learning rules used with associative systems. Primarily, these analyses frame learning in an associative network as a process that tries to satisfy a series of constraints. In general, the point is to show that the given learning rule minimizes an error function and that it is able to deal effectively with the usual problems of error minimization such as the avoidance of local minima. The analysis of energy minimization has traditionally been applied to the problem of characterizing the properties of physical systems. This is, however, a profoundly different point of view than that normally taken by psychologists who have tended more to characterize memory in terms specific to the content and coding of the input Thus, while this type of physical system analysis has been useful, there is a second, equally useful analysis that has the potential to provide some interesting common ground between associative models and more traditional ways of modelling psychological data. What we propose is an analysis of the properties of an associative memory as a data base. The aim of this analysis is two-fold. First, it should provide a way of quantifying similarity relationships among stimuli processed by an associative memory. Second, and perhaps more importantly, it should define stimulus similarity in terms of the properties of the storage matrix formed during the learning process.

Despite the obvious and strong analogies to traditional multidimensional scaling methods of representing distance relationships among stimuli, data from associative memory models have seldom been viewed or presented in this context. We propose to show here a generalization of associative memory that will make this analogy more evident. In the "standard" or "classical" model, all the stimuli to be stored in the memory are of equal importance, and all the units composing the memory are equivalent and independent. The generalization described in this paper allows to store stimuli of differential importance in a memory composed of units being also of differential importance (and/or being non-independent). The importance of units and stimuli are formalized as sets of weights. Specifically, the generalization will provide a division of the original memory in such a way as to partition out two sets of weights that correspond to the importance of individual stimuli in a set and individual components or "features" of the stimuli. Most models of the distance relations among stimuli have adopted either an euclidean or a city-block distance for the space; our generalization will provide distance relations in a weighted Euclidean space. These weights will be shown to have meaningful interpretations for the associative model, for the multidimensional model and for some kinds of psychological data.

From a psychological point of view, the analysis proposed is potentially quite useful for a number of reasons. First, it provides a quantitative model of how the components of inter- and intra-stimulus similarity contributes to the behaviour of the associative system. This is relevant in that one of the most interesting and successful uses of associative systems in psychology has been to model the formation of concepts and prototypes from exemplar data (Knapp & Anderson, 1984). Generally, these psychological data come from sorting or categorization tasks through which perceived distance measures may be derived and the stimuli may be plotted in a low dimensional space that represents a best-fit to the data. It has been shown theoretically (Abdi, 1987) that most of the current models of concept formation can be mimicked by connectionist models. The model described in this paper allows the straightforward derivation of representations for auto-associative memories.

In the current connectionist models, all the neuron-like units are of equal importance, and completely independent. Similarly, all the stimuli are of equal importance. This assumption may be quite unrealistic in some cases. This paper describes a generalization for a class of connectionist models: the linear auto-associators, or auto-associative memories. In these models, a set of stimuli is stored in a memory. When presented with a degraded stimulus, an auto-associative memory is able to reconstruct the original stimulus. Auto-associative memories can be interpreted as content-addressable memories (Hopfield, 1982), or categorizer (Anderson *et al.* 1977). The generalization allows stimuli and units to be of differential importance and to be non-independent.

11.2 The "classical" auto-associative model

The "classical" auto-associative model appears frequently in the network model literature (e.g. Anderson, Silverstein, Ritz & Jones, 1977; Hinton & Anderson, 1981; Kohonen, 1984). Its basic features are briefly reviewed here inasmuch as they will be useful in the following sections
Stimuli are represented by column vectors whose components code the value of the features used to describe the stimuli, or equivalently, the components of the vector give the input values for the basic units (e.g. neurons) of the neural network. Thus, the i th stimulus described by J features will be represented by a $J \times 1$ vector: f_i. It is generally assumed for convenience that the vectors are normalized (i.e., $f_i^T f_i = 1$). The set of J stimuli is stored in a $I \times J$ matrix $\mathbf{F}$ in which the ith row stands for f_i. The storage of f_i in the memory is given by the auto-correlation matrix $A_i = f_i f_i^T$ The retrieval of the ith exemplar is obtained by computing $\hat{f}_i = A_i f_i = f_i f_i^T f_i = f_i$. To store I stimuli in the same memory $\mathbf{A}$, suffice to "integrate" the different matrices A_i:

$$\mathbf{A} = \sum \mathbf{A}_i = \sum \mathbf{f}_i \mathbf{f}_i^T = \mathbf{F}^T \mathbf{F} \tag{1}$$

The retrieval of the i th exemplar stored in $\mathbf{A}$ is given by:

$$\hat{f}_i = \mathbf{A}\mathbf{f}_i = \sum_{k=1}^{I} \mathbf{f}_k \cdot \mathbf{f}_k^T \cdot \mathbf{f}_i = \mathbf{f}_i + \sum_{k \neq i} \cos(\mathbf{f}_k, \mathbf{f}_i) \cdot \mathbf{f}_k \tag{2}$$

Note that when f_i is orthogonal to $f_{i'}$ for all i different from i', then $f_i = \hat{f}_i$. In general, the quality of the retrieval is estimated by comparing $\hat{f}_i$ with $f_{i'}$. A popular measure is $\cos(\hat{f}_i, f_{i'})$.

11.3 Generalized auto-associative model

Let M be a $I * I$ matrix of constraints on the stimuli. M can express a set of *a priori* or *a posteriori* constraints brought to bear on the stimuli. A particular case is to differentially weight the stimuli (i.e. to give different masses), in this case, the matrix M is a diagonal matrix.

Along the same lines, let W be a $J * J$ matrix of constraints on the features, which can represent the *a priori* constraints built-in by the "wiring" of the network, or some *a posteriori* constraints. A particular case is to differentially weight the features used to describe the stimuli, in this case, W.is diagonal. In this paper, W and M are assumed to be *semi-definite positive*.

The effect of the two matrices may be interpreted as a *deformation* or *filtering* of the stimuli set. Thus, F is transformed in $\tilde{F} = M^{1/2} F W^{1/2}$. Equivalently, W can be interpreted as a re-coding schema for the original stimuli so that f is recoded in $\tilde{f} = W^{1/2} f$ *prior to storage into the memory*. Similarly, M represents the interference between the stimuli, when or after they have been stored in the memory. Different varieties of interference can be thought of, but only a differential weighting of the stimuli seems straightforward at the moment. Consequently, in the following section, we assume that is a diagonal matrix where m_i stands for the ith diagonal element of M

For convenience (but without loss of generality) the vectors f_i are normalized in the metric defined by W (i.e., $f_i^T W f_i = 1$). The cosine in the distance defined by W between two vectors is given by:

$$\cos_w(f_i, f_k) = \frac{f_i^T W f_k}{(f_i^T W f_i)^{1/2}(f_k^T W f_k)^{1/2}} = \frac{f_i^T W f_k}{\|f_i\|\|W\|\|f_k\|\|W} = f_i^T W f_k \qquad (3)$$

Given these notations, then the "generalized" auto-associative memory is given by:

$$\tilde{A} = \tilde{F}^T \tilde{F} = W^{1/2} F^T M F W^{1/2} \qquad (4)$$

The retrieval from the auto-associative memory is:

$$\hat{f}_i = \widetilde{A}\ \widetilde{f}_i = \widetilde{A}^{1/2}f_i \tag{5}$$

$$= \ w^{1/2}\left(m_i f_i + \sum_{k \neq i} m_k \cos_W(f_i, f_k) f_k \right) \tag{6}$$

Note that when f_i is orthogonal to $f_{i'}$ for all i different from i' (i.e., $f_i^T W f_{i'} = 0$) then $\widetilde{f}_i = m_i W f_i = m_i\ \widetilde{f}_i$ Consequently $\cos(\widetilde{f}_i, f_i) < 1$ as well as $\cos_W(\widetilde{f}_i, f_i) < 1$ *even when* f_i *is the only stimulus stored in the memory.* However, $\cos(\hat{f}_i, \widetilde{f}_i) = 1$ when f_i is the only stimulus stored in the memory, or when all the stimuli stored are orthogonal. This suggests that the quality of the storage should be evaluated with $\cos(\hat{f}_i, \widetilde{f}_i)$.

The term m_i corresponds to a general amplification of the stimulus, by the matrix. In order to evaluate its intensity, it is sufficient to compute the ratio $\hat{f}_i / \widetilde{f}_i$.

In sum, the generalized memory acts as a filter that deforms the input to take into account the constraints imposed by the W matrix, when one stimulus is stored.

11.4 Maximal responses of an auto-associative memory

When the stimulus set is composed of mutually orthogonal stimuli (in the distance defined by W), then the $\widetilde{f}_i$'s are stored perfectly since the cosine between $\hat{f}_i$ and $\widetilde{f}_i$ is equal to 1. In the more realistic case when the stimuli are not orthogonal, the memory will not give a perfect response to a stored stimulus. Actually, the memory will be prone to *"false recognitions"*. In particular, the memory will reconstitute perfectly some stimuli that have not been stored. These stimuli, denoted u_i are defined by the equation:

$$\widetilde{A}\widetilde{u}_i = \lambda_i\ \widetilde{u}_i \qquad \text{with } \widetilde{u}_i^T\widetilde{u}_i = 1 \tag{7}$$

which classically defines the eigenvectors of $\widetilde{A}$ (with 1 denoting the eigenvalue). From u_i it is possible to define the *"generalized eigenvectors"* of $\widetilde{A}$ by the equation:

$$u_i = W^{-1/2}\widetilde{u}_i \text{ where } u_i^T W u_i = 1 \tag{8}$$

11.5 More on the eigenvectors of A and $\widetilde{A}$

11.5.1 *Eigenvectors as "Prototypes"*
The eigenvectors u_i correspond to the maximal responses of the system, under the constraints expressed by W and M; hence they are "prototypes" spontaneously extracted

by the memory as a simple consequence of the storage mechanism. It should be emphasized that the generalized eigenvectors $\mathbf{u}_i$ are different from the standard eigenvectors of the matrix $\mathbf{A}$.

Since the matrix $\widetilde{\mathbf{A}}$ is symmetric, the eigenvectors are orthogonal, and the eigenvalues are non-negative. The matrix $\mathbf{A}$ can be reconstituted as:

$$\mathbf{A} = \sum \lambda_i \mathbf{u}_i \mathbf{u}_i^T = \mathbf{U} \, \Lambda \, \mathbf{U}^T \quad \text{with } \Lambda : \text{diagonal matrix of eigen values.} \qquad (9)$$

The similarity with equation (4) is obvious, the eigenvalues l_i correspond to the m_i's and express the importance or the mass of the $\mathbf{u}_i$'s in the reconstitution of $\mathbf{A}$.

$$\mathbf{F} = \mathbf{V} \, \Lambda^{1/2} \mathbf{U}^T \quad \text{where } \mathbf{V}^T \mathbf{M} \mathbf{V} = \mathbf{U}^T \mathbf{W} \mathbf{U} = \mathbf{I} \qquad (10)$$

11.5.1 *Eigenvectors as "global, macro or holistic features"*
The matrix $\mathbf{A}$ can be optimally reconstructed (in a least-square sense) by a small number of eigenvectors. Along the same lines, $\mathbf{F}$ can be reconstituted from the eigenvectors $\mathbf{u}_i$. The reconstitution corresponds to the *generalized singular value decomposition* of $\mathbf{F}$ under the constraints imposed by $\mathbf{M}$ and $\mathbf{W}$:

The matrix $\mathbf{V}$ contains the generalized eigenvectors of the matrix $\mathbf{F}\mathbf{F}^T$ under the constraints given by $\mathbf{M}$ (i.e., $\widetilde{\mathbf{V}} = \mathbf{M}^{1/2}\mathbf{V}$ with $\widetilde{\mathbf{V}}$ eigenvector matrix of $\mathbf{F}^T$). As each $\mathbf{f}_i$ may be reconstituted by a weighted sum of $\mathbf{u}_i$'s, the $\mathbf{u}_i$'s can be interpreted as *"global, macro or holistic features"* to be distinguished from the *"local or micro"* features used to describe the stimuli.

11.5.3 *Eigenvectors and generalized principal component analysis*
It has been pointed out previously (Anderson *et al.*, 1977) that the eigenvectors of the matrix $\mathbf{A}$ may be interpreted as the principal components of the features set (i.e. the features are projected on the "stimuli eigenvectors"). This procedure would correspond to a *"Q-Analysis"* in the factorial analysis terminology. With a generalized auto associative memory, a generalized principal component analysis is performed by the $\mathbf{u}_i$'s eigenvectors. The projections of the features are given by:

$$\mathbf{P} = \Lambda^{1/2} \mathbf{U}^T \qquad (11)$$

The eigenvalues correspond to the variance of the feature projections on the axis. Along the same lines, the $\mathbf{V}$ matrix performs a principal component analysis of the stimuli set. The projections of the stimuli are given by:

$$Q = V\Lambda^{1/2} \tag{12}$$

As a consequence, the distance between stimuli represented as points in the weighted euclidean space of the features is "optimally" decomposed along the v_i 's. Precisely, the distance between stimuli is obtained by:

$$d_w^2(i, i') = (f_i - f_{i'})^T W(f_i - f_{i'}) \tag{13}$$

$$= (q_i - q_{i'})^T W(q_i - q_{i'}) = \sum_{j=1}^{K^*} \lambda_j (q_{i,j} - q_{i,j'})^2 \tag{14}$$

where K^* is the number of non-zero eigenvalues of V or U ($\min\{I,J\} \geq K^*$), and $q_{i,j}$ is the coordinate of the projection of the ith stimulus on the jth component. This suggests the use of generalized principal component analysis to display the stimuli as they are "perceived" by the auto-associative memory.

11.5.4 *Widrow-Hoff learning procedure (alias Delta rule)*
In order to increase the performance of the system, some learning procedures may be used. The most popular is the Widrow-Hoff procedure (also called Delta-rule). Basically, the difference between the input and the output is used to correct the matrix $\tilde{A}$ in a step by step manner, as shown by the following equation:

$$\tilde{A}_{t+1} = \tilde{A}_t + \eta(\hat{f}_i - \tilde{f}_i)\tilde{f}_i^T \tag{15}$$

where $\tilde{A}_t$ denotes the matrix $\tilde{A}$ at time t, h an arbitrary positive constant, and i being randomly chosen. It can be shown (e.g. Kohonen *et al.*, 1981, Kohonen, 1984) that this procedure converges to

$$\tilde{A}^* = \tilde{F}^+\tilde{F} = \tilde{U}^T\tilde{U} \tag{16}$$

where $\tilde{F}^+$ denotes the pseudo-inverse of $\tilde{F}$.

11.6 A neural model for face perception

In this section, we present some connectionist approaches to the problem of face processing. The first subsection exposes the selection of features for describing faces. The second section deals with the transfer of learning for faces transformed by spatial filtering. In the third section, we show that an auto-associative memory will spontaneously extract face-prototypes as a consequence of the storage of different faces.

11.6.1 *Features for faces: micro features vs elaborated features*
A first approach to code face information in long term memory is to propose a coding scheme in terms of *elaborated features*. According to this coding scheme a face will be separated into nose, mouth, chin, hair, etc. Each of these elaborated features will have one level among several possible levels (e.g., a nose can be straight, aquiline...). The recognition of a face will be equivalent to identifying the correct level of the elaborated features.

Such an approach is indeed intuitively appealing. Leonardo da Vinci supported it in his *Tratado della Picturia*. This approach is also the basis for some well-known methods of reconstruction of faces by eyewitness (e.g. Photofit or Identikit). However, although we are able, if needed, to describe a face using elaborated features, the following psychological evidence suggests strongly that we do not use such a coding scheme to store information in long term memory:

(1). Eyewitnesses find it hard to describe unknown faces with such a coding scheme (Loftus, 1979; Yarmey, 1979), even when they are asked to do so with faces that are present (Klatsky & Forest, 1984).

(2). The reconstruction of faces using systems like Photofit or Identikit is very poor *even when the face to be reconstructed is available.*

(3). Attempts to improve the performance of eyewitness by improving their ability to code a face in elaborated features fails or even leads to a *decrease* in their performance (Woodhead, Simmonds & Baddeley, 1979).

(4). There is no correlation between the ability to describe a face in terms of elaborated features and the ability to recognize faces (Goldstein, Johnston & Chance, 1979).

(5). By contrast, holistic coding activities increase memory task performance. Specifically, subjects who rate faces for subjective qualities (honesty, likability, intelligence...) perform better on recognition tasks than subjects who rate faces for elaborated features. Even if the difference is small, it is reliable (Patterson & Baddeley, 1975; Bower & Karlin, 1974). In general this effect is interpreted within the "levels of processing" framework. It is worth noting that subjects find meaningful such questions about the holistic properties of faces and show a clear agreement among subjects (Abdi, 1986).
(6). Recognition of familiar faces is resistant to change in the elaborated features (glasses, change in hair style, absence or presence of facial hair (e.g. Galper & Hochburg, 1971;

Pittenger & Shaw, 1975), or to modifications of the elaborated features as involved for example in aging (Seamon, 1980a,b; Bahrick *et al.*, 1975).

(7). Transformations of faces that increase the saliency of the elaborated features (e.g., caricatures, drawing) actually *decrease* subjects' performance in perceptual and mnemonic tasks (Loftus & Bell, 1975; Hagen & Perkins, 1983; Tversky & Baratz, 1985).

(8). The configuration of elaborated features is a better predictor than the elaborated features themselves in reaction time studies (Sergent, 1986a). Moreover, performance can be affected by transformations that do not affect the elaborated features, such as mirror transformation (McKelvie, 1986) or spatial filtering (Millward & O'Toole, 1986; Sergent, 1986b).

Thus, it seems preferable to code the faces in terms of *"micro-features"* rather than in terms of elaborated features. A primary advantage of a low level code such as pixels or lines is that it avoids coding dilemmas such as deciding "what type of chin a given person has", or even, "is the type of chin a relevant feature for a face". Moreover, the necessity of assuming the existence of pre-processing systems able to extract elaborated features can be eliminated.

Such an approach has already been shown to be feasible and fruitful. O'Toole, Millward & Anderson (1987) used pixels and lines in a series of computer simulations of the recognition transfer between spatially-filtered versions of the same faces. These simulations were done in conjunction with a series of experiments that tested the same type of recognition transfer with human subjects.

In O'Toole *et al.* (1987), observers viewed low-pass (L), high-pass (H), or normal (N) unfiltered faces in a learning phase. Afterward, in a test phase, the subjects were tested in a two-alternative forced choice recognition task. They were asked to find which of two faces was presented in the learning phase. These pairs of test faces were presented either as L, H, or N faces; thus, all possible transfer cases were observed. The results of the O'Toole *et al.* experiment (1987) are presented in Table 11.1

O'Toole *et al.* also simulated the transfer using a connectionist model. Faces were digitized and represented by 900-pixel vectors. The communication between units was limited to a neighbourhood of five units. To improve storage, the Widrow-Hoff procedure was used for five trials per stimulus. Test trials were simulated by pairing each face vector learned by the model with a new one. Each face vector was then recalled, and the cosine between input and output was computed. The system was said to have "recognized" the face in the pair with the highest cosine. The results are given in Table

11.2. The general pattern of results of the experiment and the simulation is highly similar as indicated by the strong correlation between the two sets of results [$r(7)=.88$]. Specifically, both human subjects and simulations show a clear specificity encoding effect (Tulving, 1982): the transfer is optimal when encoding and test are performed under the same conditions.

Table 11.1. *Probability of target detection (human subject)*

	Test Normal	Test Low frequencies	Test High frequencies
Learning Normal	.82	.73	.62
Learning Low Frequencies	.66	.71	.54
Learning High Frequencies	.61	.60	.77

O'Toole *et al.* demonstrated that a connectionist model can simulate the behavior of human subjects with a good accuracy. Recently, Ellis, Young, Flude & Hay have suggested that some repetition priming effect of face recognition may be best explained by connectionist models. In the following section it is shown that a auto-associative memory may exhibit spontaneously a *cognitive* behavior, namely the extraction of face prototypes from a set of faces.

Table 11.2. *Probability of target detection (computer simulation)*

	Test Normal	Test Low frequencies	Test High frequencies
Learning Normal	.82	.73	.62
Learning Low frequencies	.66	.85	.70
Learning High frequencies	.60	.55	1.00

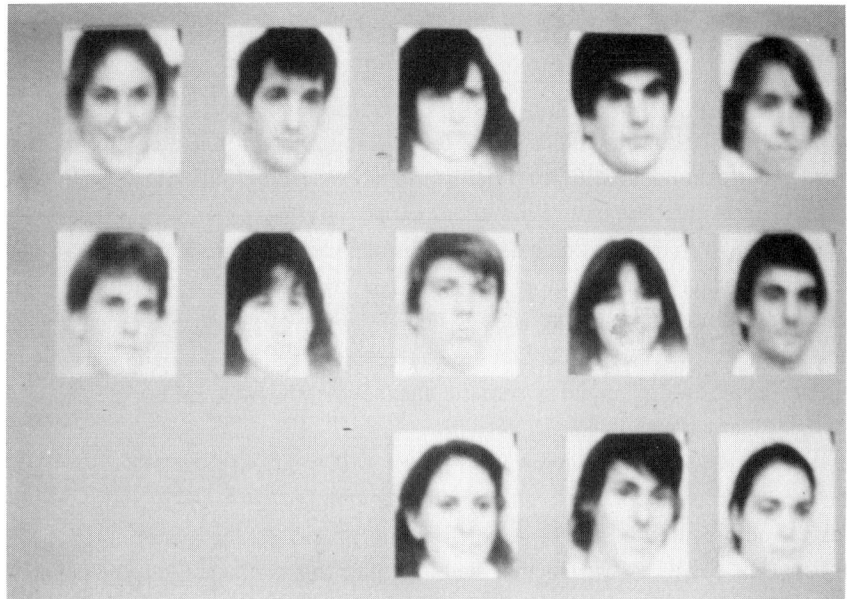

Figure 11.1 A sample of the faces stored in the auto-associative memory

11.6.2 *Face prototype abstraction by an auto-associative memory*

Material. Photographs of thirty-two Brown University undergraduates (16 males and 16 females) were used as stimuli. All the models wore white drapes to hide their clothing. None had a beard or wore glasses in the photographs. In order to increase the "ecological validity" of the experience, the photographs were not scaled nor were the poses (i.e. some faces are photographed full view, some

other are almost 3/4; however, none are profile). Some exemples are displayed in figure 11.1.This lack of control is thought to show the resistance to noise of connectionist memories. The photographs were digitized to give a 71*71=5041 pixel-vector whose components give the light intensity of the pixels (from 0 to 256).

Procedure. The faces were given a unitary weight. The matrix $\mathbf{F}$ was rescaled to be a correspondence-matrix (i.e. the sum of its elements is one, and elements are positive or null). The luminance of the screen was maintained constant for each face; as a consequence the sum of each row of the matrix $\mathbf{F}$ is constant and equal to $f_{i.}$ =1/32 The units (i.e., the pixels or the neurons corresponding to the perceptive field) were weighted using an "informational" scheme. The general idea was that the importance of a neuron should be inversely proportional to its use or to its probability of firing. The matrix $\mathbf{W}$ was a diagonal matrix with diagonal elements. The matrix $\widetilde{\mathbf{A}}$ was constructed following equation (4).

$$w_{jj} = 1 / \sum_{i=1}^{I} f_{ij} \qquad\qquad (17)$$

Results. According to the predictions of the theoretical section, the eigenvectors of the matrix $\widetilde{A}$ correspond to the "optimal stimuli". As figure 11.2 illustrates, they are remarkably face-like. The first[1] eigenvector expresses what is common to the set of faces and could be interpreted as a "face detector" (as opposed to anything being non-face like). The second third and fourth vectors correspond to "prototypical faces" which are created by the memory from the original faces as a consequence of the storage process. It should be stressed that these prototypical faces are not actual faces. The following vectors can be interpreted as the "noise" in the system (i.e. the fact that the faces are not precisely scaled, that the poses are different, etc...).

Correspondence analysis interpretation of the eigenvectors. As pointed out previously, the eigenvectors of the matrix $\widetilde{A}$ can be interpreted as the generalized principal components of **A**. With the particular set of weights that we have used, the eigenvectors perform a *correspondence analysis* of the faces (Benzécri, 1973; Greenacre, 1984). As a consequence, it is possible to draw a graph of the faces as they are "perceived" by the system by projecting the faces onto the eigenvectors, that procedure being equivalent to a correspondence analysis (recall that the strong property of correspondence analysis is the so-called "dual representation": it is possible to represent in the same space both rows and columns of the data matrix). Figure 11.3 displays the positions of the faces in the space defined by the first two eigenvectors. As can be seen, the major opposition is between male and female, which is coherent with the empirical results obtained for humans.

11.7 Discussion

These first results clearly constitute an encouraging first step toward a comprehensive connectionist model for face perception. Some developments of this class of model look particularly promising. A first approach will be to use these systems to simulate "face-ogens" abstraction (Bruce, 1986; Bruyer, 1987), a process identical for faces to Morton's logogens (1969). In particular, connectionist models present spontaneously a "priming" behaviour: the recall of one face will prime the recall of similar faces stored in the memory. (cf. Anderson & Mozer, 1981).

---

[1]Actually what we call here the first eigenvector is the second. The first eigenvector is, in fact, a *trivial vector* which expresses only the fact the rows of the matrix **F** sum to one (cf. Lancaster & Timenetsky, 1985)

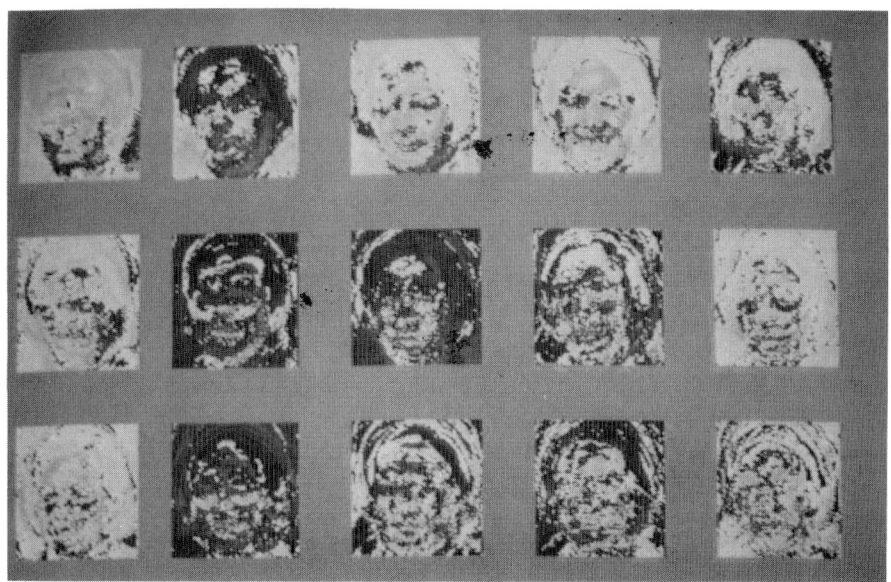

Figure 11.2 The first 15 eigenvectors of the auto-associative memory. The corresponding eigenvalues are: .020 .018 .012 .011 .010 .008 .008 .008 .008 .007 .007 .007 .007 .006 .006 .006. The "percentage of inertia" are: 10.8 8.6 6.1 4.8 4.6 4.1 3.9 3.7 3.5 3.4 3.3 3.2 2.9 2.8 2.7

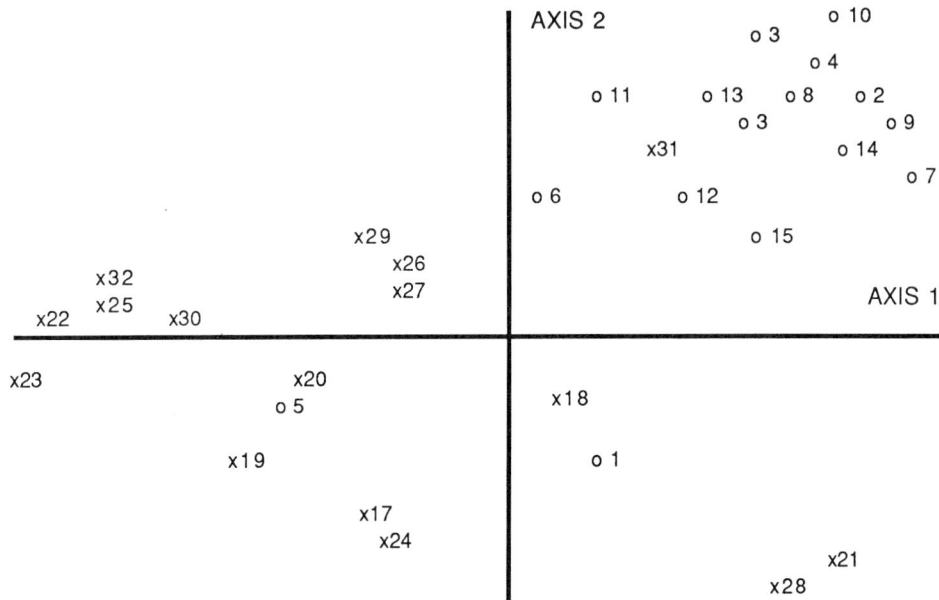

Figure 11.3 Correspondence analysis of the faces: Axes 1 & 2, l_1=.020, t_1=10.82, $l l_2$=.0175, t_2=8.63

Male faces are preceded by X, female faces by O. (see text for explanations)

A second approach will aim toward the modelling of context effects (Tiberghien, 1986). In order to do so, some extraneous information (i.e. visual, semantic, or some description of the situation) should be added to the code for faces. This can be done by embedding the units coding the faces within a larger set of units coding the extraneous information Then, the model will present some *madeleine de Proust* 's behaviour: a context associated with only one face will be able to reconstitute the face. (cf. Knapp & Anderson, 1984)

A third approach will deal with the development of facial expressions. A prediction is that if one face is stored with different expressions, then the first eigenvector should represent an expressionless face and the successive eigenvectors should correspond to different "faceless" expressions. These predictions will be dealt with in forthcoming studies

However, the current model is only partial. Specifically, the faces should be pre-scaled even if approximately and they should be coded in micro-features before being stored in the memory. Moreover, some cognitive processes such as conscious search, decision processes, imagery, etc. do not easily fit into that framework. Despite its shortcomings, the current model is able to give an account of some important cognitive processes such as transfer of learning, prototype extraction, etc. and would be able also to mimic most of the current models of face perception (see Bruyer, 1987, for a recent review of these models).

References

Abdi, H. (1986). Faces, prototypes and additive tree representations, in H.D. Ellis, M.A. Jeeves, F. Newcombe, A. Young (Eds.), *Aspects of face processing* Dordrecht: Nijhoff.

Abdi, H. (1987). Do we really need a contingency model for concept formation ? *British Journal of Psychology*, **78**, 113--125.

Anderson, J.A., Mozer, M.C. (1981). Categorization and selective neurons. In G.E. Hinton & J.A. Anderson (Eds.), *Parallel models of associative memory,* Hillsade: Erlbaum.

Anderson, J.A., Rosenfeld, E. (1987). *Neurocomputing: some   important papers*, Cambridge: MIT Press.

Anderson, J.A., Silverstein, J.W., Ritz, S.A., Jones, R.S. (1977). Distinctive features, categorical perception, and probability learning: some applications of a neural model, *Psychological Review,* **84**, 413--451.

Bahrick, H.P. (1983). Memory for people, in J. Harris (Ed.), *Everyday memory, actions and absentmindedness*, London: Academic Press.

Bahrick, H.P., Bahrick, P.O., Wittlinger, R.P. (1975). Fifty years of memory for names and faces: a cross-sectional approach, *Journal of Experimental Psychology: General*, **104**, 54--75.

Benzécri, J.P. (1973). *L'analyse des données*, Paris: Dunod.

Bower, G.H., Karlin, M.B. (1974). Depth of processing of faces and recognition memory, *Journal of Experimental Psychology*, **103**, 751--757.

Bruce, V. (1986). Recognising familiar faces. In H.D. Ellis, M.A. Jeeves, F. Newcombe, A. Young (Eds.), *Aspects of face processing,* Dordrecht: Nijhoff.

Bruyer, R. (1987). *Les mécanismes de reconnaissance des visages*, Grenoble: Presses Universitaires de Grenoble.

Davis, G.M., Ellis, H.D., Sheperd, J.W. (1978). Face recognition accuracy as a function of mode of presentation, *Journal of Applied Psychology*, **62**, 180--187.

Da Vinci, L. (1882). *Trattato della Picturia*, Vienna: H. Luwig.

Ellis, A.W., Young, A.W., Flude B.M., Hay, D.C. (1987). Repetition priming of face recognition, *Quaterly Journal of Experimental Psychology*, **39a**, 193-210.

Galper, R.E., Hochberg, J. (1971). Recognition memory for photographs of faces, *American Journal of Psychology*, **84**, 351--359.

Goldstein, A.G., Johnson, K.S., Chance, J.E. (1979). Does fluency of face description imply superior face recognition? *Bulletin of the Psychonomic Society*, **13**, 15--18.

Greenacre, M.J. (1984). *Correspondence analysis*, London, Academic Press.

Hinton, G.E., Anderson, J.A. (1984).*Parallel models of associative memory,* Hillsdale: Erlbaum.

Hopfield, J.J. (1982). Neural networks and physical systems with emergent collective computational abilities. *Proceedings of the National Academy of Science, USA,* **79**, 6871--6874.

Hopfield, J.J. (1984). Neurons with graded responses have collective computational abilities, *Proceeding of the National Academy of Sciences, USA,* **81,** 3088--2558.

Klatzky, R.L., Forrest, F.H. (1984). Recognizing familiar and unfamiliar faces, *Memory & Cognition,* **12,** 60-70.

Kohonen, T. (1977). *Associative memory: A system theoretical approach,* Berlin: Springer Verlag.

Kohonen, T. (1984). *Self organization and associative memory,* Berlin: Springer Verlag. Lancaster, P., Tismenetsky, M. (1985). *The theory of Matrices,* New York: Academic Press.

Loftus, E. (1979). *Eyewitness testimony,* Cambridge (MA): Cambridge University Press

McClelland, J.L., Rumelhart, D.E. & Hinton, G.E. (1986). The appeal of parallel distributed processing. In D.E. Rumelhart & J.L. McClelland (Eds.), *Parallel distributed Processing,* Cambridge: MIT Press.

Millward, R.B., O'Toole, A.J. (1986). Recognition memory transfer between spatial-frequency analyzed faces. In H.D. Ellis, M.A. Jeeves, F. Newcombe, A. Young (Eds.), *Aspects of face processing,* Dordrecht: Nijhoff.

Morton, J. (1969). Interaction of information in word recognition, *Psychological Review,* **76,** 165-178.

O'Toole, A.J., Millward, R.B., Anderson, J.A. (1987). *A physical system approach to recognition memory for spatially transform faces,* unpublished manuscript: Brown University.

Patterson, K.E., Baddeley, A.D. (1975). When face recognition fails, *Journal of Experimental Psychology: Human Learning & Memory,* **3,** 406--417.

Pittenger, J.B., Shaw, R.E. (1975). Aging faces as viscal-elastic events, *Journal of Experimental Psychology: Human Perception & Performance,* **104,** 374--382.

Rumelhart, D.E., McClelland, J.L. (1986). *Parallel distributed processing,* Cambridge: MIT Press.

Seamon, J.G. (1980b). *Memory & Cognition,* New York, Oxford University Press

Sergent, J. (1986a). An investigation into component and configural processes underlying face perception, *British Journal of Psychology,* **75**, 221--242.

Sergent (1986b). Microgenesis of face perception. In H.D. Ellis, M.A. Jeeves, F. Newcombe, A. Young (Eds.), *Aspects of face processing*, Dordrecht: Nijhoff.

Tiberghien, G. (1986). Context effects in recognition memory of faces: some theoretical problems. In H.D. Ellis, M.A. Jeeves, F. Newcombe, A. Young (Eds.), *Aspects of face processing*, Dordrecht: Nijhoff.

Woodhead, M.M., Baddeley, A.D., Simmonds, D.C.V. (1979).On training people to recognise faces, *Ergonomics*, **22**, 333-343.

Yarmey, A.D. (1979). *The psychology of eyewitness testimony,* New York: Free Press.

ARGUMENT FOR REAL NEURAL NETWORKS

This chapter is solely intended to provide the viewpoint of an experimental neurophysiologist dealing with artificial neural networks as tools for simulation of simple models of certain nervous structures. The conjunctive association of both approaches has strongly emphasized the necessity to use a formalized language as a link between these rather far away fields. As no such language is yet available one might be tempted to build one. Without such a link, indeed, the much sought after and needed cross fertilization between these different domains may be hindered for still an unpredictable period of time.

Since the early 1980s artificial neuronal networks (ANN) built up by the coupling of a number of formal neurons (FN) have received a great deal of attention and numerous studies have been devoted towards unveiling the limits and intricacies of their complex properties. Although some of the results had already been mathematically studied in the 1960s and 1970s, in particular by Caianello, Widrow, Amari, Kohonen and Grossberg, this renewed interest stemmed mainly from Hopfield's 1982 paper. By greatly simplifying the existing models Hopfield was able to solve some of the equations governing the dynamics of these systems. The results confirmed, very elegantly, that a class of global properties emerge from such networks, global properties which can not be directly deduced from the simple rules governing each individual element and the coupling between them. Another important result of the abovementioned paper was the demonstration of the close relationship between these types of networks and those of magnetic Ising systems, thus extending previous suggestions by Little (1974) and Little & Shaw (1978) who had already pointed out some of the analogies between ANN and statistical physics. A later generalization (Hopfield, 1984 ; Hopfield & Tank, 1986) done by computing the dynamics with FN having a continuous range of responses, instead of FN with only two states, opened the pathway to conceiving electrical circuits with global functions derived from ANN. It is therefore not surprising that the most numerous contributions in this field come from the physical, mathematical and electronics communities (e.g. Bienenstock *et al ,* 1986 ; IEEE 1st ICNN, 1987 ; Kohonen, 1984 ; Wolfram, 1986).

A symptomatic and noteworthy point is that **all** these contributions (since the original paper by Mc Culloch and Pitts in 1943) have claimed to be directly inspired by the Neurosciences, a remark which also stands for the contributions from the other two big communities engaged in the study of ANN, psychology and artificial intelligence (Grossberg, 1982 ; Haugeland, 1981 ; Minsky & Papert, 1969 ; Rumelhart & Mc Clelland, 1986 ; Mc Clelland & Rumelhart, 1986). The influence exerted by brain studies appears to find it roots mainly in the results derived from two very different levels of experimental approach. On one hand is what can be viewed as a 'global' level where the focus is on unveiling the properties exhibited by higher mental functioning, and on the other hand the 'infracellular' level of the physico-chemical mechanisms of membrane and cellular integration and firing. It must be pointed out here that these two levels are far from representing the whole range of the research modalities that allow us to gain insight into the understanding of the CNS. Moreover the question is open as to whether the above mentioned levels are sufficient or even adequate for a fruitful interaction between the domains of artificial and real neural networks.

Apart from the strictly genetical, ontogenetical and phylogenetical approaches - which have in common a dissection of the nervous system in 'blocks' submitted to biological rules that are, in part at least, governed by trends exterior to the nervous systems *per se* - the organization and functioning of the nervous system can be experimentally dealt with along five different lines :

1. Properties of and interaction between membrane patches and intracellular metabolism (transmitter release, receptors, channels, second messengers, synaptic plasticity, etc ...).

2. 'Repertoire' performed by different cellular types, be it neuronal or glial (firing rates,extracellular buffering, response characteristics, potentiation, etc).

3. Dynamical range of restricted networks of neurons (essentially input - output transformation in precise subsystems).

4. Global properties of systems (i.e. visual cortex, reflex centers, oculomotor coordination, etc).

5. Generalisation rules for CNS parts (vision, movement, learning, memory, etc).

As can immediately be noted these different approaches differ essentially in the "resolving power" with which the reality of the CNS is tackled and are therefore tightly complementary. There appears a linear progression from "simple" to "complex", from "element" to "group" to "system". A very general trend - that has been confirmed by 150 years of neurobiological research - is that, with a global view at any "magnification factor", the rules that appear to govern the properties of that given level can not be directly deduced from those that seem to control the immediate one-step more elementary one. Naturally this could be strongly advocated as a justification for the relevance of transposition of results from ANN studies to the neurobiological universe, **given that the simplification procedure (SP) that allows system modeling be clear and adequate**. The basis for this SP is that limited details in a given system (network) can be skipped as "irrelevant" and nevertheless allow a good predictability of the overall system dynamics just by the simulation of the "main" phenomena (Gelfand & Walker, 1984). The question is therefore to appreciate if that holds for a crosstalk between artificial and real neural networks and, if it does, what is the exact range of validity of the SP. This problem must be approached with caution and I would like to present hereafter some arguments for a strategy to access the different parameters necessary to achieve such a goal.

The prime difficulty stems from the need to classify what seems important - and must therefore be integrated - and what seems secondary, or irrelevant, - and can be skipped - in defining a model from the known morphofunctional data of a real network. This holds for the two constitutive elements of a network : the neuron properties and the wiring.

(A) Neuron properties appear to be much more complex than was formerly thought. They seldom are relay stations (Barlow, 1961) but typically transform their inputs to produce a new output function by a cascade of stages from postsynaptic dendritic membrane centripetally to the trigger zone of the initial segment and further out to the presynaptic axonal bouton (Calvin & Graubard, 1977). Even the rules that govern transmitter induced changes in membrane voltage of spines (Coss & Perkel, 1985) and the influence of dendritic activation on the voltage variations at the somatic level (Rall, 1977) have been greatly refined (Rall, 1981 ; Horwitz, 1981 ; Koch *et al.*, 1983 ; Miller et al, 1985 ; Sheperd et al, 1985 ; Sheperd & Brayton, 1987). The simplest schematic relationship that can be built to list the factors controlling neuronal input - output transformations shows that, in the present state of knowledge, there are no less than twenty of them ranging from nature and pattern of input connectivity to quantitative data of cell anatomy and intrinsic membrane properties (Burke, 1987).

If a more detailed analysis on each of these factors is sought the picture becomes even more intricate as can be seen in reviews on voltage dependent conductances (Adams, 1982), cell morphology (Hillman, 1977), generation of spike trains (Calvin, 1975) or release mechanisms at central synapses (Korn & Faber, 1987). Moreover the classical chemical-type neurons do not represent the whole range of existing relationships between pre and postsynapic elements (e.g. Benett, 1966 ; Roberts & Bush, 1981 ; Furukawa & Furshpan, 1963 ; Fujita & Kobayashi, 1979 ; Axelrad & Korn, 1982 ; Changeux, 1986).

Thus the morphological **and** physiological personality of each neuron type is **unique** and must be extensively labeled.
 Plasticity of synapses (Hebb, 1949) will not be discussed here.

(B) The same complexity and detailed diversity appear also from studies of the connectivity blueprint. It is clear that each portion of the CNS has a specific composition in cell types, fibers and pattern of communication (Cajal, 1909,1911 ; Lorente De No, 1988 ; Braitenberg, 1977). In the mammalian cerebral cortex where general trends of organization are found (Mountcastle, 1978) the classification in different zones is established on many precise factors and can lead to such an extreme morphology as the rat barrel field somatosensory cortex (Woolsey & Van Der Loos, 1970). The importance of this wiring, expressed as an index proportional to the extent of the neuropil, is stressed by the fact that its development during phylogeny is parallel to the "abstract" capabilities linked to the cortex. Even in a structure as regular (and usually cited as "crystal-like") as the vertebrate cerebellar cortex a differentiation between folia can be evidenced when more precise morphological characteristics are studied (Lange, 1982, Bishop, 1987). The connectivity must therefore also be considered as a unique feature of a real neuronal network and its exact characteristics know so as to be embedded in the ANN diagram.

This is even more important if one holds in mind that far from being passive transmitting lines axons can act as complex filters differentially conveying the spike trains along their numerous collaterals, a feature which is usually omitted (see Waxman, 1978).

It is revealing that recent reports on ANN with very precise and different types of associative properties have, empirically, been constructed with wiring diagrams of far apart topologies (Sejnowski & Rosenberg, 1986 ; Dehaene *et al.*, 1987), thus suggesting that, indeed, the specificity pertaining to circuitry is essential for the sculpting of the functional possibilities of networks.

Another very important aspect of real neuronal networks that has no counterpart whatsoever in ANN is related to the fact that all biological systems are in a permanent search for equilibrium due to the many contradictory **constraints** they are submitted to. It is this everlasting fight which is the *primum movens* for survival and it is not seriously possible to consider that the gradual making up of the CNS has not been strongly influenced by these stringent limitations. A major point is then to establish the whole set of variables which can act by 'putting constraints' on the basic wiring and fundamental properties of the elementary nodes in the ANN. These constraints will provide the setting in which the network will be forced to function, thus giving different "flavours" to the types of transformations the ANN will be able to perform (see for instance Marr's computational theory : Marr, 1982).

Although many such constraints can be listed the main two seem to be the time constants used in a system and the way the transiting information is represented, or coded. The necessity to use all or none spikes to convey information over long distances results in the necessity to simulate strictly these temporally organised trains in artificial systems, the usual way being by random number generation. Attention must then be paid to the validity of this generator, most of them not being really random and, thus, introducing biases resulting in undesirable cycles. As for the temporal constraint it is certainly one of the most powerful. Indeed the networks must be organized so that the result of the transformation should be attained by a "single-shot" of processing, as in real life. The usual neurophysiological literature where the evoked activity of a given neuron to an electrical or natural stimulation of the periphery is represented by post stimulus time histograms or by means of latency blurrs the fact that the network rules of construction must be such that it will generate the adequate response by a single cycle of computing and not after n repetitions.

To attempt, then, to bridge the gap between ANN modeling and real CNS analysis it is necessary to apply, **simultaneously**, modeling and experimental approaches to a neurobiological system whose morphological structure and physiological functioning are well enough understood so that the **predictive** value of a simplified model could be **experimentally tested** given strict conditions of **analogy**. Furthermore, for this strategy to yield interesting correlations it must be used by addressing problems at a level of organization at which approaches have similar and homogeneous resolving powers. The vertebrate cerebellar cortex seems one of the best candidates for such a cooperative investigation due to its specific characteristics. This nervous structure has indeed:

a) a limited number of cellular types (five) with only one, the Purkinje cell (PC), having an axon efferent to the structure, all other neurons having an intracortical distribution of their axon.

b) a remarkable morphological organization in regular layers, each with specific patterns of fibers and cell to cell contacts.

c) only two inputs (the mossy and the climbing fibers) where each one is distinctly recognizable by its histological and physiological properties.

d) an invariant topological construction along the two main axes of the extension plane of the cortex (the rostro caudal/sagittal and latero-lateral ones).

e) a great identity of the basic structure of this cortex during phylogeny, a fact in favour of a specific and common function throughout evolution and whatever additional afferents it receives (Cajal, 1911 ; Eccles, Ito & Szentagothai, 1967 ; Llinas, 1969 ; Ito, 1984).

Although the cerebellar structure is one of the best known in the CNS there are still many unknown and controversial issues. One must then proceed by steps during the simplification procedure and it appears evident that the trial and error process which is usual in scientific activity will lead in the future to selecting those paths which seem the most fruitful for a **predictive interaction** of the experimental and theoretical approaches.This interaction must, in particular, be focused on the **informational transfer capacities** of networks, a concept which can be fully approached only by analysing the entropic properties of the system (Giraud *et al.*, 1985, Axelrad *et al.*, 1987).

(supported by a grant from 'Fondation Simone & Cino Del Duca').

References

Adams, P. (1982). *Trends in Neurosciences*, **5**, 116-9.

Axelrad, H. & Korn, H. (1982). The Cerebellum : New Vistas, In :*Experimental Brain Research*, eds. S. Palay & V. Chan-Palay, suppl **6**, 412-39.

Axelrad, H., Bernard, C., Cottrel, M. & Giraud, B. (1987). 1st ICNN, *Proceedings. IEEE*, eds. M. Caudill & C. Butler, **IV**, 59-66.

Barlow, H.B., (1961). In : *Sensory Communication*, ed. W.A. Rosenblith, 217-34, MIT Press.

Benett, M.V.L. (1966). *Annals of the New York Academy of Sciences*, **137**, 509-39.

Bienenstock, E., Fogelman, F. & Weisbuch, G. (1986). Disordered systems and biological organization, *Computer & Systems Sciences Series*, eds. E. Bienenstock, F. Fogelman & G. Weisbugh, **20**, Springer Verlag.

Bishop, G.A., Blake, T.L. & O'Donoghue, D.L. (1987) In : *New concepts in cerebellar neurobiology*, ed. J.S. King, 26-56, Alan R. Liss.

Braitenberg, V. (1977). *On the texture of Brains,* Springer.

Burke, R.E. (1987). *Trends in Neurosciences*, **10**, 42-5.

Cajal, S. Ramon. Y. (1909-1911). *Histologie du Système Nerveux*, Maloine.

Calvin, W.H. (1975). *Brain Research*, **84**, 1-22.

Calvin, W.H. & Graubard, K. (1977). In : *The Neurosciences : IVth Study Program*, 513-24, MIT Press.

Coss, R.G. & Perkel, D.H. (1985). *Behavioral and Neural Biology,* **44**, 151-85.

Dehaene, S., Changeux, J.P. & Nadal, J.P. (1987). *Proceedings of the National Academy of Sciences*, USA, **84**, 2727-31.

Denker, J.S. (1986). *Neural Networks for Computing*, eds. J.S. Denker, American Institute of Optics.

Eccles, J.C., Ito, M. & Szentagothai, J. (1967).*The Cerebellum as a Neuronal Machine*, Springer.

Fujita, T. & Kobayashi, S. (1979). *Trends in Neurosciences,* **2**, 27-30.

Furukawa, T. & Furshpan, E.J. (1963). *Journal of Neurophysiology*, **26**, 140-76.

Gelfand, A.E. & Walker, C.C. (1984). *Ensemble modeling*, ed. M. Dekker.

Giraud, B., Bernard, C. & Axelrad, H. (1985). *C.R. Acad. Sci. (Paris)*, **301**, 565-70.

Grossberg, S. (1982). *Studies of mind and brain*, D. Reidl.

Haugeland, J. (1981). *Mind Design*, ed. J. Haugeland, MIT Press.

Hebb, D.O. (1949). *The organization of behavior*, Wiley.

Hillman D.E. (1977). *The Neurosciences, 4th Study Program*, 477-98, MIT Press.

Hopfield, J.J. (1982). *Proceedings of the National Academy of Sciences*, **79**, 2554-8.

Hopfield, J.J. (1984). *Proceedings of the National Academy of Sciences*, **81**, 3058-92.

Hopfield, J.J. & Tank, D.W. (1986). *Science*, **233**, 625-33.

Horwitz, B. (1981). *Biophysical Journal,* **36**, 155-92.

IEEE First International Conference on Neural Networks (1987).

Ito, M. (1984).*The cerebellum and neural control*, Raven Press.

Kohonen, T. (1984). *Self Organization and Associative Memory*, Springer.

Koch, C., Poggio, T. & Torre, V. (1983). *Proceedings of the National Academy of Sciences*, **80**, 2799-802.

Korn, H. & Faber, D. (1987). *Synaptic Function*, ed. Edelman, Gall & Cowan, 57-108, John Wiley & Sons.

Lange, W. (1982). In : The Cerebellum : New Vistas, *Experimental Brain Research*, eds. S. Palay & V. Chan-Palay, suppl **6**, 93-107.

Little, W.A. (1974). *Mathematical Biosciences*, **19**, 101-12

Little, W.A. & Shaw, G.L. (1978). *Mathematical Biosciences*, **39**, 281-90

Llinas, R. (1969). *Neurobiology of Cerebellar Evolution and Development*, ed. R. Llinas, American Medical Association.

Lorente De No, R. (1938). In : *Physiology of the Nervous System*, ed. J.F. Fulton, 274-314, Oxford University Press.

Marr, D. (1982).*Vision*, Freeman.

McClelland J.L. & Rumelhart, D.E. (1987). *Parallel Distributed Processing*, eds. J.L. McClelland & D.E. Rumelhart, **II**, MIT Press.

Mc Culloch, W.S. & Pitts, W. (1943). *Bulletin of Mathematical Biophysics*, **5**, 115-33.

Miller, J.P., Rall, W. & Rinzel, J. (1985). *Brain Research*, **325**, 325-30.

Minsky, M. & Papert, S. (1969). *Perceptrons*, MIT Press.

Mountcastle, V.B. (1978). In : *The Mindful Brain*, eds. G.E. Edelman & V.B. Mountcastle, MIT Press.

Rall, W. (1977). In : *Handbook of Physiology*, **I**, The Nervous System, ed. E.R. Kandel, ch. 3, 39-97, American Physiological Society.

Rall, W. (1981). In : *Neurones without impulses*, eds. A. Roberts & B.M.H. Bush, 223-54, Cambridge University Press,.

Roberts, A. & Bush, B.M.H. (1981). In : *Neurons without impulses*, eds. A. Roberts & B.M.H. Bush, Cambridge University Press.

Rumelhart, D.E. & McClelland, J.L. (1987). *Parallel Distributed Processing,* eds. J.L. McCleland & D.E. Rumelhart, **1**, MIT Press.

Sheperd G.M. & Brayton, R.K. (1987). *Neurosciences,* **21**, 151-65.

Sheperd, G.M., Brayton, R.K., Miller, J.P., Segev, I., Rinzel, J. & Rall, W. (1985). *Proceedings of the National Academy of Sciences,* USA, **82**, 2192-5.

Sejnowski, T.J. & Rosenberg C.R. (1986). NETtalk, Technical Memo, Johns Hopkins University.

Waxman, S.G. (1978). In : *Physiology and Pathobiology of Axons*, ed. S.G. Waxman, Raven Press.

Wolfram, S. (1986). *Theory and Applications of Cellular Automata*, ed. S. Wolfram, World Scientific.

Woolsey, T.A. & Van Der Loos, H. (1970). *Brain Research,* **17**, 205-42.

13 *J . Demongeot and C. Robert*

A STUDY OF DIFFERENT UNCERTAINTY COEFFICIENTS USED IN ARTIFICIAL INTELLIGENCE : TOWARDS A NATURAL DEFINITION OF WEIGHTS IN SEMANTIC NETWORKS

13.1 Introduction

Firstly we will discuss classical uncertainty coefficients used for inference in knowledge bases : Mycin, Sam, plausible or fuzzy reasoning. We show internal contradictions in the algebra defining operations on these coefficients ; it is due to the fact that the two references, the probabilistic (when the uncertainty is maximal) and the logic ones (when the uncertainty vanishes) are not considered as limit cases of these models of inference, and that seems to be unrealistic.Then we propose a generalization of the bayesian networks based on the definition of an hamiltonian function on a convenient network, whose coefficients are learnable. Finally, we show how one can relate their calculation to the Roc-analysis, when vertices of the knowledge network are defined from medical scores.

13.2 Somes types of uncertainty ... and imprecision

13.2.1 *Uncertainty coefficients*

The tentative of quantification of human opinions and judgments is not recent (Laplace, 1814) (Poisson, 1837), but the systematic use of computers now permits complex calculations on the algebra of uncertainty coefficients : these coefficients are combined in order to give a weight of truth to elementary predicates or to any combination of them (see for example Kanal & Lemmer, 1987 and in press). As noted, for example, in Rotterdam *et al.* (1986) or by Horvitz and Heckerman in Kanal & Lemmer (1986), the operations defined on these coefficients are often inconsistent. This is due in general to the fact that the choice of the algebra is made by mixing the logical and the probabilistic references, without searching to have these references as limit cases as the uncertainty decreases or increases; this absence of reference leads to a correct choice under certain hypotheses, but incorrect in others. For example, if $P \cup P'$ and $P \cap P'$ denote respectively the logical union and intersection of the predicates P and P', we can define the uncertainty coefficient $c(P \cap P')$ and $c(P \cup P')$ in many ways :

- $c_1(P \cap P') = \min (c_1(P), c_1(P'))$
- $c_2(P \cap P') = c_2(P) c_2(P')$
- $c_3(P \cap P') = \max (0, c_3(P) + c_3(P') - 1)$
and
- $c_1(P \cup P') = \max (c_1(P), c_1(P'))$
- $c_2(P \cup P') = c_2(P) + c_2(P')$
- $c_3(P \cup P') = \min(1, c_3(P) + c_3(P'))$.

It is easy to prove that c_1 operations hold if $P > P'$ or $P < P'$, c_2 operations hold if P and P' are independent and c_3 operations are valid only if $P \cup P' = \Omega$ or $P \cap P' = \emptyset$. The results of the operations above, frequently used in the Sam, Mycin, plausible or fuzzy algebras of uncertainty coefficients can lead to very different results ; if $c(P) = c(P') = 1/2$, for example, we have :

$c_1(P \cap P') = 0.5$, $c_2(P \cap P') = 0.25$, $c_3(P \cap P') = 0$
and
$c_1(P \cup P') = 0.5$, $c_2(P \cup P') = 0.75$, $c_3(P \cup P') = 1$.

The circumstances described in the example above show the maximal differences between the coefficients ; when the value of the uncertainty coefficient of P and of P' tends to 0 or to 1, this discrepancy disappears. However, this shows the necessity of defining carefully these operations.

13.2.2. Uncertainty and imprecision

We can distinguish between four types of uncertainty or imprecision of the common language used to express the knowledge, each involving a specific sort of quantification ; we will describe briefly these four types below :
a) "Mary is tall"
We can quantify the notion of tallness by using a fuzzy function f defined on the set of

possible heights to [0,1] (see for example Dubois, 1983 or Prade, 1985).

b)"Mary will have a fever"

We can choose P in [0,1] representing the probability of the event "Mary will have a fever"

c) "Mary killed the cat"

If there are three suspects, we can define a subjective evidence weight following the Dempster-Shafer approach (see for example Spiegelhalter, 1986) in order to quantify the degree of culpability of each suspect.

d) "Mary is ill with disease D"

In the absence of other information, we quantify the uncertainty by the prevalence of the disease D in the whole population.

In the examples above, we met a semantic imprecision in a), the probability of an event in b), a subjective probability in c) and a statistical uncertainty in d). Defining a system of weights quantifying this uncertainty or imprecision consists of choosing the type of coefficients, then choosing the type of operations on these coefficients. In the following pages, we propose a way to take into account this management of the uncertainty in a semantic network.

13.3 Uncertainty in semantic networks

13.3.1 *Definition and propagation of the certainty in a semantic network*

Following Sowa (1984), we define a semantic network as " the collection of all the relationships that concepts have to other concepts, to percepts, to procedures, and to motor mechanisms" of the knowledge. This network can be represented by a graph G, whose vertices represent predicates about these different entities of the knowledge (see for example Sowa, 1984 or Andreassen & Wellman, 1987, for the building of such a graph). The realization of the predicate associated to each vertex can be represented by the realization of a boolean or continuous random variable. In the following, we will propose an approach in the boolean case (see Robert, in press) for the general case and for a medical application), then each vertex v will can take the state s(v) equal to 0 or 1, the value of the state being random. We can distinghish between three kinds of vertices :

- primary vertices, whose values are fixed from the beginning by observation of facts (in medicine, by observations of symptoms in a patient).For these vertices, the uncertainty is suppressed by the observation.
- intermediary vertices, whose values are determined by iterating the process of propagation of the certainty in the network (these correspond in medicine to intermediary concepts like syndromes or diatheses)

- final vertices, whose values are fixed at the end of the propagation (in medicine, these vertices can be represented by diagnosis, prognosis or therapy).
Let us denote respectively by V(P), V(I) and V(F) these three sets of vertices.

We define now the uncertainty in the network by building on the state space of the graph G a sequence of probability measures $\mu(t)$: it is easy to show that this state space is isomorphic to the set P(V) of all the subsets of the set V of the vertices of G, by identifying each subset of V to the configuration of states 0 or 1 of vertices which has exactly its values 1 on this subset. All the measures $\mu(t)$ give a probability 1 to the value 1 for random variables s(v), where v belongs to V(P). The measure $\mu(0)$ contains this primary, almost sure, information on V(P) and eventually a bayesian information on V(I) and V(F). It is well known (see for example Demongeot, 1987, Demongeot & Tchuente, 1987, or Demongeot, Goles & Tchuente, 1985) that $\mu(t)$ can be defined by a hamiltonian real function U(t) defined on P(V), called the potentiel of the network; the one to one relation between $\mu(t)$ and U(t) is given by:

For any A in P(V), $\mu(A) = \exp(U(t)(A))/Z(t)$, where Z(t) is a normalization constant.

We show also that U(t) can be defined in a unique way by taking :

$U(t)(\emptyset) = 0$ and, for any A in P(V), $U(t)(A) = \sum_{A \supset B} J(t)(B)$, where J is called the interaction of U.

J(t) is a function defined on P(V) by its one to one relation with U(t) :

For any A in P(V), $J(t)(A) = \sum_{A \supset B} (-1)^{|A \backslash B|} U(t)(B)$

The propagation of certainty is called deterministic, if we decide the state s(v)(t+1) by calculating the quantity :
$u(v,t) = U(t)(\{v\} \cup A(t) \cap \mathcal{V}(v)) - U(t)(A(t) \cap \mathcal{V}(v))$,

where A(t) denotes the configuration reached at iteration t and $\mathcal{V}(v)$ represents a neighborhood of v' corresponding to the range of the "causality" of the network, and after, by deciding :

$s(v)(t+1) = 1$, if $p(v,t) = \exp(u(v,t))/(1 + u(v,t)) > 1/2$
$s(v)(t+1) = 0$, elsewhere

The propagation is called stochastic, if we make the choice above with the probability p(v,t). At the end of the propagation, i.e. when the measure $\mu(t)$ has reached its limit, we can classify the final vertices v of V(F) by calculating the measures μ([v]), where [v] denotes the set of all configurations having the state 1 in v : then the hierarchy of possible decisions proceeds directly from this ordering. Note that the final measure μ(∞) satisfies in general to a variational principle, if it is the Gibbs measure associated to the limit potential U(∞) : it is ameasure of maximal entropy among a certain family of measures (see for example Demongeot (1987), Lippmann (1987) and Omohundro (1987)).

If the J(t)'s are independent on t, the network is called unlearnable ; if not, it is called learnable and we can choose many way of learning (like Hebbian rule - see for example Fogelman Soulié *et al.*, 1987) or empirical frequency rule (see below). In the case of an unlearnable network, the convergence of the propagation is ensured in the both deterministic and stochastic cases (see for example Demongeot & Tchuente, 1987). In the learnable cases, there exists a certain lot of theoretical results of convergence and many "proofs" by simulation (see Demongeot & Hervé, in press). Let us note that the propagation of certainty described above presents similarities with the propagation of information in the graphs (see lectures of the Colloquium CNRS 276 "Théorie de l'information", in particular the papers by Schneider, Terrenoire & Tounissoux, Losfeld & Comyn, Devijver, and by Forest, 1978).

13.3.2 *Examples of interactions*

We give here only introductory examples (see Robert, in press, for a more complete study) :

a) Example 1 (Spiegelhalter, 1986)
Spiegelhalter starts from the observation that in Emycin, we can show contradictions as the following : let us suppose that the certainty factors of the rules :R1 "if disease 1, then medication 1" and R2 "if disease 2, then medication 2" are respectively .6 for R1 and .9 for R2 ; if the uncertainty coefficients c(disease 1) and c(disease 2) are respectively .9 and .7, the application of the operations on weights in Emycin leads to prefer medication 2 although disease 1 appears most probable. The apparent inconsistancy comes from the fact that no indication is given of the support for medication 1 if disease 1 is not true. For this reason, he proposes for the interaction J({v,v'}) the following formula :

$$W(v,v') = Log(P(v \mid v')P(v' \mid v)/(P(v \mid \daleth v')P(v' \mid \daleth v)))$$

$$J(\{v,v'\}) = W(v,v') + W(\daleth v, \daleth v'),$$

where P denote the empirical statistical probability of occurrence of events corresponding to the vertices.

We can observe that the definition of W, called the weight of evidence is completely symmetrical. The interaction J({v}) is chosen equal to LogP(v). All other interactions are equal to 0.

b) Example 2 (Kim & Pearl, 1983)
They take J(t)(A) equal to 0, if |A| > 1 and they define J(t)({v}) as follows :

$$J(t)(\{v\}) = \sum_{v' \varepsilon \, \mathcal{U}(v) \cap A(t)} Log \, P(v \mid v')$$

The non-realization of the v''s brings any information on the realization of v. This example shows that the concept of bayesian network can be considered as a particular case of the semantic networks defined by a general potential U (see Kim & Pearl, 1983 ; Pearl, 1985 ; Andersen *et al.*, 1986 ; Zrida *et al.*, 1987, and Andreassen & Willman, 1987), because, in the stochastic version of the network, the limit measure $\mu(\infty)$ is that having the maximum entropy and compatible with the initial knowledge on V(P) and with the conditional probabilities P(v|v') (if we suppose the stochastic independence between the v' of $\mathcal{U}$(v)).

c) Example 3
We can take for J({v,v'}) the symmetric expression :

$$J(\{v,v'\}) = Log(P(v|v')/P(v))$$

and, for J({v}), the same expression as in Example 1.

13.3.3 *A simple example of learning*

In the three examples above, the interaction is defined from the empirical probability P ; its frequential estimation allows the learning ; we can proceed as follows, for the probability P(v|v') for instance :

- we ask the expert for a first bayesian preestimate : P(v|v') = .6 ± .2 for example
- because this first estimation corresponds to a frequential calculation, taking into account roughly the experience of the expert, we can evaluate the approximate size n of the pseudo-sample used by the expert : if that corresponded to a real sample, the standard variation .1 would be calculable by the formula :

$$.1 = (P(v|v')(1-P(v|v'))/n)^{1/2}, \text{ then } n \approx 100 \, P(v|v')(1-P(v|v'))$$

- for each new case giving an activation of v and v', we calculate the new probability P'(v|v') by :

$$P'(v|v') = (nP(v|v')+1)/(n+1),$$

and we iterate this process with P' and n' = n+1. That allows the evolution of P, hence of J and U by taking into account new cases or old observations contained in a data base, we can relate automatically to the expert system in order to improve the precision of the uncertainty coefficients (for more details, see for example Robert *et al.*, 1988, and Robert, in press).

13.3.4 *Other propositions of learning*

The optimal choice of the variables appearing in vertices of the semantic network is crucial : it can be improved by searching the combinations of observed variables, whose predictive power is maximal ; for these variables, probabilities like P(v|v') are maximal and the network tends to the state closest to the purely logical one. This possibility is offered by techniques like factorial analysis, which gives the linear combinations of initial variables susceptible to make the best discrimination between the nearest vertices (see for example Robert *et al.*, 1986 and 1988, and Rialle, 1988). Other non-linear (polynomial for example) combinations are possible, but they are more complicated to obtain, because they demand factorial analyses on successive powers of initial variables. After this choice, it is possible, by using the Roc-analysis, to calculate the predictive value of such "super-variables", called scores in medical environment : this Roc-analysis give the best production rules, in the case of a boolean semantic network (see Robert *et al.*, 1986).

13.4 Conclusion

After some remarks and criticisms about the classical uncertainty coefficients, whose algebra of operations is often inconsistent, we propose a definition based on the notion of a potential on a semantic network ; that generalizes the notion of bayesian network (see Andreassen & Willman, 1987, and Pearl, 1985). Such a potential can be learnable in certain cases and it permits the final decision, optimally under certain criteria. For the systematic use of maximal entropy measures and best discriminant scores, and for an application in the therapy of child meningitis, we refer to Robert (1988 and in press).

References

Andersen, S.K., Andreassen, S. & Woldbye, M. (1986). Knowledge representations for diagnosis and test planning in the domain of electromyography. In : *European Conference on Artificial Intelligence*, ed. L. Steels, pp. 357-368. Brighton.

Andreassen, S. & Wellman, M. (1987). Munim - On the case for probabilities in medical expert systems - a practical exercise. In : *European conference on artificial intelligence in medicine*, Marseilles Aug. 87. AIME, eds J. Fox, M. Fieschi & R. Engelbrecht, pp. 149-160. *Lecture Notes in Medical Informatics* , **33,** Springer Verlag, New York.

Demongeot, J. (1987). Random automata networks. In : *Automata networks in computer science*, eds F. Fogelman Soulié, Y. Robert & M. Tchuente, pp. 47-57. Manchester University Press. Manchester.

Demongeot, J., Goles, E. & Tchuente, M. (1985). *Dynamical systems and cellular automata*. Academic Press. New York.

Demongeot, J. & Tchuente, M. (1987). Dynamical systems and cellular automata. In : *Encyclopedia of Physical Science and Technology*, pp. 464-472. Academic Press. New York.

Demongeot, J. & Hervé, T. (to appear). Theoretical study and simulation on hypercube T 20 of a general neural network. In : *Neuro 88*. Paris.

Devijver, P.A. (1978). On the amount of information conveyed by nearest neighbors and its use in pattern recognition. In : *Théorie de l'information, Colloque International CNRS 276*, pp. 353-362. Editions du CNRS. Paris.

Dubois, D. (1983). *Modèles mathématiques de l'imprécis et de l'incertain en vue d'applications aux techniques d'aide à la décision*. Thesis, Grenoble.

Fogelman Soulié, F., Gallinari, P., Le Cun, Y. & Thiria, S. (1987). Automata networks and artificial intelligence. In : *Automata networks in computer science*, eds. F. Fogelman Soulié, Y. Robert & M. Tchuente, pp. 133-186. Manchester University Press. Manchester.

Forest, F. (1978). Notion d'information acquise lors du cheminement sur un graphe. In : *Théorie de l'information, Colloque International CNRS 276,* pp. 373-379. Editions du CNRS. Paris.

Kanal, L.N. & Lemmer, J.F. (1986). Uncertainty in artificial intelligence. Series *Machine Intelligence and Pattern Recognition,* vol. 4. North Holland. Amsterdam.

Kanal, L.N. & Lemmer, J.F. (in press). Uncertainty in artificial intelligence II. Series *Machine Intelligence and Pattern Recognition.* North Holland. Amsterdam.

Kim, J.H. & Pearl, J. (1983). A computational model for causal and diagnostic reasoning in inference systems. In : *Proceedings 8th International Joint Conference on Artificial Intelligence,* pp. 190-193. IJCAI. Karlsruhe.

Laplace, P.S. (1814). *Essai philosophique sur les probabilités.* Courcier. Paris.

Lippmann, R.L. (1987). An introduction to computing with neural nets. *IEEE ASSP Magazine,* 4-22.

Losfeld, J. & Comyn, G. (1978). Information généralisée et analyse de données. In : *Théorie de l'information, Colloque International CNRS 276,* pp. 343-351. Editions du CNRS. Paris.

Omohundro, S.M. (1987). *Efficient algorithms with neural network behavior.* Report 1331. Department of computer science of the University of Illinois. Urbana.

Pearl, J. (1986). A constraint-propagation approach to probabilistic reasoning. In : *Uncertainty in artificial intelligence,* eds. L.N. Kanal & J.F. Lemmer, pp. 357-370. North Holland. Amsterdam.

Poisson, S.D. (1837). *Recherches sur la probabilité des jugements en matière criminelle et en matière civile.* Bachelier. Paris.

Prade, H. (1985). A computational approach to approximate and plausible reasoning with applications to expert systems. *IEEE Trans. Pattern Analysis and Machine Intelligence,* **7,** 260-283.

Rialle, V. (1988). Data analysis as an aid to learning and knowledge base making in a medical field. Chapter 27, this volume.

Robert, C., Zarski, J.P. & Demongeot, J. (1986). Utilisation de la notion de score comme outil décisionnel en médecine - Propositions pour l'aide à la fabrication automatique de règles de production. In : *A.I. Biomed 86*, pp. 234-244. CRIM. Montpellier.

Robert, C., Duhamel, A., Rialle, V. & Vila, A. (1988). Using clinical datafiles in building expert systems. Chapter 28, this volume.

Robert, C. (in press). Observable networks : a Markov field approach for probabilistic reasoning. *Artificial Intelligence.*

Rotterdam, E.P. & de Vries Robbé, P.F. (1986). A critical comment on certainty factors. In : *A.I. Biomed 86*, pp. 245-248. CRIM. Montpellier.

Schneider, M. (1978). Généralisation du théorème de l'information transmise par un questionnaire. In : *Théorie de l'information, Colloque International CNRS 276*, pp. 399-406. Editions du CNRS. Paris.

Sowa, J.F. (1984). *Conceptual structures*. Addison-Wesley. London.

Spiegelhalter, D.J. (1986). A statistical view of uncertainty in expert systems. In : *Artificial intelligence and statistics,* ed. W.A. Gale, pp. 17-56. Addison-Wesley. Reading.

Terrenoire, M. & Tounissoux, D. (1978). Information et conservation du flux dans des processus d'interrogation arborescents. In : *Théorie de l'information, Colloque International CNRS 276*, pp. 407-415. Editions du CNRS. Paris.

Zrida, J., Birdwell J.D. & Cockett J.R.B. (1987). Uncertain knowledge representation via stochastic decision trees. In : *Cognitiva 87*, pp. 111-116. Cesta. Paris.

SPEECH AS A NEURAL OBJECT REPRESENTED BY A RANDOM FIELD

14.1 Introduction

Both in the fields of A.I. and cognitive science, one faces the problem of choosing an appropriate representation of the objects processed by the systems. In the first part of this book, we could appreciate how the representation of knowledge closely influences the organization of the rules applied to those objects.

This question is rather difficult in cognitive science because there are two possible ways for dealing with the brain capabilities :

- the "downward" approach, due to experimental psychology, proposes some internal representation of our sensory perception. It is then possible to describe some basic cognitive behaviours of the brain and their mechanisms. Tasks like pattern classification, associative memory, or image restoration can be realized by classical machines (linear systems) or by networks of simple units using some neural connectionist concepts. We would like to point out about this later methodology that only the systems (assemblies of formal neurons) incorporate some connectionist notions while the objects processed by those systems have a common representation which is not at all close to the neural system. Nevertheless neural network models developed in this context are able to contain a very large number of units. This is essential according to the concept of the collective properties of the neural system.

- the "upward" approach consists of recording the electrophysiological data (single neuron activities) of the peripheral sensory systems like the cochlea, the retina, etc..., or the cortical neural layers if possible, in order to describe the primary neural coding of the information.Such an approach requires the recording of several simultaneous spike trains activities but it is not yet possible to record a very large number of neuron activities at the same time; some multi-electrode techniques are actually under development but they don't really allow the recording of independent activities.

There finally appears a kind of duality between the downward and the upward approaches; on the one hand, the former is based on the connectionist concept but omits physiological data : the algorithms (neural networks) have a great ability to perform some information processing that belongs to high level cognitive behaviours; this property basically comes from the fact that the networks are made of a very large number of units. On the other hand, the latter approach is close to the biological and physiological reality but cannot access to the concept of the collective behaviour of the neural system because it can only deal with several single neurons at the same time, not a large number.

In order to simulate the collective properties of a network, one needs to make some strong simplifications : the neurons and the synaptic rules are very simple functions and the processed objects have no temporal nature (Static patterns). In Kohonen (1984) and Hopfield (1982) for instance, the patterns are clearly static images, and even in Tanks *et al.* (1987) each detected segment of speech is a binary static vector. The elimination of the time dimension in neural modelling is very common and we shall now introduce a new concept for the representation of neural activity which provides a compromise between the simplifications necessary to the downward approach and the biological reality due to the upward approach. The activity of an assembly of neurons (the neural object) will be represented by a random field; as a consequence this representation induces a new way of describing a neural network. Though this representation is general, we shall develop its description in the context of speech coding inside the auditory system.

14.2 The specificity of the neural signal

Neural activity is made of spike trains emitted by the neurons which are represented by temporal stochastic renewal point processes (see figure 14.1). The fact that the neuronal signal is a random process seems very noticeable because this stochasticity appears in the temporal behaviour of the signal and should so be taken into account in a good representation of the neural signal. As we shall manage with the speech signal, the temporal dimension of the neural signal obviously remains one of our major problems. Different authors (Kohonen 1984, Tanks *et al.* 1987) consider speech as a sequence of events , that a neural network may classify ; but in doing so, they consider that the events themselves have been previously detected. This detection is generally made by a very simple analysis of the speech signal which performs the interface level between the external acoustic signal and the neural system. As this interface is physiologically provided by the cochlea whose the main property is tonotopic selectivity, the interface is realized by a spectral representation of the signal : a collection of band pass filters roughly reproduces the frequency analysis realized by the basilar membrane (inside the cochlea) of the peripheral auditory system (see figure 14.2). The quantization of the energy in each band provides a succession of vectors every 5 or 20 ms which represent the signal. As far as speech perception may be reduced to the four steps of figure 14.3, this kind of representation of the speech signal avoids the main difficulty of the signal representation involved in levels 2 (interface between the physical and the neural signal) and 3 (multineuronal activity) so as to pay entirely attention to the level 4 (information processing) while the representation of the input signal remains close to its physical nature. This approach typically belongs to the connectionist field of research: the function performed by the level four can be applied to any (usually physical) objects; as the representation of those objects (network inputs) is not appropriate to the neural nature, one needs to "overcomplicate" the treatments of the level four in order to get some good results; the actual solution is either to supervise the treatment, or to use very long learning algorithms.

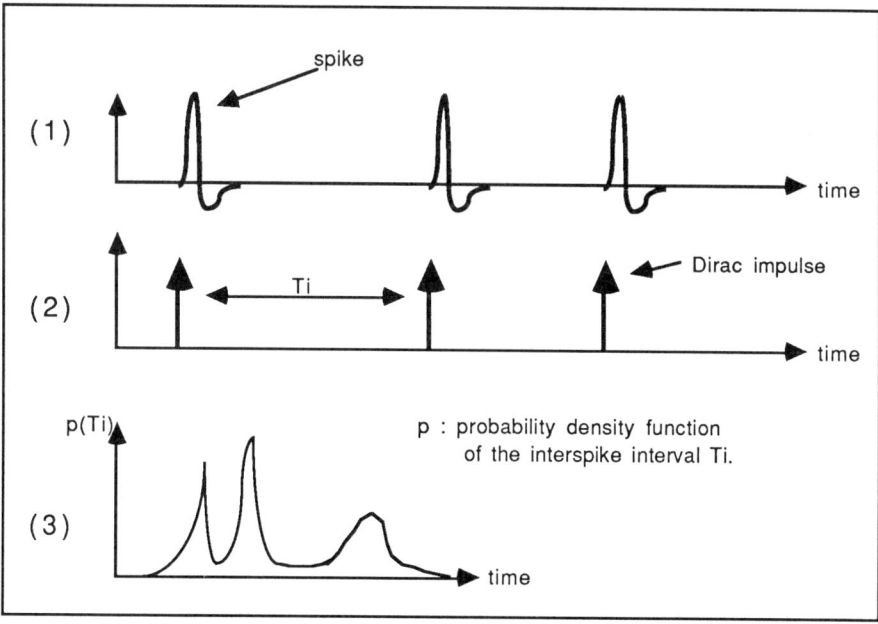

Figure 14.1. The spike trains (1), which are the neuronal activity, are represented by temporal point processes (2). Under stationary conditions, the probability density function of the interspike intervals Ti can be estimated by a histogram (3). This pdf entirely represents the random process; in the case of the auditory nerve fibres activity, the pdf measured in response to a vowel is synchronized on the main spectral components (formants) of the vowel, which can be found back in the Fourier transform of the pdf. This synchronization effect proves the temporal coding of the information inside the random spike trains.

In order to show why spectral representations of speech are insufficient to describe the real coding known, up to now, at the auditory nerve level, we shall briefly review the main properties of this neural coding.

Though the tonotopy of the peripheral auditory system remains a basic coding of the signal, it is a property related to a first order statistical measure of the auditory nerve fibres activity because the selectivity of a fibre to a pure tone is measured by its mean discharge firing rate (see figure 14.2). It has been well known for several years that there exists a fine temporal coding of information inside the interspike interval distribution. It is possible to find, under certain conditions, the spectral components of the acoustic stimulus by calculating the Fourier transform of the interspike interval probability density function (Delgutte 1980, Sachs *et al.* 1980).

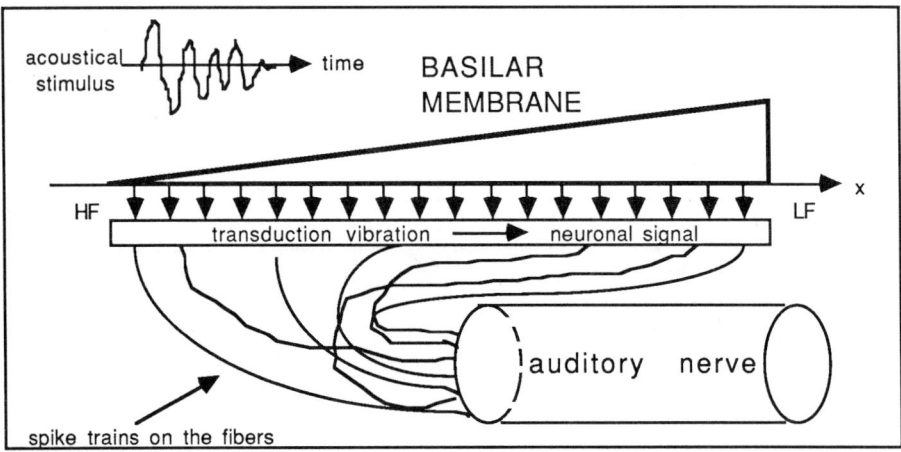

Figure 14.2. The basilar membrane inside the cochlea transforms the acoustic signal in a neural object. Because of its increasing thickness all along its axis x (35 mm long) each frequency component of the signal is selectively encoded at one point of the axis. The mechanical vibrations of the membrane at each point x are transformed in a neuronal signal generated on the auditory nerve fibres. The highest frequencies (HF) are encoded at the beginning (basis) of the membrane and the lowest (LF) are encoded at its end (apex). This is known as the tonotopical property of the peripheral auditory system.. The selectivity of a fibre to its characteristic frequency is measured through the mean discharge rate of the fibre in response to a succession of acoustic pure tones.

A deeper analysis of this temporal coding is necessary in order to understand its particular specificity. From the statistical point of view the information carried by the random process (interspike intervals distribution) is effective if there are enough realizations of the process. Let us say that we need about 500 spikes for each distribution representing the temporal coding of a vowel at one point x of the basilar membrane. As a vowel is recognized in about 50 ms and given a mean firing rate of 200 spikes per second, there is about 10 spikes on a fibre during 50 ms. In order to obtain our 500 spikes, this distribution must be spread over several fibres (about 50). The fact is that from each internal hair cell. (located at one point of the basilar membrane) there are about 30 auditory nerve fibres which are supposed to carry the same information. This temporal coding must thus have also a spatial dimension.

As a conclusion we can say that neural coding just after the interface between the external physical stimulus and the neural system, is temporal, stochastic and spatially distributed on many fibres because of the tonotopy and the interspike interval code. We propose a representation which takes into account all these properties.

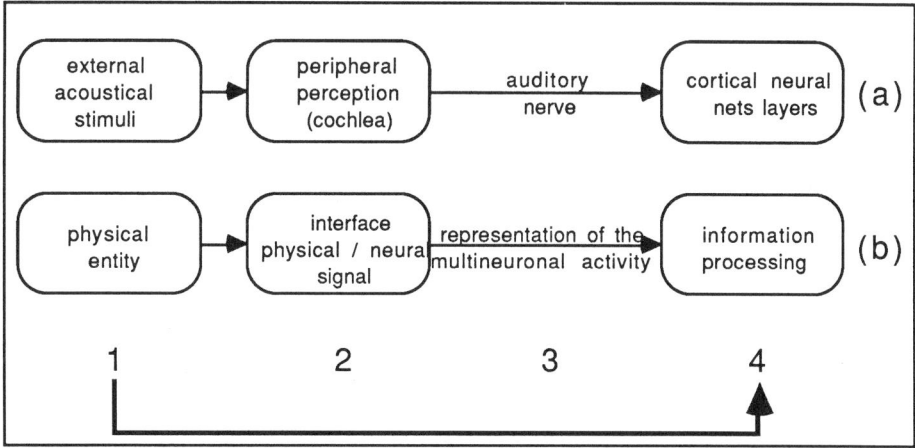

Figure 14.3. Auditory perception can be shown in four steps. Because of the difficulty of representing the speech signal and its neural nature at step 3, neural network modelling pays most attention to the functional ability of cognitive high levels (step 4) so as to apply those functions to the physical objects (step 1) which have no neural nature. We propose a multineuronal representation of the speech coding at level 3 based on the properties of the interface provided at step 2 and based on the neural nature of the signal at step 3.

14.3 The random field as a concept for describing the multineuronal activity.

14.3.1 *The ear-th representation*
Let us consider N spike trains representing the activity of N auditory nerve fibres or of N neurons of a neural network. The ear-th representation whose name is closely induced from the initial understanding of the ear by T. Herve (sic!), is based on the three following steps.

- Each spike train is first sampled at the frequency $1/\Delta t$, so that each spike represented by a Dirac impulse - see figure 14.1 - falls in an interval $[k\Delta t , (k+1).\Delta t]$. Δt is shorter than the refractory period and the boolean variable M_k is 1 if a spike is emitted during the interval $[k.\Delta t,(k+1)\Delta t]$, else it is 0.

- Let now be given N spike trains $M(i,j)$, where (i,j) denotes an arbitrary 2-dimensional organization of the emitting neurons on a square lattice, part of $\mathbb{Z} \times \mathbb{Z}$ with $1 \leq i \leq n$, $1 \leq j \leq n$ and $n \times n = N$.
We can build a succession of binary matrices M_k such that each term $M_k(i,j)$ is 1 if there is a spike in the interval $[k.\Delta t,(k+1)\Delta t]$ of the train (i,j), else $M_k(i,j)$ is 0. The figure 14.4 shows this transformation for 4 spike trains.

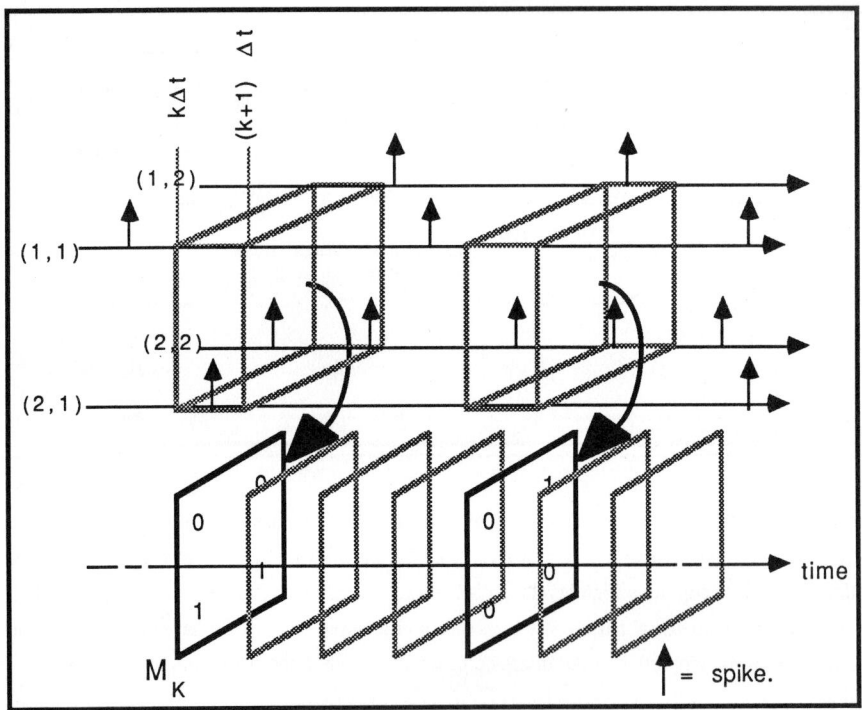

Figure 14.4. Transformation of four spike trains emitted on fibres (1,1), (1,2), (2,1), (2,2) into successive binary matrices. The temporal succession of these matrices M_k obtain at $K.\Delta t$ will be analyzed like the realizations of a random field defined on four sites.

- The new concept that we introduce now, consist of considering the successive boolean matrices M_k like the realizations of a random field defined on a finite set of N sites of $\mathbb{Z} \times \mathbb{Z}$. Each term (i,j) of M_k is the state of the site (i,j) at time $k.\Delta t$ (with $1 \leq i \leq n$, $1 \leq j \leq n$ and $n \times n = N$), so that M_k represents a **configuration** of the random field. The 2D organization is arbitrary, and there is no conceptual argument against a 3D one, but we shall see later why this choice is very convenient in the case of the modelling of a

2-dimensional neural network.

14.3.2 *Parameters of a random field*

A random field is entirely defined by the interaction potentials $J_U(A)$ of its configurations A, which are the parameters of its Gibbs measure associated to the potential U; the estimation of these potentials is made by the Gibbs sampling technique Geman *et al* (1984) . Among all the possible configurations, let call :

  - "ø" the configuration whose every sites are in the state 0,

  - "n-uplet" any configuration whose every sites, but n, are in the state 0.

With N sites, there will be N possible singletons, $\binom{N}{2}$ pairs, etc..., $\binom{N}{n}$ n-uplets.

The following equations provide the way of calculating an interaction potential $J_U(A)$:

$$J_U (A) = \sum_{B \subset A} (-1)^{|A \backslash B|} U (B) \tag{0}$$

If a potential $J_U(A)$ is charged, i.e significantly different of 0, this means that the sites of this configuration have some spatial interaction and that the occurrence of this configuration cannot be explained as the coincidence of its under-configurations.

Suppose, now, that the N spike trains represent the activity of N isolated fibres of the auditory nerve, whose activity may be considered like N statistically independent stochastic point processes. As the state of a site (i,j) depends on the realization of the interspike interval density of the considered fibre (i,j) without, in that case, any local interaction between the sites, the interaction potentials of the associated Gibbs measure will be null, except those of the singletons whose value is closely related to the mean $\mu(i,j)$ interspike interval of each train (i,j).

Such a random field is called trivial; a trivial random field will represent, for us, the activity of N fibres of the auditory nerve and will be the input excitation of our intermediary neural network.

14.3.3 *The neural network*

As our aim here is not to insist on the network, we shall briefly describe its structure. It is made of 64 neurons (i,j), $0 \le i \le 7$ and $0 \le j \le 7$, providing a plane organization; a spike emitted by the neuron (i,j) excites its four nearest neighbours and inhibits the eight next nearest neurons through synaptic weights. We have introduced a short term plasticity law so that the connectivity may change quickly in response to short variations induced by a speech signal. Each neuron has an external input via a synaptic contact with one fibre of the auditory nerve . Here are the equations of the network:

a) Time sampling period: Δt ; $t = k.\Delta t$.

b) Neuron output : $o_{i,j}(k) = 1 \Rightarrow$ occurrence of a spike at time $k.\Delta t$. eq. (1).

   $V_{i,j}$ is the excitatory / inhibitory neighborhood (neurons (m,n)) of the neuron (i,j) .

$$o_{ij}(k) = H \left[\sum_{(m,n) \in v_{ij}} w_{m,n}.e_{m,n}(k) - s_{ij}(k-1) \right] ; H(t) = 1 \text{ if } t > 0, \text{ else } H(t) = 0 \quad (1)$$

c) $S_{i,j}(k)$ is the threshold of the neuron i,j. eq.(2).

$$S_{i,j}(k) = S_{ij}(k-1) + \sum_{(m,n) \in V_{ij}} W_{m,n} . e_{m,n}(k) \quad (2)$$

d) Short term plasticity rule: $w_{m,n} = w_{m,n}(k_0)$ as long as $k_0.\Delta t \leq k.\Delta t \leq k_0.\Delta t + 3$ ms, so that the weights change every 3 ms. eq. (3,4,5).

$$|w_{m,n}(k)| = |w_{m,n}(k-1)| + \Omega[e_{m,n}(k-1) , o_{i,j}(k)]. w_{m,n}(k-1). \quad (3)$$

$$\Omega(0,0) = 0, \Omega(0,1) = \Omega(1,0) = - \text{ß}, \Omega(1,1) = \text{Nf: for excitatory synapses.} \quad (4)$$

$$\Omega(0,0) = 0, \Omega(0,1) = \Omega(1,0) = \text{Nf}, \Omega(1,1) = - \text{ß: for inhibitory synapses.} \quad (5)$$

As the output activity of the network is made of N spike trains, it can also be represented as a random field. According to our description of neural activity, a **neural network** appears like a kind of **parallel random automaton network** to which we have added an innovation process (input random field) and whose activity is an output random field. The estimation of the interaction potentials of this random field provides the means to characterize the function realized by the network; we now explain how it is possible to get information about the pseudo-physiological behaviour of the network through the measurement of the Gibbs parameters.

14.4 Simulation and results

14.4.1 *Input random field*
In the simulation we present here, an input random field is obtained from sixty four independent spike trains. The interspike interval distribution of each train is a normal distribution N (μ,σ). The case when all the trains follow the same distribution is called the homogeneous input random field otherwise it is a non-homogeneous one. It is important to notice that in the homogeneous case the interaction potentials of the singletons are all

equal; in the non homogeneous case the interaction potentials of the singletons are equal only if the concerned normal distributions have the same mean. According to the arguments developed in part 14.2, there should be a group of fibres discharging along the same interspike interval distribution; in the non-homogeneous case, we consider thus only two different distribution at the same time: a group of fourty height fibres (distribution N_1) and a group of 16 fibres (distributions N_2); Those 16 fibres are located at the sites (i,j) such that $4 \leq i \leq 7$ and $0 \leq j \leq 3$ - see figures of section 14.4.4 -.

The important parameter in our representation is the sampling rate of the spike trains. In order to remain consistent with both the speech domain and the physiological data we choose $\Delta t = 100 \ \mu s$ -see Delgutte (1980). One should notice that if Δt is to small, only $\emptyset$ and configurations of singletons will occur: this physically means that one looks at the activity of each site so closely that it becomes independent of its neighbours. On the contrary, if Δt is to large (while always shorter than the refractory period of a neuron (1ms)), configuration of triplets, quadruplets will occur in such a way that it may be impossible to estimate their associated interaction potential because of their increasing number (there are $[N! \ / \ n!(N-n)!]$ possible configurations of n-uplets). In a study that is not to be developed here, we showed that only configurations of pairs and singletons are significantly charged; one can then either choose Δt short enough so as to mainly get configurations of singletons and pairs, or calculate the interaction potentials of pairs and singletons from the occurrences of the higher n-uplets.

We present in part 14.4.2 and 14.4.3 two simulations:

- the first one shows how the ear-th representation allows to deal with some temporal parameters close to the speech signal.

- the second shows that the concept of interaction potentials provides a mean to retrieve the concept of tonotopy through the spatial organization of the singletons.

14.4.2 *Network's stationarity*

The stationarity of the input random field is conditioned by the stationarity of the acoustical signal used as a stimulus of the auditory peripheral system. A vowel can merely be modeled like a 200 ms long stationary signal so that the activity of the auditory nerve is assumed to be stationary in response to a vowel, Delgutte (1980).

The stability of the output random field in response to a stationary input one is obtained when the Gibbs measure settles after a transient time. A simple means providing the proof that the random field is in a Gibbs state, is to verify the stability of the estimated interaction potentials.

In our simulations, the convergence to a Gibbs state always occurs, whatever the kind of input interspike interval distribution. This suggests that the system is ergodic. We can also analyze the convergence through the stability of the synapses: as we introduced a short term plasticity law, the weights of the synapses can move towards their stable values over a short time; this time is closely linked to the transient time of the synaptic weights that we measure. It is then satisfying to notice that the **mathematical measure** of the transient time corresponds to a **biological behavior**.

The ergodicity is an essential property and we noticed that the duration of the transient time varies from 20 to 100 ms, depending on the initial state of the neurons; if most of the neurons are in their refractory period at the beginning of an excitation, the transient time is rather long. We can easily compare this property to a temporal context effect: if a previous excitation has left the neurons in their refractory period, they need a longer time to deliver their output and stabilize their connectivity.

This phenomena is common in biological systems and our representation is able to take into account such a temporal behavior. The concept of the context effect is fundamental in the speech studies: the perception of a stop-consonant, for instance, is conditioned by the length of a 50 ms long silence just before its burst . As the burst lasts 20 to 40 ms, one may suppose that during the silence, the neural system comes back to a state which allows its neurons to deliver a quick response to the burst. Our simulations based on the variation of a silence length between two stationary excitations have shown that the transient time obtained in response to the second excitation is effectively sensitive to the previous context and is shorter when the silence is longer -see figure 14.5. A typical result of this experiments appears in the table 14.1.

Table 14.1 *Variations of the convergence time Tcv2 of the output random field in response to a stationary stimulus as a function of a previous silence duration Ts - see figure 14.5 - .*

Ts (ms)	1 0	2 0	3 0	5 0
Tcv2 (ms)	3 3	2 7	1 8	1 8

Simulations were realized on a large number of different input random field. The simulation corresponding to the above table was performed with the homogeneous random fields I_1 generated from $N(8ms,1ms)$ and I_2 generated from $N(4ms,1ms)$. The duration T1 of I_1 was such that a Gibbs state was reach before the silence (Tcv1 < T1); Tcv2 is measured through the stability of the interaction potentials of I_2 (variations of 5% around the stable values). Notice that Tcv2 becomes shorter when Ts is long enough and reaches a limit (18 ms). This means that, according to our formalism, Ts has a perceptive role when shorter than 30 ms.

14.4.3 *Tonotopy and Gibbs measure*

In order to see how far our representation of neural activity is appropriate to the neural coding of speech, we realize a simple experiment:

As the tonotopy can be found at every level of the auditory chain, its fundamental to encode it in the network output random field. Knowing the fact that the network is excited by a non-homogeneous random field, the output random field must statistically contain this non-homogeneity. As we explained it in 14.4.1, such an input random field gets the information from two points of the basilar membrane providing the to different interspike interval distributions N_1 and N_2. In order to show that the network is able to detect this non-homogeneity in the fine temporal activity of the fibres and not only in the different mean discharge rates of the two kinds of spike trains, we choose the distributions N_1 (8ms, 1ms) and N_2 (8ms,2ms) for which the standard deviations are different. The results of these simulations are shown in figures 14.6 and 14.7. One can notice that some aggregations of potentials of singletons appears; they are clearly located on the two different areas that were previously defined like the areas excited by the two groups of fibres so as to give a way of detecting the underlying tonotopy. This simple simulation permits to conclude that the network reinforces the "contrast" between two different areas of its input activity (this property was expected) and that The ear-th representation give the right tools for describing the temporal behaviours of the network.

14.5 Conclusion

We have presented a new representation of multineuronal activity; we try and show how a close knowledge of the nature of the neural object has influenced our modelling. The speech coding background that is our basis for describing this approach must not hide its general character . As we try to deal with neural network modelling we need to have a look at neural coding and neural capabilities. The first one is given by the electrophysiology and the second is given by the experimental psychology; a great temptation would be to make an exclusive choice between this two approaches. We try to explain how a reflection on classical neural modelling and the will to take into account a physiological reality, leads to the ear-th representation. As a consequence the mathematical background induced by the representation of the neuronal signal strongly influences the representation of a neural network: a neural network is then described like a kind of parallel random automaton net excited by a innovation random process. This provides a mathematical way of dealing with biological parameters (synaptic weights, convergence time, stability,spatial interaction) through the definition of some statistical measures. The notion of synaptic connections, for instance, is difficult to follow either in the biological systems or in the simulated models; it can now be related to a small number of parameters (potentials of singletons and pairs).

We think that such an approach is powerful because it gives a theoretical background for the analysis of the simulations, and it takes into account all the intrinsic properties of the processed (neural) object , that is its stochastic, temporal and spatial (distribution over a large number of units) nature.

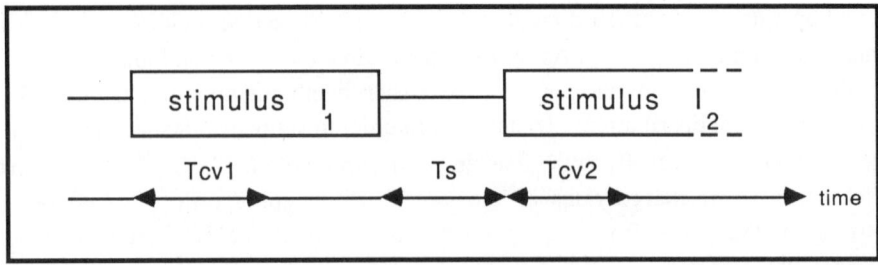

Figure 14.5 In response to the stationary stimuli I_1 and I_2 (input homogeneous random fields) we measure the convergence time T_{cv2} as a function of the silence duration T_s introduced between I_1 and I_2. T_{cv2} is estimated through the stability of the interaction potentials of the random field measured in response to I_2.

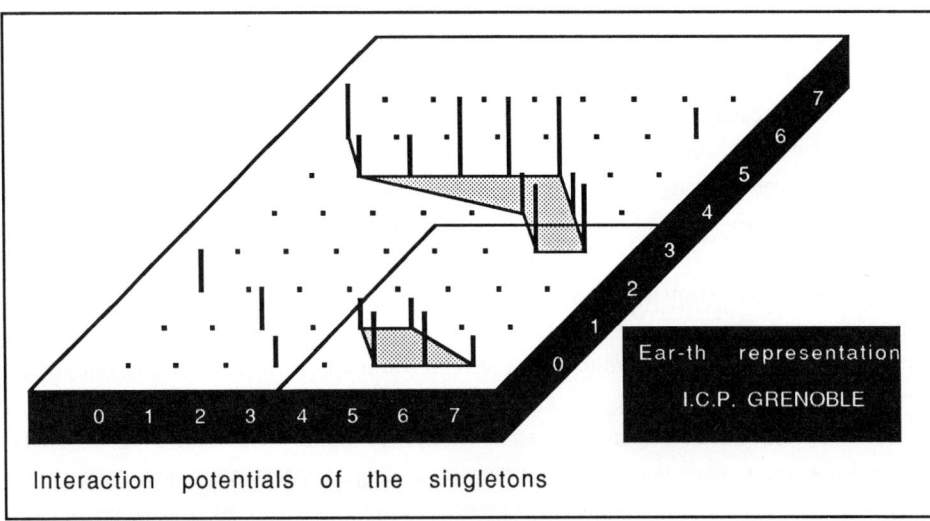

Figure 14.6 In response to a non-homogeneous input random field two aggregations of potentials of singletons (in the dashed areas) appears that show how the network has detected the underlying tonotopy induced by the fine different temporal activity of the input fibres in the concerned areas. This simulation is obtained for N_1 (8ms, 1ms) and N_2 (8ms,2ms) with the parameters Nf = 6 and β = 0.04.

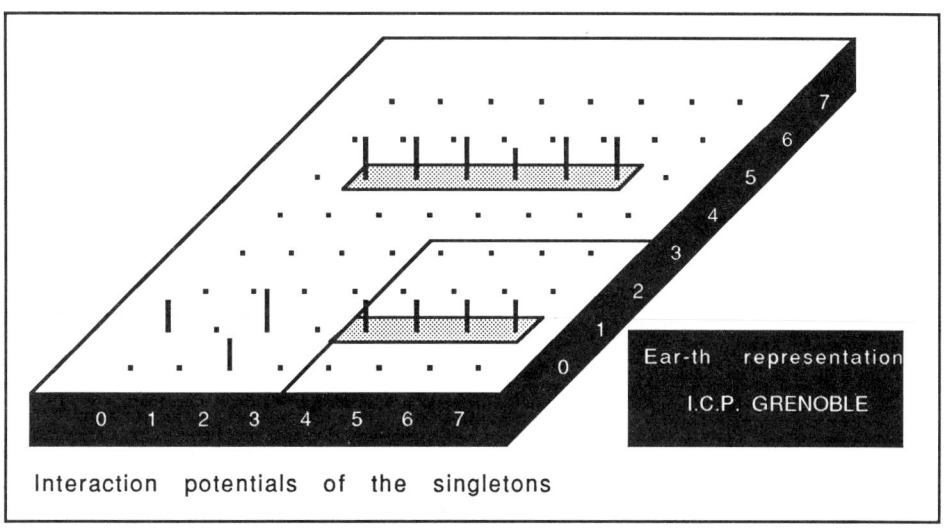

Figure 14.7 Same simulation as in figure 14.6 with Nf = 6 and β = 0.05. Notice that the choice of different values for the synaptic parameters allows to increase the size of the aggregation of potentials of singletons.

References

Chau, K.S. & Chong, H. (1985). *Journal of Advanced Applied Probability,* **17**, 666-78.

Delgutte, B. (1980). *Journal of the Acoustical Society of America,* **68**, 843-47.

Demongeot, J., Tchuente, M. & Goles, E. (1983). Dynamical systems and cellular automata. Academic Press.

Demongeot, J. & Tchuente, M. (1987). *Encyclopedia of physical science and technology,* Academic Press, **4**, 464-72.

Geman, S. & Geman, D. (1984). *IEEE Transactions in Pattern Analysis,* **6**, 721-41.

Herve, T., Dolmazon, J.M. & Demongeot, J. (1987). *Proceedings of the IEEE. International Conference on Speech and Signal Processing,* **1**, 161-64.

Hopfield, J.J. (1982). *Proceedings of the National Academy of Science. U.S.A.,* **79**, 2554-58.

Kohonen , T. (1984). Self organization and associative memory. Springer verlag edition.

Von der Malsburg, C. & Bienenstock, E. (1987). Disordered system and biological organization. Springer Verlag, Berlin.

Perkel, D.H., Gerstein, G.L. & Moore, G.P. (1967). *Biophysical Journal*, **7**, 391-418.

Preston, C. J. (1974). Gibbs measures on countable sets. Cambridge University Press.

Sachs, M.B. & Young, E.D. (1980). *Journal of the Acoustical Society of America*, **68**, 858-75.

Tanks, D. & Hopfield, J.J. (1987). *Proceeding of the National Academy of Science. U.S.A.* **84**, 896-1900.

15 *C. Jutten, J. Hérault and A. Guerin*

IN.C.A. : AN INDEPENDENT COMPONENTS ANALYSER BASED ON AN ADAPTIVE NEUROMIMETIC NETWORK.

15.1 Introduction

Since the boolean model of Mac Culloch and Pitts in 1943 (Mac Culloch *et al.*, 1943), formal neurons have developed to include adaptive features, for instance Adaline (Widrow, 1962), the Perceptron (Rosenblatt , 1960) or the Informon (Uttley, 1970). These kind of adaptive models are very successful since the 70s, and especially 80s, where they follow an exponential development, as shown by the very important number of publications and books on this topics.

One of the principal applications of these adaptive networks is the design of Associative Memories (Anderson , 1977; Kohonen, 1984; Hopfield, 1982) which functions consist in coding and classification operations (hetero-associative memory) or of recall with correction (auto-associative memory). The significance of such devices is clear for Pattern Recognition, and numerous examples have been published to illustrate this field.

Unfortunately, the capacity of these memories is limited to a little number of patterns: about 0.15 time the number of "neurons" with binary output, so long as the prototypes (patterns) presented during the learning phase are orthogonal two by two. In fact, if prototypes are not orthogonal, this capacity decreases drastically (Amit *et al.*, 1985). In order to get good performances, it is necessary to apply some pre-processing: for instance, Kohonen proposes a Laplacian operator (Kohonen, 1984) which increases the "orthogonalisation" between input patterns.

In all these applications, the patterns are in fact vectors: for example, an image can be represented by a vector, according to the concatenation of the successive rows of this image, each pixel of the image corresponds to a particular component of the vector. In our approach, we consider each component of the vector as a time signal: the vectors presented to the network are now samples of multidimensional signal. It is actually this kind of signals the Central Nervous System processes: optical, auditory, olfactory, etc. sensors give to the Central Nervous System numerous signals that we can consider as one multidimensional signal. Moreover, these various sensors are sensitive to many sources, and even though sources are independant (i.e. orthogonal), the mixings at the outputs of the sensors are no more independent, because each component is the result of the superposition of many sources.

A pre-processing device, able to "orthogonalize" the signals issued from these sensors proves to be a necessary interface between natural signals and associative memories. We propose in this paper an adaptive algorithm, based on a highly connected neuronal network with synaptic plasticity, which extracts all independant signals from mixed signals, i.e. which acts as an Independent Components Analyser (IN.C.A.). Before dealing with this problem, we want to emphasize the originality of this work:

i.   Our model processes time dependent signals, as the Central Nervous System does.

ii.   Our model is based on a neuromimetic recursive architecture, with plasticity properties. Such architectures are current in the Central Nervous System, at the sensory and cortical levels.

iii. The connections between formal neurons must be asymmetric. If symmetry is an acceptable property for physical interactions, it is not true for biological systems.

iv.   The adaptation rule is a local rule, which must be asymmetric. The asymmetry is effective by the product of two non-linear functions f and g.

v.   Most adaptation rules perform a maximization of correlation. On the contrary, our one lies on an independence test : it performs, in particular, a minimization of correlation.

vi.   The learning is permanent. The adaptive network is able to fold the solution if the mixture is moving.

In brief, biological systems are inspiration sources for engineering. This assertion continuously influences our approach and constitutes perhaps the principal reason of its originality.

15.2 The problem

15.2.1 *Generalities*

Source discrimination by an array of sensors is a fundamental problem in Signal Processing:

i. in radar or sonar applications, with the help of an array of antennas, the problem consists in the detection of the presence or in the localization of a known source (Nicolas *et al.* , 1985), or even in the elimination of a scrambling source, which is generally an unknown source (Christophe *et al.* , 1985).

ii. in teleconference studios, this problem is a very difficult one: when several speakers are talking simultaneously, signals and echoes are mixed. Moreover, the problem doesn't reduce to a simple speaker recognition task, but it is necessary tó extract the signal emitted by a particular speaker from all other signals. At present, there is no satisfactory solution to this problem, called the "cocktail party effect" (Strube, 1981).

In Signal Processing, to resolve this problem, in any particular application, *a priori* knowledge about the signal, signal properties or external medium properties is essential, which limits the impact of existing solutions. We may also note, that all the studies on this subject have used adaptive filtering technics (Macchi, 1981), based on stochastic approximation algorithms.

To solve the discrimination problem, we present a novel and very powerful adaptive algorithm :

- no *a priori* knowledge about the sources is necessary,

- the only assumption is statistical independence of sources,

- this algorithm is able to extract *simultaneously* all the sources with a good accurancy (-20 to -25 dB),

- sources can be stochastic or determinist, with wide or narrow bandwidth, non-stationary, etc.,

- this algorithm applies to a large variety of signals of various nature; here are a few examples :

* channel separation in presence of noise and crosstalk,

* processing of handwritten text,

* 3-D processing in binocular vision which leads to a standard object representation and to unveiling of 2-D or 3-D object nature.

The method originality lies in a recursive architecture, in combination with a non-linear adaptation law, derived from architectures and learning processes within Nervous System of Vertebrates. This algorithm is at present simulated both on a microcomputer and on a specific processor (Guérin, 1987) designed and built in our laboratory..

15.2.2 *Equations*

Let there be an array of sensors, each sensitive to an unknown linear combination of n sources $X_j(t)$. The response $E_i(t)$ of the sensor i is:

$$E_i(t) = \sum_{j=1}^{n} a_{ij} . X_j(t) \qquad 1 \leq i \leq n \qquad (1)$$

with matrix and vectorial notations:

$$E(t) = A.X(t) \qquad (2)$$

where $E(t)$ is the vector of components $E_i(t)$,

A is a square n-matrix of elements a_{ij},

$X(t)$ is the vector of components $X_j(t)$.

At every time t, the only information known is the vector $E(t)$. Now, we state the problem of sources discrimination in these terms:

Hypothesis 1 : $X(t)$ components are unknown and are statistically independent sources.

Hypothesis 2 : the linear transformation represented by the matrix A is regular; the inverse matrix A^{-1} exists or, which is equivalent, determinant of A is non zero.

Hypothesis 3 : the unknown mixing matrix A is supposed time independent.

Question : is it possible, only with the help of observation of E(t), i.e. without *a priori* knowledge neither about mixing matrix A, nor about the source X(t), to discover the primary signal X(t) ?

Response : there is no classical solution to this problem which on this form is a new problem, more general than classical sources discrimination problem in Signal Processing. We propose an adaptive algorithm to solve it.

15.2.3 *Principles of solution*

We use a recursive architecture (figure 15.1) made up of n fully interconnected operators. Each operator N_i receives a mixed signal $E_i(t)$ from sensor i and weighted outputs of the others operators N_j ($j \neq i$) : - $C_{ij}.S_j(t)$ and the output $S_i(t)$ of operator i is defined by:

$$S_i(t) = E_i(t) - \sum_{j \neq i} C_{ij} . S_j(t) \qquad (3)$$

In vector notation,

$$S(t) = E(t) - C.S(t) \qquad (4)$$

where C is a square n-matrix of coefficients C_{ij} with $C_{ii} = 0$.

We deduce :

$$(I + C).S(t) = E(t) \qquad (5)$$

where I is the n-square identity matrix, and if we assume:

$$E(t) = A.X(t) \qquad (6)$$

we get :

$$S(t) = (I + C)^{-1}.A.X(t) \qquad (7)$$

if the matrix $(I + C)^{-1}$ exists.

To solve the discrimination problem, the outputs $S_i(t)$ must be equal or at most proportional to $X_j(t)$:

* Outputs are equal to primary signals, i.e.

$$S(t) = X(t) \qquad (8)$$

$$\text{and } (I + C) = A \qquad (9)$$

is a solution.

* Each output $S_i(t)$ is proportional to the source $X_i(t)$:

$$S_i(t) = d_{ii}.X_i(t) \qquad (10)$$

$$\text{or } S(t) = P.X(t) \qquad (11)$$

Then

$$(I + C)^{-1}.A = D \qquad (12)$$

or

$$(I + C) = A.D^{-1} \qquad (13)$$

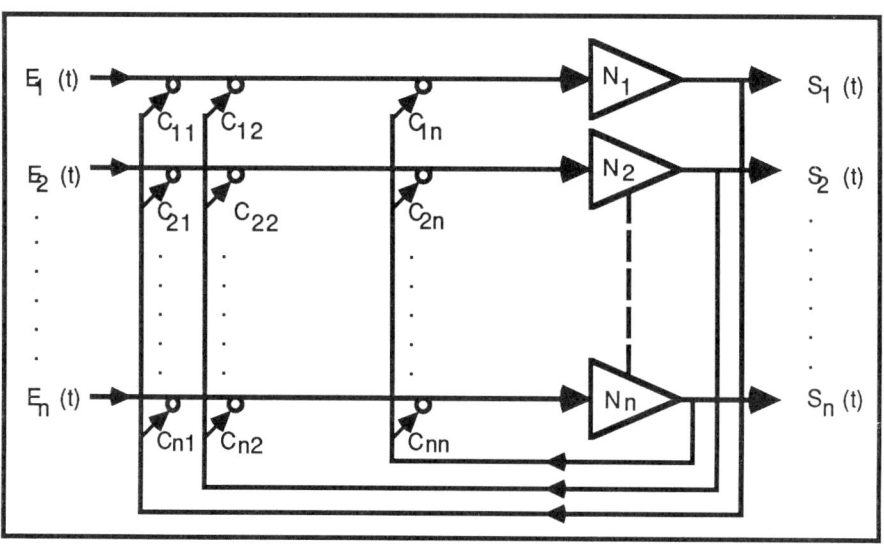

Figure 15.1. Network fully interconnected. Each triangle N_i is an operator of which the output is S_i. The horizontal line on the left of each operator i is an addition line, which output S_i is equal to $E_i - \Sigma\, C_{ij}.S_j$.

* In the most general case, output $S_i(t)$ is proportional to a source $X_j(t)$ ($i \neq j$), and

$$S(t) = P.X(t) \qquad (14)$$

where P is now a square n-matrix, with n non zero elements, derived from a diagonal matrix D by permutation of rows.

Thus, source discrimination is possible, if C of coefficients C_{ij} exists and fulfills the relation (13) where D would be a permutation of a diagonal matrix and I is the matrix Identity of order n.

We prove later that every element C_{ij} ot the matrix C can be computed by an iterative method, with the help of an adaptation law derived from an independence test of the outputs $S_i(t)$ and $S_j(t)$. Before explaining of this law, we shall propose to illustrate the algorithm performances by a few examples.

15.3 Simulation results

15.3.1 *2-source problem*
We begin this study with the easiest case, that of discrimination of two sources (figure 15.2). In this case, we consider only two sensors, two operators and also two coefficients C_{ij} : C_{12} and C_{21}. We present here three examples: in the first one, we built ourselves the mixing matrix A, which therefore allows to verify convergence and accuracy of the algorithm because we can easely calculate the theoretical solution ; in the second one, we describe a possible application to binary channel separation in the presence of noise and crosstalk (modelled by the mixing matrix A); the third one is an application to hanwriting processing, where the mixing is unknown.

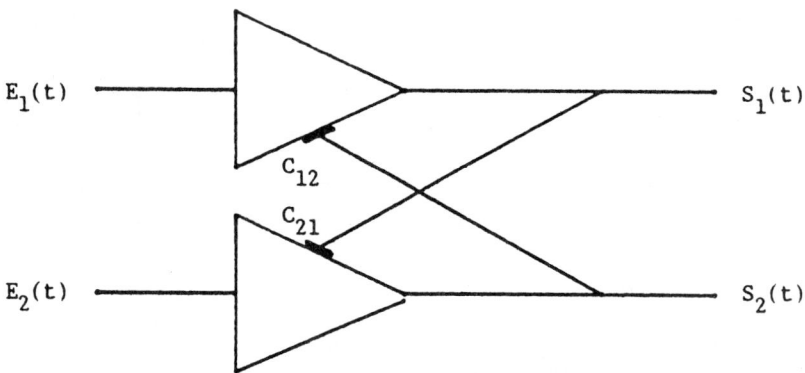

Figure 15.2. 2-operator network. In this case, we have only two coefficients, C_{12} and C_{21}.

Example 1 : We choose a regular mixing matrix A. then we consider two signals $X_1(t)$ and $X_2(t)$, with any range of properties: determinist or random, with large or narrow bandwidth, etc. but satisfying the independence assumption (hypothesis 1 in § 15.2.2). At every time t, we choose $X_1(t)$ and $X_2(t)$, and we compute the mixing inputs $E_1(t)$ and $E_2(t)$; then we deduce:

$$S_1(t) = E_1(t) - C_{12}(t).S_2(t)$$

$$S_2(t) = E_2(t) - C_{21}(t).S_1(t)$$

(15)

If the operators N_1 and N_2 are linear:

$$S_1(t) = \frac{E_1(t) - C_{12}(t).E_2(t)}{1 - C_{12}(t).C_{21}(t)}$$

$$S_2(t) = \frac{E_2(t) - C_{21}(t).E_1(t)}{1 - C_{12}(t).C_{21}(t)}$$

(16)

Equations (16) are valid if $1 - C_{12}(t).C_{21}(t) > 0$, i.e. if $(I + C)^{-1}$ exists. Then we compute the new values of matrix C elements according to the adaptation law:

$$C_{ij}(t + 1) = F [C_{ij}(t), S_i(t), S_j(t)]$$

(17)

After 500 to 1000 network iterations with adaptive modifications, we note that:

$$< dC_{ij} / dt > = 0$$

(18)

where $< . >$ represents time averaging symbol: the algorithms converges. Figure 15.3.c displays trajectories of points $(C_{12}(t), C_{21}(t))$ in the plane (C_{12}, C_{21}) leading to the theoretical point P^*. In this example, the sources $X_1(t)$ and $X_2(t)$ are random signals with uniform probability density. At the beginning of learning ($C_{12}(0) = 0, C_{21}(0) = 0$), the outputs $S_1(t)$ ans $S_2(t)$ are proportional to inputs $E_1(t)$ and $E_2(t)$, i.e. the outputs consist of a linear combination of the primary sources $X_1(t)$ and $X_2(t)$ (figure 15.3.a). After the algorithm converges (figure 15.3.b), $S_1(t)$ and $S_2(t)$ are continuously proportional to $X_1(t)$ and $X_2(t)$ respectively: now we see a rectangular distribution, because $X_1(t)$ and $X_2(t)$ are independent signals; if the signals $X_1(t)$ and $X_2(t)$ themselves were also produced by a mixing matrix B of more primary signals $Y_1(t)$ and $Y_2(t)$, the outputs $S_1(t)$ ans $S_2(t)$ would be proportional to $Y_1(t)$ and $Y_2(t)$.

Example 2 : Let us consider now two binary transmission channels, with additive noise and crosstalk, modelled by a linear combination of channel sources (figure 15.4). At channel outputs, we get mixed noisy signals. By applying our algorithm, it is possible to extract both binary signals, without any mismatch, after about 1000 iterations.

Example 3 : Input distribution consist of sloping handwritten text (figure 15.5). At any time t, we draw a point of this text, characterized by cartesian coordinates, $E_1(t)$ and $E_2(t)$. $E_1(t)$ and $E_2(t)$ are the component of the input vector E(t). We use the same 2-operator architecture as in the two previous examples, but here the mixing matrix is unknown. After learning over 500 to 1000 points of the text, the algorithm converges, and in the plane (S_1, S_2) text lines and letters are straightened.

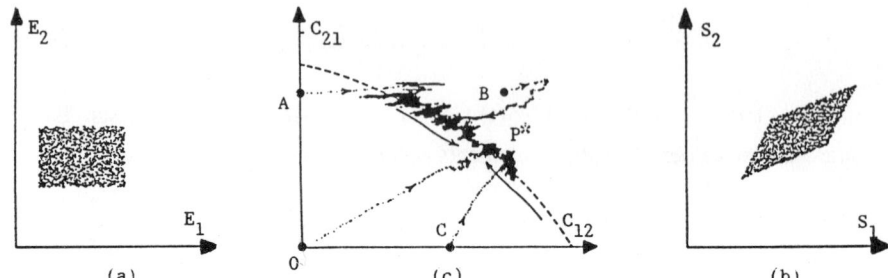

Figure 15.3. 2-operator problem.

a. Outputs distribution in cartesian plane (S_1, S_2) at time $t = 0$. It is equivalent to inputs distribution.

b. Outpus distribution in the same cartesian plane after convergence.

c. Trajectories of points $(C_{12}(t), C_{21}(t))$ for various initial conditions.

In this example, $X_1(t)$ and $X_2(t)$ are random sequences generated by the computer.

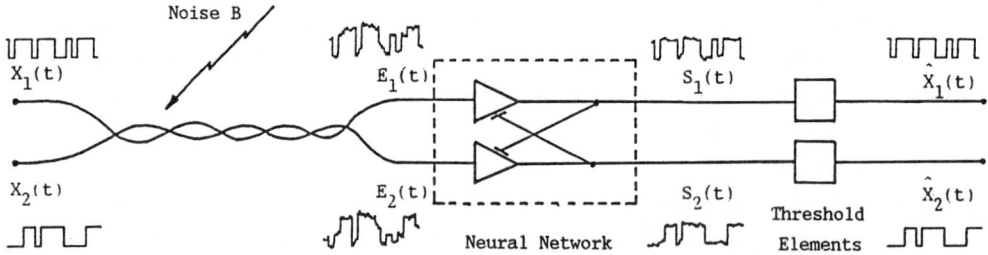

Figure 15.4. Application to transmission lines with crosstalk in the presence of noise.

Input lines are unknown binary signals, $X_1(t)$ and $X_2(t)$, disrupted by additive noise B and crosstalk; signals $E_1(t)$ and $E_2(t)$ at line output are noisy mixing of signals $X_1(t)$ and $X_2(t)$. By applying our algorithm, it is possible to separate $X_1(t)$ and $X_2(t)$: $S_1(t)$ and $S_2(t)$ at operator output demonstrate the processing efficiency. thus, with the help of a simple threshold element, it is easy to discover the two binary signals $X_1(t)$ and $X_2(t)$.

15.2.4 *More general results*

Problem generalization to a n-operator architecture is theorically straightforward. But in practice, simulation is very difficult because of the computing duration and of the C_{ij} trajectories and outputs S_j distributions which distributions are n.(n - 1) and n-dimensional spaces, respectively. We have simulated a stereoscopic vision model which uses a 4-operator network.

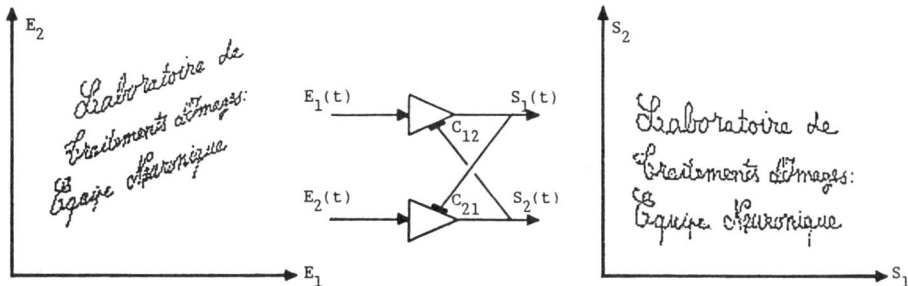

Figure 15.5. Application to handwritten text processing.

Inputs are cartesian coordinates E_1 and E_2 of sloping text points. After algorithm convergence, network outputs correspond to new coordinates associated with straightened lines and letters of the initial text.

Example 4 : An object (figure 15.6.) in a 3-D cartesian space (u_1, u_2, u_3) is seen by two receptors R and R' (for example two TV cameras). The object forms in the retina of each receptor two different images (binocular disparity) $I(E_1, E_2)$ and $I'(E_1', E_2')$.

At any time t, we illuminate with a laser a random point $M(u_1, u_2, u_3)$ of this object. We observe a luminous point $P(E_1, E_2)$ in the image I and another one $P'(E_1', E_2')$ in the image I'. We associate with the point M the 4-component vector E(t) :

$$\begin{vmatrix} E_1 \\ E_2 \\ E'_1 \\ E'_2 \end{vmatrix}$$

By means of random points illumination, we obtain a random vector series E(t), which provides input vectors of a 4-operator adaptive network. By applying the discrimination algorithm, we observe convergence of the 12 coefficients C_{ij} after about 3000 iterations. In the output space, we note that one output (S_4) is equal to zero ; the distributions of the others outputs are represented by projections on the three planes (S_1, S_2), (S_1, S_3) and (S_2, S_3) as we can see on the figure 15.6.

We recognize front, side and top views of the original object :
- $S_1(t)$ contains width information,
- $S_2(t)$ contains length information,
- $S_3(t)$ contains height information.

It is important to note that computing architecture shows the object by a standard representation, which is unknown to the receptors.

Example 5 : We use the same experimental device as in example 4, but we replace the 3-D object by a photograph of this same object. After convergence, outputs $S_1(t)$ and $S_4(t)$

are equal to zero. The network discovers the dimensional nature of the object (the photograph is a 2-D object) seen by the two cameras (figure 15.7.).

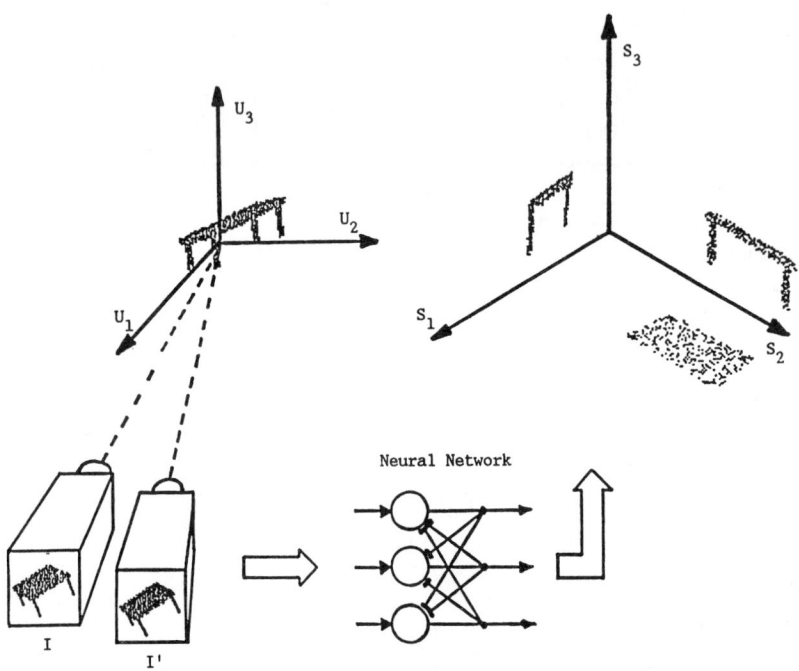

Figure 15.6. Application in stereoscopic vision.

The two TV cameras develop two different images I and I' of the 3-D object (a table). At network output, we can see a standard representation of the object "table".

15.3 **How is it possible ?**

15.3.1 *Adaptation law principles*

In part 15.2.3, we have sketched the processor architecture in the general case (figure 15.1) and we have shown that the coefficients of the matrix C can be computed by an adaptive learning process derived from those known in Central Nervous System of Vertebrates. In line with various studies (Hebb, 1949; Rauscheker and Singer, 1981), we suggest this adaptation law:

$$dC_{ij} / dt = - \gamma.C_{ij} + a.f(S_i).g(S_j) \tag{19}$$

where f and g are two functions, a is the adaptation gain and γ is a "forgetting" coefficient which is not essential. Subsequently, in the following, we always take this coefficient equal to zero. We can abstract operators network and adaptation law equations by the two relations:

$$S_i = E_i - \sum_{j=1}^{n} C_{ij}.S_j \qquad 1 \le i \le n \text{ and } j \ne i$$

$$dC_{ij} / dt = a.f(S_i).g(S_j) \qquad i \ne j$$

(20)

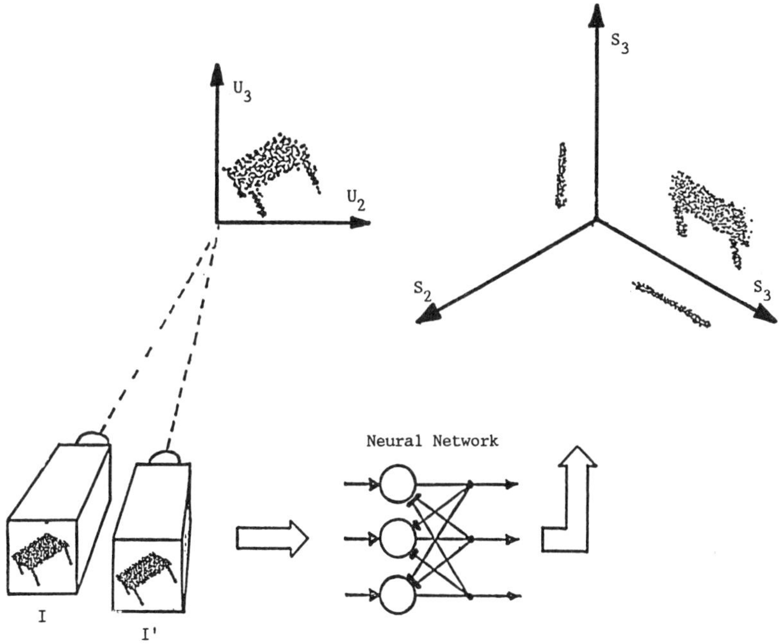

Figure 15.7 Application to stereoscopic vision.

Now, the object seen by the two cameras is a photograph of the table. The network discovers the 2-D nature of this object.

From these equations, the function of every operator can be viewed as modelling the input signal $E_i(t)$ according to a linear combination of outputs signals $S_j(t)$; this model would carry an estimation of $E_i(t)$:

$$\hat{E}_i = \sum_{j \ne i} C_{ij} . S_j$$

(21)

With this assumption, output $S_i(t)$ would be the estimation error:

$$S_i = E_i - \hat{E}_i \tag{22}$$

We assert, if this is true, that the adaptive process must aim to minimize a particular function of this error. According to equations (7), (11) and (12), after the algorithm convergence, the error is proportional to a particular primary source $X_i(t)$. the number of unknown variables in this problem corresponds to the number of coefficients C_{ij} ($i \neq j$) that the algorithm must compute, i.e. $n.(n - 1)$.

15.3.2 *Selection of the adaptation law*
The problem formulated in this way has the same equations than classical problems of adaptive filtering have. We thus use the same method which consists of minimizing an error function, for example, the mean square error in relation to the coefficients C_{ij}.

$$<S_i^2> = < (E_i - \hat{E}_i)^2 > \tag{23}$$

Now let us calculate partial derivatives of the error with respect to each coefficient C_{ij}, by using zero mean variables denoted $s_i = S_i - <S_i>$ and $e_i = E_i - <E_i>$:

$$\frac{\partial}{\partial C_{ij}} < s_i^2 > = < \frac{\partial}{\partial C_{ij}} s_i^2 > = 2 < s_i \frac{\partial s_i}{\partial C_{ij}} > \tag{24}$$

From equation (2) applied to zero mean variables: $s = e - C.s$, let us deduce:

$$(I + C).s = e \tag{25}$$

and after derivation with respect to C_{ij}:

$$(I + C) \frac{\delta s}{\delta C_{ij}} + \begin{pmatrix} 0 \dots 0 .. 0 \\ \dots\dots\dots\dots \\ 0 \dots 1 .. 0 \\ \dots\dots\dots\dots \\ 0 \dots 0 .. 0 \end{pmatrix}. s = 0 \tag{26}$$

In this relation, all elements of the second matrix are equal to zero, except the one located on row i and column j, which is equal to one. If matrix $(I + C)^{-1}$ exists, we can write:

$$\frac{\delta s}{\delta C_{ij}} = - \begin{pmatrix} 0 \dots q_{1i} .. 0 \\ 0 \dots q_{ni} .. 0 \end{pmatrix}. s \tag{27}$$

This matrix has only one non zero column , the column number j, which elements are those of $(I + C)^{-1}$. Let us deduce:

$$\partial s_k / \partial C_{ij} = - q_{ki}.s_j \qquad (28)$$

and, in particular for $k = i$ (connection from S_j to S_i), we obtain:

$$\partial s_i / \partial C_{ij} = - q_{ii}.s_j \qquad (29)$$

Let us multiply by s_i:

$$s_i.(\partial s_i / \partial C_{ij}) = - q_{ii}.(s_i.s_j) \qquad (30)$$

and let us average:

$$\partial <s_i{}^2> / \partial C_{ij} = -2.q_{ii}.<s_i.s_j> \qquad (31)$$

We get a partial minimum of error $<s_i{}^2>$ when the crosscorrelation $<s_i.s_j>$ is equal to zero. By using stochastic gradient algorithm, we obtain the following adaptation law which allows to hit this minimum value:

$$dC_{ij} / dt = a.s_i.s_j \qquad (32)$$

This law proves that on average, coefficients C_{ij} don't vary if operators outputs S_i and S_j are statistically independent. This is true if, according to relations (11) and (12) , each component of S is proportional to a particular component of X. Unfortunately, independence is a sufficient condition but not a necessary condition: equation (31) is only a covariance test. So, matrix C, solution of equations (11) and (12) cannot be computed exactly by the rule proposed in (32) which involves:

$$dC_{ij} / dt = dC_{ji} / dt \qquad (33)$$

This condition is unacceptable and reduces the number of independent variables to n. $(n - 1) / 2$.

That is why we propose another law, derived from the previous one, which introduces dissymetry in the relations dC_{ii} / dt and dC_{ji} / dt. We select, in equation (32) two odd functions f and g such as the product $f(s_i).g(s_j)$ is different from the product $f(s_j).g(s_i)$. Experimentally, we get good results with the following kind of rules:

$$dC_{ij} / dt = a.s_i{}^3.Arctan(s_j) \qquad (34)$$

In fact, the mean values s_i and s_j cannot be computed exactly, and we only have estimations of these mean values. According to this remark, equation (34) becomes:

$$dC_{ij} / dt = a.s_i^3.Arctan[b.(S_j - <S_j>)] \tag{35}$$

or, which leads to the same results:

$$dC_{ij} / dt = a.S_i^3.Arctan[b.(S_j - <S_j>)] \tag{36}$$

where b is a real constant.

The estimated average $<S_j>$ can be computed, for instance, by a simple first order low-pass filter:

$$<S_j(t)> = S_j(t) * exp(-t/T) \tag{37}$$

where * denotes the convolution product, and T is the time constant of the filter.

In fact, several laws based on many possible functions f and g are suitable, and more explanations about the design of this rule can be proposed (Jutten, 1987).

15.3.3 *2-dimentional solution*

The problem is limited here to a 2-operator network, receiving two inputs, $E_1(t)$ and $E_2(t)$, which are unknown linear combinations of the primary signals $X_1(t)$ and $X_2(t)$, and we can assume:

$$E_1(t) = a_{11}.X_1(t) + a_{12}.X_2(t)$$

$$\tag{38}$$

$$E_2(t) = a_{21}.X_1(t) + a_{22}.X_2(t)$$

Let us suppose that the operators N_1 and N_2 are linear and let us substitute $E_1(t)$ and $E_2(t)$ from equations (38) in equation (16):

$$S_1 = \frac{(a_{11} - C_{12}.a_{21}).X_1 + (a_{12} - C_{12}.a_{22}).X_2}{1 - C_{12}.C_{21}}$$

$$\tag{39}$$

$$S_2 = \frac{(a_{21} - C_{21}.a_{11}).X_1 + (a_{22} - C_{21}.a_{12}).X_2}{1 - C_{12}.C_{21}}$$

Looking at these two equations, we can easely deduce a possible solution: a primary signal (for instance $X_1(t)$) will be discriminated by an output (for instance $S_1(t)$) if the other primary signal (X_2) is eliminated, which is possible if its coefficient $(a_{12} - C_{12}.a_{22})$ is equal to zero. Thus, we get two different solutions:

Solution 1 : $S_1(t) = a_{11}.X_1(t)$ $C_{12} = a_{12} / a_{22}$

                                    if   (40)

                $S_2(t) = a_{22}.X_2(t)$ $C_{21} = a_{21} / a_{11}$

Solution 2 : $S_1(t) = a_{12}.X_2(t)$ $C_{12} = a_{11} / a_{21}$

                                    if   (41)

                $S_2(t) = a_{21}.X_1(t)$ $C_{21} = a_{22} / a_{12}$

Among these two solutions, only one is acceptable, considering network stability: the loop gain must always be less than 1, i.e. that we must verify $C_{12}.C_{21} < 1$. Let us write this condition using the results of (40) and (41):

(40) involves $C_{12}.C_{21} = (a_{12}.a_{21}) / (a_{11}.a_{22}) < 1$ (42)

(41) involves $C_{12}.C_{21} = (a_{22}.a_{11}) / (a_{12}.a_{21}) < 1$ (43)

These two conditions are clearly uncompatible. Each solution corresponds to a condition for the mixing matrix A:

$$\text{if Det(A)} > 0, \text{ we retain the solution 1,}$$
$$\text{if Det(A)} < 0, \text{ we retain the solution 2.}$$

Thus, it is clear that according to values of coefficients of mixing matrix A, one of the two solutions is impossible. The theoretical solution is associated in the space (C_{12}, C_{21}) with the point P^* (see figure 15.3.).

15.3.4 Generalization

In the previous parts of this paper, we deal with a very simple, almost utopic problem. In this part, we give some results about more practical problem.

i.   This method can be generalized to a n-operator network to process n-source mixing.

ii.   We cannot strictly prove algorithm convergence: several studies about convergence of adaptive algorithms (Honig, 1983; Weiss and Mitra, 1979) demand many assumptions which are not very realistic for actual signals: stationarity, mixing condition, etc. Moreover, for many practical applications in adaptive filtering: echo canceller (Gritton and Lin, 1984) or equalizer (Macchi and Guidoux, 1975), these conditions are not valid, but algorithms and even devices work with good results anyways.

iii.   We have also studied cases, where the number p of primary independent sources is different of the number n of the sensors (Jutten, 1987). In practice, this case is very important, because the number of independent sources is unknown.

p < n : after convergence, p operators among the n operators of the network extract the p independent sources; the n - p remaining operators outputs are equal to zero.

p > n : there is more sources than operators. Theoretically, we cannot find exact solutions, because the problem is undetermined. However, network provides very satisfiying solutions.

iv. When the mixing is non-linear, the algorithm also provides good results (Hérault *et al.*, 1985 ; Jutten, 1987); examples 4 and 5 in part 15.2.4 demonstrate it perfectly: the images I and I' are generated from homographic transform of the initial object.

v. Learning is permanent: adaptation gain remains constant, which involves the drawback of a limited convergence accuracy, but allows to follow possible drifts of mixing, the causes of which can be various:

- ageing of the sensors,
- relative movement between the object and the cameras in stereoscopic vision,
- speakers movements in the problem of the "cocktail party " effect.

vi. It is also very important to insist on the following property of this method: the algorithm does not process directly the signals but designs a linear model of the mixing A, which explains that the nature of the sources is without relevance : sources can be deterministic or stochastic signals, with narrow or wide bandwidth , etc.

15.4 Conclusion

We would like to reiterate the novel aspect of this problem, for which the only application studied via classical methods is the processing of the "cocktail party " effect. At present time, results are not very satisfactory (Strube, 1981). We think that our algorithm provides a new and powerful approach to this difficult problem. Moreover, the various examples described in the part 15.2 of this paper prove the generality of this algorithms and suggest various applications (Jutten, 1987). In particular, it can be a very powerful pre-processing technique to increase performances of associative memories.

Independent Component Analysis (IN.C.A.) provided by this processing departs from the classical orthogonal decompositions (for instance, Principal Component decomposition), where one wants to find the best projection axis (principal axis, i.e. the one where variancy is maximum), of the distribution. Such processing is very useful to simplify decision operations, but it must be noticed that on this axis, we have always a mixing of sources signals (Jutten, 1987). In contrast, our algorithm discovers from the received signals all the independent signals necessary and sufficient to synthetize those received: it performs a decomposition by means of orthogonal functions, very different from decompositions as Fourier series or the Karhunen-Loève transform.

Using Fourier series, one chooses an orthogonal basis composed of an infinite number of components which are sine and cosine functions of various frequencies. This base is not specific, and consequently cannot be the simplest base. Our algorithm provides the simplest orthogonal base, composed of the smallest possible number of independent sources $X_i(t)$ (more complex than sine functions) and able to provide all the signals $E_j(t)$ by linear combinations of these sources $X_i(t)$.

In Karhunen-Loève transform, one also finds a representation by orthogonal functions linked to initial distribution. However, these orthogonal functions are still mixtures of primary sources. They obey only a zero covariance test and not an independence test as the transform derived from our algorithm.

In order to implement this solution to a n-source discrimination problem, it is necessary to increase computing speed. This is possible for many reasons :

- the network of operators does not need a great computation accuracy : one percent is greatly sufficient,
- each operator executes independently simple calculations (sums of products), easy to realize with parallel architecture,
- simulations demand large Input/Output capabilities, without speed reduction,
- operators must be fully interconnected.

A specific computer based on systolic architecture and both pipe-line and parallel CPU has been designed in our laboratory (Guérin, 1987). Computation speed is about 50,000 times better than the speed of classicals microcomputers (with programs written in compiled Basic run on HP 9816), but Input/Output requirements slow down a little the device. We also have studied a VLSI design of such a processor (Nunzi *et al.*, 1986). At present, the main problem is due to the great number of interconnections (n.(n-1)), which renders problematic an extension to larger network. Hybrid solutions (serial and parallel architecture) have been obtained, based on a circuit composed of several elementary cells, and very easy to extend. Each cell corresponds to a particular coefficient C_{ij} and is able to perform product $C_{ij}.S_j$ as well as the up-date of the coefficient C_{ij} according to an adaptive rule. Moreover, communication is possible from a cell to its neighbours, resolving the interconnection problem.

References

Amit, D., Gutfreund, H. & Sompolinsky, H. (1985). Spin-glass models of neural networks. *Physical review A*, **32**, 2 , 1007-18.

Anderson, J. A. (1977). Neural models with cognitive implication. In: *Basic processes in Reading*, Eds. D. Laberge & S.J. Samuel , Hillsdale, N.J. Erlbaum.

Christophe, F., Morisseau, C. (1985). Elimination auto-adaptative de brouilleurs par une méthode du gradient appliquée à un réseau lacunaire., *GRETSI* , 677-82.

Mc Culloch, W.S. & Pitts, W.H. (1943). A logical calculus of ideas immanent in nervous activity. *Bulletin of Mathematical Biophysics*, **3**, 115-33.

Gritton, C.W.K. & Lin, D.W. (1984). Echo cancellation algorithms. *IEEE Transactions on Acoustic, Speech and Signal Processing Magazine*, 30-7.

Guérin, A. (1987). C.R.A.S.Y. Un Calculateur de Réseaux Adaptatifs Systolique. Application au calcul neuromimétique. Thèse de Docteur-Ingénieur, I.N.P. Grenoble.

Hebb, D.O. (1949). The organization of behaviour. Wiley, New-York.

Hérault, J., Jutten, C. & Ans, B. (1985). Détection de grandeurs primitives dans un message composite par une architecture de calcul neuromimétique en apprentissage non supervisé. *GRETSI*, 1017-22.

Honig, M.L. (1983). Convergence models for lattice joint process estimators and least squares algorithms. *IEEE Transactions on Acoustic, Speech and Signal Processing*, **31**, 415-25.

Hopfield, J. (1982). Neural networks and physical systems with emergent computational abilities. *Proceedings of the National Academy of Science of USA*, **79**, 2554-8.

Jutten, C. (1987). Calcul neuromimétique et Traitement du Signal. Analyse en Composantes Indépendantes. Thèse d'Etat es Sciences Physiques. I.NP.-U.S.M. Grenoble.

Kohonen, T. (1984). Self-Organization and Associative Memory. Springer Verlag.

Macchi, O. (1981). Le filtrage adaptatif en télécommunications. *Annales des Télécommunications*, **36**, 615-25.

Macchi, O. & Guidoux, L. (1975). Un nouvel égaliseur : l'égaliseur à double échantillonnage. *Annales des Télécommunications*, **30**, 331-8.

Nicolas, P., Vezzosi, G. (1895). Localisation de sources ponctuelles avec une antenne de géométrie inconnue. *GRETSI*, 331-7.

Rauscheker, J.P. & Singer, W. (1981). The effects of early visual experience on the cat's visual cortex and their possible explanation by Hebb synapses. *Journal of Physiology*, **310**, 215-39.

Rosenblatt, F. (1960). Perceptron simulation experiments. *Proceedings of the I.R.E.*, **3**, 48.

Strube, H.W. (1981). Separation of several speakers recorded by two microphones (Cocktail-party effect). *Signal processing*, **3**, 355-64.

Uttley (1970). The Informon : a network for adaptive Pattern Recognition. *Journal of Theoretical Biology*, **27**, 31-67.

Weiss, A., Mitra, D. (1979). Digital adaptive filters : conditions for convergence, rate of convergence, effects of noise and errors arising from the implementation. *IEEE Transactions on Information Theory*, **25**, 637-52.

Widrow, B.(1962). Generalization and information storage in networks of Adaline neurons. In: *Self-Organizing Systems* ., Eds. M.C. Yovits, G.T. Jacobi & G.D. Goldstein, Sparten books, Washington.

NATURAL AND ARTIFICIAL MEMORY SYSTEMS

16.1 Introduction

The capacity to store and retrieve information is a property common to biological organisms and certain artefacts. In a very general way such entities, whether natural or artificial, can be described as systems, that is, as sets of interdependent events, phenomena or processes functioning as a whole. A system can be characterized by an action equation which accounts for its response (performance) and by a transition equation which describes its changes in state, that is, its trajectory (learning).

The study of systems includes theory that was originally inseparable from cybernetics. Natural and artificial systems may differ according to the nature of the data they process. From this point of view distinctions can be drawn between mechanical systems (movement), energy systems (energy) and information systems (information). But systems can be further differentiated according to their level of complexity. Thus physicochemical systems are, for example, contrasted with biological systems and social systems. Finally, types of architecture and processing can also provide criteria for a taxonomy. Thus closed systems can be distinguished from adaptative systems and self-learning from memory systems.

But what is a memory system ? Or, if one prefers, what are the structural and functional properties which justify the claim that a system has a memory ? In a first approximation a memory system can be characterized as a system capable of retrieving, in whole or in part, faithfully or with distortion, one of its earlier states in order to reproduce it or to have it interact with its current state. A system of this type is characterized by a one-way trajectory which may be adapted or not (but this depends radically on the point of view of the observer of the system). A memory system necessarily comprises some feedback capacities, be they small or great. An elementary memory system may be made up of a single feedback loop, which Von Foerster (1965) called a 'cognitive tile'. However the most complex memory systems are the result of the recursive embedding of a large number of such loops.

A complete description of a memory system should therefore specify its design, the nature and format of elementary units of information and the properties of its encoding, storage and retrieval functions. It is obvious that the human cognitive system is one of the most complex memory systems known. A lot of effort has gone into attempts at a satisfactory description of its structure and functioning. Nevertheless models are purely metaphorical in nature (Roediger III, 1980) and human memory has been compared in turn to a wax tablet (Plato, Aristotle) to vast palaces (St Augustine, James), to muscular strength (Woodworth), to the computer (Simon, Feigenbam), to a library (Broadbent), to a hologram (Pribram), to a tape recorder (Posner), to a lock (Kolers), to a dictionary (Loftus), and even to a garbage can (Landauer).

There has been an overabundance of metaphors but so far no description which can claim the general assent of researchers in cognitive sciences. Nowadays models of human memory fall into rival classes according to whether or not they derive from the design and functionalities of computers of the Von Neumann type.

16.2 Symbolic information processing

The symbolic information-processing models of human memory assume more or less complete isomorphism between the human memory system and artificial memories that we are at present capable of building.

16.2.1 General properties

These 'information-processing' models assume that human memory can be described as an information processing system made up of elementary processing modules arranged in sequence. This organization may be strict, that is, a module can be applied to data only after it has been fully processed by the lower level module. However, sequential organization is not incompatible with a serial, parallel or cascade processing model (Mc Clelland, 1979). The activation of the various modules and the transfer of whole sets of processes defined by design of this sort is applied to discrete information units stored in specific loci of permanent memory. This sort of spatial organization of memory information is one of the most striking properties of 'data-processing' models (spatial metaphor).

The model of human memory worked out by Atkinson & Shiffrin (1968) may be taken as a prototype of this class of models since they draw distinctions between short-term memory (highly similar to the buffer of the computer), a long term memory (which can be compared to the central memory of the computer) and control processes (like the computer control unit). Each processing module has specific properties: limited or unlimited capacities, serialization or organization of information and information decay or interference, to mention only a few.

A more recent model is that proposed by Anderson (1983), under the name ACT*. He differentiates a working memory in which the current situation and outcome of memory processing are represented. This transitory working memory is in constant relation with a long term memory of the declarative type and a long-term memory of the procedural type. The former stores factual or conceptual data in a semantic network; the latter stores procedures in the form of more or less compacted production rules (ifthen). These procedures are applied to declarative knowledge and to representations of current situation in working memory. This can give rise to or modify declarative knowledge, generate or modify new procedures and also modify the current state of working memory.

Both the above models have the general characteristics of 'information-processing' models: modularity, sequential organization, control processes, discrete memory units, spatial organization of memory traces. Their functional designs differ however since Atkinson & Shiffrin's model (1968) is of rather basic data processing structure whereas Anderson's (1983) bears more resemblance to expert systems.

16.2.2 *Specific problems*

Obviously not all the problems raised by the functioning of human memory are a matter of choice of architecture. Problems to be solved are in fact of three sorts:

a) What is the nature and the format of memory encoding and how is sensory and perceptual information transformed into permanent or transitory memory representation units ?

b) What are the processes, deliberate or automatic, through which memory information can be retrieved or reactivated ?

c) Finally, how is information organized in permanent memory ?

16.2.2.1 Coding format and encoding process

The variety of sensory information received by the memory system is considerable (different sensory modalities, visual images or scenes, speech, symbols). This sensory and perceptual information is first transformed or encoded before being represented in memory. The nature of this encoding has given rise to a fair number of experimental controversies and theoretical debates. Paivio (1976) defended the hypothesis of the double (verbal and iconic) encoding for perceptual information. Double encoding is supposed to affect mainly images and perceptual scenes, its efficiency decreasing with concrete words and even more with abstract ones. This position was attacked by Anderson (1978) who put forward the hypothesis that all perceptual information is encoded in abstract and propositional form regardless of its original nature (iconic or verbal). However attractive this interpretation may seem it does not suffice to account for the empirically observed superiority of iconic over verbal memory. In view of this experimental failure it is understandable that several researchers (Kosslyn & Pomerantz, 1977; Pylyshyn, 1973) should prefer the option of different encoding levels:

a) A deep level of encoding, abstract in nature, which can be formalized propositionally.

b) A more superficial level where iconic and verbal codes may co-exist. Here the date-processing metaphor is obvious since the first level of encoding can, for example, be compared to computer machine language and the second level to multi-format representation which can be generated by this language on the outputs of the system.

Is there any real need moreover to distinguish between two specialized processing modules for memory information? In other words is there any need for separate short-term and long-term memories with different structural and functional properties: decay of trace and absence of organization in one case, interference and organization in the other, for example. The fact is that this theoretical distinction can be dispensed with and some do prefer to speak of the activated portion of permanent memory as working memory, corresponding to the current situation or blackboard of computer scientists. At the present time a good deal of research is being done on the laws of activation processes and of spread of activation in permanent memory.

16.2.2.2 Retrieval in memory.

Information processing models of human memory assume that memory representations are stored in permanent memory once and for all (except in cases of damage to the neurological hardware). They are stored at specific loci in memory space. Thus, in data-processing models, permanent memory is spatially organized and can be directly accessed.

Access to memory representations is possible through an automatic or deliberate sequential search process, structured by relations of a semantic order. This search metaphor is the necessary corollary of the spatial metaphor. From this point of view, for all the sophistication of its hypotheses of memory organization and the retrieval procedures involved, the 'data-processing' model is not fundamentally different from the vast palaces of memory of St Augustine or the memory theatre of the Renaissance Kabbala (Yates, 1975). Only the technical reference is different, electronic space replacing town planning space. The underlying logic is the same in spite of the miniaturization of referential space through advances in micro-technology.

In view of this situation how can we explain the phenomena of 'forgetting' so characteristic of human memory ? Here there is one distinction that plays an important heuristic role: that between the concepts of availability and accessibility in memory. It is claimed that a memory representation is always available in permanent memory but may temporarily be inaccessible. In other words what we call 'forgetting' results from a failure of the search process in memory space as a result of interference between memory representations or by reason of a deficiency of triggering ones and the orientation of memory search. Contextualist theories (Tulving, 1985; Tiberghien, 1986a) have made it clear that forgetting is linked to absence of similarity and of semantic compatibility between contextual conditions of the creation of memory trace and contextual conditions of retrieval. Admittedly another cause is frequently cited: forgetting through encoding failure (failure to construct or consolidate a permanent memory trace). But this is really pseudo-forgetting since the representation is never actually stored in permanent memory and can not be accessible because it is not available.

16.2.2.3 Organization of memory
Thus 'symbolic information processing' models assume memory to be a sort of space. Admittedly this space can be viewed as subject to no definite laws of organization since Landauer (1975) worked out a model of memory in which laws of storage and search process are not determined by the nature or characteristics of memory information. Memory space is three dimensional and proximity of storage addresses in this space is determined solely by temporal proximity of successive encoding. The search process results from activation diffused symmetrically in all three dimensions at constant speed. A process of this sort is both serial and parallel and the order of access to various loci in space is strictly random. Here memory is totally passive and unorganized, efficiency depending solely on the spatial scope of search. As Landauer states: ordering in a memory of this sort is more like that of waste in a garbage can than that of lexical items in a dictionary (Landauer, 1975 p. 302). In spite of its apparent structural and functional simplicity this waste paper model does account effectively for a certain number of learning and forgetting phenomena. It should be pointed out, however, that out views of this sort are in a small minority; most 'data-processing' models conceding that permanent memory is structured and that memory representations do not all have the same status.

Thus Tulving (1983) distinguishes memory representations of a semantic nature from those of an episodic nature. The former is factual or conceptual knowledge independent of the personal experience of the individual, the latter refers to autobiographic, personally experienced knowledge corresponding to events localized in time and space. Semantic representations are seen as highly organized on the basis of conceptual relations, whereas the encoding of episodic representations is seen as mainly temporal. Moreover access to semantic representation is seen as largely automatic, whereas access to episodic representation is the outcome of a deliberate choice of the individual.

The memory traces of episodes in various contexts may lead to the generation of a semantic representation (abstraction and schematisation processes) whereas the memory trace of an episode in constant context preserves the contextual specificity and thus the episodic character (specification process). Tulving also maintains that access to the two classes of representation involves different mechanisms: resonance between memory representations and perceptual experience or inference and reconstructive processes. Furthermore access to semantic representations does not modify the state of the memory system whereas access to episodic memory does affect memory traces. The distinctions between episodic and semantic memory has played a leading heuristic role in the study of phenomena of retrieval and forgetting. There is strong experimental evidence in its favour since the amnesic syndrome characteristically involves perturbation of the episodic memory while the functioning of semantic memory remains relatively intact.

Nevertheless, on the theoretical level the relations between the two types of memory are far from clear: is it necessary to dissociate them so radically ? Should episodic memory be regarded as embedded in semantic memory ? Is the distinction really necessary; isn't the semantic register rich and flexible enough to encode both concepts and personally experienced events ?

Besides, the above distinction does not cover all memory representations as Larsen (1985) has most pertinently shown. He draws a distinction between situational specificity (strong or weak) and personal specificity (strong or weak). The crossing of these two dimensions defines four classes of representation: episodic representations of strong situational and personal specificity: semantic representations of weak situational or personal specificity; representations related to personal identity, of weak situational and strong personal specificity and finally, historic or factual representations of strong situational and weak personal specificity. Clearly Tulving's dichotomy lumps together identity representations and episodic ones on the one hand and historical and conceptual representations on the other. But it is not inconceivable that the four classes of representation and modes of access to them may not be strictly reducible (Tiberghien and Audeghy, 1985).

There is another distinction which is rather popular at the moment, that between declarative and procedural representations. The criterion here is very different since declarative knowledge is made up of representation of facts or events which can be consciously recalled and verbalized whereas procedural knowledge (cognitive or motor skills) cannot be consciously recalled and is hard to verbalize. These two classes of representation may be stored in different memory modules and organized in specific ways. Thus Anderson (1983) assumes that declarative representations are organized on the basis of a semantic network and procedural knowledge on that of a production system. This distinction serves to show how the supposed structuring of memory representation is linked to descriptive models. The three main models used to describe declarative knowledge are: list structure; tree structure or semantic network and schemata.

Declarative representations can be easily rewritten as formulae consisting of a predicate associated with one or several arguments. This sort of structure is easy to translate into programming language LISP (Anderson, 1983). It is also possible to describe a body of declarative knowledge in the form of a semantic network consisting of nodes linked by various logical relationships (agent, object, etc.). These two formalizations are quite isomorphic and it is theoretically possible to pass at any moment from one to the other.

The last type of formalization of declarative knowledge concerns much larger sets from network units or lists. A schema is the product of the integration and generalization of specific items of knowledge. Whereas a proposition may be general or specific, a schema is always a very general representation of a set of characteristic features of an object or a situation but is not a full description. For example the schematic representation of a 'fish' bears only on features essential to the recognition of this category of animal. Schematic representation must not be confused with a prototypic representation which is simply a specific and representative exemplar of a category of objects or situations. A prototypic representation always provides a full description of the object or a situation (example: 'sparrow' can be taken as a prototype of the category 'bird'). The advantage of schematic and prototypic representations is that they make it possible to encode large sets of knowledge in a concentrated and readily accessible form. The synthetic nature of such knowledge is in clear contrast with the basically analytic character of propositional representation.

Procedural knowledge is much less amenable to formalization by reason no doubt of its dynamic, automatic and 'non verbalizable' character. Knowledge like this requires direct temporal encoding and involves more or less complete causal relations. The stimulus-response paradigm proposed by behaviourism was one of the earliest attempts to formalize procedural knowledge. Procedural knowledge required for the performance of a complete action is described as a succession of links between stimuli and responses, the latter in their turn producing stimuli, thus ensuring the continuity of the procedural sequence. However in this sort of description behaviourism obviously could not include the least non-observable phenomenon. The stimulus-response schema and its mediational variants was irreconcilable with the concept of mental and memory representation. Furthermore, in this conception of the problem the stimuli and responses were quite definite and highly specific events. But the fact is that the human subject often responds to configurations of stimuli and produces responses of too complex an organization to fit into such a summary description.

Production systems are an attempt to overcome the above difficulties. This formalization derives from the work of the mathematician Post (1943) on rewriting rules. Newell and Simon (1972) used this in an endeavor to describe the behavior of the human subject in problem-solving situations. This is the type of formalization that gave rise to expert systems which play such an important part in artificial intelligence at the moment. A production rule is made up of condition and action parts. Both of these may include several conditions and several actions which makes possible a much closer description of action sequences triggered by configurations of events. Moreover, contrary to the stimulus-response paradigm, production rules may be general or specific and also allow for the description of mental representations (knowledge, goal).

Finally, action schemas (scripts, scenarios) make it possible to give a schematic description of procedural knowledge. There is a clear isomorphism between these procedural schemata and declarative schemata just as there is a relative isomorphism between production systems and semantic networks. Action schemata are structured, stereotyped, complex action sequences (example: restaurant script, administrative formalities scripts, flight procedures script for air-traffic controllers). They are general bodies of knowledge resulting from the integration of numerous experiences in similar situations and are easily activated. Like declarative schemata, action schemata are highly flexible for, although parameters are predetermined for some of their dimensions, they are optional for others.

Symbolic information processing models of human memory have given rise to much more precise descriptions and formalizations of what was often vaguely referred to as knowledge. The effort of classification has made possible the development of systems for handling knowledge based on one or the other of these types of formalization. Technological successes in imitating and simulating memory are however confined to perfectly circumscribed situations and the degree of generality of knowledge taxonomies may often be questioned. Several problems are still pending:

a) What, for instance, is the relationship between semantic and episodic knowledge ?

b) How can procedural knowledge be built up from declarative knowledge and vice-versa ? How can the following bi-polar factors be integrated into taxonomies of this sort: general-specific, automatic-deliberate, verbalizable-non verbalizable ?

c) Last, but not least, is the proliferation of varying systems of knowledge due to anything more than playing around with re-writing rules ? In other words the types of formalization briefly described here are relatively interchangeable. Does this not mean that the diversity of knowledge forms and their modelisation have something in common which can only be modelled at a lower level of description ? Other models can be used in an endeavour to explore this hidden lower level of the structure of human memory.

16.3 Connectionist and neo-connectionist model of human memory

All the models described above are based on a certain number of assumptions that can in fact be radically challenged. This shift in view-point will rely necessarily on other analogies for human memory. Symbolic information processing models of human memory are the consequence of the fascination of so many researchers with the efficiency and versatility of artificial data-processing systems. But, when all is said and done, what remains to be explained is real human memory, memory as displayed by a natural machine whose efficiency and versatility are, after all, so much greater than those of even our most efficient artefacts.

It is true that although we know the structure and composition of the machines we build, we know almost nothing about the design architecture and functionalities of our own central nervous system. Date-processing metaphors cannot break through the barrier of 10^{10} neurons of the human brain. 'Natural' modelisation, simplified to a reasonable degree might be preferable to complex technological modelisations which have, in view of the state of our neurological knowledge, virtually no chance of validation. At the end of the Second World War cybernetics had already taken up the challenge and certain of its conjectures, regarded at the time as rather wild, are now being taken seriously, mainly because symbolic calculation power is now reaching theoretical limits.

16.3.1 *General properties*

Symbolic information processing models of human memory draw a careful distinction between the structure of a memory system (architecture design) and its functionalities.

This modular conception may be rejected in favour of a theoretical view in which structure can no longer be dissociated from its functions. For instance, a functional network is a special structure of data-processing in which knowledge is no more than the state of the system at a given moment. Furthermore, the assumption of a strictly sequential architecture design of human memory collapses when neurological and behavioral data are examined closely. The central nervous system is characterized by numerous feed-back loops and a high degree of interaction between its parts. The sensitivity of human activities to context effects, which was discussed earlier, is probably the behavioral consequence of the massively parallel organization of the central nervous system. Another property of human memory is its highly adaptive, and even auto-adaptive character since new forms of knowledge can be generated from a variety of experiences. Such auto-adaptation is obviously not a feature of our existing artificial memories or at least the programming heuristics at present being applied only allow restricted 'rediscoveries' that up to now hold no surprise for the human programmer. Another property of our memory is the continuous character of the processing of information which cannot easily be reduced to discrete units. What are, for instance, the discrete units that make face recognition possible ?

Finally the above models all rely to a greater or lesser extent on a spatial metaphor where each memory trace is stored in a definite locus in memory space. This metaphor may be escaped from and it is possible to conceive of memory systems in which information is not precisely located but spread over the whole of the system (distributed memory). All the information contained in the system would, in a sense, be localized in all its parts.

16.3.2 *Connectionist models*

The architecture of connectionist and neuro-mimetic models is a systematic application of these principles. Architecture of this sort takes the form of a network of 'neuromimes'. Each neuron modelised is characterized by a variable synaptic weight. Input information modifies the synaptic weight of the neuron but, and this point is crucial, output information feeds back to the whole set of neurons.

Here we have a system wholly looped back on itself. If a definite pattern of information is presented to this system, synaptic weights will be modified as a function of time and may tend to a point of equilibrium. This state may be identified as the trace of the pattern in the neuromimetic network. The permanent feedback system explains why the representation of a memorized pattern cannot be located precisely in the neuromimetic structure. Here the whole is not the sum of the parts but in a certain sense the whole is in each part of the network.

Thus in the last analysis it is a configuration of synaptic weights that is encoded by the neuromimetic system. A system of this sort can learn and memorize patterns (pattern here refers to an ordered set of values). Memory can be distributed, that is, entirely delocalized, and the notion of memory search or retrieval is rather meaningless when the problem is viewed in this way. In a connectionist system retrieving information simply consists of reproducing the memorized pattern in the presence of an access key (Ans, 1986).

At present a number of studies are being done on architectures of this sort. They involve simulating the behaviour of neuromimetic network on the digital computers at present available. Matrix computation is obviously the most appropriate mathematical formalization for these trials since the feedback loop mentioned earlier defines a matrix ; the values on the matrix represent the synaptic weights at a given moment. In elementary situations simulations like these can account for cued recall, recognition and even recognition of prototypes. However it is not yet at all clear how these models could be used to account for contextualist laws of human memory (auto-association and hetero-association). Moreover any increase of the number of neuromimes entails a considerable increase of the amount of noise in the pattern reproduced in the presence of an access key. Finally there is no guarantee of the system's achieving equilibrium since this is actually the outcome of self-adaptation. The achievement of equilibrium is highly dependent on the initial values attributed to synaptic weights.

It must further be noted that these architectures are only partially consistent with our neurological and neurophysiological knowledge. Admittedly, the central nervous system's capacity for recovery after injury is far from negligible and this is an argument in favour of distributed memory. Furthermore, the existence of feed-back loops in the CNS has been known for a long time. However, various brain structures are also relatively specialized and it would be inaccurate to say that everything is connected with everything else. Need we remind ourselves again that the relation between neuromimetic architecture design and the brain is also highly metaphorical ?

16.3.3 *Neo-holographic models*

Thus symbolic information processing and 'neuro-mimetic' models can be taken as radically opposed. However there are some models which fall between the two extremes ; the neo-holographic models for example.

Neo-holographic models assume that human memory, like a hologram, has the property of distribution of information throughout the whole of memory space. But whereas neo-connectionist architecture designs associate this notion of distribution with the actual structure of neuromimes, neo-holographic models restrict it to the concept of trace. Both classes of models reject the spatial metaphor but though neo-connectionist models assume memory to be structured as a network, neo-holographic models retain the functional and modular view of symbolic information processing models. Neo-holographic models include a set of sequentially organized information processing modules. Neo-holographic memory does not have the self-adapting character of neuromimetic models since it is strictly bound to input and output and does not have the complex feed-back structure of neuromimetic models. Finally neo-holographic models process discrete units of information which can be dissociated from processing modules ;

in neuromimetic networks on the contrary both structural and functional information is made up of continuous variations of the configuration of synaptic weights. Seen in this way the concept of (active and intentional) memory search is meaningless in both types of models. Whereas learning and retrieval processes are clearly dissociated in neo-holographic memory, they have no differentiated theoretical status in neuromimetic memory.

The CHARM (Composite Holographic Associative Recall Model) model devised by Eich (1982) is one of the best worked out neo-holographic models of the last decade. The model describes information entering the memory system as patterns of features encoded in the form of positive or negative numeric values of variable similarity.

With this model it is possible to account for interference phenomena, recall situations and prototype extraction. It is even possible to formalise context effects. However CHARM is only applicable to recall situations and extension of it to recognition situations raises problems, the solutions of which are by no means clear (auto-convolution, decision processes).

16.4 Conclusion

In the attempts to explain the structure and processing laws of human memory there are two main research directions or, if one prefers, two contrasting modelisation styles:

a) A 'bionic' (or neuromimetic or computer bionic) style which draws inspiration from the structural and functional properties of the central nervous system for its models and perhaps for machines in which their essential properties could be preserved.

b) A symbolic information processing (or computer-symbolic) style in which the inspiration for description and explanation of natural processes is drawn from the structural and functional properties of artefacts within the scope of present day technology (the approach of classic artificial intelligence).

This opposition is in part the consequence of the uncontested monopoly of symbolic computers of the Von Neumann type. The technological success of these information systems has ended up by convincing many researchers that the human cognitive system is governed by the same computational rules. This monopoly situation has favoured the proliferation of symbolic information processing models of human memory especially since the only tools available for simulation were of the Von Neumann type. The situation may change however if machines of a different type can be wired up to give performances equal or superior to those obtained with earlier designs. Once we actually get round to the wiring up of neo-connectionist machines, it will no doubt become possible to judge the real efficiency of the underlying models.

From a theoretical point of view, this tension between radically opposed types of architecture is the symptom of unresolved debate.

a) Is memory organized or not ? In the affirmative, what is the nature of this organization and how can it be formalized (propositional logic, semantic network, production system) ?

b) Is memory localized or distributed ?

c) Is retrieval in memory the consequence of an oriented and perhaps deliberate search process and/or does it simply result from a 'resonance' or 'echo' mechanism which includes a greater or lesser amount of noise?

On these points there is total opposition between symbolic information processing and connectionist models. We have seen, however, that some mixed models have managed to emerge and these attempt to integrate concepts and mechanisms from both the computer-symbolic and the neuro-bionic trends (see for example CHARM, Minerva 2 of Hintzman, 1984). This theoretical solution should not be neglected as it may be the most apt to take into account the complexity of the empirical data on the functioning of human memory that has been gathered so far. We have, in fact, seen that none of the models accounts satisfactorily for the distinction between semantic (or conceptual) and episodic memory. But there is a great deal of experimental evidence for this distinction, the most spectacular being that of amnesic syndromes in which episodic memory alone is affected. Nor does any model integrate context effects in a really satisfactory way, in particular where recognition situations are concerned.

In our view, these difficulties can be traced back to the basically asymmetrical character of human memory. The human brain is probably a mixed system and perhaps doubly so. Indeed there is no reason not to suppose that there are different structural and functional levels of information processing; 'neuromimetic' and symbolic information processing architecture are not really on the same level. On a lower level of neuronal organization information might be distributed and on a higher level it might, after a reunitarisation process, be quite localizable and expressible in symbolic form (Hofstadter, 1985). A system of vertical and horizontal connections of this type is not incompatible with the column architecture of cortical cells. This would explain the fact that some brain damage is reversible and some is not. The relative hemispheric specialization is also a problem that has not yet been integrated into existing models. It is true that it is not yet by any means clear what might be the structural origin and functional significance of this specialization (parallel, analogic, iconic, or contextual processing for the right hemisphere and sequential, digital, verbal, or local for the left). Though it is not yet really understood, this hemispheric differentiation is one more argument in favour of a model of an asymmetrical type with both the symbolic properties of 'data-processing' models and some analogical properties of connectionist models.

Further, human memory seems to provide for both automatic retrieval (resonance) and deliberate, active, orientated search. There is no point in attempting to explain only one of these aspects and ignoring large amounts of experimental data (Tiberghien & Lecocq, 1983; Peris & Tiberghien, 1984): retrieval in memory is at least partially a process of intentional search guided by contextual information associated with the act of remembering (Tiberghien, Cauzinille & Mathieu, 1979; Tiberghien, 1984; Tiberghien, 1986b).

The really striking factor of the present situation is, finally, a considerable destabilisation due to the theoretical opposition between basically antagonistic models. It is to be expected that this situation will give rise to attempts at unification and the exploration of new avenues. Some important problems have been temporarily neglected as well.

Sooner or later they will have to be raised. I refer in particular to the integration of the affect, which may also be a form of knowledge, into models of human memory (Mandler, 1985). But this is another and so far unwritten story...

References

Anderson, J.R. (1978). Arguments concerning representations for mental imagery. *Psychological Review*, **85**, 249-77.

Anderson, J.R. (1983). *Architecture of Cognition*. (MA) Harvard University Press.

Ans, B. (1986). Mémoire associative et réseaux adaptatifs. *Neuro-sciences et sciences de l'ingénieur*. IIIème Journées, Marseille ronéotypé.

Atkinson, R.C. & Shiffrin, R.M. (1968). Human Memory: A Proposed System and its Control Processes. In: *The Psychology of Learning and Motivation: Advances in Research and Theory*, Eds. K.M. Spence & J.T. Spence, New York: Academic Press.

Eich, J.M. (1982). A composite holographic associative recall model. *Psychological Review*, **89**, 627-61.

Hintzman, D.L. (1984). Minerva 2: a simulation model of human memory. *Behavior Research Methods, Instruments & Computers*, **16** (2), 96-101.

Hoffstadter, D. (1985). *Göder, Escher et Bach: Les trois brins d'une guirlande éternelle*. Paris: Inter Editions.

Kosslyn, S. & Pomerantz, J.R. (1977). Imagery, propositions and the form of internal representations. *Cognitive psychology*, **9**, 52-76.

Landauer, T.K. (1975). Memory without organization: properties of a model with random storage and undirected retrieval. *Cognitive psychology*, **7**, 495-531.

Larsen, S.F. (1985). Specific knowledge and knowledge updating. In *Foregrounding backgrounding*., Eds J. Allwood & E. Helmquist, Stockholm: Doxa.

Mandler, G. (1985). *Cognitive Psychology : An Essay in Cognitive Science*. Hillsdale, N.J.: Lawrence Erlbaum.

Mc Clelland, J.L. (1979) On the time relation of mental processes : an examination of systems of processes in cascade. *Psychological Review*, **86**, 287-330.

Newell, A. & Simon H.A. (1972). *Human Problem Solving*. Englewood Cilffs, NJ: Prentice Hall.

Paivo, A. (1976). Imagery in Recall and Recognition. In: *Recall and Recognition*, Ed. J. Brown, Londres, Wiley.

Peris, J.L. & Tiberghien, E. (1984). Effets de contexte et recherche conditionnelle dans la reconnaissance de visages non familiers.*Cahiers de Psychologie Cognitive*, **4**, 323-34.

Post, E.L. (1943). Formal reductions of the general combination decision problem. *American Journal of Mathematics*, **65**, 197-268.

Pylyshyn, Z. (1973). What the mind's eye tells the mind's brain: a critique of mental imagery. *Psychological Bulletin*, **80**, 1-24.

Roediger III, H.L. (1980). Memory metaphors in cognitive psychology. *Memory & Cognition*, **8**, 231-56.

Tiberghien, G. (1984). Just how does euphoria work ? *The Behavioral and Brain Sciences*, **7**,   255-56.

Tiberghien, G. (1986 a). Intelligence, mémoire et artifices. In: *Psychologie, Intelligence artificielle et Automatique*, Eds. J.M. Hoc & G. Tiberghien, Bruxelles: Mardaga.

Tiberghien, G. (1986 b). Context and Cognition. *European Bulletin of Cognitive Psychology (Cahiers de Psychology cognitive)*. Special issue, **6**, 105-21.

Tiberghien, G. & Audeghy, N. (1985). La planification du dialogue dans les systèmes de communications automatisés. *Cognitiva 85 : de l'intelligence artificielle aux biosciences*. Paris: CESTA.

Tiberghien, G., Cauzinille, E. & Mathieu, J. (1979). Pre-decision and conditional search in long-term recognition memory. *Acta Psychologica*, **43**, 329-43.

Tiberghien, G. & Lecocq, P. (1983). *Rappel et Reconnaissance*. Presses Universitaires de Lille.

Tulving, E. (1983). *Elements of Episodic Memory*, Oxford University Press.

Von Foerster, H. (1965). Memory without record. In: *The anatomy of memory*, Ed. D.P. Kimble, Palo Alto: Science and Behavior Books.

Yates, F. (1975). *L'art de la mémoire*, Paris: Gallimard.

PART 3

MEDICAL DECISION MAKING AND EXPERT SYSTEMS IN BIOMEDICINE

The early 1970s saw the birth of the expert system concept. The early 1980s have seen a certain flowering of it, but at the same time, we have met some important difficulties in putting this concept into practice and making it really useful in everyday life for human investigation.

Although a range of expert system (ES), most of them being based on production rules, are famous, pure artificial intelligence (AI) is not enough to solve complex problems. Cognitive science, however, both embodies and enhance AI, as the conference on which this book is based has shown.

Indeed, the third day of this three-day conference succinctly but convincingly illustrated some well-grounded methods of AI and their limits, however the research trend that emerged is pushing back those limits.

We shall not commit the fault and the injustice of classifying the various chapters into arbitrary and limiting categories, nevertheless we can discern three main axes that every chapter more or less contains:

- the first axis is the affirmation or the confirmation of a methodology for expert system building. This methodology is undoubtedly extremely difficult to establish and seems to be partially re-invented with the building of every new expert system.

- the second axis is the integration of specialized expert systems as a part of more complex processes. Integration is essential because of the necessity to export expert systems from their place of inception and make them fully operational, and also to verify their indispensability and the reasons for putting them at the heart of vast research and development issues.

- the third axis corresponds to the fundamental research and conceptual innovation in AI and ES, in particular, knowledge representation, inferential strategies, knowledge acquisition and learning, etc.

Finally, we hope that readers will benefit greatly from their reading of the chapters, and will find some responses to their questions.

17 *P. Aubas, M. Chein, O. Cogis and P. Dujols*

AN AI APPROACH TO THE FOLLOW-UP
OF CLINICAL ONCOLOGY THERAPEUTIC STRATEGIES

17.1 Introduction

We are concerned with application domains where parts of the knowledge are imprecise, incomplete and/or doubtful and where "la connaissance est de nature largement implicite, où elle repose sur des présupposés ou des arguments souvent implicites et où elle se traduit par des savoir-faire pratiques ou des productions discursives" (Borillo, 1984).

As with any application, some usual analysis, in the conventional data processing sense, is to be performed. But it won't suffice to produce knowledge that is stable enough, nor all the knowledge eventually needed in order to solve the problem.

It is possible to analyze some parts of the knowledge beforehand, that is before running a complete version of a program using real data samples, and this knowledge will be implemented using conventional models. But it turns out that this is not possible for all the knowledge involved in the process.

In order to express some parts of his/her knowledge, and ultimately give it a definite model, a domain specialist needs to be able to test and modify, in a non monotonic incremental way, what he/she thinks is involved in the problem solving process (bearing in mind that parts of it might eventually appear as inaccurate), through first program versions running on relevant real data samples.

From now on, this paper will refer to this kind of knowledge only, that is knowledge to be "elicited" interactively by running a program, testing and incrementally modifying both the data structure and the way to handle it (Keravnou *et al.*, 1986).

Thus the models we are looking for should be more flexible than conventional ones. For instance we assume that it is not possible to decide beforehand what will be the objects if one intends to use an object oriented approach, nor to specify the relation fields if relational data bases are to be thought of. These elements are to evolve while things are taking place and it might even be an extra difficulty to decide on whether this and that should be an object, a relation, an attribute, a value or whatsoever.

And because it will be the expert responsibility to "debug" the knowledge representation, the model must be simple enough to be understood by the domain expert (a doctor, a go player, a headmaster...), any specialist interested in his/her own domain and not willing to become a computer science expert.

The system this paper deals with is based on rooted trees with labels attached to edges and leaf nodes (that is nodes which are end-points on the tree), which we call "i-trees" (Chein et al., 1986). This model bears what we think to be nice qualities, as labelled rooted trees are :
   - well known and well studied as abstract items,
   - easy to modify and work upon,
   - easy to understand by non trained persons,
   - easy to implement.
In addition we can view a labelled rooted tree as one knowledge unit and take advantage of the versatility of its possible interpretations, for instance :
   - as a "semantic" access to information attached to the leaf nodes : sequences of edge labels (usually words referring to the domain knowledge) leads from the root to some leaf node and thus to the label attached to that node;
   - as a "grouping" of sentences expressed by the specialist, if edge labels are significant enough so as to strongly suggest a "sentence" when "reading" a path from the root to the leaf node;
   - as implementing K-ary relations or predicates : the edge labels of some path can be understood, some as part of the relation or predicate name, others as name of the k-uple elements;
   - as recording "objects" implemented as sub-trees.
As the knowledge elicitation and setting up take place and the general structure becomes clearer, we formalize the structure through the notion of genericity, a binary relation among i-trees which :
   - takes into account the conventional notion of instantiation in a specific way,
   - expresses the implicit structure induced by the data processing
   - stands as a first design of the knowledge organization.

The data processing itself is made by means of a few basic tree manipulating functions which are used basically in a reflex oriented programing way. This seems to be relevant to many "practical know-how" involved in the application domains we are interested in (Chein et al., 1986 1987). We do not address the dynamic aspect of our exploratory programing work in this paper, confining ourselves in its static aspects.

In section 17.2 we present a formal definition of i-trees and their handling.

In section 17.3, as an illustration of our approach, we briefly sketch the static knowledge used in performing the first generic task (in the sense of Chandrasekaran, 1986) of our medical application, namely "patient entry in a protocol".

In section 17.4 we briefly state a few aspects of the progress of our work.

17.2 i-Trees and Genericity

17.2.1 *i-Trees*

17.2.1.1 1-Trees

An l-tree T is $T = (X, U, E, e)$ where :

- (X,U) is an oriented rooted tree, with X the set of nodes and U the set of edges;
- $e : U \to E$ is a mapping, with E the set of edge labels.

A rooted path labelling of T is either any sequence $(e(u1), e(u2),..., e(uk))$, $k \geq 1$, where $(u1, u2,..., uk)$ is a path in T starting at the root of T, or $\neg$ the empty sequence.

The family of rooted path labellings of T is denoted by $a(T)$ or $s(T)$ when it is restricted to paths in T from the root to leaf nodes of T (that is corresponding to maximal paths in T). $a(T)$ and $s(T)$ are families rather than sets because of possible duplicities (two different paths might have the same labelling).

We define a hierarchy for l-trees :

class I : any l-tree
class II : l-trees T for which $s(T)$ is a set
class III : l-trees T for which no element of $s(T)$ is the labelling of any other rooted path
class IV : l-trees T for which $a(T)$ is a set ; l-trees in class IV are called injective l-trees and if T is an injective l-tree, $a(T)$ is called the set of accesses to T.

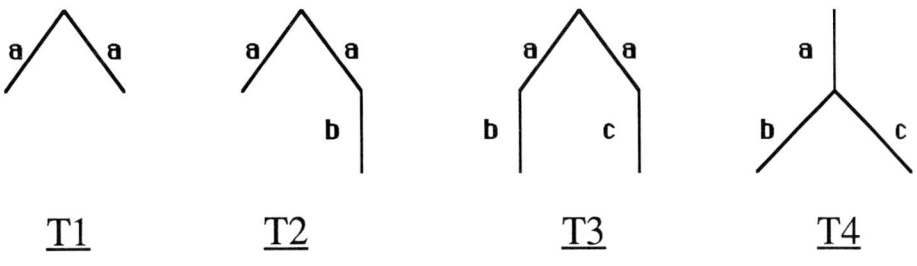

Figure 17.1. Examples of l-trees

- $T_1[I - II, T_2 [II - III, T_3 [III - IV, T_4 [IV$
- $I 1 II 1 III 1 IV$
- $T [II$ iff any element of $s(T)$ is associated to exactly one leaf node of T

- T [III iff any element of s(T) is associated to exactly one node of T (this is a leaf node)
- T [IV iff any element of a(T) is associated to exactly one node of T

iff ¢ x, y, z [X, xy, xz [U implies e(xy) ≠ e(xz) (that is e is locally injective).

T å$_p$ T' stands for the following :
- there exist edges xy and xz in T' with same labelling e(xy) = e(xz)
- T is obtained from T' by identifying y and z (e.g. T3 å$_p$ T4).

å$_p$ induces an order relation on class I denoted by <$_p$ for which the set of minimum elements is IV. Moreover , given any T [I , there exists a unique T$_0$ in IV such that T$_0$ <$_p$ T, and T$_0$ is denoted by i(T). Note that <$_p$ is compatible with the number of nodes of l-trees.

¬$_i$ denotes the equivalence relation on class I defined by : T ¬$_i$ T' iff i(T) = i(T').

The hierarchy of l-trees is partitioned by ¬$_i$ in such a way that :
- equivalence class of T in IV is the singleton {T}
- equivalence class of T in III is the interval for <$_p$ with i(T) as minimum and with maximum element the star of maximum rooted paths in T (that is the l-tree for which the root is the only node to have possibly more than one successor and with same maximum rooted paths as T);
- equivalence class of T in II is the interval for <$_p$ with i(T) as minimum element and with maximum element the star of rooted paths in T.

17.2.1.2. Sums of products and normal forms.
Let ¬ { E and let E be recursively defined by :
    - ¬ [E
    - I being some set if a$_i$ [E and P$_i$ [E for i [I, then Σ a$_i$ p$_i$ [E
E is called the set of E-expressions.

If the sum is thought as associative and commutative , one can define a one-to-one correspondence between l-trees and E-expressions :
    - ¬ corresponds to the l-tree with one node
    - the sum of two E-expressions corresponds to the identification of roots
    - the product a P, with a [E and P [E, corresponds to the identification of the endpoint of an edge labelled "a" with the root of the l-tree corresponding to P.

If one considers the sum to be a boolean sum with ¬ being neutral and if one uses the left distributivity of the product , one can get the E-expression corresponding to i(T) from the E-expression corresponding to T .

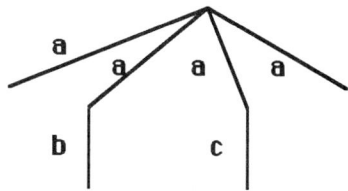

Figure 17.2. Example : corresponds to a¬ + ab¬ + ac¬ + a¬ rewritten as 2a + ab + ac .

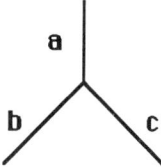

Figure 17.3. Example : corresponds to a(b+c).

Orthogonality.

Let E* be the set of finite sequences of elements of E . If m [E* and T [IV then m ˘ T
iff one of the following is true :

(i) m=¬

(ii) T= ¬

(iii) T= Σ a¡ T¡ with m = am' and a ≠ ai for all i .

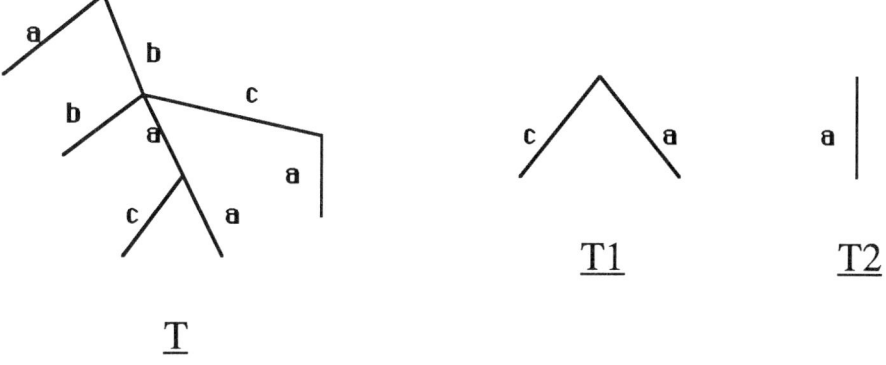

Figure 17.4. Example : (T, ba)| = (T1, ¬), (T, ab)| = (¬ , b), (T, bcd)| = (T2, d)

Normal form.
The normal form (T,m)| for a pair (T,m) is defined as :
   - (T,m) if m ˘ T
   - otherwise (Tj,m')| with T =Σ aᵢ Tᵢ , m = am' and a = aj for some j.

17.2.1.3. Finite languages on E

A language on E is any subset of E*, that is any set of finite sequences of elements of E.
A prefix language is a language L such that no word m [L is a left factor of any other
word m' [L (that is m'= mm" for some non empty word m" [E* is impossible).
   Through s(T), there is a one-to-one correspondence between the set of finite prefix
languages on E and class IV (injective l-trees).

17.2.1.4. i-Trees.

An i-tree is a T= (X, U, E, e, F, f) where :
- (X, U, E, e) is an injective l-tree,
- f : lf-->F is a mapping from the set of leaf nodes of (X, U) to some set F of values
(use symbol ¬ in F if one doesn't want f to be defined over all lf).
The class of i-trees is denoted by i .
The product-sum expressions can be extended to i-trees by using values at leaf nodes , if
any, in place of ¬ , thus yielding an E-F-expression for any T [i.

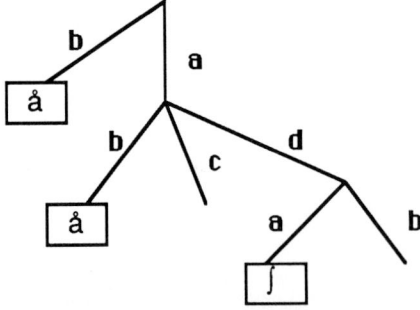

Figure 17.5. Example : corresponds to   bå + a(bå + c¬ + d(a∫ + b¬))

   F-E-expressions are easily implemented using LISP . With the above example :
   (b (å) a (b (å) c (nil) d (a (∫) b (nil)))) .

17.2.1.5. A set of basic functions

The i-trees are handled through some basic partial functions summarized below, using i
to denote the set of i-trees and L the set of edge labels sequences:

   graft : i x L x i   ---------> i

let T$_1$, T$_2$ be i-trees, L an edge labels sequence and T = graft (T$_1$, L, T$_2$)

let L$_1$ be the largest left factor of L which is an access to T$_1$, say to node x of T$_1$, and let L$_2$ be the remaining right factor of L

T = graft (T$_1$, L, T$_2$) is obtained from T$_1$ by:

- adding to T$_1$ from x a new path with edge labelling L$_2$ leading, say, to new node y
- identifying y with the root of T$_2$
- suppressing (and thus loosing) the value attached to x in case x was a leaf node in T$_1$

pick :   i x L   --------> i

if L is an access to T , say to node x, then pick (T, L) is the sub-i-tree of T with root x; otherwise, it is undefined.

cut :   i x L   ---------> i

if L is an access to T, say to node x, then cut (T, L) is the sub-i-tree of T obtained by suppressing from T the edge leading to node x together with the sub-i-tree of T with root x; otherwise, it is undefined.

Normal forms are easily extended to i , and if ˙ is a basic function while   (T,m)| = (T',m') then ˙ (T, m, rest) = ˙ (T', m', rest) . Therefore basic functions need to be defined when m˘T only.

17.2.1.6. Virtual i-trees

If i (F = 0, some leaf nodes might be labelled using values that are i-trees themselves, thus leading to a natural notion of virtual i-trees and virtual accesses, used in a conventional way, when one wants to make use of a top-down decomposition of a too-large i-tree.

Virtual i-trees can be taken into account by slightly changing the orthogonality and normal form definitions :

if T = ¬ , that is if T is reduced to a single root and leaf node x, and if the value of f(x) is in turn an i-tree T' then :

- m ˘ T iff m ˘ T'
- (T,m)| = (T',m)|

The two preceding points yield extension of basic functions to virtual i-trees.

17.2.2. *Genericity*

17.2.2.1. l-tree Genericity

Let ¥ : E --> E' a mapping. ¥ can be extended to E*, and then to languages by :

¥ (e1e2...ek) = ¥ (e1) ¥ (e2)...¥ (ek) , where e1, e2...ek [E , and ¥ (¬) = ¬
¥ (L) = { ¥ (m) ; m [L} , ¥ (ø) = ø.

Let T = (X, U, E, e) be an injective 1-tree. T ¥-generates T , or is a ¥-generic for T,
or T is ¥-generated from T when T is the injective 1-tree T = i (X, U, E', ¥ ο e).

Because of the one-to-one correspondence between injective 1-trees and prefix
languages the ¥-genericity notion can equivalently be defined through languages, for T
¥-generates T   iff s(T) = ø(¥(s(T))) , where when L is some language, ø(L)
stands for the language obtained from L by taking away from L any word which is prefix
of some other word in L .

T is said to be totally ¥-generated by T when ¥(s(T)) = ø(¥(s(T))) and partially ¥-
generated otherwise.

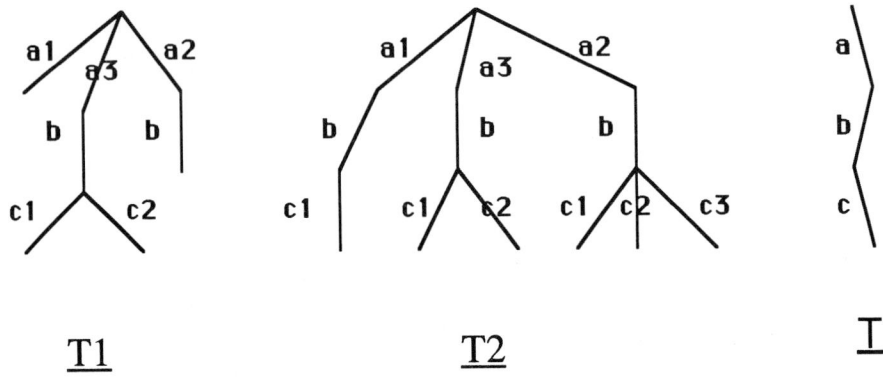

Figure 17.6. Example : ¥(a_i) = a ,   ¥(b) = b ,   ¥(c_i) = c , for all i .T_1 is partially ¥-generated
from T, and T_2 is totally ¥-generated from T.

17.2.2.2. i-tree Genericity

Let T a 1-tree ¥-generated from T . Any node x in T has a corresponding node in T,
namely the node y pointed in T by ¥(c) if c [a(T) points on x in T. Let $¥_n(x)$ denote
y . Now let T = (X, U, E, e, F, f) be an i-tree , ¥ : E-->E' and ® : F--> F' some
mappings. The genericity relation is extended to i-tree in the following way : T is ®-¥-
generated by T if T = (X, U, E', e', F', f) [i with e' = ¥ ο e , and for every leaf
node x in T , $¥_n (x)$ is a leaf node in T and ®(f(x)) = f'($¥_n(x)$)).

17.3 **Examples from the medical application**

In terms of therapeutic strategy in Oncology, each problem is to be considered on three
different "view-points", namely : "Treatment", "Disease", "Ill-patient". "Ill-patient" view-
point, i.e. a patient affected by a disease, models physiological functions and their

disturbances (etiologies, consequences). "Disease" view-point describes the natural history of the neoplasms (treated or not), the means and the methodology used for that description. In the "Treatment" view-point the therapeutic protocols are formalized with a conceptual hierarchy, i.e. : protocol, therapeutic sequences and courses, drugs and their side-effects... Moreover, in the different view-points, the concepts and their manipulating functions are described in different and complementary ways.

The first medical task to be performed, namely "patient entry in a protocol", requires knowledge from the three above-mentioned view-points, each view-point being built from one or several knowledge units :
- treatment is made of "protocols", "courses", "chemotherapic drugs", "drugs side-effects",
- disease is made of "disease" only,
- ill-patient is made of "physiological functions", "laboratory exams", "ill-patient",

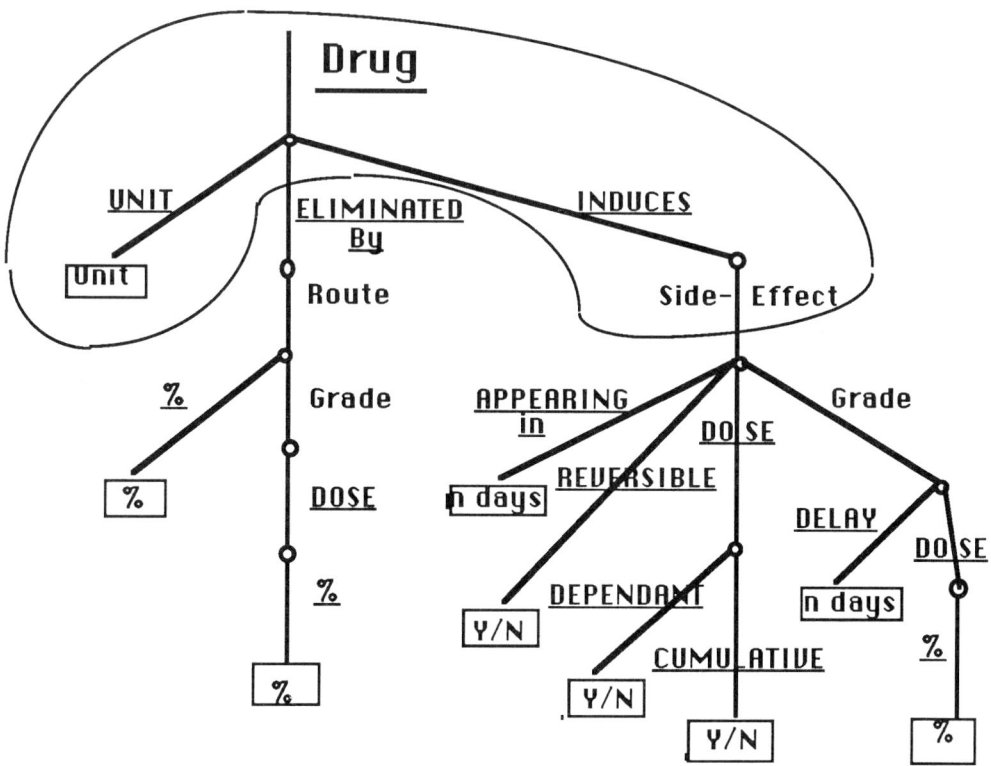

Figure 17.7. Example : the generic "chemotherapic drug".

This description of the knowledge units (implemented as i-trees) is the result of the numerous modifications of the expert's initial proposals. These modifications were realized by the expert during his programing validation. One can hope that for this first medical task, "patient entry in a protocol", a quite stability of the description of the knowledge units is reached. On the other hand, new modifications will be needed to realize tasks as : "follow-up in the protocol", "choice of the best protocol".

In the figure 17.7. right most path one can see a 3-ary relation between a drug, a side effect and a grade. If the value of the leaf node is added then the relation is 4-ary.

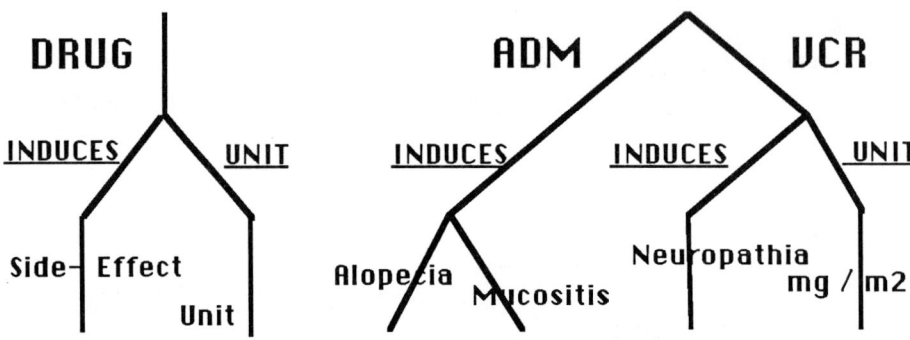

Figure 17.8. A possible concretization of the encircled part of the generic "chemotherapic drug" from figure 17.7.

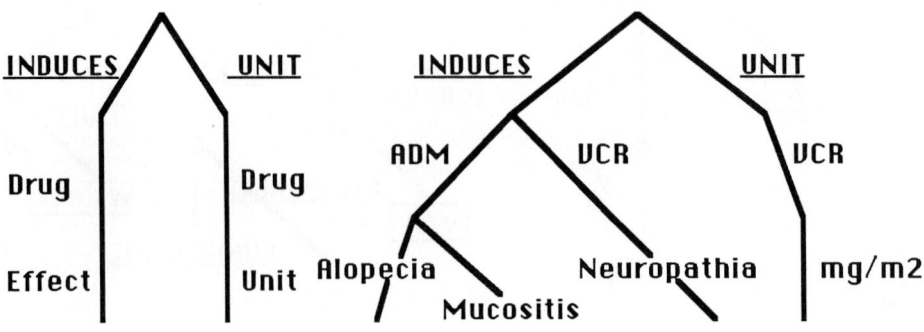

Figure 17.9. "INDUCES" is now viewed as a binary predicate and "UNIT" is viewed as an unary predicate.

In figure 17.8., the path, "ADM, INDUCES, Alopecia", corresponds to the sentence "The ADM (Adriamycin) induces alopecia". Again, from figure 17.8., the sub-i-tree with the edge "VCR" (Vincristin) as its starting edge can be viewed as the description of some "object" VCR.

If logical programing is intended, one might prefer figure 17.9. to figure 17.8.

As an illustration, figure 17.10. shows the generic "protocol" as used in the first medical task.

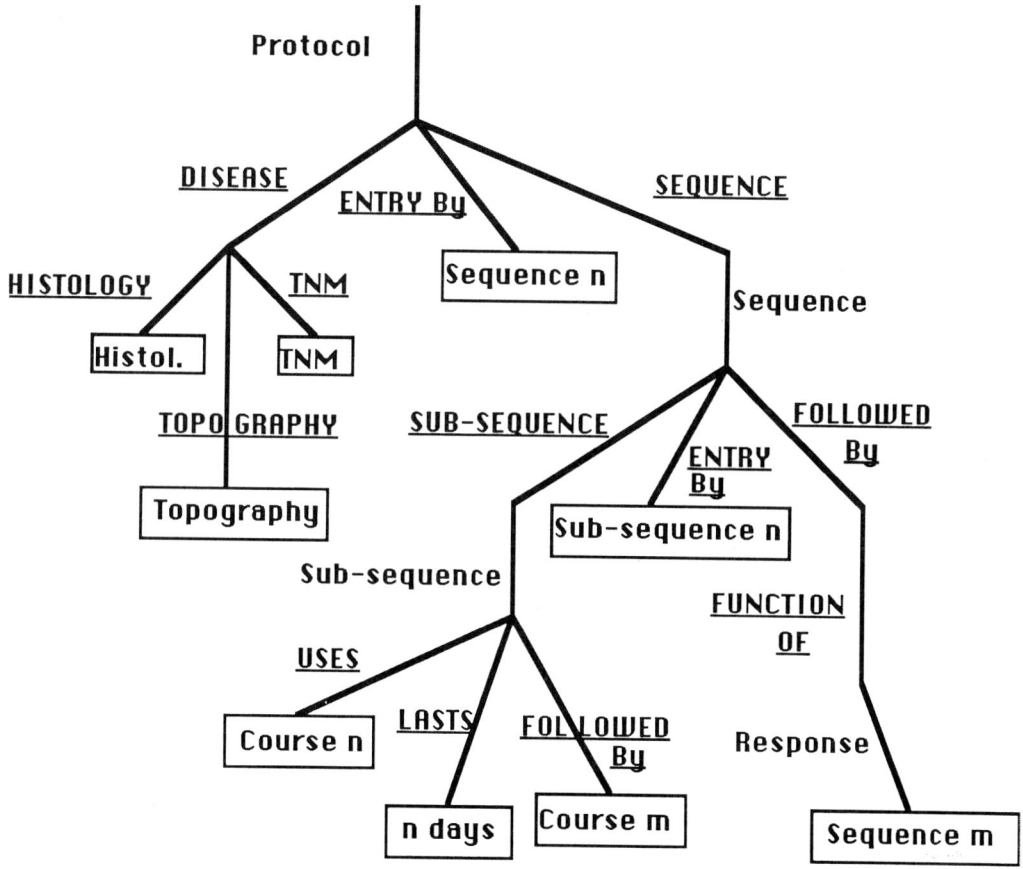

Figure 17.10. The generic "Protocol".

17.4 Developing State

17.4.1 *Informatics view-point*

Using Common-LISP on a VAX-Station, a prototype has been achieved which performs the "patient entry in the "extensive small-cell lung carcinoma" protocol" task.

Besides a simple language designed as to handle the basic i-trees manipulating functions in a reflex oriented way, the prototype includes :

- a graphic human-machine interface (HMI) for the creation, modification and management of the i-trees,

- a "natural language" HMI for a translation of expert's sentences,expressing the knowledge from the different view-points : generics being previously entered, sentences are, when possible, "translated" into paths of concretization of these generics.

At present time, we are also working on :

- a more convenient language for reflex-oriented programing,

- the handling of some integrity constraints between concretizations of the generic i-trees,

- problems reacted to automatizing evolution or changes of knowledge structures. This problem, up to now little studied, raised because our system is meant to be a "Knowledge Formalizing Tool" and has to cope with kind of "no-structure - structure - new structure" sequences.

- a formal semantics in order to discuss control, equivalence and halting problems.

17.4.2 *Medical view-point*
The examples above-presented are parts of the knowledge yet implemented to allow the task "patient entry in the "extensive small-cell lung carcinoma" protocol".

To be able to realize other generic tasks, as "follow-up in the protocol", the expertise is now focused on time and coherence management. The formalization of the time used by the agendas (i.e. therapeutic anticipations) seems to be easily feasible, knowing scheduling organization problems. On the other hand more difficult would be some time management problems as those concerning the evolution of the disease or the fit of patient's history to protocol temporal description...These problems of time and coherence will impose the construction of more sophisticated models.

17.5 Acknowledgement

M. Gandara, C. Ortiz, S. Poltoratzky and D.Vella have contributed to the medical project development. This project is supported by the EEC (ESPRIT Project 1592/86, Therapy Advisor in Oncology) and by the ARC (Association pour la Recherche sur le Cancer - Project 6536/85).

References

Borillo, M. (1984). Informatique pour les Sciences de l'Homme., Mardaga, Brussels.

Chandrasekaran, B. (1986). Generic Tasks in Knowledge-Based Reasoning : High-Level Building Blocks for Expert System Design. *IEEE Expert*, Fall 86, 23-30.

Chein, M. & Cogis, O. (1986). Les i-arbres. *Actes du CIIAM 86*, Hermès, Paris, 683-704

Chein, M. & Cogis, O. (1987). Dilem(2) : Genericity. RR 35/87. CRIM, Montpellier.

Keravnou, E.T. & Johnson, L. (1986). Competent Expert Systems. Kogan Page, *McGraw-Hill International Book Company*, New-York.

18 *R.Beuscart, M.C. Beuscart, A. Duhamel and the SES Group.*

THE SEPTICEMIA - EXPERT - SYSTEM (S.E.S.)

18.1 Introduction

In acute infectious diseases with bacteriemia, unless the sequence of clinical signs can be reversed early, the mortality rate may be 50% or higher. Suspected or proved bacteriema must be promptly treated with antimicrobial drugs. The selection of the inital treatment depends on the most likely source of organism.

However, bacteriologic identification is genrally obtained after a 48 h waiting period. During this time, some characteristics are suggestive of the type of bacteria: antibiotic therapy may then be guided by clinical and simple biological findings.

To help the physician in the choice of the best antibiotic therapy , we designed an Expert System called S.E.S.: "Septicemia Expert System".

18.2 Epidemiologic network

In France, 19 Infectious-diseases departments are linked by an Informatics network. Each department has a micro-computer and a software to acquire precise information about septicemia and severe infectious diseases. A database (SES-DIFF2) was developed using MULTILOG data-base software on MS-DOS. 1200 items by case can be recorded.

Much information is collected: patient's antecedents, medical history of the disease, drugs prescribed before hospitalization. During the presence of the patient in the department of Infectious disease, clinical examinations, biological informations, therapeutics are recorded at days 2, 4, 8, 16. The software was conceived to make the use of this huge document easy. Each medical department stores its own cases and can exploit them.

The data from the 19 hospitals are centralized in Lille and epidemiologic studies can be performed: description of the most frequent forms of septicemias; links between clinical, biological and bacteriological findings; prognostic factors; differences between nosocomial and non-nosocomial bacteriemias (Mouton *et al.*, 1986).

The results of these epidemiologic studies can be sent to each centre through the network.

18.3 The expert system

The Expert System (SEPTICEMIA EXPERT SYSTEM) was simultaneously developed by 40 physicians of the 19 departments.

This expert system was built in two parts which correspond to different steps of reasoning:

18.3.1 *Diagses*
DIAGSES is a knowledge base for the discrimination between bacterial infections. Using DIAGSES, a physician can identify which agent is responsible of the infection.

DIAGSES uses clinical information such as:
   - Age, sex.
   - previous hospital treatment before the septicemia
   - Cancer or immuno-depression
   - Clinical history (fever, shock, consciousness)
   - Suspected or proved infectious localizations...

DIAGSES uses some biological data:
   - Number and percentage of neutrophils.
   - Blood urea, glycemia, creatinin...

Only clinical and biological data are necessary for the interrogation of DIAGSES: one hour after the admission of an infected patient in a Internal Medecine Department, the physician has these data and only these ones. From this information, DIAGSES infers the most likely bacterial infection(s), and defines which new examinations may be useful.

DIAGSES contains 800 rules. DIAGSES is built using the formulation of inference rules handled by the software SAM. Two sorts of rules can be distinguished:
   1) Assertions:
      These rules define the field of the knowledge, the medical characteristics of infectious diseases, the relations existing between items. These rules are not real inference rules since they don't make the reasoning progress.
   2) Inference rules:
      These rules express the knowledge of the physicians and make the reasoning progress from clinical signs to syndromes, from associations of syndromes to the diagnosis, from the diagnosis to recommended complementary examinations . There is an organisation of the rules inside the knowledge base. The different chapters of rules

correspond to the clinical forms of septicemias the physician observes. So the knowledge base is divided in paragraphs such as:

- Immuno-depression and Septicemia.
- Renal septic localizations and Septicemia.
- Neurologic syndroms and Septicemia.
- ...

The correction of inexact rules and the adaptation of certainty coefficients are facilitated by this organization.

SES reasons at a high-level of medical knowledge, as an expert. SES is not able to infer that "headache, diarrhoea, nausea, photophobia" evokes meningitis. This semiological level, which is time-consuming in expert systems was avoided. SES takes information as "meningitis, purpura, shock evokes Meningococcemia". SES uses high-level information that a medical doctor (and even medical student) must be able to infer from his own findings. DIAGSES gives further knowledge that the non-expert physicians do not have: as an expert, the response of DIAGSES is "This septicemia is probably caused by staphylococcus aureus, or perhaps streptococcus A".

18.3.2 *Abses*

ABSES is a second knowledge base containing reasoning rules on antibiotics, authorized pharmacologic associations, treatment duration.

ABSES can be used immediately after DIAGSES, using the response proposed by DIAGSES. As DIAGSES's response is the name of a bacteria, this name can be included for the interrogation of ABSES. In this case, only the germ has to be introduced. Other data as medical history, clinical and biological observations precedently used by DIAGSES are kept by ABSES.

But the physician can also use ABSES when bacteriological results are available to adjust the antibiotic therapy when septic localization make the antibiotics prescription difficult. In this case ABSES is interrogated alone. The physician must specify medical history, antecedents, the sites of septic localization, the nature of the infectious agent.

The response of ABSES consists of:

1) The list of antibiotics usually prescribed.

2) The mode of prescription (mono or bi-antibiotic therapy).

3) If a bi-antibiotic therapy is proposed, the possible associations of antibiotics are listed.

4) The precautions for antibiotics use are recalled.

If allergies or other medical limitations for using antibiotics (e.g. renal insufficiency) are specified during ABSES interrogation, the list of the possible antibiotics will be reduced.

18.4 Software

SAM is an expert system software which was written by O. Gascuel (1985) to help physicians in the realization of medical expert-systems . It uses two formulations to express the knowledge: descriptive rules and inference rules.

18.4.1 *Descriptive Rules*
The description of the objects of the base and of the links between these objects is simplified by the use of two representations:

- Some objects $X_1, X_2,..., X_p$ CONSTITUTE an object Y.
  Some signs constitute a syndrome; some syndromes constitute a disease, some examinations contitute a protocol...

- Two objects are mutually exclusive:
  IF A is true THEN B is false;
  IF B is true THEN A is false;

  These two rules can be replaced by one rule:

  A and B ARE-MUTUALLY-EXCLUSIVE;

18.4.2 *Inference Rules*
In SAM, we find two sorts of rules:

- Certain knowledge. This type of knowledge is expressed with the verb IMPLIE:

ex: Septicemia and septic bone localization IMPLIE long term antibiotic therapy;

- Uncertain knowledge. These rules explain uncertain knowledge with different possible conclusions for a same premise. Sam uses coefficients of certainty as MYCIN (Shortliffe *et al.*, 1975).

As Example:

IF ENDOCARDITIS AND TOXICOMANIA

THEN STAPHYLOCOCCUSS IS THE MOST PROBABLE <.90>

OR STEPTOCOCCUS <.50>.

SAM is written in FORTRAN. It achieves forward reasoning but may also be used backwards. SAM is linked with two other programs SYNONE and GLOSE:

SYNONE: this program understands hundreds of medical words, their synonyms, rectifies orthographic faults and guides the physician through menus of interrogation.

GLOSE: Glose creates french or english natural language to express the results of the Expert System session, which are normally expressed in a table and includes them in grammatically correct sentences.

18.5 Multicentric expertise

The SES Study Group gathers the major French experts in the field of infectious diseases. 40 physicians worked on this project. A special methodology was used to induce the collaboration of all these medical experts and to build a coherent knowledge base while they could disagree on particular points of diagnosis or treatment.

18.5.1*First step*
The SES group was divided in four parts. This division was realized taking geography in account. France was cut in four districts: North-West (Lille), East (Nancy), South-East (Grenoble), South-West (Toulouse). Each region gathered the medical teams of four or five universitary hospitals and was centered by a town in which reunions took place. In each region, a physicician was chosen to centralize data and information. He took upon himself the responsibility of the organization of the work in his district.

Each group had to define the rules for a particular area of the knowledge base.The knowledge of septicemia could be infered from scientific publications, but there were two points of view:
- - 1- Septicemia induced by a micro-organism:
  Septicemia and staphylococcus aureus
  Septicemia and pneumococcus

  ...

  In these publications, we found information concerning the clinical features of the disease, the biology, the most frequent septic localization...

- - 2- Septicemia and clinical information:
  Septicemia and Cancer
  Septicemia and Meningitis
  Septicemia and AIDS

  ...

  In these publications, we found which are the most frequent bacteria associated with a pathology .

We kept this dual expression of the knowledge for building the rules base. So, a group had to write the rules about 'Septicemia and Staphylococcus Aureus' and another had to express the knowledge about bone septic localization in septicemias. Some rules were common. The cooperation of the two teams produced a coherent knowledge on the subject. When an agreement was obtained, the rules were put in the base for testing.

18.5.2 *Second step*

There were monthly meetings between the experts of a region. These reunions were necessary to collect the expertise, to resolve conflicts between contradictory rules of decision, to compare bibliographic data and clinical experience. After these meetings, the decision rules written by the group were sent to the other groups in France for advice and criticism.

There were trimestrial meetings of the entire group, in Paris. During these meetings, the knowledge was discussed, the translation of this knowledge in inference rules was explained in order to obtain a general agreement. Informaticians, scientists and statisticians attended these meetings to explain what was possible to do and why some demands were unrealizable. Some clinical cases were proposed for testing the expert System.The confrontation with clinicians' expertise was fruitful. At the end of these national sessions, an agreement was reached.

18.5.3 *Third step*

When the knowledge base was complete, twenty physicians were invited in Lille to test the expert system. During three days, they had to study the performances of SES with clinical cases of growing difficulty. A first evaluation of SES in the field of diagnosis and therapy was done. The System was corrected during this real-time confrontation: some rules were excluded, new therapeutic agents were introduced, many certainty factors were modified. After this last optimization, SES was presented and evaluated.

18.6 Evaluation

18.6.1 *First validation*

115 cases of septicemia were collected during summer 1986. These records were well documented: symptoms, biological findings, bacteriology, antibiotic therapy, prognosis. At this level, only DIAGSES (Diagnostic Expert System) was evaluated.

The six or seven most important signs or syndromes of each case were kept for the interrogation of DIAGSES. The System answered giving one, two or, at maximum, three possible germs.A comparison between DIAGSES responses and the bacteriological data is summarised in TABLE I. We could consider that a 'germ named first' is a good response; and we can qualify a germ named second or third as 'a good advice'

TABLE 18.I : *First validation (115 cases of septicemias) of DIAGSES. The response of DIAGSES may be uncertain and several germs (2 or 3) proposed.*
Germ named first : good response
Germ named second or third: good advice

Germ named first	59 %
Germ named 2-3	27 %
Inexact responses	14 %

18.6.2 *Second validation*

40 clinical examples of septicemia were proposed by physicians who did not belong to the SES Group : 2O easy cases and 2O difficult ones. These cases were introduced and the responses of SES were recorded. Non-expert medical practitioners (residents, non-expert hospital physicians) who were attending a post-universitary teaching agreed to give advice for diagnosis and therapy. The comparison between SES and non-expert physicians is resumed in TABLE 2.

Table 18.2..a : *EASY CASES*

	SES	Non- experts (means)
Germ named first	70 %	58 %
Germ named 2-3	30 %	31 %
Inexact responses	0 %	11 %

Table 18.2.b : *DIFFICULT CASES*

	SES	Non- experts
Germ named first	50 %	10 %
germ named 2-3	35 %	8 %
Inexact responses	15 %	82 %

18.6.3 *Validation with the epidemiologic data-base.*

In 1986, 350 cases of the database were used to test the two expert Systems, DIAGSES and ABSES. The Diagnosis performances are similar to those presented in Tables I and II: 60% of the germs were correctly identified (first place); a good advice (2nd-3rd place) was given for 25% of the cases.

18.6.4 *To test ABSES*
We retained the germ found by the bacteriological examination. However, some cases were excluded because the patients were treated according to experimental protocols. In all the other cases, the treatment prescribed by ABSES was good. There was **no error of prescription.**

At this time (1987), there is a link between the epidemiologic data-base and the expert system which allows a great scale testing of the two expert-systems. 947 cases of septicemias will be used in the next months. We hope to discover inconsistencies, inaccuracy, mistakes, repeated errors.

18.7 **Discussion**

SES is not the first expert system designed to help physicians in the managing of infected patients. The most famous medical expert system is certainly MYCIN which was designed for the diagnosis and treatment of severe infectious diseases with bacteriemia. As SES, MYCIN had two steps of reasoning:
1. identification of the germ
2. antibiotic therapy.

As opposed to MYCIN, SES is only a clinical tool. Bacteriological findings and microscopic characteristics of the germ are not included in SES. MYCIN mixes two types of reasoning rules:

* rules of germ identification with bacteriological definitions: form of the bacteria, colour staining, and so on... These rules are not known by clinicians but only by bacteriologists.

* rules of therapy including bacteriological identification and clinical observation to infer the best antibiotic treatment.

SES is only reasoning from the point of view of the clinician : in ABSES and in DIAGSES, the left part of the rule is only composed with clinical descriptions, syndromes, medical history of the patient, infectious sites... No microscopic definitions are used. SES utilizes only clinical or epidemiological information.

So, the knowledge bases contain two types of rules.

(1) heuristics, giving the knowledge of the experts: bibliographic data, experience, intuition.

(2) Epidemiologic data: the results of epidemiologic studies are included in the knowledge bases. Here are some examples:
- Some varieties of infectious diseases, described in specialized literature were not observed in any of the 19 Infectious-Diseases departements, within 2 years. Because of this extremely rare occurence, the rules concluding to this pathology were excluded (example : some types of Gram negative endocarditis).
- Some links exist between information of different nature: these links must be taken into account. If different data are reinforcing themselves, the results of the Expert System would be biased.
- The epidemiology of Infectious diseases shows that the prevalence of the germs is evolving with time, the hospitalized population, the patients. AIDS is an example of a new epidemiologic factor creating a favourable situation for the emergence of septicemia.

Reggia (1985) enumerates the *LIMITATIONS OF CLINICAL MEDICAL DECISION SYSTEMS*:
1. The lack of large relialable data for testing
2. The problem of transferability
3. The physician resistance
4. The maintenance.

1. SES was developed jointly with an epidemiological database which contains now more than 900 cases of septicemia recorded in different Infectious Diseases Departments in France. The exploitation of this database is only beginning. The software link between the database and the expert systems will give us great information about the reliability of SES, but also the evolution of the epidemiology of septicemia, according to the variations of the pathogenicity of the germs, and the presence of favouring factors (cancer, AIDS).

2. The problem of transferability is solved in France because of the presence of medical experts coming from all the parts of France. Geographic considerations can be taken into account. There is an agreement between the experts.
All the physicians will be able to use SES by the means of the TELETEL network, without high-cost investment. We avoid also the problem of repeated releases.

3. "Physician resistance to using CMD Systems may be facilitated by the lack of responsibility of the expert system designers" Gascuel (1985). The two expert Systems, ABSES and DIAGSES are signed by the 'LIGUE FRANCAISE POUR LA PREVENTION DES MALADIES INFECTIEUSES'. This league gathers the major part of the French medical experts (clinicians and bacteriologists) in the field of Infectious

Diseases. The French TELETEL network allows each physician to use the expert system from his office at low cost.

4. Maintenance of the Expert System: The SES Group continues to study the epidemiology of septicemias and severe infectious diseases, to publish the results of these works. Bi-annual meetings of the whole SES Group are provided: new information is shared which will permit the maintenance of the inference rules and the building of additional information systems.

18.8 Conclusion

SES is a clinical tool designed for physicians in a situation of emergency: diagnosis and treatment of severe infectious diseases including bacteriemia. SES is divided in two parts: DIAGSES for the identification of the most likely infectious agent; ABSES for treatment counselling. Antibiotic information is also available on SES, concerning the mode of utilization of the prescribed antibiotics (Posology, mode of administration, complications, limits, ...).

SES is a very fast expert system. 3 or 4 minutes are only necessary to interrogate DIAGSES and ABSES. 2 minutes are sufficient for the interrogation of ABSES alone.

SES is a medical tool, realized by medical doctors for their colleagues. If validated, it will be diffused throughout the French-speaking medical community, using informatics networks.

References

Gascuel, O. (1985). Un système expert pour la réalisation de diagnostics, *Technique et Sciences Informatiques*, **4**, 359-72

Mouton, Y, Beuscart, R, Blanc, D. & SES Group. (1986). French multicentric Septicemia Expert System study (SES) : First epidemiological results., XXVIth *ICCAC*-New Orleans, abstract n° 1242.

Reggia, J.A. & Tuhrim, S. (1985). An overview of methods for Computed-Assisted Medical Decision Making., In: *Computer-Assisted Medical Decision Making*, **2**, Springer-Verlag. New-York.

Shorliffe, E.H., Davis, R., Buchanan, B.G., Axline, S.G., Green, C.C. & Cohen S.N. (1975). Computer-based consultations in clinical therapeutics-explanation and rule acquisition capabilities of the MYCIN system., *Computer and Biomedical Research* , **8**, 303-20.

19 *M.C. Beuscart-Zéphir and R. Beuscart*

AN AUTOMATIZED MENTAL TEST :
TOWARDS A COMPUTER-ASSISTED COGNITIVE DIAGNOSIS

19.1 Introduction

The present research is concerned with three topics :
- artificial intelligence,
- cognitive psychology, which investigates mental processes involved in cognitive functions such as memory, problem-solving, etc...
- psychometrics, which involves theoretical and methodological study of mental tests (we shall refer especially to intelligence tests).

Our purpose is to identify the mental operations involved in a concrete intelligence test, the Passalong, subtest of the Alexander Battery. This test has been automatised. In the future, an expert-system should allow an automatic classification of the subjects, according to the mental processes recorded.

19.1.1 *Psychometrics : the mental tests-problem*
Usually, mental tests have good methodological characteristics. They are discriminant, reliable and empirically valid. So they allow the establishment of pronostics, which permits for example the orientation and counselling of the subjects. Generally, mental tests are assessed by standardized performances, for example number of correct responses in limited time. Unfortunately, most of these tests were created by the 1930s. They were elaborated empirically, from clinical intuitions so they are not based on modern theories of cognition, which appeared in the 1960s. Generally, the users do not know the processes or mental operations involved in these tests. So, these instruments do not allow the establishment of a cognitive diagnosis of the subjects.In short, Psychometrics needs theoretical validation of its instruments, and therefore a rapprochement has taken place between psychometrics and cognitive psychology.

19.1.2 *Mental tests and cognitive psychology*

The first attempts of rapprochement are due to Carroll and Hunt. Carroll (1976) first considered psychometric tests as cognitive tasks. Hunt (1974, 1975) investigated correlations between psychometric and experimental tasks. Then Sternberg (1977, 1985) realized the componential analysis of psychometric tests. These studies are based upon models of cognition derived from information processing approaches (Newell and Simon, 1972). Nevertheless, the results are somewhat disappointing, because of the weakness of the correlations, and for causal interpretations are sometimes difficult to establish.

So far, developments of cognitive psychology in the probem-solving area (Holyoak 1984, Richard 1982) have not been utilized to study psychometric tasks. But most of the tests could be considered as problems and this could lead to the study of problem-solving's strategies.

For example, J.F. Richard (1982) studied Tower of Hanoï 's solving and, on this occasion, created a particular method of protocol analysis which could be transfered to the study of mental tests. Richard's research is interesting too because of its inductive point of view. The author uses a Tower with 3 stems and 3 disks ; he records all the movements (displacements) each subject realizes and so collects protocols of 495 children aged 7. The analysis of protocols leads to divide them in "episodes". Richard's assumption is that an episode characterizes a type of representation of the knowledge relative to the game, and corresponds to a particular system of manipulating rules. Then the author elaborates a model, based on protocols' analysis ; this model sets forth the rules underlying the movements of the subjects, and characterizing the corresponding represention of the task. The model also provides for the series of episodes. But this model has not yet been implemented on a computer, and therefore Richard cannot validate the simulation of sequences of episodes, which could only account for each protocol.In short, the protocol analysis seems to be a fruitfull method, and may lead to simulation. But this method is not easy to use. For example, Richard's protocols lack for data : all the displacements are coded, but not the corresponding times. The observers only noted the perceptible breaks (pauses), which contribute to determine the beginning of a new episode . Evidently, this method can suffer from subjectivity. Moreover, data collection has required the contribution of about 10 observers. To overcome these disadvantages, we have choosen to automatize the task, i.e. data collection and analysis.

19.2 Method

19.2.1. *The psychometric task : The Passalong, of Alexander Battery.*

In the view of its author, the Alexander battery measures concrete intelligence, which can be defined as the aptitude underlying good performances in technical learning channels. This battery was created in 1935, revised in 1946. One of the subtests, the Passalong is constituted of a thin wooden case, in which are placed rectangular or square wooden blue or red pieces. One of the border of the case is blue, the opposite one is red. In the initial state, the blue pieces are along the red border, the red pieces are along the blue border. Subjects must move the pieces, without getting them out of the case, so that the red piece comes along the red border. Subjects can help themselves by looking at a full-sized figure, showing the final state. The final state is always symetrical to the initial state (fig. 19.1).

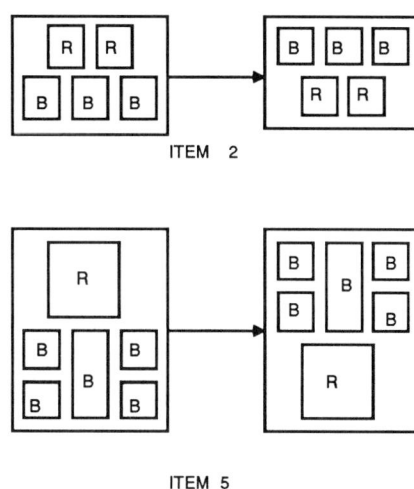

Figure 19.1: Initial and final states for items 2 and 5.

Generally, the winning strategy works for all the items : it consists in moving the blue pieces to create an empty space under the red piece(s), so that it can be driven along the red border. The test is composed with 9 items of increasing difficulty. These items must be solved in limited time. Quality of performance depends on the number of solved items and on the time necessary for solving each problem.

19.2.2. Automatization

The Passalong has been equiped with an electronic system which registers all the movements of the wooden pieces, and the time between two successsive manipulations.

The Passalong can be considered as a 3 x 2 (items 2 and 3) and then 4 x 3 (items 4 to 9) matrix, in which there are always one or two uncovered places "the gaps" (and 5 or 10 places covered by the red and blue pieces). So, each blue and red piece was equiped with a magnet, oriented along the diagonal axis. Under the bottom of the case, we fixed some ILS which are opened when there is a gap over them. So, at each time, we can know the location of the one or two gaps. This electronic system is connected with an Apple II acquisition card equiped with a clock. For each movement, the location of the gaps, and the moment at which the movement took place, are registered. The registration ends when the task is finished , or when the examiner stops it, or when the time allowed is overstayed. The automatized Passalong is identical with the common Passalong, so the subjects sit a standard examination.

At the end of the registration, the examiner executes the reconstruction of the series of manipulations, for only the gaps were registered. But the inital states are well-defined as well as the constraints of movements (vertical or horizontal), so the reconstruction is easy.

At the end of the reconstruction, we have at our disposal, for each subject, nine protocols (one for each item). Each protocol comprises 2 data for each movement : the coded configuration (state), and the time this configuration has been executed.

The coded configurations are then tanslated into figures which represent unambiguously each state. The illustrations make the psychological analysis easier. The states on which the subject paused are underlined.

The coded protocols are then analyzed on a computer, by an automata. The program enumerates and records the different states, which constitute the nodes of the automata. When recording, the program creates links between the nodes and counts how many times the path to solution crossed each node. The program also counts the different links between two nodes. One node has at least one link to another (in this case, it is a cul-de-sac) ; generally, it has two links with two other nodes. When the automata enumerates 4 different links between a node and the others, this node becomes a "pivot". The automata also enumerates the "Aller-retours", when the subject passes again across the same nodes, exactly in the opposite order. Pivot states and Aller-retours movements are illustrated fig. 2. On this figure, we see that subject passed through 9 different states, as follow : 1-2-3-4-5-6-3-2-7-1-7-2-3-8-9.

So, on this protocol, there is an Aller-retour : 3.2.7. - 1 - 7.2.3 which is labeled   AR 1->3, depth 3. (Subject passes on 3 states from the cul-de-sac). There is also a pivot , configuration 3, for this configuration communicates with four others : 2-4-6-8.

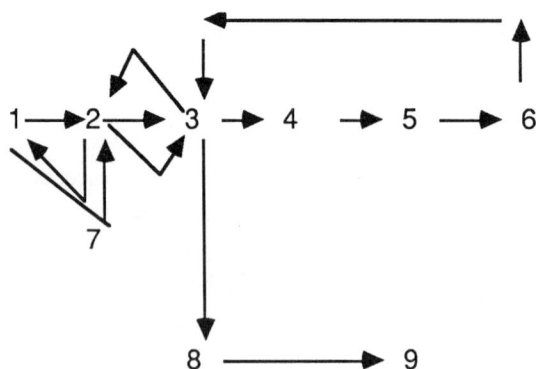

Figure 19.2:   Coded protocol involving an aller-retour and a pivot.

aller-retour: 3-2-7-1-7-2-3

Pivot : **3** : 3-(2 and 4 and 6 and 8)

In sum, the informatic analysis provides the following informations : total number of states, number of different states, number of pivots and their identification (coded state) and location in the protocol, number of Aller-retours, their depthness, identifcation and location. The total solving time is recorded during the examination.

19.2.3. *Subjects*
25 children (mean age : 11 ; 2) sat the automatized test.

19.3 **Results**

A first rough analysis of protocols leads to ascertain some facts :

19.3.1 *Information provided by the automatized analysis*
This information seems relevant to cognitive analysis. For example, the pivots correspond to sections of the path to solution where the subject had some difficulties. Most often, pivots concern movements whose aim is to create an empty space under a (big) red piece (cf fig. 3).

Learning processes related to this problem are proved to be important to the issue of the test, and must be transfered from an item to the next ones.

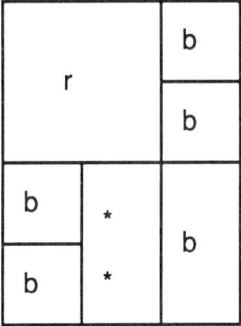

Figure 19.3. State A, which is a frequent pivot of item 5.

19.3.2 *The pauses.*
Another important information concerns the pauses, whose duration and location characterize the subject's ability to anticipate and become conscious of the problems. For example :

- when they face a difficulty, and after one or two unsuccessful attempts, **performing subjects** have a long pause, one or two states before the solution-state. Usually, after this break, they drive the pieces to the solution-state without doing any error. In this case, the pause could indicate a change of episode.

- when they face a difficulty too, **failing subjects** try to execute a lot of movements, without any pause. When they luckily reach the solution state resolving the difficulty , they can have a pause on this solution state or on the next one. So, for these subjects, pause does not always indicate a change of episode, but seems to correspond to the time necessary to recognize an hazardly obtained solution.

19.4 Simulation

19.4.1 *Simulation : Some elements of the model*

If we consider the nine items of the Passalong as nine problems the subjects have to solve, then the whole test can be viewed as a learning set for solving these problems.

This learning could be described as a set of rules that the subject could acquire after or during each item. Resolving subject would have to organize these rules, and could use them according to the configurations he is faced with, along each item.

As an illustration, we present a prototype of model for items 2 and 3. Item 1 is a training one.(See fig. 19.4).

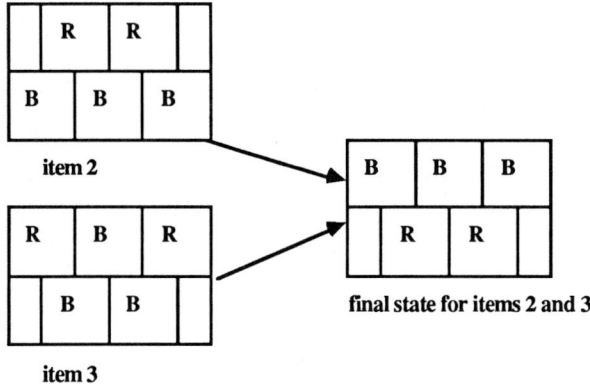

Figure 19.4: Initial and final states for items 2 and 3.

At the beginning of the test, for the first item, subjects could have identified and stored some rules either from the observation of the training item (cf. Fig. 19.5) or from the instructions. Instructions explain to the subjects they must reproduce the final state figured on the card, and drive the red pieces along the red border and the blue ones along the blue border.

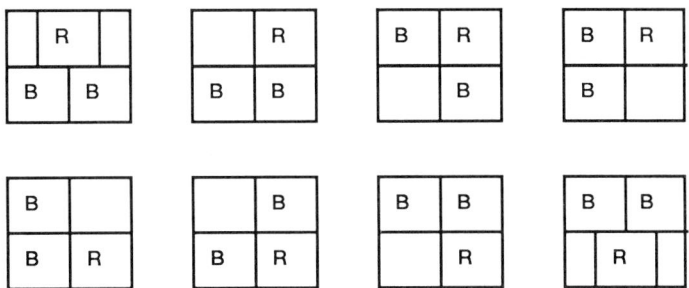

Figure 19.5: Training item. **B**: blue pieces - **R** : red pieces.

1 - from the observation of the training-item, the subjects can store general rules such as :
G1 : make all the pieces turn around the borders of the case, until the final state is
reached. More precisely : any empty square of the matrix gets the value of the preceding
square ; the preceding square gets value "empty".
G2 : Don't turn back, except if there are some constraints such as cul-de-sac, error,
breaking of a superordinate rule etc...

2 - From the instructions, subjects can store operating or manipulating rules, more
precise, such as:
M1 : if there is an empty square such as a red piece can be driven along the red border,
then do   this movement.
M2 : if there is an empty square such as a blue piece can be driven along the blue border,
then do this movement.
M3 : if there is no empty square allowing aplication of M1 or M2, then do anyone
movement, at random.

3 - Subjects could also have stored unconsciously some mental or perceptive
reservations, such as :
R1 : don't insert a blue piece between 2 red pieces or, stronger : don't separate the two
red pieces.
R2 : don't insert a red piece between two blue pieces.

   With the few rules above, we can simulate the principale solving procedures for item2 :
- Procedure A : if subject utilizes only G1 (and G2) he effects a just turn-around strategy,
labeled procedure A (see fig. 6)

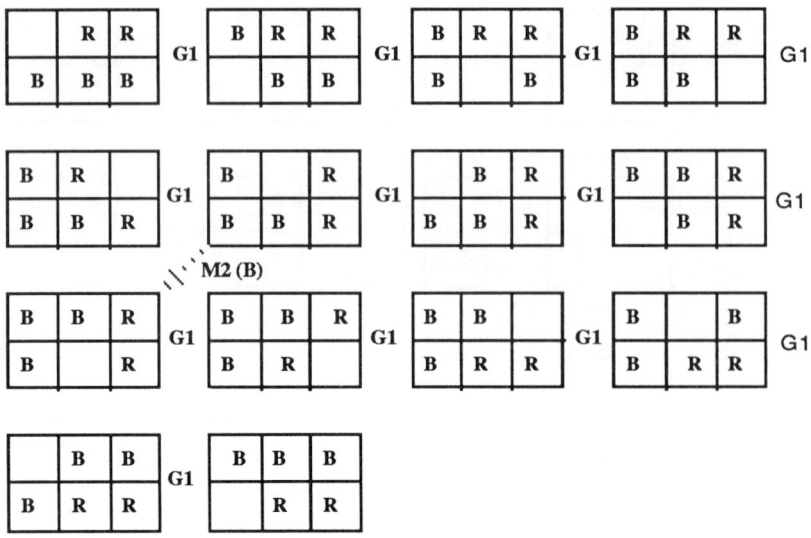

Figure 19.6 : Procedure A (G1-G2) and Procedure B (M2-G1-G2).

- Procedure B : it differs slightly from procedure A : at step n°7 of procedure A, the subject applies M2, which leads directly to state n°9 of procedure A. Stored rules are organized as follows: (see fig. 19.6).

   M2 -> G1 (M2 dominates G1)

- Procedure C : subject here applies essentially operating rules (see fig. 7). Usually, in this procedure, subject separates the two red pieces and move them independently. In this case, rules are settled as follow : (M1 - M2) -> M3, not R1, G2.

   It can be noted that there exists a variation of procedure C, which we did not illustrated here, and which does not lead the subject to separate the red pieces : at step 4 of the procedure, the subject moves the 2nd red piece instead of the blue one. In this case, rules can be settled as follows :

   (M1, M2) -> M3, G2.

- Procedure D: (see fig. 19.8) from the beginning, (is it at random or is there a rule underlying this movement ?) the subject separates the two red pieces and inserts between them a blue one. In this case, rules can be settled as follows :

   (M2 -> M1) -> M3, non R1, G2.

   These rules were formulated with Prolog and the model was implemented on VAX. The program currently produces all the procedures available for items 2 and 3.

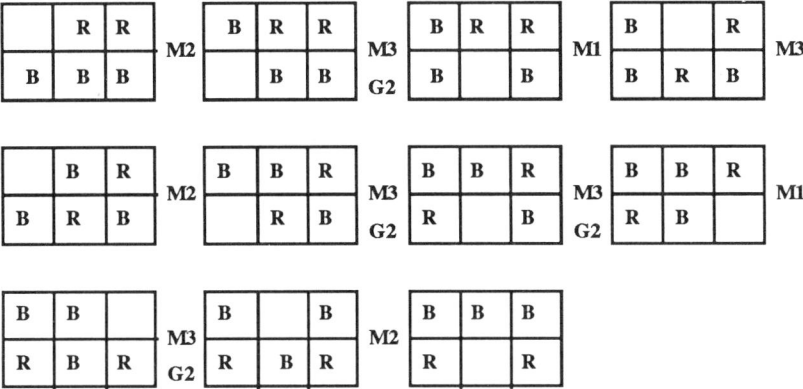

Figure 19.7 Procedure C (M1,M2,M3,G2)

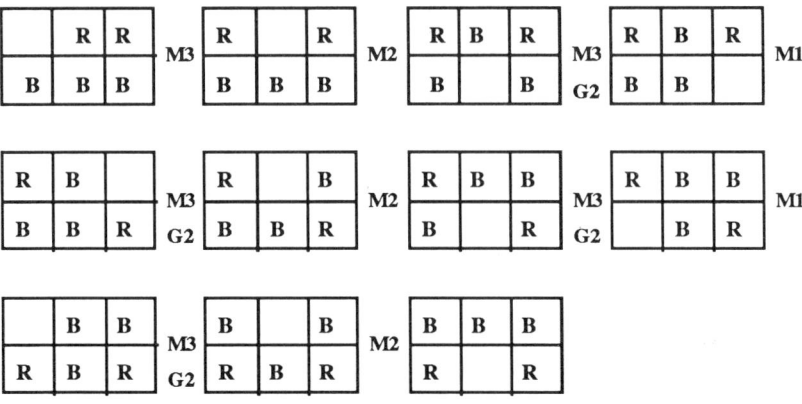

Figure 19.8 : Procedure D (M2,M1,M3,G2)

19.4.2 *Test of the model : protocols'analysis*

We analyzed subject's protocols of items 2 and 3 in order to confirm the following assumptions :

- subjects apply the rules of the model (or their negatives) ; these rules are adequate to explane all the movements ;
- individual differences depend on organization of the rules (meta-rules) ;
- pauses and/or aller-retours often indicate changes of episodes.

This qualitative analysis seems conclusive, for the subjects examined. As an illustration, we present several subjects'protocols characterizing the different types of strategies available for items 2 and 3 in our sample.

Subject 1 : Anne-Sophie, item 2 (see fig. 19.9)

Anne-Sophie applies procedure A throughout the resolve of the item. However, we note a typical pause on the third configuration where M1 is applicable. We can suppose Anne-Sophie considered the application of rule M1, and finally did not apply it. Therefore, rule M1 is available in working memory. On the other hand, we note there is no pause on the sixth configuration where rule M2 is applicable. So, the rule M2 is not available in working memory. The final diagnosis of rules can be settled as follow : two rules, G1 and M1 are available, but only G1 is utilized. The structure of the rules is : (G1 -> M1), G1 dominates M1.

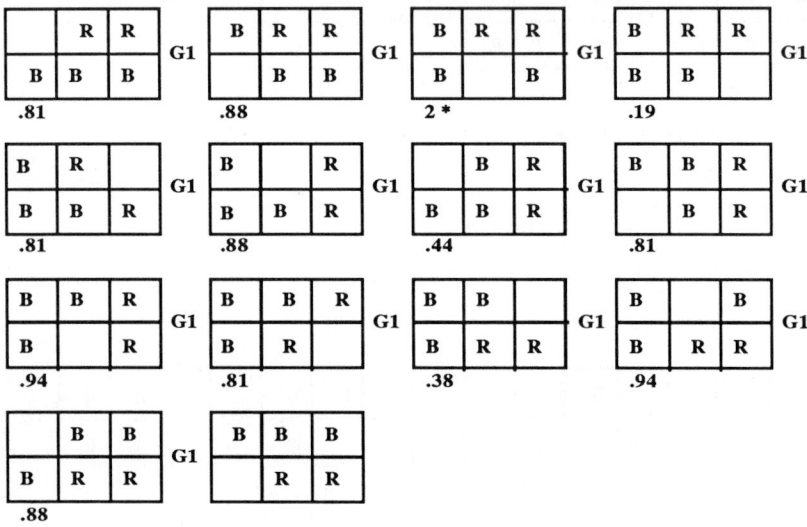

Figure 19.9: Anne-Sophie, item 2 - Rules (G1 - M1)

mean time = 0.82 sec - s.d. = 0.44 sec. - limit for pauses (*) = 1.55 sec.

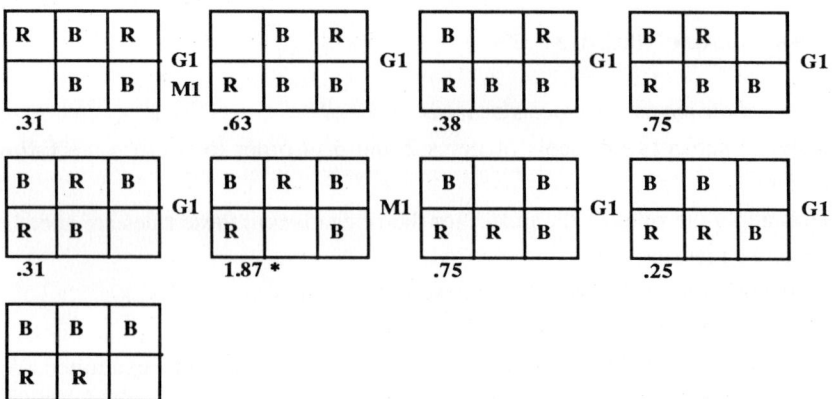

Figure 19.10: Julien, item 3 - Rules (M1-G1)

mean time = 0.71 sec - s.d. = 0.55 sec - limit for pauses (*) = 1.61 sec

Subject 2 : Julien, item 3 (see fig. 19.10)

As he did for item 2, Julien applies procedure A. But on this particular item, this procedure alone cannot lead to the solution. Effectively, Julien pauses on configuration 7, then applies M1, so that he can terminate by applying G1. The diagnosis is settled as follow : (M1), and then (next episode):

(M1-> G1).

Subject 3 : Karine, item 2

Karine presents a typical case of conflict for the choice of hierarchy of the rules. Her protocol can be divided in two episodes :
* the first episode includes states one to six. All along this episode Karine applies procedure A. There is no pause on state 3, neither on state 6. We cannot infer that M1 and M2 exist in working memory. For this first episode, the only rule available is G1 ;
* the second episode begins on state 7, with a pause and a return to state 6, that allows the application of M2; so the subject introduces a new rule, which dominates the preceding one. The structure of the rules is now : (M2 -> G1). We can note that, for item 3, Karine implements the same structure: (M2 ->G1).

19.5 Conclusion

At present, tests computerisation is developing broadly. But this computerisation does not renew Psychometrtics. Generally, it consists in the automatisation of the data analysis, but the data are the same as before computerisation, even if the analysis is refined. Sometimes, the test is translated on the computer: instead of writing his answer with a pencil on a sheet, the subject answers directly on the computer to the questions written on the screen. In this case, we do not know if the task is psychologically equivalent to the standard ones. This type of computarisation does not lead to new data, which should allow new qualitative analysis such as cognitive process analysis.

On the contrary, the computerisation of a performance test, for example the Passalong, which involves the automation of the task, and its link with an expert-system, leads to collect new data (protocols), although the subject sits standard examination. This method leads to an accurate analysis of mental operations involved in the test.

Our observations are consistent with findings in the problem-solving area. For example, we meet again the concept of series of episodes (Richard, 1982) in the solving procedures.

Our method also permits to identify processes underlying individual differences of procedures. In this case, individual differences lay principally in meta-rules, that is in organization and structure of the rules.

However, it will be necessary to connect the rules diagnosis with existing models of cognition if we want to explain why there exist such individual differences in the meta-rules.Then, we shall be able to develop an expert-system for computerised-assisted-diagnosis, in which the data base will include the knowledge of the psychologist. This knowledge is partly elaborated from the observations and interpretations of the individual differences demonstrated by the protocols' analysis, i.e. rules diagnosis.

In sum, the automatized Passalong, at present, led for the first items to the implementation of a satisfactory model, and it allows the development of an expert-system which aim is to provide an automactic diagnosis of rules and meta-rules. These first results seem encouraging. The Passalong and other automatized performance tests (which are to be created) could be for the psychologists a good instrument of computer-assisted cognitive decision making. For the future, they could contribute to develop a real individual computer-assisted learning.

References

Caroll, J.B. (1976). *Psychometric tests as cognitive tasks : A new "structure of intellect".* In: *The nature of Intelligence*, Ed. Resnick, LB. Hillsdale N.J. : Lawrence Ertbaum associates.

Holyoak, K.J. (1984). *Mental models in problem-solving.* In: *Tutorials in learning and memory,* Eds. Anderson, J.R. & Kosslyn, S.M. : San Francisco, Freeman.

Hunt, E. (1974). *Quote the Raven ? Never More !* In: *Knowledge and cognition*, Ed. Gregg L. Hillsdale N.J. Lawrence Erlbaum associates.

Hunt, E., Lunneborg, C., Lewis, J. (1975) : what does it mean to be high in verbal ? *Cognitive psychology*, **7**, 194-227.

Newell, A, Simon, HA (1972). *Human problem solving.* Ed. Englewood Cliffs N.J. Prentice Hall.

Richard, JF (1982) : Planification et organisation des actions dans la résolution du problème de la tour de Hanoï, par des enfants de 7 ans. *L'année psychologique*, **82**, 307-336.

Sternberg, R.J. (1977) : Intelligence information processing and analogical reasoning: the componential analysis of human abilities, Hillsdale N.J., Lawrence Erlbaum associates.

Sternberg, R.J. (1985) : Cognitive approaches to intelligence. In: *Handbook of intelligence*, Ed. Wolman, B., New-York, Chichester, Wiley.

VERIFICATION OF MEDICAL KNOWLEDGE MODELS USING FREE TEXT ANALYSIS

Amongst the models of medical knowledge, one has historically been privileged because of its spontaneous use by the physicians, the medical narrative. The narrative is the first step of information mediation in the medical approach and thus closely reflects the diversity and the evolutionary of nature medical reality. In this respect, medical narrative can be considered to contain the clinical aspect of medical knowledge.

We present here a tool able to extract the semantic content of medical narrative in order to control the adequacy of established knowledge models.

20.1. The medical narrative contains the patient clinical history

Every spontaneous exchange of information between physicians is mediated by natural language narratives. These narratives contain the synthetic data of the clinical history of the patient, as in the medical chart, discharge summaries, surgical or radiological reports or progress notes. Besides the reporting of every clinical event, the natural language is the only support of the interpreted knowledge, and then of the synthetic views on the patient. The numbers contained in the medical chart (lab results, body measurements, etc) are rough or primary data because they are not interpreted by the physician's knowledge (Roger, 1982).

The diagnosis alone does not for two reasons fully describe the patient's state of health:

1. The severity stage is not enclosed in the diagnosis label. The state of health of a cirrhotic patient relies, for example, besides the etiology, on the stage of severity of the disease, expressed in terms of liver function tests or of degree of portal hypertension (episodes of ascites, of gastrointestinal bleeding due to esophageal varices), as well as on the presence of associated diseases. The evolution of these

complications is also of primary importance : are they constant in frequency and severity or do they become more and more frequent and severe ? These observations appear mainly in the medical narrative, the numbers being of secondary importance.

2. The diagnosis label represents a short cut to the patient's real disease, as if all the diseases with the same label would give the same clinical picture and the same clinical course. To give a patient a diagnosis label corresponds to identify him to an hypothetical "mean" patient, as if all patients bearing an "acute appendicitis" would present themselves with identical clinical findings. The particuliar data that express the gap between the clinical state of an individual patient and its corresponding diagnosis label lies in the free text.

20.2. How to verify the adequacy of medical knowledge models

The power of a knowledge model greatly depends on its ability to adapt itself to the reality it has to describe (see figure 20.1). It is particularly true in the medical domain where the reality itself is constantly moving.

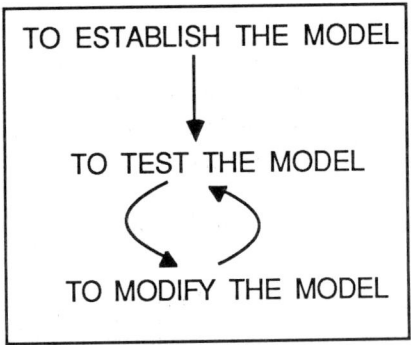

Figure 20.1. Step-by-step adaptation of the model to the reality

As it is impossible to directly use the semantic content of a patient in order to test the adequacy of a given model, another medium of information must be invoked. The clinical narrative, by its position in medical communication, is the best medium of medical reality, reflecting its properties of diversity and evolution as well as common sense. The actually less bad way to test the adequacy of knowledge models is to confront them to the semantics of clinical narratives such as discharge summaries which are striking summaries of the patient clinical histories.

N. Sager described an audit tool for healthcare evaluation, by comparing the content of a free text discharge summary to a reference table which specifies the elements of information to be found in such a document for a given disease (Sager, 1983). Such an evaluation tool can also be used in a "reverse manner" in order to test the adequacy of the model to fit the reality, as does ONCOCIN. When a physician who fills with ONCOCIN an oncological protocol does not give the prescribed medication, this choice is reviewed by experts who decide of an eventual modification of the protocol (Shortliffe, 1981).

The present paper describes a tool for evaluation of medical models based on the analysis of the narrative.

20.3. Knowledge representation of medical narratives

The medical approach represents itself a model of the patient's reality. The patient lives a sequence of health states, occuring before, during and after hospitalisation, successively modified either by the pathological process of the disease or by the healthcare actions (see figure 20.2).

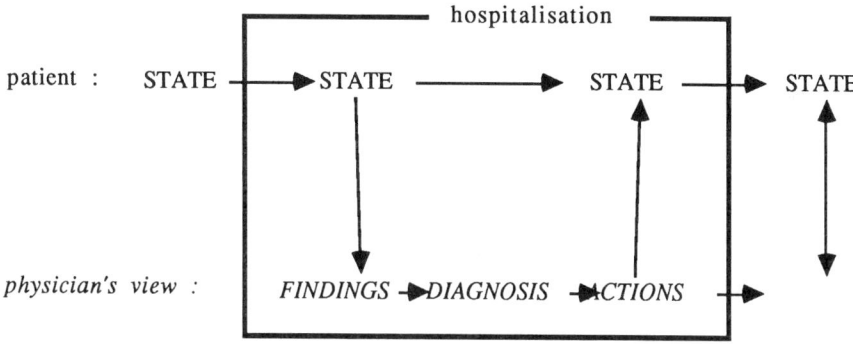

Figure 20.2. sequence of state of health of the patient and of medical inferences during an hospitalisation. (times goes from left to right : before during and after the hospitalisation)

The medical approach first relies on the clinical findings successively experienced by the patient and observed by the physician. By the aid of his knowledge, the physician then interpretes these findings, generates an hypothetical diagnosis and try to prove or refute it with the support of paraclinical procedures. The diagnosis is settled step-by-step, allowing therapeutical actions. Evolution of the disease process will be another factor in the evaluation of the diagnosis. The medical approach builds up a loop betwen the patient's reality and the consequences of the healthcare actions.

MAMIS, our tool of extraction of the semantic content of the clinical narratives processes the textual knowledge first by the recognition of the medical expressions and secondly by the restitution of the sequence which binds these expressions (MAMIS stands for "Multi-Link Medical Information System"). The three semantic categories of the expressions reflect the different steps of the medical approach (see figure 3). Each expressions can furthermore be characterized by different weights and confidence assessments : stages ("absence of", "risk of", "appearance", "increased", "unchanged", "decreased", "end of", "past") and level of certainty ("sure", "probable", "foreseen") (Frutiger *et al.*, 1980).

The time relation is of primary importance between the medical events. But besides the simple temporal <u>sequence</u> of the observed events, physicians build a network of relations reasoning between these events. These relations (mainly corresponding to the verbs found in the narratives) are enclosed by MAMIS in three categories :

- **"induces"** describes the physiopathological sequence of the disease, going from the etiologic agent of the disease to its complications, or going from a treatment to its effects ; "causes", "is complicated by" belong to the same category (e.g. "hepatitis is complicated by a cirrhosis" or "aspirin induces a diminution of fever") ;

- **"reveals"** goes up the physiopathological sequence, showing the cause of a clinical finding, etiological process of a disease or the result of a paraclinical procedure; "shows" and "evokes" are part of this category (e.g. "fever and hepatomegaly evoke an hepatitis" or "a chest X-ray reveals a lobar pneumonia") ;

- **"motivates"** describes the trigger of a medical action - either diagnostic of therapeutic - (e.g. "the suspicion of a gastroduodenal ulcer motivates an endoscopy" or "the bleeding motivates emergency blood transfusions").

Each of these categories symbolizes a set of other verbs ; "leads to" or "provokes" belong to the "induces" category (Borst *et al.*, 1984). These relations respect the sense of the chronological sequence, as seen in the following two sentences, "a pleural puncture reveals a hemothorax" and "a pleural puncture provokes a hemothorax" where the two verbs place the expressions in a reverse chronological order.

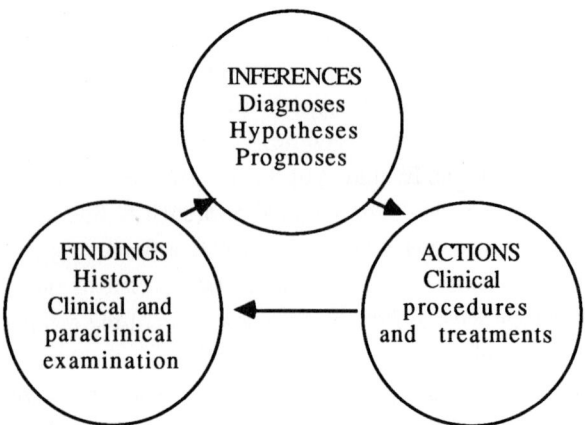

Figure 20.3. Semantic categories of medical expressions

20.4. Extraction of the semantic content of the medical narratives

The analysis of the narratives by our system is first accomplished by recognizing the medical expressions and secondly by analyzing the sentence.

The medical expressions are handled by a semantic network that mainly achieves the following two functions :

- **uniformisation** :
  The aim of this function is to recognize and uniformize the different words or combination of words than can have the same meaning, such as "Crohn's disease", "regional enteritis" or "granulomatous enteritis". Graitson gives an example of several hundreds of synonyms of an expression (Graitson, 1983). The semantic network completes this function either by direct synonymy or by combination of terms (e.g. "vesicular lithiasis" is related to "cholelithiasis").

"Patient known for an arterial hyp   ertension, hospitalised for abdominal pain irradiating in the   right lower quadrant which evokes an appendicitis"

PATIENT
      KNOWN
            FOR ARTERIAL HYPERTENSION
      HOSPITALISED
            FOR ABDOMINAL PAIN
                  IRRADIATING
                        IN RIGHT LOWER QUADRANT
                  EVOKES
                        APPENDICITIS

The different expressions are repr   esented on a hierarchical structur   e that respects the attachment between th   em. It is not possible to make the   right attachment between "hospitalised"   and "patient" (and not between "ho   spitalised" and "hypertension") without a sema   ntic analysis of the expressions.

Figure 20.4. Example of sentence analysis with attacment of the precisions betwwen expressions.

- **affiliation of expressions**
  Each recognized expression is affiliated at least to one specific semantic class. The different precisions of an expression can be recognized and characterized by the semantic network, such as the numerous features of a pain :"triggered by", "modified

by", "irradiating into", "colicky", "sharp", etc. The affiliation of a verb to its category is handled at this level (e.g. "shows" will be affiliated to "reveals"). The semantic class is defined by the relative position of the expression into the semantic network, allowing the multi-affiliation.

The sentence analysis is actually carried out by a simple syntactic parser written in Pascal, based on a programming language parser (Wirth, 1976). The sentence is broken in expressions, precisions and relations. These precisions are fragment of sentences successively superposed in order to fully describe an element, such as a patient, a finding, etc (e.g. "75 year old patient", "known for a lung cancer", "hospitalised for chest pain", or "colicky abdominal pain", "increased by the meals"). The main function of the parser is to accomplish the right attachment between expressions (see figure 20.4).

20.5. Conclusion

We describe here the system called "MAMIS", a extraction tool of the knowledge contained in the medical narratives knowledge, which restores the semantic sequences between the medical expressions. These sequences express the relations between the findings and the diagnosis, between the successive stages of a disease, as well as between the motives of the medical actions and their resulting effects.

The tool is designed to allow the verification of the knowledge models by the aid of their confrontation with the semantic content of the discharge summaries, which actually represent the best synthetical views of the patient clinical history.

The narratives are analysed by the aid of a semantic network that recognizes and handles the expressions and then by a parser that accomplished the attachment between these expressions.

Several discharge summaries in the field of digestive surgery have been analysed. A junction with a more powerful syntactical parser is planned in order to enlarge the treated domain.

20.5. Acknowledgements

Fonds National Suisse de la Recherche Scientifique, grant 3.920-0.83

References

Borst, F., Wehrli, E. & Scherrer, J.R. (1984). "Medial, a Natural Language Processing System for Medical Records". In: *Medical Informatics Europe 84 Proceedings* (Springer-Verlag, Berlin,), eds. F.H. Roger, J.L. Willems, R. O'Moore & B. Barber, 128-33.

Frutiger, P., Rossier, P. & Scherrer, J.R. (1980). "On-line ICD/SNOMED Encoding by Physicians in the HIS DIOGENE". In : *Medinfo 80,* Lindberg, Kaihara, eds. IFIP, North-Holland Publishing Company, 1290-4.

Graitson, M. (1983). "Aspects du traitement computationnel des données médicales en langue naturelle". *Thèse,* Université de Liège, Faculté de Philosophie et Lettres.

Roger, F.H. (1982). "Le résumé du dossier médical, indicateur informatisé de performance et de qualité des soins". *Thèse d'Agrégé de l'Enseignement Supérieur.* Université Catholique de Louvain, Faculté de Médecine.

Sager, N. (1983). *"Natural Language Information Processing* ", Addison-Wesley Publ. Comp, London.

Shortliffe, E.H. (1981). "ONCOCIN, An Expert System for Oncology Protocol Management". In : *Proceedings of the 7th International Joint Conference on Artificial Intelligence*, Vancouver, 876-81.

Wirth, N. (1976). "*Algorithm + Data Structures = Programs*", Prentice-Hall Inc., Englewood Cliffs, New Jersey.

THE SKILL DIMENSION :
ACQUISITION OF EXPERT BEHAVIOUR

21.1 Behaviour acquisition and knowledge elicitation

Most expert systems, either in medicine or in other application domains, are built assuming that when functioning they should indeed be experts right away. Knowledge engineering for such systems is seldom related to the human behaviour acquisition processes. In that respect, machine learning - a field concerned with developing computational theories of learning and constructing learning systems - is obviously central to the progress of AI knowledge representation methodologies (Michalski, 1986).

Production rules are a well-known knowledge representation scheme that has been heavily used in medical problem solving modelling (Shortliffe, 1976; Szolovits, 1982). Learning has been studied in Medicine, particularly by processing of rules and increasing their quantity and quality. The model we describe departs from these previously introduced acquisition mechanisms: the intelligent agent does not improve performance by increasing its knowledge base, but by building symbolic expectations enabling him to focus its attention on relevant hypotheses before starting the actual problem solving process.

Medical problem solving can be formalized into two different consecutive tasks, namely generation of initial hypotheses and evaluation of the latter (Norman, 1979). While the evaluation process might itself force the evocation or generation of new hypotheses to investigate, focus on the initial hypotheses is based on data gathered from the patient's complaints and from a set of discriminant cues the physician has learned from experience. Through successive evaluation of cases the medical expert acquires this first-look ability to pre-structure the problem.

Our study of knowledge acquisition processes, with clinical diagnosis as a workbench application domain, stressed out the following points (Rappaport *et al.*, 1984):

- Knowledge acquisition and behaviour acquisition are intertwined processes. Performances of problem solving tasks by an intelligent agent in the process of learning, alter and are altered by knowledge acquisition processes. Knowledge acquisition is not to be considered without reference to the agent acquiring knowledge.

- Behavior acquisition is constructing or modifying representations of what is being experienced. Learning is thus an adaptive process, based on interactions with the environment. Representation of these interactions and their use for oncoming problem solving activities change as the agent accumulates experience.

- The problem solving oriented knowledge representations are symbolic in nature. The cognitive processes at work are essentially construction and modification of symbolic representations of sets of concepts, through the analysis of past and current experience.

The strong dynamic relation between the environment and the intelligent agent during learning activities is then the core of knowledge elicitation processes, whether they are automatized or not.

21.2 Acquiring medical expert behavior

21.2.1 *The SKP simulation program*

An expert behavior acquisition simulation program, named SKP - standing for Symbolic Knowledge Processing -, was developed at the Robotics Institute, Carnegie-Mellon University, to test and refine the model. The SKP simulation program is organized around three consecutive modules: a production system for performing the diagnosis task, a knowledge acquisition module, and a first-look signs generator module.

The performance module is a production system producing a diagnosis. It operates in forward chaining on initial patient complaints and first-look signs, if any, synthesised by the generator module. Two different knowledge bases were developed as test domains: Birth Control Prescription Aid, and the Etiologies of Hypertension. The respective sizes of the knowledge bases were of 50, and 45 rules.

Production firings are recorded during operation of the performance module and input to the knowledge acquisition module. Each performance produces a trace - the list of fired rules - that is aggregated to clusters of previously recorded traces, according to a proximity measure. The proximity of two lists of rules is defined as the symmetric difference between the set of data that lead to the firing of the rules. It is a symbolic distance measure since these data are not all necessary numerical. New clusters are built when a trace is too distant from previously created clusters. Since the clustering algorithms operates on list of signs, clusters are partially ordered by the inclusion relation.

The third module extracts first-look signs from the set of clusters. For each least specific cluster (maximal with respect to the inclusion relation) of this dynamic memory, signs shared by its member traces are added to the initially empty list of first-look signs. These signs are then added to patient's complaints to direct the performance module on the next case.

As mentioned before, the first-look signs constitutive of the general expectation of the medical expert are not improved by means of statistical analysis of previously solved cases. The processing of these discriminant signs is symbolic, and this accounts for the instability of human thought, disturbed by a single, significantly unexpected event, but then well remembering this disturbance. The first-look signs are patient-independent but experience-dependent. They might be altered by exposure to a series of similar cases or a few very unusual ones and thus represent the physician's state of expectation.

21.2.2 *Skill refinement from learning by practice*

Figure 21.1 presents results drawn from a set of experiments run through the expert behavior acquisition simulation program with the Etiologies of Hypertension knowledge base. The accuracy of the initial focus of attention is computed as the distance between the set of hypotheses generated by the first-look signs alone, and the hypotheses evaluated and confirmed by the performance production system. This proximity thus denotes the accuracy of the concept-driven initial focus of attention, while the performance module is both data-driven (patient's complaints) and concept driven (first-look signs).

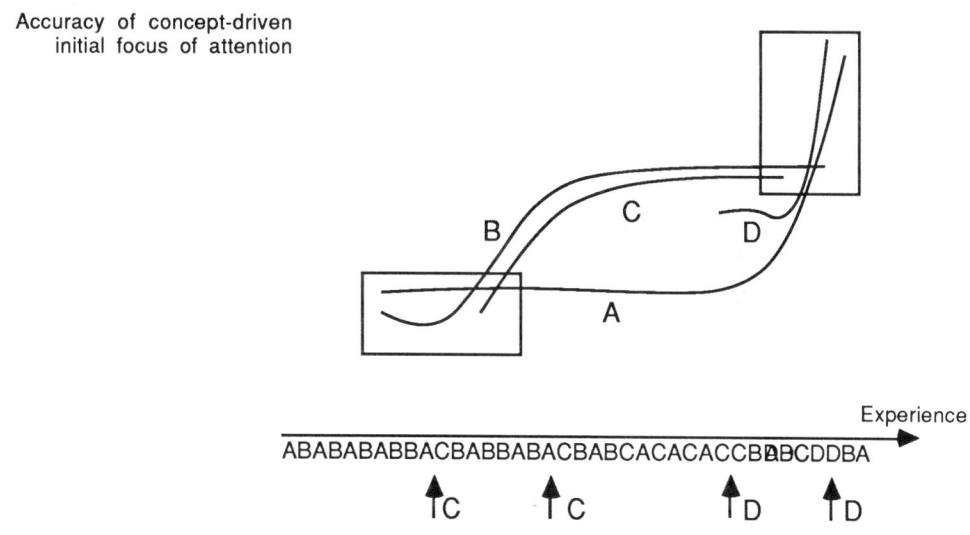

Figure 21.1 : In the Etiologies of Hypertension testbench, the system is presented with two quite different cases, named A and B. After presenting a consistent population of cases A and B, unexpected cases, named C and D, are occasionally presented. Particular occurrences of unexpected case enhance the initial accuracy of the first-look signs, even for common cases A and B as well as for uncommon cases C and D.

Case A is a hypertension induced by a fibromuscular disease of the renal artery,
Case B is a hypertension induced by an important stress,

Case C is a hypertension due to a hyperthyroidism,

Case D is a hypertension due to an acute glomerulonephritis.

In abcissa, the course of the system's experience is shown, with the series of cases it encountered. Arrows point to the important events. The two rectangles indicate the general situation of the system with regard to its first-look generation capacity, at the beginning and further during its experience.

Solution paths (chains of rules applied to solve the case) are recorded from the rule-based problem solver and input to the dynamic memory. These solution paths act as presentations for a version space (Mitchell, 1982) partially ordered by the inclusion relation. Since the knowledge base is defined a priori and is not altered by the learning process, the version space is finite, and the number of clusters generated is usually few. First-look signs are then used by the performance production system to focus its attention right away on the relevant hypotheses.

Evolution of first-look signs:

{ RAPID-ONSET; SEVERE-HIGH-BLOOD-PRESSURE; SYSTOLIC-HIGH-BLOOD-PRESSURE; ABDOMINAL-BRUIT }

This set of first-look signs is produced before the event C. They are definitely relevant to cases A and B. RAPID-ONSET, SEVERE-HIGH-BLOOD-PRESSURE and ABDOMINAL-BRUIT are characteristic of A (hypertension induced by a fibromuscular disease of the renal artery), while SYSTOLIC-HIGH-BLOOD-PRESSURE is relevant to B (hypertension induced by an important stress).

{ ANXIETY; SYSTOLIC-HIGH-BLOOD-PRESSURE; ABDOMINAL-BRUIT; WEIGHT-LOSS; PALPABLE-THYROID-GLAND; PALPITATIONS; PERMANENT-TACHYCARDIA }

After presentation of case C (hypertension due to hyperthyroidism) and new instances of A, and B, the first-look signs are modified. RAPID-ONSET, and SEVERE-HIGH-BLOOD-PRESSURE are removed. Signs relevant to C are added, reflecting the perturbation to the so far homogeneous A, and B population.

{ SEVERE-HIGH-BLOOD-PRESSURE; AGE; PROTEINURIA; RECENT-STREPTOCOCCAL-INFECTION; ABDOMINAL-BRUIT }

When case D (hypertension due to an acute glomerulonephritis) is presented the first-look signs are modified to reflect the various populations (A, B, and C) and the accommodation this second perturbation. AGE is a common sign for case A, B, C, and D while PROTEINURIA, and RECENT-STREPTOCOCCAL-INFECTION are characteristic of case D. Signs SEVERE-HIGH-BLOOD-PRESSURE, AGE, and ABDOMINAL-BRUIT denote expectation of instances of case A.

Figure 21.2 : In the Etiologies of Hypertension testbench the evolution of the set of the first-look signs generated by the third module reflect the homogeneous A, and B cases population as well as accommodation of perturbation (cases C and D of hypertension). The final expectation built by the system allows the performance module to be focused directly on discriminant signs of populations A, B, C, and D. The accuracy of the diagnosis process is then enhanced by this experience-driven initial focus of attention. Without this set of first-look signs, the performance module would require exhaustive and systematic data gathering on the case before assessing its relation to A, B, C or D.

From a medical standpoint, concept clusters built by the system during successive case evaluations refer to actual therapies or ways of reasoning in the medical fields chosen . From a behavioral standpoint, the evolution of the system tends to reach a general, optimal state of expectation, as shown in Figure 21.1 by the two rectangles. Examination of first-look signs shows they contain condensed information on past experience (cf Figure 21.2). This synthesis takes into account the numerous usual events, as would a statistical analysis of cases, as well as the few occasional unexpected occurences of unusual cases. Whereas common cases are handled on the basis of the greater amount of recorded similar cases, unexpected cases can induce specializations allowing new similar unexpected cases to be handled on the basis of the previously encountered particular instances. Extraction of first-look signs thus qualifies as a derivational analogy process (Carbonell, 1986).

21.3 Skill dimension in behavior classifications

Earlier studies of skill refinement have stressed out three major dimensions along which cognitive behavior can be classed : a task dimension, a processing dimension, and a skill dimension. Any behavior on a given task will, with practice, shift from the problem-solving to the cognitive skill end of the skill dimension (Card *et al.*, 1983). This accounts for the evolution captured in Figure 21.1 where simulated medical behavior shifts from pure data driven problem-solving to experienced management of the focus of attention.

This study in the medical field provides some indication that, as behavior becomes highly skilled (final rectangle in Figure 21.1), some of it may become organized differently. More specifically, first-look signs appear as a concept-driven mechanism of a specific structure that differs from the data-driven evaluation process.

Cases presented to the program induce a partition of the behavior stream into unit tasks. For each medical case, the problem-solver first acquires the case data and then evaluates the relevant hypotheses. Unit tasks thus have a well-defined internal structure and serve as a control construct for the problem-solver. The important point about the acquisition phase of the unit task, is that more than just a task is acquired (medical data and cues) - with the first-look signs, a method for accomplishing the task is also acquired (apply relevant rules for investigating hypotheses evoked by first-look signs).

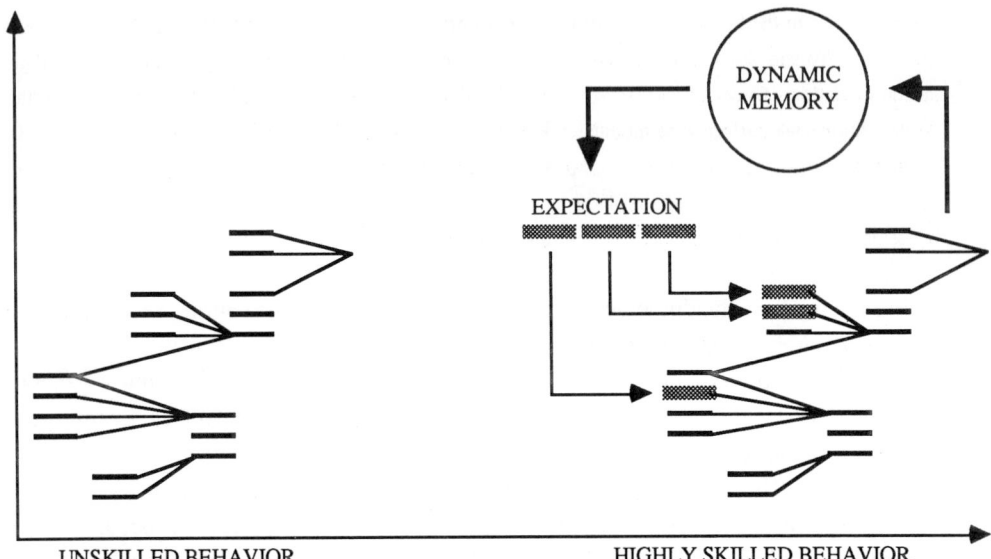

UNSKILLED BEHAVIOR   HIGHLY SKILLED BEHAVIOR

Figure 21.3 : The skill dimension of behavior space.
Skill is one of the features that distinguish novice from expert behavior. On the unskilled end of the skill dimension, novice behavior is pure problem-solving. Systematic application of book-knowledge, encoded as production rules in our model, yields solution to problems presented to the performance module.

On the high end of the skill dimension, experts appear to focus their attention on salient features of the problem, thereby guiding the problem-solving performance. This expectation-driven problem solving is made possible through a shift in knowledge structure. Experience accumulated through repetitive processing of problems is not encoded into new or modified rules, but aggregated in a dynamic memory from which an average expectation is extracted.

This general expectation is used to correctly point out the salient features of cases so far processed and thus direct the attention of the performance module on the relevant hypothesis when a new case is presented. This ability to judge where to focus its attention is quite characteristic of expert behavior.

Experiments with the model showed that behavior organisation during acquisition phase and during evaluation phase of the case were definitely of a distinct nature (cf Figure 21.3). When first-look signs are produced, they directly evoke initial hypotheses to investigate. The evaluation of the generated hypotheses then guides the data gathering process. First-look signs thus constrain the set of candidate rules for evaluation to those production rules that are relevant to the generated hypotheses.

This shift in structure accounts for the skill refinement observed in the field of medical problem-solving in our experiments (Chauvet, 1985). This indication of different behavior organisations seems somewhat contrary to the notion of homogeneous organization apparently implied by the skill dimension classification. Since problem-solving behavior is simply the less skilled end of this dimension, it is not a separate species of behavior nor a separate class of tasks, and one would thus expect quantitative rather than qualitative improvement along this skill dimension. While this is the case for highly-skilled automatic behaviors, gradually developed with extreme practice, some cognitive skill behavior were shown to be very resistant to becoming automatic. It seems unlikely that medical case-solving could ever become extensively automatic.

21.4 Problem-solving and knowledge acquisition tools

This study indicates the need for basic research work in the field of knowledge acquisition in various application domains, as problem solving software tools now emerge on the market. The current limitations of such problem solvers are their dependency towards human experts for consistently acquiring knowledge. Results drawn on our experimentation in the medical field, and particularly the simulation of expert behavior acquisition, provide theoretical and applicative guidelines for future work :

- Knowledge acquisition should take into account the agent. Problem solving is an acquired ability and is strongly related to adaptive learning. This work thus emphasises problem-solving oriented knowledge representations for future problem solving activities. The extraction of first-look signs illustrates the need for considering both data-driven guidance and concept-driven guidance for the problem solver.
- Pre-structuring the problem space for managing the focus of attention of the problem solver is characteristic of expert behavior. Although we have been working under the assumption that this pre-structuring ability , symbolic in nature, might be acquired by processes close to derivational analogy, this is by no means the only scheme of skill refinement by learning from experience. Depending on the task performed by the problem solver, alternative propositions were made : the chunking model of practice is an example of such an architecture. Interestingly enough, expert behavior acquisition is obtained by weak methods in previously mentioned work.

This paper, along with the other mainstreams of research work in AI, argues for task-oriented concept-driven software tools for automatizing knowledge acquisition. A possible architecture for such learning systems stems from this study , encompassing a problem-solver operating in a given task problem-space interacting with a focus of attention manager overlaying a pre-structure on the problem space. Managing the focus of attention is itself considered as problem-solving in a higher problem-oriented problem-space. Operation of a weak method on multiple problem-spaces is also found in research works on algorithm design, and organisational behavior.

References

Card, S.P., Moran, T.P. & Newell, A. (1983). The Psychology of Human-Computer Interaction. Lawrence Erlbaum Associates, Publishers.

Carbonell, J.G (1986). Derivational Analogy: A Theory of Reconstructive Problem Solving and Expertise Acquisition. In: *Machine Learning: An Artificial Intelligence Approach,* **II**, Morgan Kaufmann Publishers, 371-93.

Chauvet, J.M., (1985). Genetic Epistemology. *AI Magazine,* **6**, 18-9.

Michalski, R.S. (1986). Understanding the nature of learning: Issues and research directions. In: *Machine Learning: An Artificial Intelligence Approach,* **II**, Morgan Kaufmann Publishers, 3-25.

Mitchell, T.M. (1982). Generalization as Search., *Artificial Intelligence,* **18**.

Norman, D.A. (1979). Analysis and Design of Intelligent Systems. In: *Human and Artificial Intelligence.,* North Holland Publishing Company.

Rappaport, A.T., Chauvet, J.M. (1984). Symbolic Knowledge Processing for the Acquisition of Expert Behavior: A Study in Medicine. Carnegie-Mellon University, The Robotics Institute, Technical Report CMU-RI-TR-84-8.

Shortliffe, E. (1976). *Computer Based Medical Consultations: MYCIN.* American Elsevier.

Szolovits, P. (1982). *Artificial Intelligence and Medicine,* Westview Press.

22 *Y. Chiaramella, C. Berrut, P. Cinquin*

A CONCEPTUAL MODEL FOR MEDICAL REPORTS IN A MULTIMEDIA ENVIRONMENT

22.1 Introduction

The context of this study is the definition of a multimedia data base for storing and retrieving heterogeneous data such as X-ray or MRI pictures and related textual reports containing information about these iconographic documents.

The data base aspects related to data base model, storage and access techniques were investigated by G. Munoz (Munoz, 1987) who implemented a prototype based first on the TIGRE multimedia DBMS (Lopez, & all, 1983) and later on the ORACLE DBMS. This prototype allowed to store digitalized pictures and related textual information (the medical reports) and to access these data using SQL-like queries. As an example, one could retrieve particular X-ray pictures related to a given patient over a given period, or retrieve the associated reports using the same criteria, or retrieve both information. Despite the multimedia technology involved, the very nature of the queries was hence still classical, which means that possible queries were limited by a predestined (i.e. static) semantic model imbedded in standard relational schemas.

In a second approach we were interested in allowing more sophisticated queries such as "select all the X-ray pictures where an observed lung opacity is related to lung cancer". On one hand, this kind of query clearly allows to investigate the data base in a very flexible way (for epidemiologic studies, as an example). On the other hand this approach also corresponds to the design and implementation of a more sophisticated semantic model for medical reports than one can expect to define using the relational model. The design of the semantic model and of the two fundamental processes which are first the interpretation (or indexing) of medical reports according to this model, and second the retrieval techniques of those documents based on this model, are thus the main objectives of our study in the area. In this paper we will concentrate on the semantic model design and on the indexing process.

After a short presentation of the information contained in medical reports (see section 22.2), we describe and comment the proposed semantic model in section 22.3. Then in section 22.4 we present the interpretation process which is a transformation of the natural language format of the medical reports into the semantic model.

22.2 The Medical Reports

Medical reports most often are short, hand-written documents, usually less than one page long, which are produced by specialists while they investigate medical data. They usually combine external attributes such as patient's names and dates, examination data about the special techniques used for the examination, observations and, most often, a proposed diagnosis. These three last kinds of information constitute the very content of the medical reports, in contrast with external attributes which describe the context of the examination. While external attributes are usually described in a conventional format (i.e. using specific predestined fields in the document) and are well adapted to a relational model, the content is expressed in natural language and needs a more sophisticated and flexible model.

Due to the intrinsic nature of these documents and the circumstances of their elaboration, they are both highly technical and written in a concise and direct style. Hence the basic vocabulary is mainly made of technical terms related to the technology used for the examinations, and of medical terms used to describe observations and to issue diagnosis. On the other hand, concise and direct style most often lead to rather simple syntactical structures of the sentences.

These two fundamental characteristics of the textual information we have to process (limited vocabulary and simple syntax) may allow automatic deep understanding of medical reports which, in turn, may allow the design of high-level information retrieval access techniques. In a classical approach, deep understanding means the possibility to translate natural language information in an elaborate semantic model, and high-level information retrieval techniques means the possibility to issue "content oriented" queries.

22.3 The semantic model of medical reports

22.3.1 *Main principles*
The model presented here is based on the idea of conceptual dependency introduced by Schank (1980 and 1981). Our view of this model in the particular context of the study is based on the following principles:

a) the dependency among concepts is represented by binary tree structures:

- the non-terminal nodes correspond to semantic operators which state in detail particular relationships between lower-level concepts (i.e. subtrees).

Example: the binary operator [due-to] establishes a causality relationship between its two operandi.

- the terminal nodes correspond to medical or technical terms which are simple words or compound words in common use in the domain (they in fact define the semantic domain of the application).

Example: "liver", "lung", "opacity"..

b) every sentence of a medical report is translated in such a tree which constitutes the proposed representation of the meaning of this sentence. Hence the conceptual model of a medical report is a set of such trees.

Example: the following expression is the prefixed notation of a simple binary tree which corresponds to the interpretation of the sentence "the lung opacity":

[bears-on] (opacity, lung)

c) every tree is built according to a formal model which is defined by a grammar. The language which corresponds to this grammar is called the Conceptual Language (or the target language when considering the interpretation process from the natural language to the conceptual model). We call Conceptual Report (CR) the representation of a medical report according to the semantic model.

Before going into the details of the model, we have to give some insights about these choices:

- the natural language expression of medical reports, if relatively simple, is not limited to a predestined syntax (a subset of the natural language). We thus have to deal with a simple but not strictly normalized language which the users would not usually accept, due to the corresponding constraints. Hence every a-priori design of the conceptual model using predestined static structures (such as frames) would be more difficult to match with the input data, and thus to implement.

- as the user language is not controlled, we have to deal with complex problems such as natural language ambiguities, ellipsis, paraphrasing. The solution of these problems implies transformations of syntactical and semantic structures which we estimate easier when implemented using trees.

- the organization of knowledge imbedded in medical reports clearly presents several levels of organization. As mentioned before, a medical report usually contains information about the examination, the observations made and possibly a diagnosis. Each of these elements may in turn be refined in terms of subnotions such as signs, localization and so on, the lowest level being elementary medical facts or knowledge. This obviously suggests a hierarchical conception of the model which fits well with the tree structures defined above. Moreover this hierarchy may be defined through a context free grammar where the metasymbols stand for intermediate-level concepts (such as signs, observations, diagnosis), and terminal symbols stand for atomic concepts (or self-defined concepts). The rules of the grammar provide the definition of the intermediate concepts (see examples below) and specify the possible structures of the trees. The correspondence between metasymbols and intermediate-level concepts is very important because it allows to *retrieve* these concepts in conceptual reports, using syntactical properties (hence the implicit knowledge to which they correspond may be made explicit).

22.3.2 *The Conceptual Language*

The conceptual language presents three main levels in organizing the knowledge associated to the medical report content. Metasymbols are shown in upper case characters, terminal symbols are shown in lower case characters. Terminal symbols are noun phrases (which may be reduced to a single word). We restrict the following presentation to a subset of the language (sufficient to illustrate the main principles of the model) , and which is sufficient to understand the following examples.

a) the first level expresses that a report is made of one or several sentences, and gives the formal definition of higher-level concepts related to the main components of a medical report (conceptual report, observations, diagnosis):

> CR ::= OBSERVATION
> CR ::= DIAGNOSIS
> CR ::= OBSERVATION [induces] DIAGNOSIS

> these rules define a CR (conceptual report) as possibly made of an observation, a diagnosis or an observation and a related diagnosis (the relationship being made explicit by the semantic operator).

b) the second level defines basic notions such as OBSERVATION, DIAGNOSIS and the associated sub-notions.

OBSERVATION ::= OBSERVATION [due-to] OBSERVATION
> this rule expresses that observations may be interdependent

OBSERVATION ::= SIGN [shown-by] EXAMINATION I SIGN
> this rule defines an observation as a sign revealed by an examination, or a sign alone. A sign is an observable entity, such as a volume, an area.

DIAGNOSIS ::= DIAGNOSIS [and] DIAGNOSIS
> this rule defines a diagnosis as a possible combination of several sub-diagnosis.

DIAGNOSIS ::= LESION
> this rule defines a diagnosis as the identification of a particular lesion.

SIGN ::= SIGN [has-for-value] QUALIFIER
> this rule defines a sign as being possibly related to a qualifier (such as augmentation, diminution..)

SIGN ::= SIGN [bears-on] LOCALIZATION
> this rule defines a sign as being related to a particular localization.

LESION ::= LESION [located-on] LOCALIZATION
> this rule defines a lesion as an active process in a given localization of the organism (like in "the tumor of the lung")

LESION ::=LESION [in-topologic-relation-with] LOCALIZATION
> this rule defines a lesion as a possible combination of a lesion related to a localization (like in "tumor behind costal grid").

LOCALIZATION ::= LOCALIZATION [located-on] POSITION I CONST-ORG
> this rule defines a localization as either a constituent of the organism or a more complex notion combining a localization and a particular position (like in "the upper part of the left lung").

c) The third level contains pre-terminal and terminal rules, which correspond to the lowest level concepts in the model. The set of terminal symbols is defined in a dictionary (see section 4); the sub-classes of terminal symbols (like SIGN...) are determined by assigning each term in the dictionary a *semantic class which is the corresponding metasymbol* (as an example, the term "augmentation" will be assigned the semantic class "sign" in the dictionary). Being associated to metasymbols in the grammar, the semantic classes assigned to terms are used while generating the semantic interpretation of sentences. The rules in fact control which classes may be combined to derive a correct interpretation. This approach is very similar to Semantic Grammars introduced by Fillmore (1968).

SIGN ::= *NP (SIGN),* which stands for "a term whose semantic class is SIGN" (like "volume"..).

LESION ::= *NP (lesion)*, which stands for "a term whose semantic class is LESION" (like "tumor", "cancer"..).

CONST-ORG ::= *NP (const-org)*, which stands for "a term whose semantic class is CONST-ORG" (like "lung", "elbow"..).

POSITION ::= *NP (position)*, which stands for "a term whose semantic class is POSITION" (like "fringe", "side",..).

Of course this gives only a partial idea of the actual semantic model which is made of about 60 rules; as an indication, there are 11 different semantic operators and the dictionary is organized in 24 semantic classes. The first experimentations have led to very encouraging results, which demonstrate the validity of the approach. But they also clearly show that the model has to be refined to improve the effectiveness of the process; this mainly concerns the design of updating interfaces for the dictionary , the syntactical and semantic analyzers.

22.4 The interpretation

The aim of this chapter is to describe how to transform the medical reports which are written in natural language into conceptual reports which are written in the target language described in the previous section. Through the use of syntactical and conceptual knowledge, we define an automatic process which performs this translation.

To describe this process, we first define the morphology and the dictionary we use, then the syntactic and conceptual tools, and finally we give examples of translation.

22.4.1 *The morphology*

The first step in our process is a morphological tool which recognizes each form in the text.

We process a classical morphological analysis from left to right.This analysis consists of a segmentation of each form into a root and an ending (Palmer - Berrut, 1985). The roots stand in a dictionary, the endings in several specific tables. All known segmentations of each form are stored in a dictionary.

We use a dictionary in which all the roots are factorized according to a lexicographic tree, and ordered according to a frequency criteria in order to optimize the access (Palmer, 1981). Each root end is materialized by a slot. During the analysis, when such a slot is met, a set of ending tables is ratified. The recognition is then at the same time pursued through these tables and in the dictionary without back-tracking.

22.4.2 *The dictionary*

Each form is stored with its syntactic and semantic information. The dictionary we use can be seen as a relation:

form * syntactic category * (semantic feature , semantic class)

where:

- the syntactic category is the grammatical category of the form according to the syntactic model we will define afterwards;
- the semantic feature is the semantic interpretation given to the form (according to the semantic model), and which is substituted to the form during the translation;
- the semantic class represents a metasymbol of the target language.

Examples :

(liver, substantive, (liver, CONST-ORG)).

here the semantic feature is the term itself (liver), the semantic class being CONST-ORG.

(ectopical, qualifying adjective, ([has-for-value], position, unusual), QUAL)

here the semantic feature is an expression in the semantic model: ([has-for-value], position, unusual), which gives a refined interpretation of the term. The semantic class is QUAL(ificative).

Let us remember that the aim of our process is to detect in the text medical facts and semantic links between these facts. The medical facts are expressed in this dictionary as simple features (terminal symbols of the target language) - see "liver" for example -, or as completely instantiated features (instantiated rules of the target language) - see "ectopical" for example -. On the other hand, the links between medical facts are expressed through incompletely instantiated features (un-instantiated rules of the target language). The left or right context of these forms in the reports will instantiate these features. Syntactically speaking, these semantic links are expressed in the natural language through prepositions, verbal syntagms and their nominalization.

Example : (deviate, verb, ([due-to], ([bears-on]([has-for-value], POSITION, deviation), LOCALIZATION), DIAGNOSIS)), OBSERVATION) where localization and diagnosis are notions which are not instantiated.

The result of the morphology and of the consultation of this dictionary is a network of syntactic and semantic informations; these informations can be ambiguous (for example, words representing polysemies or homographs). The aim of the syntactic component and of the conceptual component is to solve such ambiguities in order to get the translation of each report into the target language.

22.4.3 *The syntactic component*

The aim of this component is:

- to solve some syntactic ambiguities in order to simplify the semantic network;

- to give to the conceptual component a first representation of the text (the syntactic component tries to extract from the text what might be called syntactic concepts and links between these concepts).

22.4.3.1 Solving ambiguities

Through a consultation of the dictionary, the morphological analysis gives the list of all the syntactic categories of each form in the text. We can get:

- either a single syntactic category (the word is recognized without any syntactic ambiguity)
  - or several syntactic categories (the word is a homograph)
  - or no syntactic category (the word is not known in the dictionary).

A list of about fifty syntactic categories has been manually defined, this list can be divided in two groups:

- the closed categories: these are the categories which contain a finite number of words; for example articles and pronouns;
- the opened categories: these are the categories which contain a hardly numberable list of words, such as nouns, adjectives and verbs, whose content may evolve as the corpus grows.

Inside these opened categories, the irregular words which mainly come from the language's inheritance, can be considered as a stable subset which we have stored in the dictionary. We also have stored the closed categories (Grevisse, 1980). So each new word, that is to say each word which is unknown in the dictionary, is neither irregular nor member of a closed category: so it is either a noun, an adjective or a verb or an adverb. If it is a noun, an adjective or a verb, the word is regular: its different forms (feminine, plural) can be automatically deduced from standard inflexion suffixes.

The syntactic analysis first applies a syntactic filter on the list of grammatical categories obtained from the morphological step. This filter is based on positional relations between grammatical categories of consecutive words in a sentence, which is synthetically defined by a so-called "precedence matrix". If we consider the transition possibilities between grammatical categories of consecutive words as links, and categories as nodes, we can view the sentence as a (generally not linear) network. Non linearity arises when several links start from or converge to a single node: this corresponds also to an ambiguity. The filtering step first enables the syntactically correct links between nodes, but also discards unauthorized configurations (i.e. some of the grammatical categories of words may be discarded).

At the end of this step some ambiguities may still remain: some words may still have multiple grammatical possibilities, so that several pathways may still be considered in the network. The syntactic analysis then goes through a second step to solve remaining "interesting ambiguities"; i.e. it tries to linearize fragments of the network when it will help the conceptual process. That means that the syntactic component solves syntactic ambiguities only if the words attached to these ambiguities are also semantic ambiguities, so that solving the syntactic ambiguities also simplifies the semantic network. This process involves the recognition of ambiguity patterns and the application of standard solution for each of them. At the end of this step the network is linearised on portions which might be interesting for the conceptual process (partly linearized network). Hence we have solved only "interesting ambiguities" without going into deep sentence analysis (Berrut, Palmer, 1986).

22.4.3.2 A first representation of the text
The syntactic component must provide a first representation of the text for the conceptual component. That means that the syntactic component tries to represent the text as concepts and links between concepts. The problem is to know what might be called concepts and what might be called links for a syntactic purser. The approximation we made here is the following: we consider as "syntactic" concepts nominal syntagms and as links between these concepts verbal syntagms and prepositions (except "of"). Applying on the text a grammar representing these possibilities, we can extract a syntactic representation of the text.

Example: for the sentence
"condensation   du   poumon droit"
(condensation of the right lung)
we get
nominal syntagm   preposition   nominal syntagm
which could be represented

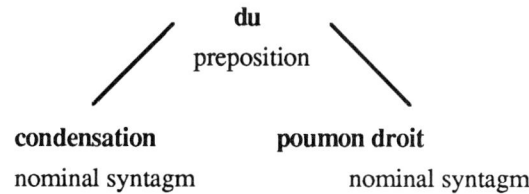

du
preposition

condensation   **poumon droit**
nominal syntagm   nominal syntagm

22.4.4 *The conceptual component*
We now consider the semantic component whose input is the representation the syntactic component delivers. Comparing this representation with the first semantic network we could have used at the end of the morphology, we now have a representation of the text according to what the syntactic component might locate as concepts and links between concepts, and also the syntactic component might have solved ambiguities.

The network we obtain is made of semantic terms (some semantic terms may have empty slots); at the moment there is no link between these semantic terms except that we know the nominal and verbal syntagms according to the syntactic analysis. We try to fill the empty slots of the verbal syntagms (or their nominalization) using their neighbors, according to the target language. This process is provided by a rewriting system (Ramos, 1987) which describes the target language. The rewriting system also provides the possibility of back-tracking when it gets semantic terms which are impossible to relate. It also provides a normalization of the conceptual reports (i.e. reports written in the target language): that means that semantically equivalent reports will become equivalent conceptual reports, even if their writings are different in the vocabulary and in the presentation (paraphrasing). An attempt to implement this solution has been made in Prolog using dictionaries of about 700 words (Yan, 1986).

Example: for the above example
"condensation   du   poumon droit"
(condensation of the right lung)
we get

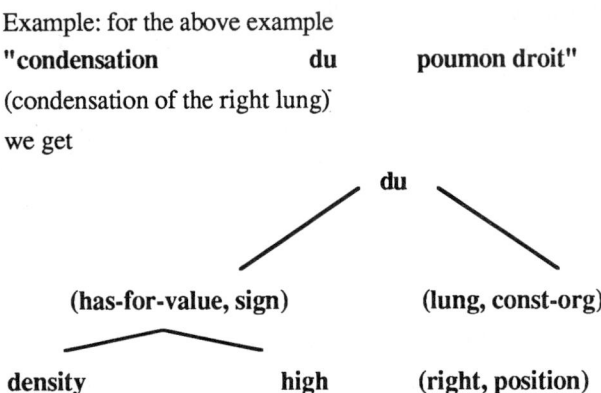

we use the following rewriting rules:
const-org position --> ([located-on, const-org, position], localization)
sign localization --> ([bears-on, sign, localization], sign)

which gives the following tree:

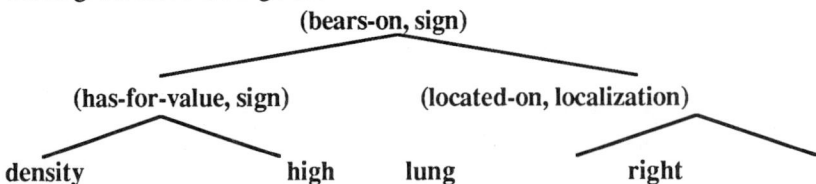

22.5 Conclusion

Given the multimedia context described above, the medical reports may thus be considered as detailed descriptions and interpretations of the associated pictures, and the semantic model which we have defined for the documents may be considered as a semantic model for the pictures themselves. The classical data base approach based on a predestined model of the data (here mainly the external attributes) combined with information retrieval techniques based on more elaborate models for document content may thus allow a more complete and flexible set of access techniques to multimedia documents.

Besides the particular application investigated in this study (namely X-ray pictures and their related medical reports) our belief is that there are many other application fields presenting the same basic characteristics and hence that the approach presented below is of much larger scope. Preliminary implementations of the model has shown good results, but there is no doubt that the model will have to be improved to undertake real size applications. We thus concentrate also on a critical aspect of this work: the design of efficient and ergonomic interfaces for the dynamic definition and updating of the model by end users. This concerns dictionary updating (with consistency check) and the updating of the rules (syntactical and semantic rules).

References

Berrut, C. & Palmer, P. (1986). Solving Grammatical Ambiguities within a Surface Syntactical Parser for Automatic Indexing. *Proceedings of the 8th ACM-SIGIR Conference,* Pisa.

Fillmore, C. J. (1968). The Case for Case. *Universals in Linguistic Theory*, 1-88. E. Bach and R.T. Harms, Molt Rinehart and Wiston (New York).

Grevisse, M. (1980). Le bon usage. Editions Hatier, Paris.

Lopez, M., Palazzo-Oliveira, J. & Velez, F. (1983). The TIGRE Data Model. *Research report Tigre 2,* Bull-LGI research center, Grenoble University.

Munoz, G. (1986). Stockage et exploitation de dossiers medicaux multimedia au moyen d'une base de données généralisée. Ph. D thesis, Grenoble University.

Palmer, P. & Berrut, C. (1985). Etude d'un analyseur de surface de la langue naturelle pour un système de recherche documentaire. *Proceedings of the 13rd ACSI conference,* Montreal.

Palmer, P. (1981). Etude de l'organisation d'un dictionnaire pour l'analyse du français. Master Thesis, Grenoble University.

Ramos, H. (1987). Une application de la réécriture à la compréhension de la langue naturelle: le traitement de comptes rendus médicaux. Master Thesis, Grenoble University.

Schank, R. C. & Birnbaum, L. (1980). Memory, Meaning and Syntax. *Research report,* **189**. Yale University, Department of Computer Science.

Schank, R.C. (1981). Representing Meaning: an Artificial Intelligence Perspective. *Cognitive Technical Report* , **11**. Yale University. Cognitive Science Program.

Yan, J. (1986). Interprétation sémantique de comptes rendus médicaux. Master thesis, Grenoble University.

23 *S. Comby, J.P. Flandrois and A. Pave*

A CONTRIBUTION TO THE STUDY OF THE DISCRIMINANT CAPABILITY OF AN EXPERT SYSTEM: APPLICATION TO CLINICAL BACTERIOLOGY

23.1 Introduction

For about twenty years, medical diagnostic problems have been approached by Artificial Intelligence (A.I.) methods and certainly contributed to the development of this field (Kleinmutz, 1984). Numerous expert systems, depending on cognitive rules, attempt to simulate human reasoning. However only a few have had practical applications to clinical routine; most of them illustrated or enhanced fundamental aspects in A.I. field.

So, the aim of our work was not to test an elaborate technology of knowledge organization or management, but to rapidly exploit an elementary inference engine (PROLOG II) in order to demonstrate the feasibility and the relevance of an expert system in a restrictive field; the clinical bacteriology of urine samples, by comparing decisions taken by the system to medical diagnoses and multivariate analyses results. Consequently, the methodological originality of the present work consisted in studying, **in a descriptive manner**, how knowledge-based systems compete with data structure analyses for discrimination. Multivariate analyses were used like a decision-aid means and then might contribute to the identification of some discriminant rules.

23.2 Origins of the study

In medical bacteriology laboratories, practitioners often have recognition problems, especially in order to choose between **significant** urinary tract **infection** and urine sample **contamination**. The answer requires medical experience. Contamination risks are indeed multiple, related to micro-organisms' ability to grow in this excretion medium (e.g. contamination by commensal vaginal flora in a female patient, or after urine catheter implant).

The availability of an expert is necessary to help decide, during an analysis:

before germ identification, which is not carried out if there are indications of contamination after direct flora or cytology examination.

before antibiogram study (in a therapeutic aim), which is not carried out if germs are assumed to be non-infectious.

The **expert system concept** provides an answer to this decision problem, because of its availability and the *a priori* medical knowledge, which is more or less formalized. However, the decision factors may be also considered as variables for mutivariate analysis:

as quantitative variables, e.g. flora and cytology enumeration (abundance classes).

as qualitative variables, e.g. inquiries about patient (age and sex) or about isolated and identified germs.

In order to compare these two methodological approaches, 200 urine screenings, including 32 sterile or insignificantly infectious cases, were used.

23.3 **Methodology**

23.3.1 *Application of Artificial Intelligence techniques the Expert System (fig. 23.1.)*
In all expert systems, the inference engine handles knowledge in order to ensure the management of reasoning.

23.3.1.1 Presentation of the inference engine: PROLOG II
PROLOG (for logical programming) seems first like a programming language, but it provides an elementary inference engine sufficient for our purpose. The representation formalism in this case is the Horn clause: an inverted production rule, the conclusion part of which appears in the rule headline. The available version, PROLOG II (Colmerauer *et al.*, 1983), is software working on Macintosh. It will be regarded in this study as a conception tool for expert system model.

Its main characteristics, as an inference engine, are briefly stated. It is an engine admitting variables, transferred to the rules as argument. It is reasoning by back-tracking (e.g. in our expert system, in order to verify a biological assumption), and the whole of the rules concerned are first explored in depth. This way is pursued up to success or failure, then the system back-tracks in order to start applicable rules which have not been tested (restriction stage). All answers to a given problem are then found (contrary to the Edinburgh's version, which stops as soon as the tracking is successful). Its last characteristic is monotony: the inference engine does not modify already established facts. This quality is well suited to a diagnostic subject that remains unchanged during an ordinary session of expert system utilization.

23.3.1.2 Knowledge representation
Knowledge is written in PROLOG, like Horn clauses. Relatively to the system architecture, different modules need to be distinguished (although their formalism is similar).

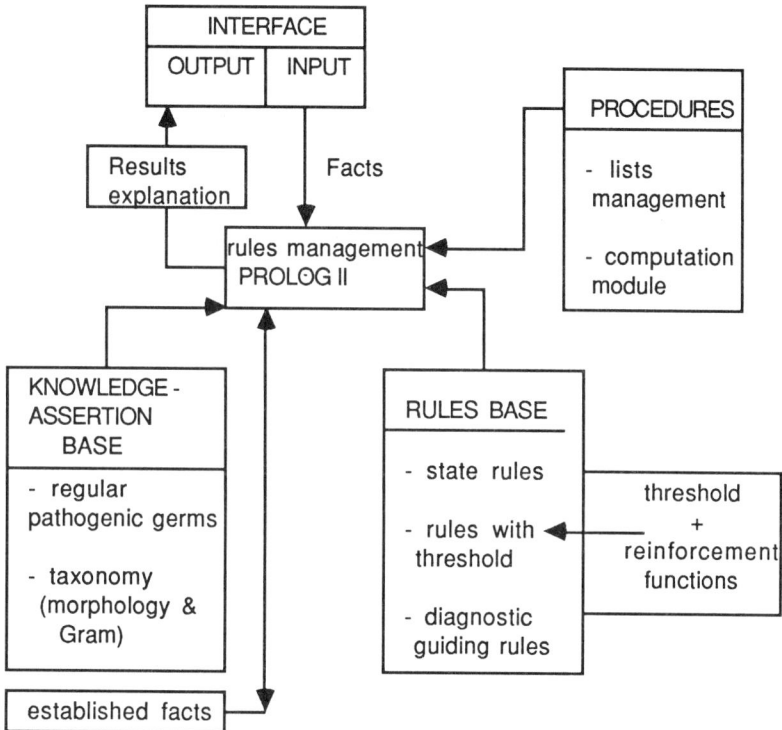

Figure 23.1. Scheme of expert system principles. See text for further details about rules and knowledge assertions.

(i) **The rule base:**
It represents the set of "savoir-faire" units, including a condition part and a conclusion part. The headline (the conclusion to verify) contains arguments which are equally transmitted as input or output parameters, according to the rule:

$$e.g. \quad pat(female, a\text{-}ge, 2, contamin)\text{-}>$$
$$val(inf(59, a\text{-}ge), 1);$$

This rule means:
    if the patient is female and 59 years older (2 input arguments, the sex which represents a condition and a-ge, a variable).

then this rule validates in favour of contamination, with a weight of 2 (2 output arguments).

Biological hypotheses (fig. 23.2.) are chained; their calling order depends on the fixed asking order of the interface. Their verification is associated with the back-tracking of different kind of rules: three sorts of weighted rules are used.

- *state rules*: their application depends on inquiriy modalities about patient (sex, age), clinical service (urology, geriatrics...), taking of urine sample (with catheter or not), kind of germ (regular pathogen or not)...

- *rules with threshold*: they test semi quantitative results about flora or cytology enumeration. They need significant thresholds, determined by physicians, in favour of the infection (e.g. polynuclears $\geq 10^4$ cells/ml) or in favour of the contamination (Gram-bacilli $\geq 10^4$ bac./ml). The rule weight is reinforced when deviation between screening results and threshold is significant (enumeration = 10 or 100 times threshold).

- *diagnostic guiding rules:* they recognize a typical biological state like the beginning of infection or an infection which is already treated with therapeutics.

For example, in the first case, after questioning, the system eliminates biologically near eventualities, like contamination before a delayed examination, or polynuclear deficiency in an immuno-depressed patient. Then, it carefully studies the number of isolated species, the predominant flora ..., trying to establish the contamination, after the reject of the infection beginning hypotheses.

The system is able to generate and test other biological hypotheses, like infection with a single species, infection with two species... In regard to its inference it can distinguish between contaminant flora and infectious flora.

(ii) **Knowledge-assertion base:**

For their application, the above mentioned rules need, partly, expert knowledge looking like assertions (the condition part of the clause is always true).

This base contains the name of germs regarded as regular pathogens of urinary tract, or as contaminants.

For example:

$$\text{patho-habit-urine(Es-coli,+0.9)->;}$$

means *Escherichia coli* is a regular pathogen with a confidence about 0.9 (the certainty of this knowledge is -1 for a regular contaminant germ and +1 for a regular pathogen).

It is completed with a brief taxonomy, where some bacterial species or genera are attached to gram and morphology.

(iii) **Fact base:**

Inference needs also information related to the current problem. The system keeps this data, like the deduction of new facts (e.g. treated infection) or the weight and number of each applied rule, in favour of infection or contamination, in order to have a trace of the reasoning.

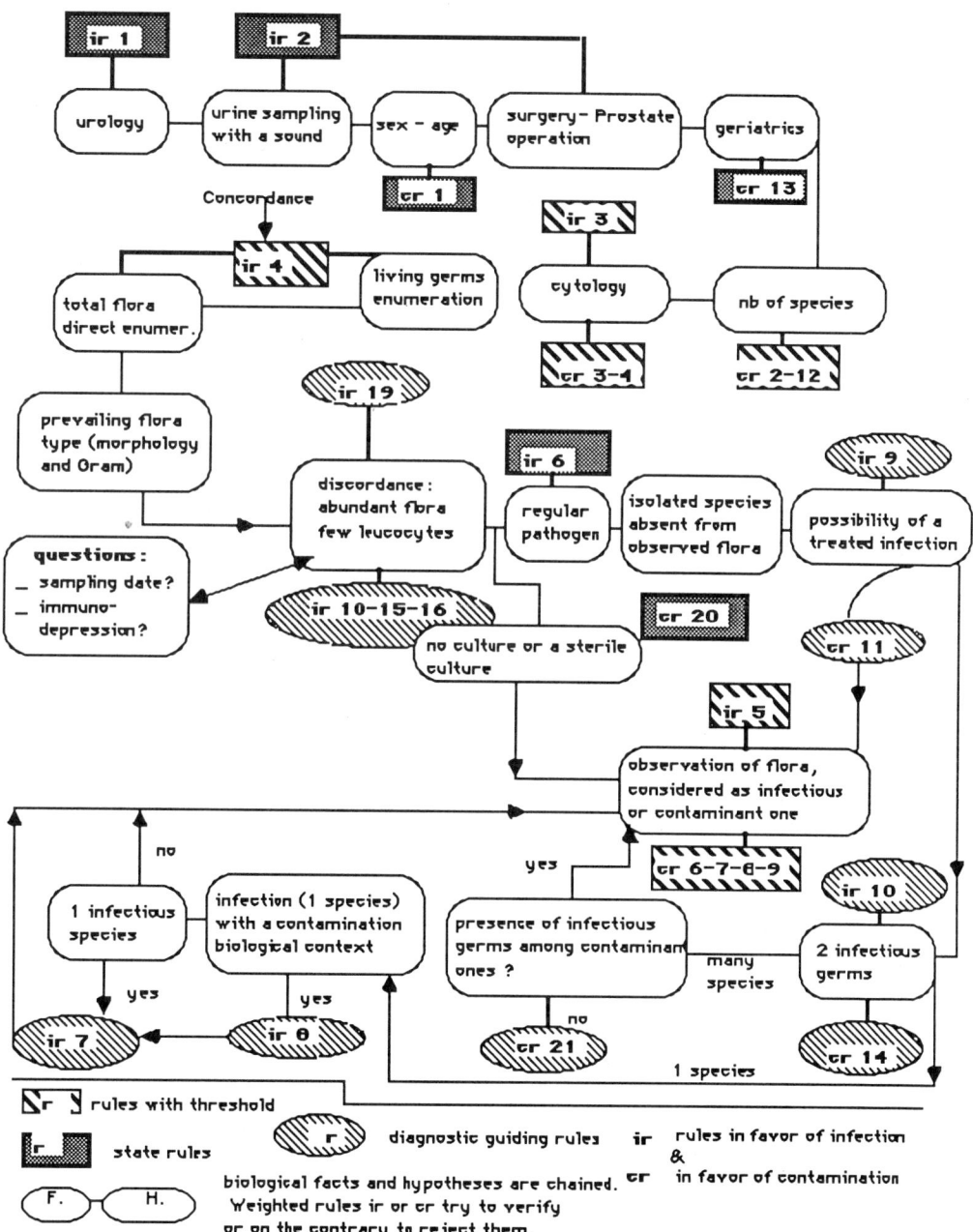

Figure 23.2. Rule chaining. Biological hypotheses are tested in turn.

23.3.1.3 Diagnostic:

After the consultation session, a decision index is given. Its computation is arbitrarily standardized between -1 and +1, like the certainty factors of MYCIN (Shortliffe *et al.*, 1975). Its empirical formula is the barycenter of applied rules weights (a.r.w.) :

$$\frac{\Sigma \text{infect. a.r.w.} - \Sigma \text{conta. a.r.w.}}{\Sigma \text{ a·r·w.}} \text{ , because :}$$

- the medical expert's diagnosis is the one which is confirmed by the greatest number of biological arguments.

- the simplicity of inference (only two final major conclusions: infection or contamination) allows us to consider more ordinary factors combination than MYCIN one.

23.3.2 *Data analysis methods*

These methods may be easy applied to screening results, if the decision factors are considered as qualitative or quantitative variables. (see list 1).

Instead of explaining their theoretical aspects (Diday *et al.*, 1982), we briefly justify their use, as descriptive means, to discriminate urine analyses and to display classifying features. The final outcome is the comparison with the expert system.

23.3.2.1 Urine screening typology.

The individuals (urine screening set) are points in the dimension space of quantitative variables or modalities. In order to make interpretation easier, points are projected on a sub-space (lower dimension) such as highest information is retained, regarding data variability.

The reduction of the number of features results from the construction of new synthetic features (factors), for coding individuals by means of their linear combination. The projection in factor planes may allow representation of individuals, with an axis system giving a satisfying discrimination between infection and contamination cases. The PCA (Principal Components Analysis) only treats numerical ordinate features. This condition will imply the selection of some variables (enumeration variables) for the analysis. The MCA (Multiple Correspondence Analysis) only treats qualitative features. The difference between these two methods is based upon the choice of the inter individuals distance: the euclidian metric (PCA) or the Khi2 metric (MCA).

23.3.2.2 Unhierarchical descending clustering.

This methodology is used as a complement to the interpretation of typology by MCA. It seems like a taxonomy, where each partition is locally optimal. The nearest individuals are brought together, according to their modalities. If a hierarchy is found, it data structure; in particular, when a class becomes individualized, this class may represent a particular infection or contamination type.

23.3.2.3 Discrimination.

The discriminant analysis determines synthetic features which have closed values for individuals from the same class and, on the contrary, opposed values for individuals belonging to different classes. The individuals' coding results from a linear combination of initial features.

Discrimination about quantitative data is equivalent to a multivariate variance analysis. To choose the best discriminant features comes down to maximizing the ratio between interclass variance and total variance. The most discriminant variables will actively contribute to synthetic feature definition (single, in the case of two populations).

Discrimination about qualitative data (Multiple Components Discriminant Analysis: MCDA) is used because modalities are almost equally represented, with a number of individuals larger than the number of modalities. This more complex methodology (Persat *et al.*, 1985) allows to consider more features for discrimination. The modality-coding, given by the analysis, is used to compute the individual-coding, by adding modality-coding of the individual.

23.4. Results

23.4.1 *Expert system diagnosis*
The comparison between this diagnosis and the physician's decision is attended with the definition of some steps and notions required for conception of systems based upon some rules.

23.4.1.1 Acceptance criterion.

At practical level: a rudimentary interface explains briefly the reasoning, especially interesting for the conception. Moreover, this software needs little memory size (82 Ko for the PROLOG environment, 17 Ko for the program itself) and the treatment runs fast (about 5 s).

At diagnosis level: we define the major risk, as the danger incurred by the patient after system decision-making (when system diagnoses contamination or not significant infection instead of infection).

An arbitrary decision threshold (indecision between -0.1 and +0.1) is chosen as safety margin: the system has not knowledge enough in order to decide (infection, contamination or insignificant), the medical expert has to conclude himself.

23.4.1.2 Successive improvements (figure 23.3.).

With the medical expert's aid, the system deficiencies are identified, and consequently corrected by adding more specialized rules. This adding does not disturb diagnostic management, but efficiency may depends on the order of rules application.

As it appears in fig. 23.3. three versions have been successively elaborated.

List 23.1. *Modalities of the qualitative variables.*

Variables for the whole of examinations (including sterile or unsignificant cases).

var.1	service	1=geriatrics
		2=urology
		3=others
var.2	sex	1=male
		2=female
var.3	age	1= <1 year
		2= 1 to 15
		3= 16 to 60
		4= > 60 years
var.4	leucocytes	1=number<10^5/ml
		2= 10^5/ml
		3=number>10^5/ml
var.5	epithelial cells	modalities 1, 2, 3 as above
var.6	cells overlaid	1=number<10^4/ml
	with bacteria	2=number≥10^4/ml
var.7	total flora	1=number<10^5/ml
		2= 10^5/ml
		3=number>10^5/ml
var.8	negat. Gram bac.	modalities 1, 2, 3 as above
var.9	positive Gram	1=number<10^4/ml
	cocci	2= 10^4 - 10^5/ml
		3=number>10^5/ml
var.10	posit. Gram bac.	modalities 1, 2, 3 as above
var.11	yeasts	1=number<10^4/ml
		2=number≥10^4/ml

--------{examinations stopped here if there is evident contamination}----------

variables for examinations with germs isolation (sterile case ?)

var.12	living germs	1=enum. <10^4/ml
	enumeration	2= 10^4 - 10^5/ml
		3= 10^5 - 10^6/ml
		4= enum. > 10^6/ml

variables for examinations with germs identification

var.13	number	1= 1species
	of species	2= 2 species
		3= 3 species and more
var.14	regular	1= yes
	pathogen	2= no

The first version is based upon single decision criterion rules, obvious for the expert: state rules and rules with threshold. The system diagnoses are the same as physician's ones in 70% of cases, but the major risk is high (>10%).

10 contaminated urine analyses are considered like sterile cases by expert system because of low germs enumeration.

The aims of **the second version** are to increase the number of ideal coincidences (from 70% to 88.7%) and to cancel the major risk. However, the system remains undecided with 8% of the analyses (rules fail or medical expert is himself undecided). The case: indecision (system) / infection (physician) does not represent a disadvantage because the doubt has to imply infection hypothesis. In front of these results there are 90% of satisfactory cases. 11 rules were added, they identify typical biological conditions, depending upon facts conjunctions. Although they are less often used than the first version ones, these rules are critical, e.g. the identification of infection with a single species implies the elimination of 6 major risk cases: the germ is considered infectious while it would be judged contaminant in an other context.

The last version attempts to reduce the number of undecided diagnoses or erroneously in favour of infection ones. 7 new urine analyses are well identified (fig. 23.3.), after the application of rules that allows for example the recognition of infectious germs among contaminant flora, relating to the significant predominance of germs, considered as infectious ones.

The system has more abilities in order to biologically decide about confused cases, like use of catheter for urine sampling, or infection with two infectious germs.

The final results amount to a satisfaction of 95% facing system diagnosis. That demonstrates the applicability of these rules (45 including 27 weighted ones) to consultation system, and the importance of ideas communication between the expert and the programmer.

23.4.2 Typology and multivariate discrimination for a decision-making

23.4.2.1 Factor representation.
Factors meaning: the first factor takes into account the greater part of the variability, it is principally defined by "the total flora", "the living germs enumeration" and "the Gram-bacilli". After MCA_1 about the whole of urine examinations (including sterile ones), we can state that modalities of these variables are ordered according to this first factor.

The variable "total flora" becomes less important after withdrawal of sterile cases. Some redundant variables ("service" and "age") are correlated with the second factor, that implies the suppression of this variable "service". The "total flora" is also ruled out (correlation with "the germs enumeration") while two additional variables ("the number of species", and "the regular pathogenicity of germs") replace the withdrawn ones for MCA_2, only about examinations where germs are isolated. While the first factor is explained by "the living germs enumeration" and "the Gram- bacilli", the second one is correlated (in an ordered manner) with "the polynuclears" and "the Gram+ bacilli" (table 23.1.).

The interest of these features for the medical decision-making is then proved. These criteria reinforce their prominent part in rules about contamination flora ("the Gram+ bacilli") or in diagnosis guiding ones (the total flora/ the polynuclear enumeration distortion).

Typology with MCA_1 displays proximity of sterility and contamination (fig. 23.4.), both distinguished by a low enumeration and few Gram- bacilli. Two groups tend to become individualized, in the majority composed by contamination and sterile analyses, or infection ones. On account of this remark, all sterile cases are ruled out.

MCA_2 displays a bad discrimination between infection and contamination (fig. 23.5.): e.g. the factor coding does not allow an accurate representation of biological states where infectious germs are different from Gram- bacilli. However a schematic clustering remains possible, the more typical MCA explanation is presented fig. 23.6. and table 23.2. , with the whole of non sterile analyses.

23.4.2.2 Visualization of the discriminant capability : discriminant analyses.
The comparison between the discriminant capability of multivariate analyses and of expert system uses the construction of histograms. The idea of decision risk is not developed, as this descriptive comparison seems sufficient.

23.4.2.2.1 Discrimination on quantitative data. If only accurately classified urine examinations (by the state rules and rules with threshold of the expert system first version) are studied, we state that discriminant analysis gives
remarkable results (fig. 23.7.) proved by PCA typology with typical grouping (fig. 23.8.). On the other hand, the most discriminant variables for the whole of non sterile examinations ("the total flora", "the polynuclears", "the Gram+ bacilli") are not satisfactory (fig. 23.9a., 23.9b.), and the expert system classifies much better. Qualitative variables have to be introduced in order to have a better discrimination, the more complex MCDA will be used.

23.4.2.2.2 Discrimination on qualitative data (MCDA). The graphical representations (fig. 23.10.) allows one to visualize the discriminant power of variables and modalities. For each variable, the individuals' canonical coding is divided into 40 classes (with the same amplitude). Each square surface (one square by class) is proportional to the number of individuals who own a modality **i** (the ordinate), and who belong to a class **j** (abscissa) of the individuals' canonical coding. In order to simplify graphics, only the profiles of surface have been drawn.

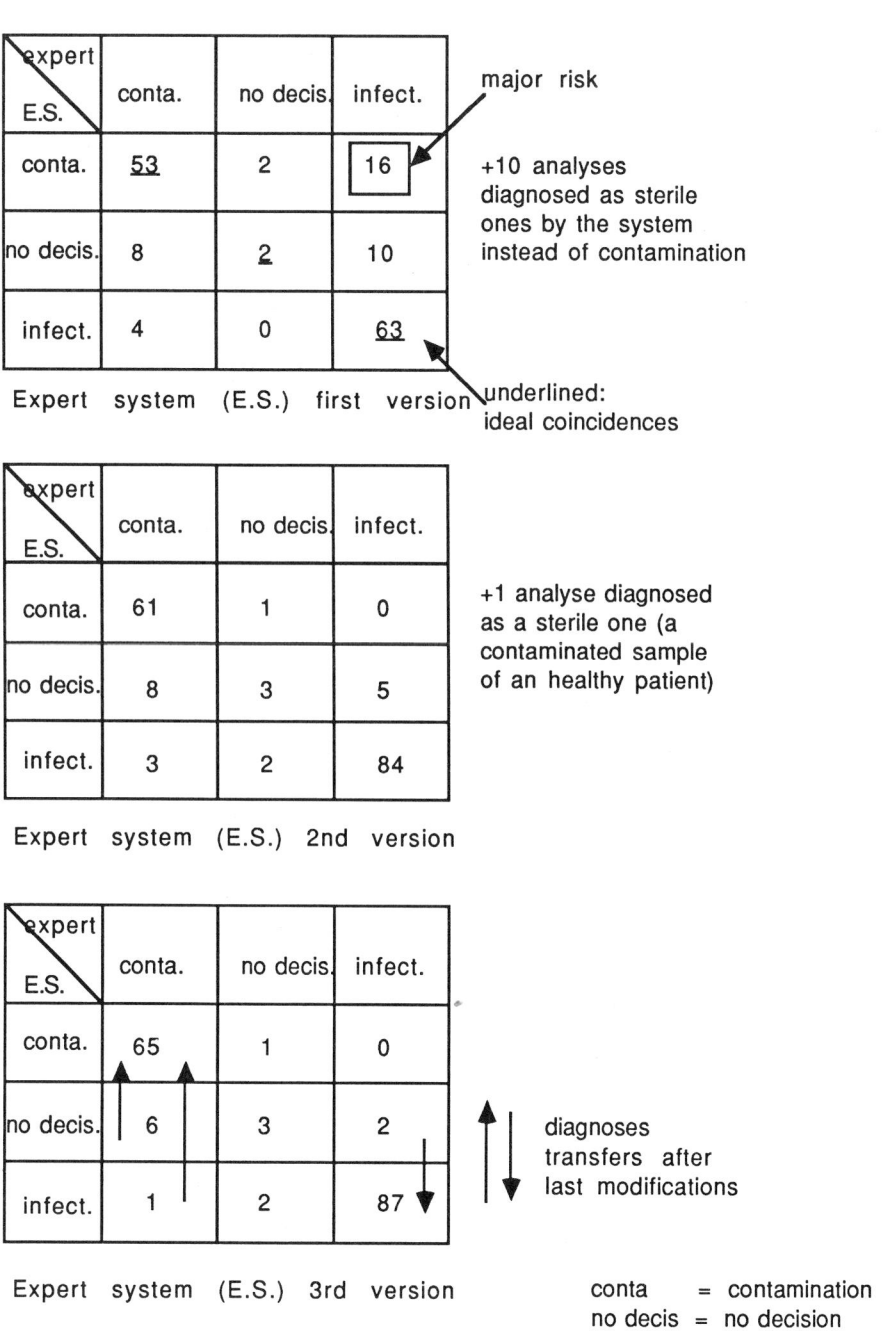

major risk

+10 analyses
diagnosed as sterile
ones by the system
instead of contamination

Expert system (E.S.) first version

underlined:
ideal coincidences

+1 analyse diagnosed
as a sterile one (a
contaminated sample
of an healthy patient)

Expert system (E.S.) 2nd version

diagnoses
transfers after
last modifications

Expert system (E.S.) 3rd version

conta = contamination
no decis = no decision
infect = infection

Figure 23.3. Comparison tables (between human experts and the successive expert system versions). 'No decision' cases are cases where 3 experts are not in agreement. In these comparisons the 32 sterile or insignificant cases (always recognized by the expert system) are taken from urine analyses.

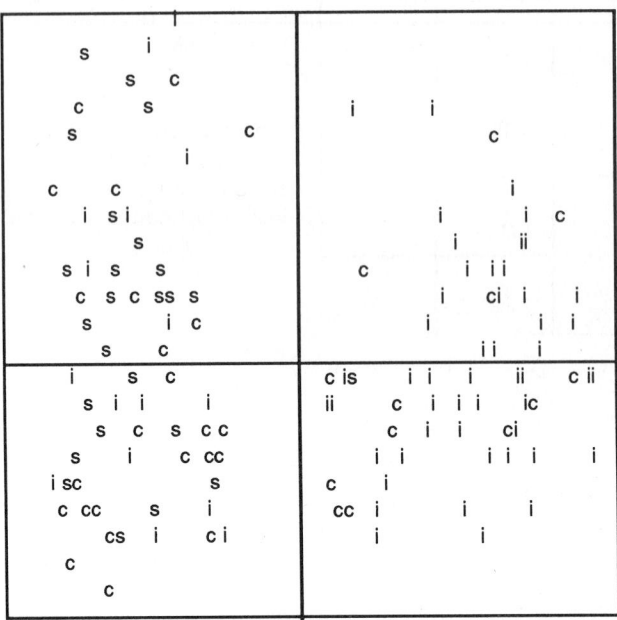

Figure 23.4. (on the left) MCA1 about the whole of examinations (including sterile and insignificant cases), in the factor plane 1x2. S=sterile, I=infection, C=contamination.

Three variables have a strong discriminant capability: "the germs enumeration", "the species number" and especially "the regular pathogens" (fig. 23.10.). The ordinal characteristics reappear in the graphical representations: the more living germs are present (increasing modalities), the more the infection hypothesis seems verified (squares of coding classes are more and more grouped near infection cases coding). The contamination diagnostic reinforcement is also found with "the number of species".

The discrimination between the two types of diagnoses is better with MCDA than with the former analysis. An estimation of bad classed or uncertain individuals is 20 for MCDA: the uncertainty area is larger than for the expert system (fig. 23.9c., 23.9d.). If the risk threshold (in a statistical meaning) were taken into account, the decision interval boundaries of expert system would be better adjusted. However the decision index might face the problem of standardization.

23.5 Discussion

Limits of classical typological methods for discrimination
With MCA or PCA, only factors which explain at the best variability, are taken into account. Although they characterize the decisions to interpret the results, they seem unsatisfying for accurate classification. These methods may be considered as preliminary

analyses (e.g. to discriminant analysis...), which display special individuals, correlation between variables...

Table 23.1. *MCA2 factor explanations (complete screenings) with the best correlations.*
The scheme of modalities coding visualizes how regular is its repartition on each axis.

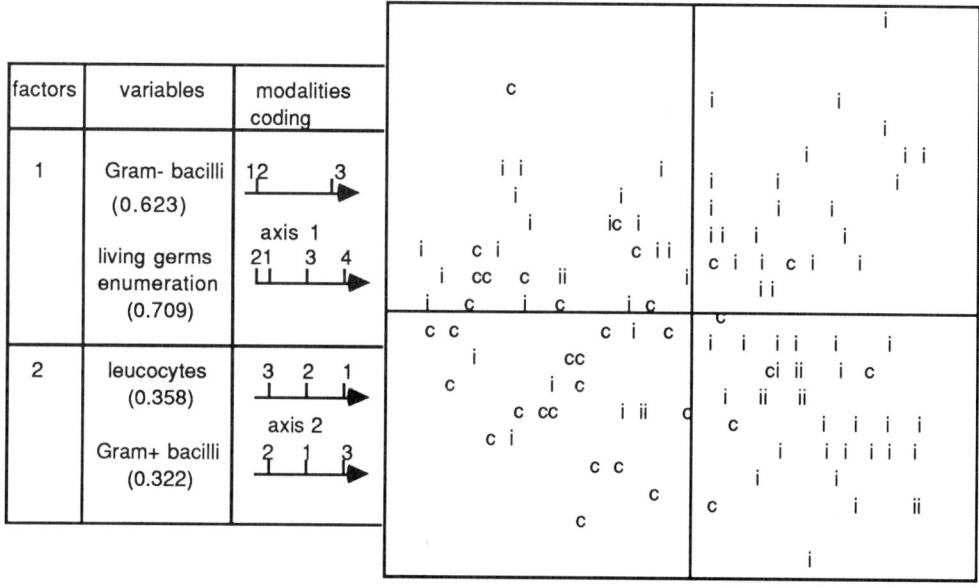

Figure 23.5. MCA2 about complete urine screenings (including germ isolation and identification). Typologies are presented in 1x2 factor plane. I=Infection, C=Contamination case.

Common characteristic between expert system and multivariate analysis:
Multivariate analyses construct a coding, linear combination of studied features. It would not be surprising if urine examinations were well classified by state rules and rules with threshold, and by discriminant analysis (or PCA). This agreement can be simplified:

urine screening results	modalities	1	2	3	final discrimination
expert system	rules with threshold	weight	=w1	=w2>w1 (reinforcement)	decision index $\Sigma_{rules} w_i$
multivariate analysis (e.g. MCA)	modalities coding	c1	c2	c3	indiv. coding $\Sigma_{Var.} a_i c_i$

So an ordinary mathematical expression is able to play the part of an expert, like an expert system with a single alternative decision criteria. Comparison between discriminant analysis and expert system:

Table 23.2. *Unhierarchical clustering the 3 main clusters.*

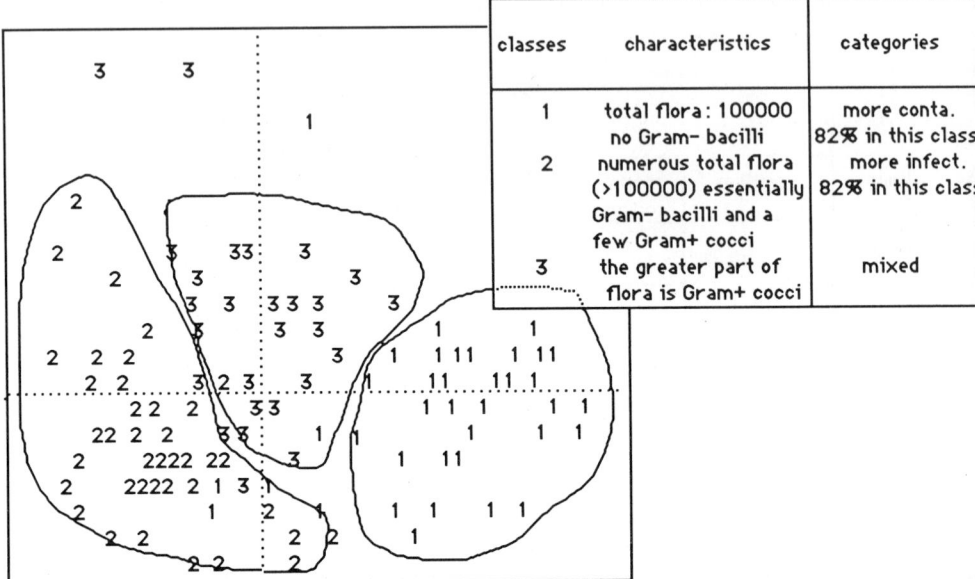

classes	characteristics	categories
1	total flora: 100000 no Gram– bacilli	more conta. 82% in this class
2	numerous total flora (>100000) essentially Gram– bacilli and a few Gram+ cocci	more infect. 82% in this class
3	the greater part of flora is Gram+ cocci	mixed

Figure 23.6. Factor representation of groups (identified by unhierarchical clustering). The meaning of each cluster is presented in table 23.2.

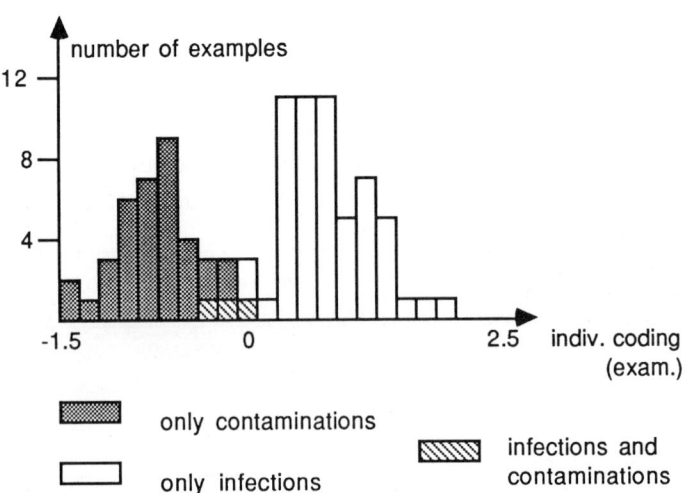

Figure 23.7. Discriminant analysis (quantitative data) with 99 examinations which are well classified by the expert system first version.

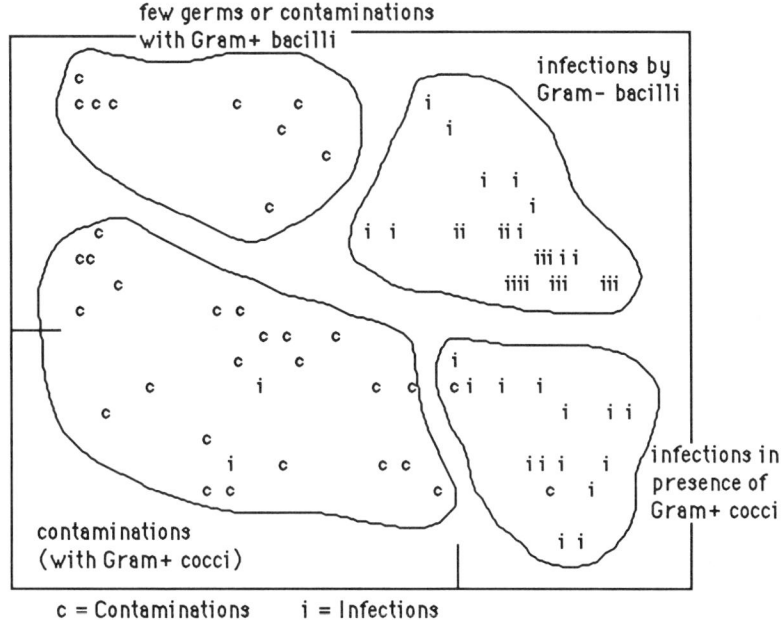

Figure 23.8. PCA about 99 individuals which are well discriminated by the first version of the expert system.

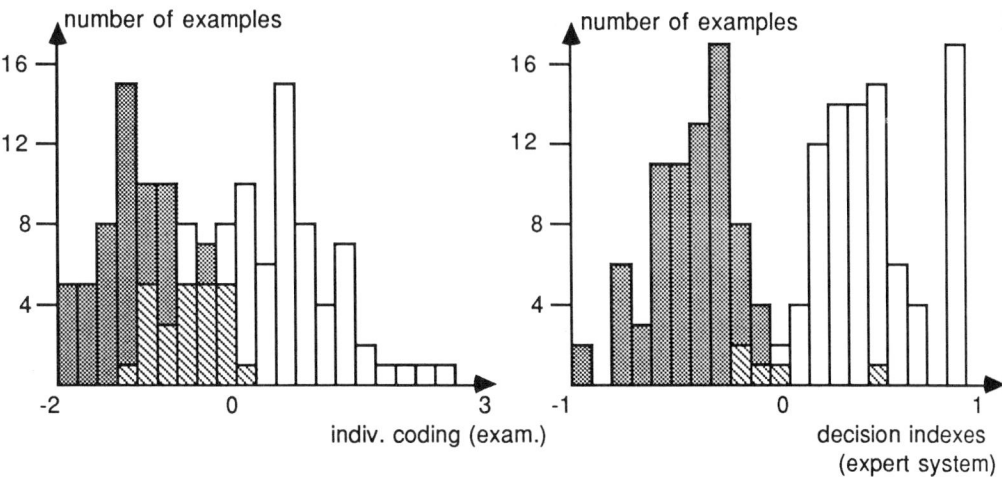

Figure 23.9.a (on the left) Discriminant analysis (quantitative data) with the whole of urine analyses.
Figure 23.9.b (on the right) Histogram of decision indexes given by the expert system (the whole of analyses).

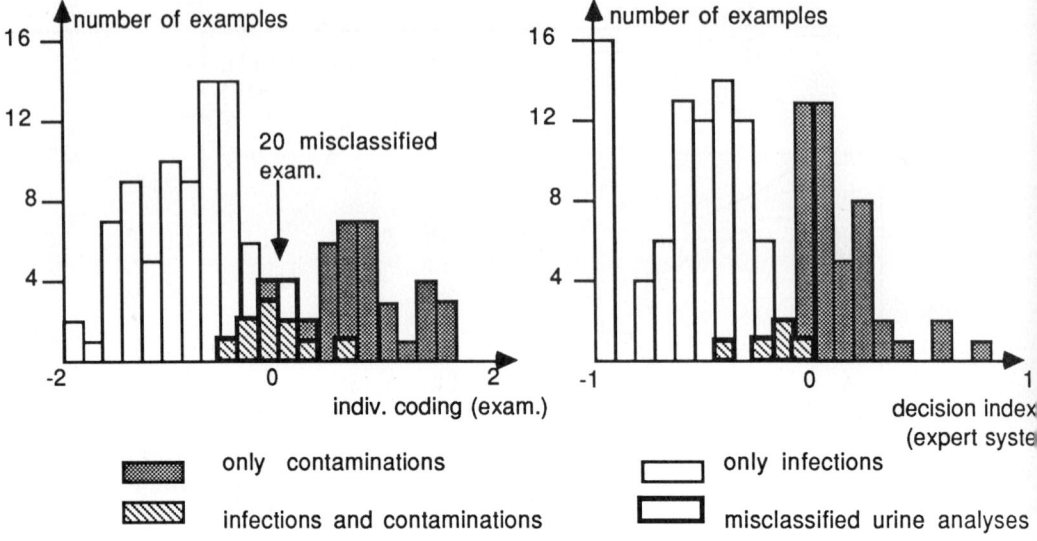

Figure 23.9.c (on the left) Discriminant analysis (12 qualitative variables) about 128 urine analyses.
Figure 23.9.d (on the right) Histogram of decision indexes about 128 urine analyses (including germ isolation and identification, then 12 qualitative variables are studied).

In order to study the two populations covering up, 20 classes with the same amplitude are defined, according to decision indexes (expert system) or individuals coding (discriminant analyses).

Because they refer to infection, or contamination predominant classes, the bad classified analyses do not necessary agree with expert system undecided diagnoses: they namely represent cases which either belong in a minority to predominant classes or belong to 'middle' classes.

1) **Agents influencing on discriminant analysis**: Discriminant analysis in its learning stage (studied in this work), depends entirely on data, and so sometimes leads to changes in methodology (e.g. if quantitative variables are not enough to discriminate). Introducing the "regular pathogen" variable has improved the results ofdiscriminant analysis. However, this feature falsifies a little the outcomes, because the rapid identification of germs is continued during examination only if these germs are significantly infectious.

2) **Capability differences between these two methodologies**: With MCDA, a feature does not discriminate if it validates either in favour of infection or conversely in favour of contamination according to the biological context. So, Gram+ cocci are generally contaminant germs, except in the case of infection with a single species. The main ability of expert system is to better recognize conjunction of facts. It can combine the features studied in a non-linear manner, conversely to multivariate analysis which is based upon a linear combination of initial features.

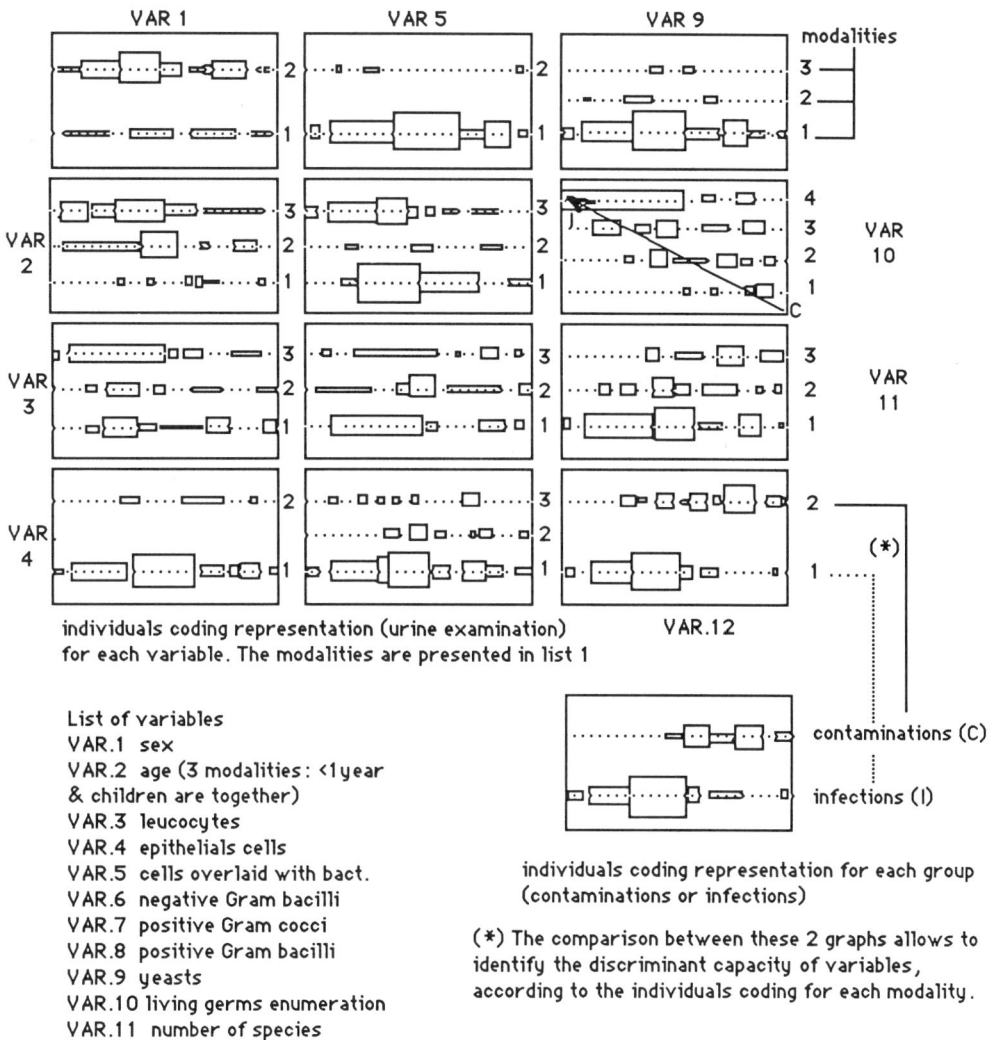

Figure 23.10. Discriminant qualitative variables (M.C.D.A.).

Furthermore, individuals whose strongly weighted modalities are inconsistent with their related discriminant class, are poorly classified (e.g. one species which is not usually pathogenic). So these poorly classified cases are now considered. Generally examinations which are not discriminated by MCDA, are well diagnosed by the expert system (17/20), and do not look like confused biological states. These are typical medical cases of infection or contamination, like infection with a single unusual pathogen, infection with two responsible species, contamination by yeasts..., the recognition of which is directly subject to coding established by data analysis.

To sum up, multivariate analysis does not allow the recognition of typical cases, as soon as the relation between variables is no longer linear. On the contrary, the expert system attempts to simulate at the best human reasoning. The modularity of the rules permits their continuous improvement it, by adding new knowledge granules, while discriminant analysis has to face the choice of variables or individual sampling. However, data analysis may contribute to the definition of decision criteria to be taken into account, and verify pertinency or importance of medical expert rules. Some rule thresholds may be identified: e.g. with the "living germs enumeration", there is evident infection, if the modality is greater than 3 (in fig. 23.10).

23.6 Conclusion

With a controlled specialization of rules, the system is able to identify a biological configuration and by extent, to discriminate two bacterial populations: contaminant (regular flora) and infection ones (pathogenic flora). The demonstration of its feasibility and interest may lead to the conception of discriminant mini-expert systems, containing some rules signification thresholds of which do not intervene in a linear manner, otherwise they are equivalent to multivariate analyses.

References

Colmerauer, A., Kanoui, H. & Van Caneghem, M. (1983). Prolog, bases théoriques et développements actuels.*Techniques et Sciences Informatiques*, **2**, 4, 271-304.

Diday, E., Lemaire, J., Pouget, J. & Testu, F. (1982). Eléments d'analyse des données. Bordas, Paris.

Kleimutz, B. (1984). Diagnostic problem solving by computer: a historical review and the current state of the science. *Computers in biology and medicine* , **14**, 3, 255-270.

Persat, H., Nelva, A. & Chessel, D. (1985). Approche par analyse discriminante sur variable qualitative d'un milieu lotique, le Haut Rhône français. *Oecologia Generalis*, **6**, 4, 365-381.

Shortliffe, E.H. & Buchanan, B.G. (1975). A model of inexact reasoning in medicine. *Mathematical Bioscience*, **23**, 351-379.

EXPERT SYSTEMS FOR
BIOMEDICAL IMAGE INTERPRETATION

24.1. Introduction

This paper presents some research issues related to the design of expert systems for biomedical image interpretation. The fields of cyto- and histo-pathology are more particularly concerned. Diagnostic formulation is progressively elaborated by examining a set of morphological indicators; these indicators are collected through the microscopic observation of the specimen which is layered on a slide and stained.

The pathologist's expertise may be drawn as comprised of:
- the ability to perceive, i.e to estimate the amount of morphological deviation, even if barely perceptible, while refering to a confusing variety of normal morphological appearances;
- the ability to diagnose, i.e to correlate morphological indicators with some potential diagnosis hypothesis;
- the ability to reason about facts, i.e to coordinate diagnostic formulation tasks and image exploration tasks in order that any final conclusion be consistently assessed; it implies developping dedicated reasonning strategies;
- the ability to coerce the overall analysis according to the specific case under study, by considering eventual specimen-specific or patient-specific circumstances.

Designing expert system within this particular field of application gives rise to challenging research issues: various knowledge levels are implied, from the early retinal level to the final diagnostic level, while involving processing activities of very different kinds, such as perceptive or deductive activities.

We have been involved within the design of expert systems dedicated to bladder cancer cyto-diagnosis and breast cancer histo-diagnosis. Both of them are conceived under a mixed object / production rule architecture, while endowed with a rich variety of functionalities, in order to capture the problems to be solved as far as possible.

Further improvements however should come from the thorough investigation of the rising representational issues. Some of these modelling issues are presented in the last part: they should be considered as a set of proposals for the design of robust expert systems in the field of biomedical image interpretation. A distributed object-oriented architecture is proposed in this framework, which is conceived as the modular networking of cooperating knowledge sources and knowledge processors.

24.2. Expert system for cytological diagnosis of bladder cancer

A prototype expert system has been developed for cytological diagnosis of bladder cancer (Pesty *et al.*, 1987). The problem to be solved is briefly presented; the modelling and processing of iconic and diagnostic knowledge is afterwards detailed.

24.2.1 *Cytological diagnosis of bladder cancer: the visual expertise*
A urinary specimen, when observed through a microscope, appears as composed of a set of cellular objects laying on a rather homogeneous background (figure 24.1). A variable amount of cells may be observed (from about fifty to ten thousands cells); these cells may appear as rather dispersed or clumped whitin more or less dense aggregates. Necrotic debris might also be observed. A cell is comprised of a nucleus and cytoplasm, which in turn may respectively display a variable amount of nucleoli and vacuoles.

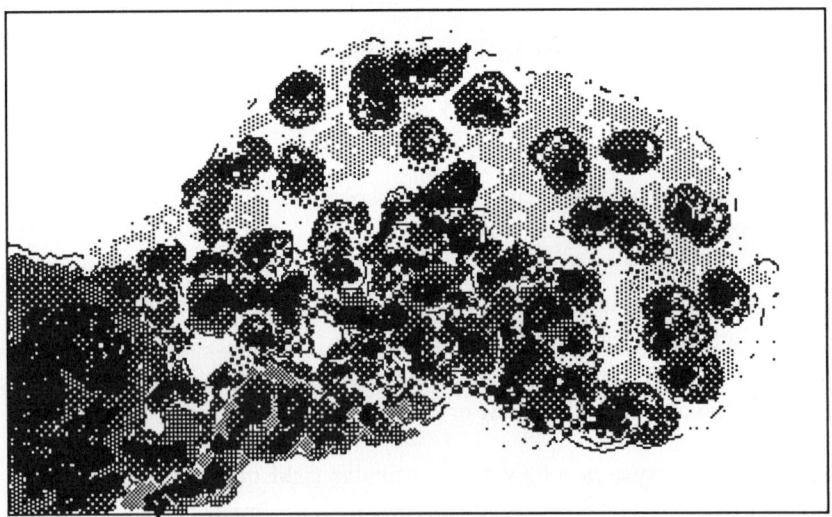

Figure 24.1. Low magnification microscopic view of a urinary specimen.

The cytologic specimen is generally observed:

- using a low magnification factor, in order to capture global morphological indicators (proliferation of cells of a specific type, detection of extraneous cells, nature of the topographical arrangements);

- using a high magnification factor, in order to capture the amount of cellular morphological deviations: it involves particularly examining their size, shape, color and texture.

Possible relationships between morphological indicators and diagnosis hypotheses have been examplified by means of an association matrix, which is displayed in figure 24.2. The degree of confidence attached to a particular morpho-diagnostic association is considered as certainly very low if denoted as "impossible" but may not be assessed with certainty if denoted as "possible".

diag. / features	negative	reactive atypia	dysplasia	papillary carcinoma	in situ carcinoma	....
. . .						
:cell size:						
< normal	imp.	imp.	imp.	imp.	pos.	
normal	pos.	pos.	pos.	pos.	pos.	
> normal	imp.	pos.	pos.	pos.	imp.	
>>normal	imp.	pos.	pos.	pos.	imp.	
nuclear membrane:						
thin	pos.	pos.	imp.	pos.	imp.	
irregular	imp.	imp.	pos.	pos.	pos.	
smooth	pos.	pos.	imp.	pos.	imp.	
. . .						

Figure 24.2. Partial view of the morpho-diagnostic association matrix. Approximately thirty morphological indicators and seven pathologies are presently concerned.

24.2.2 *Cytologic image description: the iconic knowledge*

The iconic knowledge basis is conceived as a set of objects, in the framework of Object-oriented programming (Ferber, 1985). Any object is thus defined as comprised of a set of attributes and / or a set of methods. Any object resource request or updating is performed by means of message sending. Two classes of objects are actually distinguished, which are the class Main and the class Feature.

```
(def-obj 'Main
      'm-get               "read the value of an object attribute"
      'm-put               "update the value of an object attribute"
      'm-instance          "create a new instance"
      'm-print             "describe an object"
      'm-prompt            "evaluate an attribute:  user answer-query procedure")
```

Figure 24.3. The class Main: definition of the general object handling tasks.

The class Main (figure 24.3) encapsulates a set of methods which are relevant to the definition of the general object handling tasks (reading and updating attribute values, creating and describing objects). A particular method, 'm-prompt, is dedicated to the control of a user answer-query procedure: morphological indicators are presently acquired in a qualitative form .

The class Feature (figure 24.4) is dedicated to iconic description of the specimen . It is comprised of a set of morphological indicators (attributes) and a method denoted as 'request?. Each attribute is further described by a set of properties indicating respectively the evaluation method, the possible domain of values, the message to be passed to the user, and an eventual default value. The 'request? method is invoked upon request of the system control structure; its argument is an iconic constraint of the form (Object Attribute Value). Its role is to evaluate the object attribute and to examine whether the iconic constraint is verified or not, by comparing the obtained value to the value "Value".

```
(def-obj 'Feature
      'sub-class-of         'Main
      'single-cells         '?
      'groups-&crowdings '?
      ...
      'nucleus-size         '?
      'nucleus-shape        '?
      'request?             "evaluate morphological indicator / verify iconic constraint")

(setq 'single-cells
      '$if-needed           'm-prompt
      '$possible            "yes no"
      '$message             "Are there single cells crowding?"
      '$default             nil)
```

Figure 24.4. The class Feature: iconic description of the specimen.

24.2.3 *Cytologic image interpretation :the diagnostic knowledge*

The diagnostic knowledge basis involves a set of objects describing potential diagnosis features and a set of rules describing the causal relationships between morphological indicators and diagnosis features.

A diagnosis is defined as a sub-class of the class Main. It is described by two attributes "Hypothesis" and "Confirmation". The first attribute allows storing the current diagnosis hypothesis. The value of the second attribute is significant only in case the analysis has been successfully completed, i.e the hypothesis has been confirmed. It is also comprised of the 'request? method, whose role is to verify the correspondance between current diagnosis features and eventual diagnostic constraint; it is invoked upon request of the system control structure.

The rules (figure 24.5) are defined as particular objects comprised of two attributes "Premise" and "Conclusion". The value of any of these attributes is of the form {(Object Attribute Value)}. The premise attribute defines a set of iconic / diagnostic constraint to be verified; involving a diagnostic constraint readily induces some rule sequencing constraints. The conclusion attribute exemplifies the features of the deduced diagnosis. The system is actually comprised of about seventy rules.

Rule **R5**
      'premise   '((Feature Necrotic-debris yes))
      'conclusion   '(Diagnostic Hypothesis 'High-grade-atypia)

Rule **R15**
      'premise   '((Feature Nucleus-position central)
                      (Diagnostic Hypothesis 'High-grade-atypia))
      'conclusion   '(Diagnostic Hypothesis 'Other-type-of-carcinoma)

Rule **R68**
      'premise   '((Feature Groups-&crowdings no)
                      (Feature Numerous-papillae no)
                      ...
                      (Diagnostic Hypothesis 'Other-type-of-carcinoma))
      'conclusion   '(Diagnostic Confirmation 'Other-type-of-carcinoma)

Figure 24.5. Examples of rules.

24.2.4 *The control structure of the system*

The role of the system control structure is to select and activate rules.

Rule selection is performed under a particular strategy operating at local and global levels, corresponding respectively to single diagnosis analysis and diagnosis space exploration:

- at a local level, it is based on a decomposition of the diagnostic process as comprised of two main phases, hypothesis generation and hypothesis confirmation. Rule selection is performed by means of backward chaining, some of them concluding at the hypothesis level, the other ones at the confirmation level. Hypothezing rules allow a straightforward diagnostic focussing: their premise attributes involve a restricted set of iconic constraints which appear as "possible" discriminant morphological indicator values, regarding the morpho-diagnostic asociation matrix. Confirming rules involve a large set of iconic constraints which are introduced as the negation of "impossible" morphological indicator values. An hypothesis is therefore confirmed in the case no contradictory morphological indicator value may be captured;

- at a global level, it is based on a particular ordering of the diagnostic space (decreasing gravity order). A further selection phase thus involves choosing among hypothesis or confirming rules those which conclude on the right pathology , it is performed by means of backward chaining.

Activating a rule implies evaluating its premise attribute: such processing is actually reduced, from the control structure point of view, to sending a message to the object whose analysis is requested. Featuring as well as Diagnostic objects are indeed conceived as responsible for verifying any iconic or respectively diagnostic constraint under interest ('request? method).

24.2.5 *Discussion*
The system is written in COMMON LISP and PASCAL, and runs on an APOLLO work-station (DN660 / DN3000). A multiple-window graphic interface is dedicated to the user interaction, which allows displaying the image, the trace of the rules that have been activated as well as current diagnosis hypothesis, but also to communicate in a friendly way with the user. An overall view of the system graphic interface is proposed in figure 24.6.

The system should actually be improved in order to support valuable diagnostic assessment. It should first of all be given real perceptive abilities, i.e the ability to process the image, in order to evelute quantitative morphological descriptors. Further modelling efforts should moreover be concentrated on problem solving strategy representation, in order it be more explicitly described and the system control structure part be readily restricted. The case-sensitive knowledge modelling is currently under study: it involves modelling the specimen-specific and patient-specific circumstances, as well as modelling the coercive activities by which they might constraint both problem representation and solving.

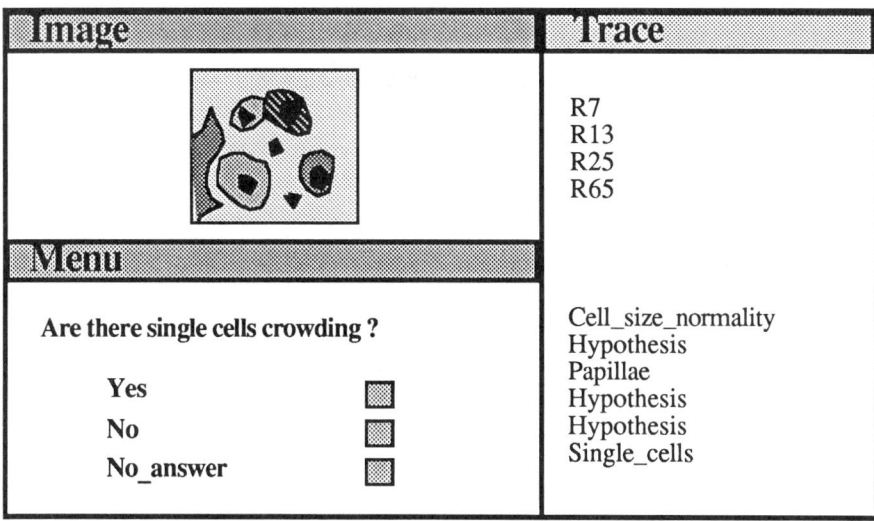

Figure 24.6. Expert system for bladder cancer cyto-diagnosis: overall view of the graphic interface.

24.3. Expert system for histological diagnosis of breast cancer

A prototype expert system has been developed for the histological diagnosis of breast cancer. The project has been conducted in close collaboration with a trained pathologist (Professor Couderc, CHU Grenoble), with the specific intent of modelling the pathologist's visual expertise (Garbay *et al.*, 1986).

24.3.1 *Histological diagnosis of breast cancer : the visual expertise*
A tissue section of the mammary gland, when observed through a microscope, appears as a complex arrangement of entities (ducts, lobules, acini, cell layers, cells ...) occurring at different organization levels of the tissue architecture (figure 24.7). The morphological appearance of these elements, as well as their topographical arrangement, provide several diagnostic indicators, which when combined in a consistent way may lead to the overall diagnosis of the suspected pathology.

The ability to diagnose thus depends on the capacity to perceive, i.e. to interpret morphological, structural and topographical aspects as abnormal; it also depends on the capacity to explore, i.e. to combine several disease indicators in order to produce coherent diagnosis. A global strategy is developed for this purpose, which is based on the top-down exploration of the image, from global architecture observation to cell morphology close examination. It involves observing the tissue images at different magnification levels, by choosing the adequate microscope objectives. A first look is obtained from the initial architectural observations : it allows generating a set of diagnostic hypotheses which ought to be confirmed during the next phases of detailed examination (Chauvet *et al.*, 1985).

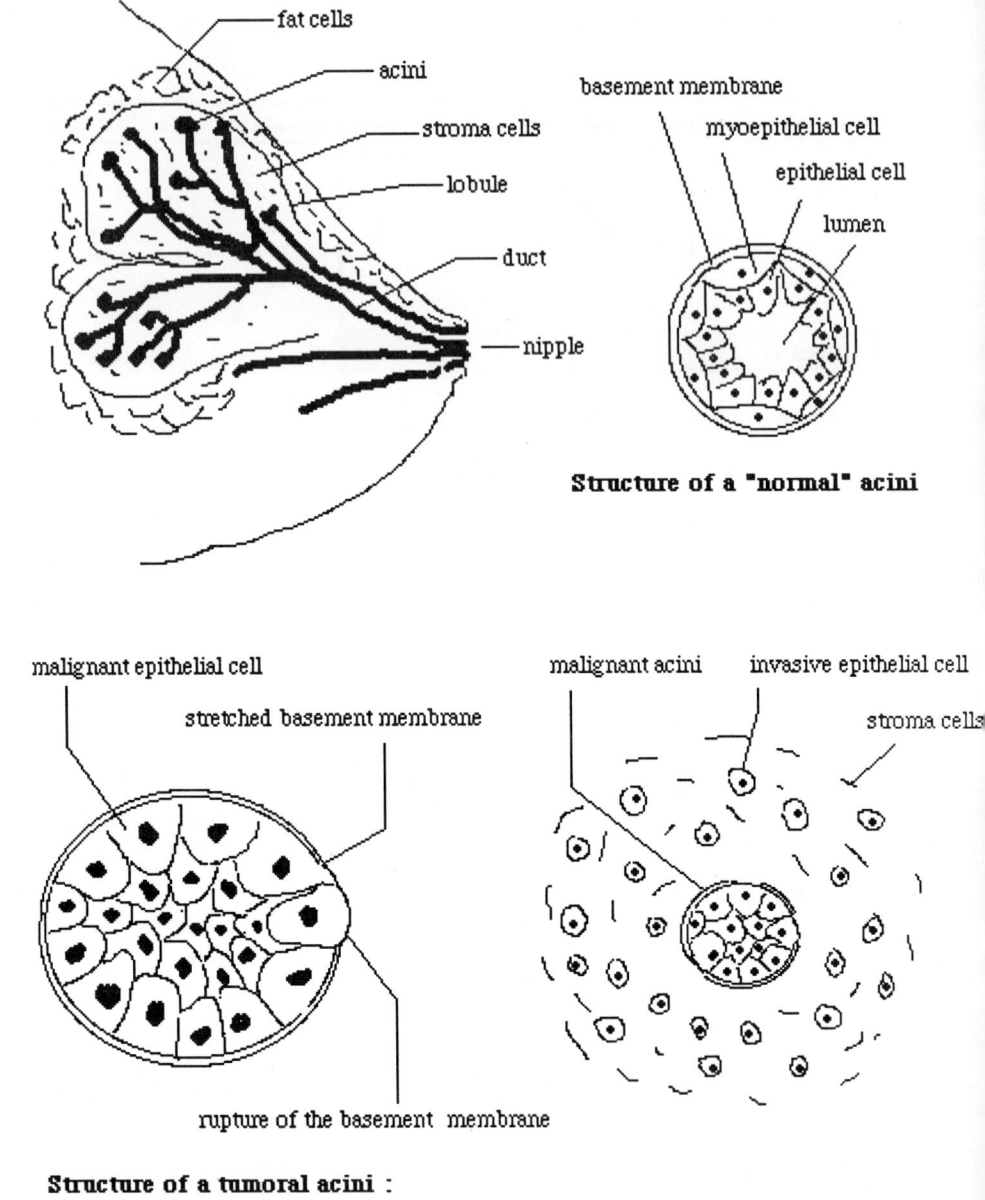

Figure 24.7. Description of the mammary gland main histological structures, examples of abnormal morphological appearances. Four types of pathology have been retained for the purpose of the study: the lobular in situ and invasive carcinoma, the canalar in situ and invasive carcinoma. In situ carcinoma may affect the morphology and the structure of entities (hypertrophy, cell proliferation). Invasive carcinoma may furthermore produce more or less severe architectural disturbances (apparition of tumor cells within the stroma, possibly self organized into linear or circular structures).

24.3.2 *Histological image description : the iconic knowledge*

As already pointed out, the ability to apprehend the iconic significance of the histological image involves the capacity to evaluate and store the features of a given entity, but also the capacity to organize these features in a coherent way, in order to keep track of all the indicators that are relevant to the same histological structure, even though they were gained through different magnification factors.

Two levels of knowledge are thus to be considered : low-level knowledge about a single event, high-level knowledge about a group of related events. Following such considerations, the iconic knowledge basis has been organized around two classes of objects, respectively the class "Entity" and the class "Meta-entity".

24.3.2.1 The class Meta-entity

The class Meta-entity encapsulates the knowledge relevant to the perception of a sequence of events. There is a one-to-one correspondance between objects of this class and the main histological structures. These objects are denoted as $Breast, $Lobule, $Acini ... They are organized in a "part-of" hierarchy.

The create-entity function is activated at each time the observation of a new event is requested by the system. Its argument is the name of a meta-entity; its role is to create a new event (GenX), to store it as the value of the meta-entity under interest, to create or update the event hierarchy. This procedure is iterated for any lower-level meta-entity. Handling the event hierarchy allows the system to keep track of the sequence of events that has been captured; handling the meta-entity values allows the system to keep track of the particular sub-sequence of events it is currently focussed on (figure 24.8).

$Breast
Value : **Gen1**
Composed-of : **($Lobule ...)**

$Lobule
Value : **Gen2**
Composed-of: **($Acini ..)**

$Acini
Value : **Gen5**
Composed-of : **($Epith-layer ...)**

$Epith-layer
Value : **Gen6**
Composed-of : **(...)**

Gen1
$Lobule : **(Gen2)**

Gen2
$Acini : **(Gen3 Gen5)**

Gen3
$Epith-layer : **(Gen4 Gen6)**

Figure 24.8. Handling the meta-entity tree: the call (Create-entity $Breast) has induced a first instanciation of the event hierarchy (Gen1, Gen2, Gen3, Gen4); the call (Create-entity $Acini) has induced its updating (Gen5, Gen6); two instances of Acini have been observed (Gen3 Gen5), Gen5 is the instance presently at hand; the procedure is repeated over the acini constituents (Epithelial cell layer here).

24.3.2.2 The class Entity

The class Entity encapsulates the knowledge relevant to the perception of a single event. It is described by a set of intrinsic, extrinsic and functional properties. Intrinsic properties allows organizing the objects into a "part-of" hierarchy, but also tying each entity to a corresponding meta-entity. Featuring objects are introduced to perform entity descriptors attachment. A partial view of the entity tree is proposed in figure 24.9.

   Extrinsic properties allow explaining the significance of the current observation (properties "Com" and "Explain") and defining the magnification factor to be used (property "Factor").

Functional properties are attached to the sole descriptive objects (property $if-needed), and define the evaluating procedures. Addressing any featuring object induces traversing the attached descriptive objects and thus invoking the evaluating procedures as a whole: it allows preserving the coherence of the system activity, from a user-defined point of view. The descriptor value, when obtained, is attached through the name of the event under study.

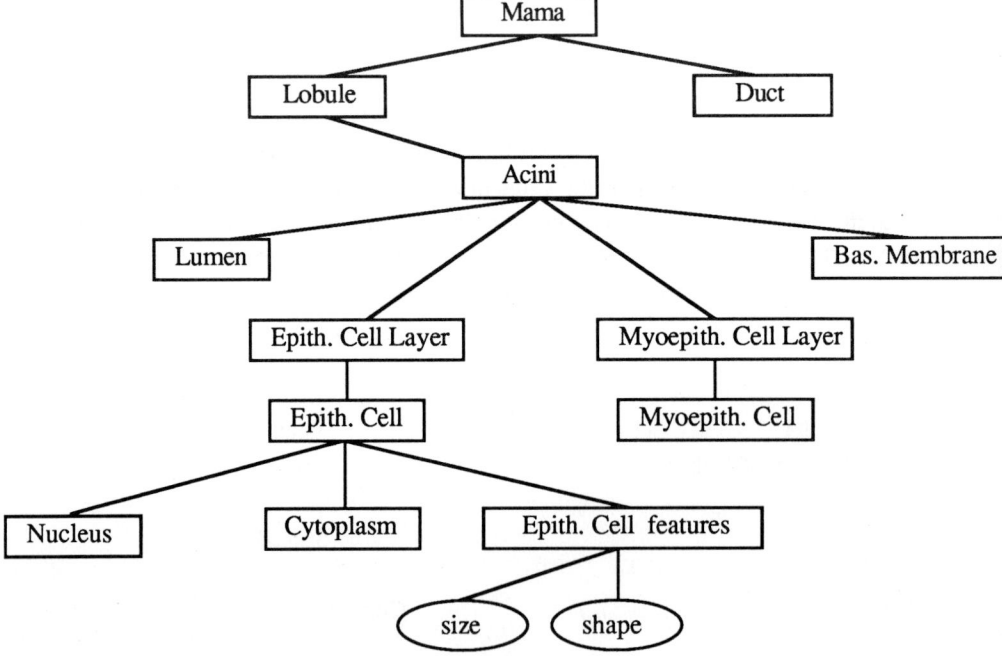

Figure 24.9. Partial view of the entity tree. A structural object is defined as composed of featuring and structural objects; a featuring object is defined as composed of a set of descriptive objects.

Two types of procedures are distinguished:
- answer-query procedures allow acquiring qualitative descriptor values. Various facilities are provided to elude the question or ask for a later answer;

- evaluating procedures allow computing quantitative descriptor values. The entity under interest is graphically delineated using either punctual, polygonal or elliptical primitives.

Activating any of these procedures first of all induces updating the displayed image. Images are organized in a hierarchy (image tree) and handled similarly to meta-entities. Meta-images are denoted by magnification factors ($X2.5, $X10, ..., $X100), and instanciated by calling the create-image function. Displaying the adequate image thus involves examining the Factor property value and selecting the image (current view) denoted by the value of the addressed meta-image.

Epithelial-cell-layer-thickness
  Factor :   **$X40**
  Com :   **"The acini epithelial cell layer is currently analyzed"**
  Explain :   **"A multiplying epithelial cell layer is a disease**
         indicator of rather high confidence degree"
  Meta-entity : **$Acini**
  Part-of :   **Epithelial-cell-layer-feature**
  $If-needed : **("How many epithelial cell layers do you observe ?**
    (answer 0 if the lumen is obstructed) (0 one many)")
  $If-awake : **($value=0)--> (Lumen-feature Presence '(not present)))**

Figure 24.10. A descriptive object involving intrinsic, extrinsic and functional properties.

The $if-awake property is finally introduced to attach some processings to be invoked as a side-effect of $if-needed procedures activation (Granger, 1985). These processings allow to preserve the coherence of the system activity, by dynamically updating the iconic knowledge basis (inhibiting potential access to inconsistent entity descriptors, for example). Some descriptor elements examples are provided in figure 24.10.

24.3.3 Histologic image interpretation: the diagnostic knowledge
The diagnostic knowledge base involves a set of rules and a set of meta-rules describing the system strategy . A diagnostic hypothesis is described by its name (Lobular-in-situ, for example), level (conceptual level currently reached by the interpretative tasks) and certainty degree (ranking from 0 to 1 and updated in proportion to the rule confidence degree).

24.3.3.1 The rules
The rules (figure 24.11) are defined as a list of the form (Conditions Conclusion). The condition part of a rule involves a set of iconic and/or diagnostic constraints which is structured using operating indicators such as "AND", "NOT", "n" or "EXC n" (depending if all constraints, the negation of a constraint, n constraints, at least or

exactly, have to be verified). The constraints are modelled using one of the following forms:

> (Name Descriptor Value)
> (Name Descriptor (?Variable))
> (HYPO Name Level (Operator Degree))

Value denotes the symbolic qualification to be obtained (hypertrophic, for example), while ?Variable denotes the name of the quantitative descriptor to be computed. (Operator Degree) defines a constraint to be verified by the diagnosis degree (< 0.4, for example).

Rule HYPO-LO-IN-SITU-8 :

((AND   (NOT (Pop-acini-feature Pop-acini-size (hypertrophic)))
                         (Acini-feature Acini-size (hypertrophic)))
            (HYPO Lobular-in-situ Hypothesis (COMB 0.05 ?Degree))))

Rule HYPO-LO-IN-SITU-4 :

((AND   (Lobule-feature Lobule-area (?area))
                         (Lobule-feature Lobule-perimeter (?perim)))
            (HYPO Lobular-in-situ Hypothesis (COMB (Shape area perim 0.15) ?Degree))))

Figure 24.11. Some rule examples; the rule confidence degree, in the second case, is updated in proportion to the shape factor value (deviation from circle).

The conclusion part of a rule is of the form: (HYPO Name Level (COMB Rule-coef ?Degree)). The function COMB defines the way of updating the diagnosis certainty degree (?Degree). Rule-coef denotes the rule confidence degree. It is updated in proportion to the observed morphological deviation, in case of quantitative descriptors handling. Reference values are provided for the purpose of such computation (Baak *et al.*, 1982). This particular feature allows increasing the diagnosis certainty degree when facing increased morphological deviations.

24.3.3.2 The meta-rules

Meta-rules are defined as a list of the form (conditions conclusion). They allow controlling the sequencing of the various diagnosis steps, by explicitating the goal to be reached in terms of a set of sub-goals (Cordier *et al.*, 1985). The condition part of a meta-rule is of the form (AND list-cond). List-cond involves a set of conditions, introduced according to either one of the following syntaxes:

> (HYPO ?X Level Degree)
> (Function Name arg1 arg2 ...)
> (Ident)

The first form allows specifying the conclusion part of the rules to be applied. ?X indicates that the operation has to be performed for all diagnostic name in Inst-list (instanciation field of the meta-rule). The second form indicates that the function of name Name is to be applied, using the provided arguments. The third form identifies the conclusion part of a meta-rule to be applied: it allows a robust structuration of problem solving strategy. Examples of meta-rules are provided in figure 24.12.

Rule Meta1
```
(    (AND         (Begin)
                  (Hypothesis-generation)
                  (Diagnos)
                  (Function Final-diagnosis)
                  (Function Eventual-feedback))
     ((CONSULTATION))
```

Rule Meta2
```
(    (AND         (Function Identify '$Patient)
                  (Function Create-entity '$Breast)
                  (Function Create-image '$X2.5))
     ((BEGIN)))
```

Rule Meta4
```
(?   (AND         (HYPO ?X Confirmation Degree)
                  (HYPO ?X Diagnostic Degree)
                  (Function Pending-indicators (quote ?X))
                  (Hypo ?X Complete-diagnostic Degree))
     ((DIAGNOS)))
```

Figure 24.12. Some of the main meta-rules: the system strategy is defined as a plan, involving a set of sub-goals.

24.3.4 *The control structure of the system*
The role of the system control structure is merely the one of selecting and activating rules, following the strategy edicted by the meta-rules (figure 24.13). Each cycle is thus comprised of two phases which are processed by using respectively backward and forward chaining:

- the selection phase consists in selecting the rules concluding on certain facts, according to the meta-rules directives (backward chaining) ;

- the activation phase consists in trying to successively activate all the rules that have been obtained (forward chaining), in order to cumulate a large amount of morphological indicators.

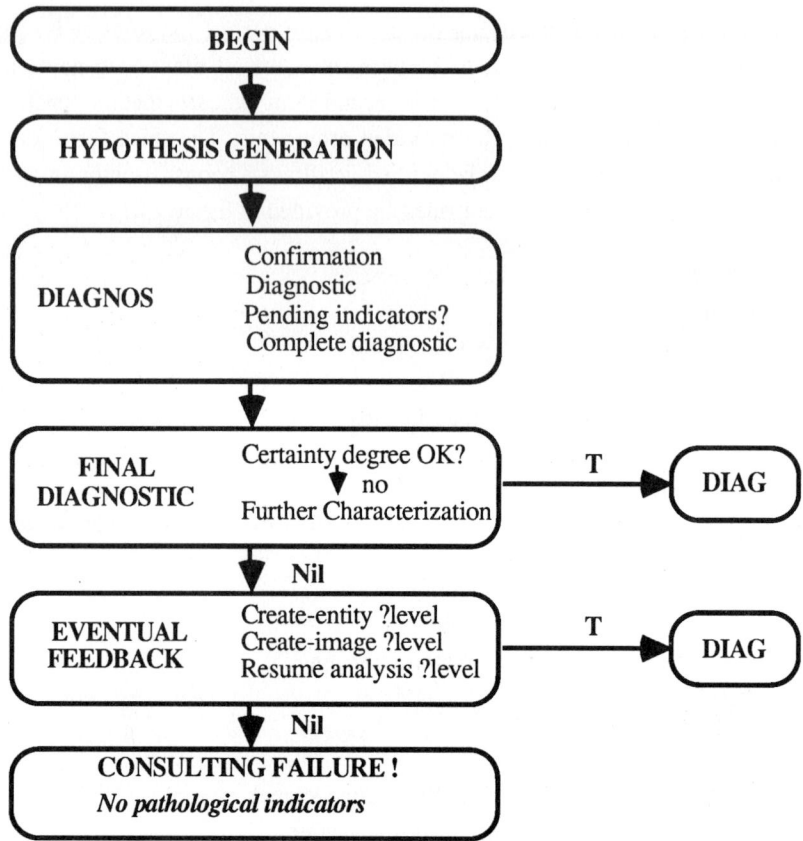

Figure 24.13. Overall view of the system strategy. The following analyzing steps are traversed:

- Begin: identify the patient, instanciate both meta-entity and meta-image trees;
- Hypothesis generation: examine the tissue architecture to produce a set of hypotheses;
- Diagnos: try to confirm each of the hypotheses by successively examining the structure and cell morphology; complete the analysis (pending indicators evaluation, pending rules activation);
- Final diagnostic: proceed to a further characterization if the diagnostic certainty degree is not sufficiently high ;
- Eventual feedback: verify the final diagnosis consistency, request a feedback in case of failure.

A feedback is requested, in case the diagnostic can not be asessed with suficient certainty. The feedback strategy involves searching for the diagnosis level at which the certainty degree increase failed to succeed. It is then considered that the morphological indicators collected through the corresponding analyzing steps are actually conveying a too weak diagnostic significance. The overall analysis has thus to be resumed from this level, in correlation with a shifting of the focus of attention: the create-entity and create-image functions are therefore activated and induce the re-instanciation of the meta-entity and meta-image trees. Such processing provides the system with the right ability of storing new morphological indicator values.

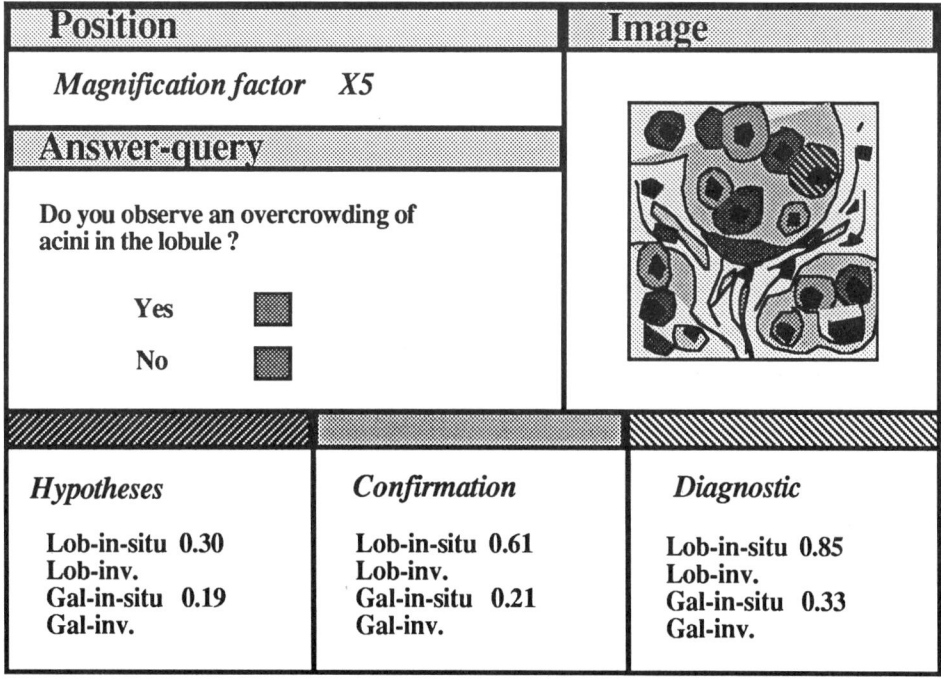

Figure 24.14. Overall view of the system graphic interface: different windows are dedicated to image and magnification factor display, explanations, comments, user answer-query and diagnosis features display, from hypothesis generation to final confirmation.

24.3.5 *Discussion*

The system is written in COMMON LISP and PASCAL, and runs on an APOLLO work-station (DN660/DN3000). A multiple-window graphic interface (figure 24.14) is dedicated to the user interaction. A limited range of morphological as well as diagnostic indicators are presently supported by the system, thus preventing him from any consistent efficiency assessment. The potential interest of the system rather arises from the rich variety of functionalities that have been investigated. Their representation and handling however suffers a serious lack of homogeneity wich impairs their right understanding and updating. Further improvements should come from their better structuration and encapsulation within dedicated objects, by using plainly the concepts of object-oriented-programming (Ferber, 1985). New research issues thus evolve: some of them are addressed in the following part.

24.4 **Designing a biomedical image interpretation system: a distributed architecture.**

These early experiments pointed to the necessity of elaborating a robust methodology of designing expert systems within the field of biomedical image interpretation. The aim of the following paragraph is to propose some research issues in designing an architecture that suits this particular field. The term architecture means a level of description of knowledge systems that specializes general Artificial Intelligence techniques to a particular class of tasks or problems (Gruber *et al.*, 1987).

Designing an architecture involves selecting adequate Artificial Intelligence low-level tools and deciding how to organize them at the architecture level, in order that they can be fitted to the required system functionalities. Selecting low-level tools involves choosing a knowledge representation method, determining the system control structure and choosing adequate resolution strategies. Organizing the low-level tools involves distributing the interpretation process and the knowledge involved among a set of sub-systems called the architecture primitives, each responsible for a well-delimitated analyzing phase. It also implies determining the kind of interaction there should be between the various primitives (communication and synchronization protocols).

Such modelling provides a high level representation of the engaged expertise, understood by both the knowledge engineer and the expert. Two basic primitives (knowledge source and knowledge processor) are firstly presented; a global architecture for biomedical image interpretation is then proposed.

24.4.1 *Knowledge sources and knowledge processors : the architecture primitives*
An image is understood by successive processings, aimed at tranforming the initial sensory informations into a more conceptual representation of the perceived scene. Such bottom-up processing is simultaneously constrained, in a top-down manner, by the instantaneous perception of both the global architecture (perceptual level) and significance (conceptual level) of the image : the notion of significance is in turn dependent on the objective as well as the expertise of the observer (Spoehr *et al.*, 1982). The way to process a given scene ultimately depends on the cicumstances of observation, i.e. on a set of case-dependent knowledge elements, which may be already available (specimen staining as well as medical past of a patient, for example).

Two fundamental capabilities are thus required, the capability to process (transform, conceptualize) and the capability to memorize (learn, store and retrieve). These capabilities are classically addressed separately in the design of an expert system, in terms of control structures and knowledge bases. When involved within the process of image interpretation, these capabilities however address knowledge elements of very different conceptual levels and consequently invoke rather dedicated processing tasks. To conceive a modular image interpretation system architecture thus implies distributing the memorizing abilities among several knowledge sources (the first type of architecture primitive), but also distributing the processing abilities among several knowledge processors (the second type of architecture primitive).

24.4.1.1 Knowledge sources

A given knowledge source (KS) is considered as dedicated to the handling of a well delimited class of knowledge. It involves a representation of the various knowledge elements (KS elements) as well as a set of activities (KS activities) acting upon KS elements and a set of meta-activities defining its own strategy (KS strategy). A KS element is represented as an object, in the framework of an object centered representation (Rechenmann, 1985), it allows the description of the concepts of the KS application domain, of their structure, attributes and relationships. KS activities are partly implicitly defined in terms of inheritance mechanisms and partly explicitily defined as production rules or procedures. KS strategy defines the optimal way to explore the KS elements. It is usually represented by a set of meta-rules.

Knowledge sources are conceived merely as active memories. Their role is to memorize, update and enrich a particular class of knowledge. They behave as long term memories by encapsulating the case-independent knowledge (expert knowledge) and also as short-term memories by grouping the case-specific knowledge (factual and circumstancial knowledge). They also play the role of interfacing the knowledge processors by giving them the ability to communicate in a synchrounous manner.

24.4.1.2 Knowledge processors

A given knowledge processor (KP) is considered as an active unit dedicated to the cooperative handling of knowledge sources that appear as related, regarding the process of interpretation. These mutual dependencies may be examplified by a set of relations tying their knowledge elements (the so-called associative knowledge).

The role of the knowledge processor is to handle this associative knowledge under a particular point of view, as formalized by a set of associative activities (KP activities). For example, the assertion "the most usefull single indicator for malignant urothelial cells is dense chromatin granules" may lead to the rule "if (Uroth-cells Chromatin-granules 'dense) then (Diagnosis Hypothesis Malignant)" . Its role is thus to transform some knowledge elements of a known conceptual level, in order to catch what they mean, or what they imply, within a different conceptual space. Activating a rule, a procedure, or any kind of activity, implies requesting some ressources of a "lower" KS and providing in turn new ressources to a "higher" KS. It is performed by sending and receiving messages to and from the concerned knowledge sources. These activities are handled according to a particular strategy (KP strategy) which edicts the way to select, apply and coordonn the KP activities.

24.4.2 Biomedical image interpretation: modelling the case-insensitive knowledge
The case-insensitive knowledge involves all knowledge sources and processors that are
relevant to the process of interpretation, considered as a general purpose process. A
global view of the corresponding architecture is proposed in figure 24.15.

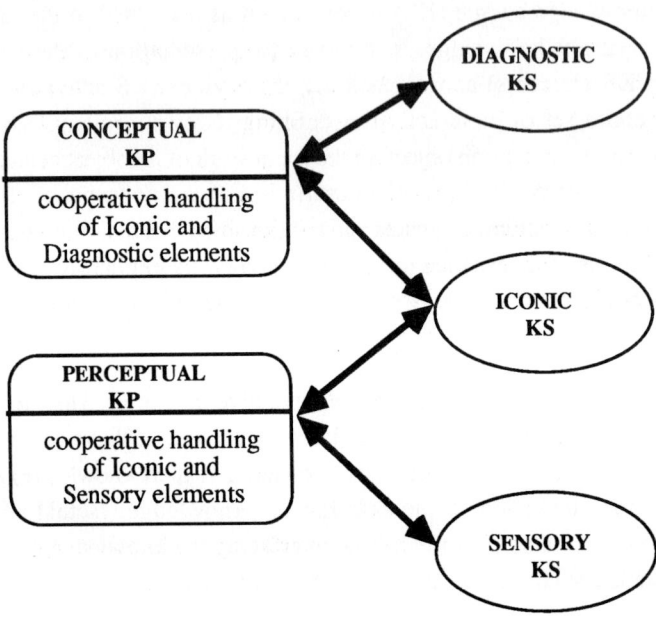

Figure 24.15. Modelling the case-insensitive knowledge sources and processors.

24.4.2.1 Knowledge sources
Several knowledge sources are distinguished, which are namely the sensory, the iconic
and the diagnostic knowledge sources.

   The Sensory KS merely involves representing the specimen to be analyzed in the form
of a hierarchy of images (KS elements) corresponding to the viewing of different
specimen fields, under different magnification factors.

   The Iconic KS involves representing the specimen to be analyzed in the form of a
hierarchy of entities (KS elements) describing the specimen components and their
features. Descriptor values are either obtained through the activation of KS activities, or
requested of the Perceptual KP. The KS strategy defines the way of exploring the image.

   The Diagnostic KS involves representing the diagnostic field under interest in the form
of a hierarchy of pathologies (KS elements). KS activities define the intrinsic conditions
(diagnostic constraints) under which the presence of a given pathology might be

hypothesized. The KS strategy defines a traversal of the tree-like structure representing the pathology space (decreasing gravity degree traversal for example).

24.4.2.2 Knowledge processors
The perceptual and conceptual knowledge processors are successively considered.

The Perceptual KP communicates with both Sensory and Iconic KS; it may also communicate with an external observer. Its objective is to exploit the Sensory KS knowledge basis in order to enrich the Iconic KS own knowledge basis. KP activities involve processing a given image in order to delineate the regions of interest and to compute the value of the requested descriptors. KP strategy defines the conditions under which either to select adequate processing tasks or to invoke the external observer for support. This local strategy is operated according to the constraints edicted by the Iconic and Sensory KS own stategy.

The Conceptual KP communicates with both Iconic and Diagnostic KP. Its objective is to exploit the Iconic KS knowledge basis in order to enrich the Diagnostic KS own knowledge basis. KP activities are defined for this purpose as a set of production rules tying diagnosis hypothesis formulation to iconic constraints verification. KP strategy defines rule selection heuristics (examining their confidence degree, for example). KS-driven strategy allows developping forward and/or backward chaining activities by defining the iconic as well as the diagnostic space to be focussed on.

24.4.3 Biomedical image interpretation: modelling the case-sensitive knowledge
The case-sensitive knowledge sources and the casual processors are firstly presented. The concepts of meta-knowledge sources and processors are then introduced and illustrated in figure 24.16.

24.4.3.1 The case-sensitive knowledge sources
The case-sensitive knowledge sources involve representing the particular case under interest. Two different knowledge sources should be addressed, which are namely the Specimen-specific and the Patient-specific KS. The Specimen-specific KS involves knowledge about the slides to be analyzed as well as their staining conditions. The Patient-specific KS involves knowledge about the patient under interest: age, sex, previous diseases and therapies, for example. Both knowledge sources share a capacity to influence problem representation and solving, under control of the casual knowledge processors, and consequently ought to be grouped within a higher level knowledge source, as described later on.

24.4.3.2 The casual knowledge processors
A casual knowledge processor communicates with one of the case-sensitive knowledge sources and one of the case-insensitive knowledge sources or processors (considered as

high-level knowledge elements). Its objective is to coerce the latter in order it fits to the situation depicted by the former. KP activities are defined for this purpose as a set of production rules. They define the circumstancial conditions under which to coerce knowledge elements or activities: in case of a pregnant woman, for example, breast cells generally display a larger size. When involving an activity, it allows constraining its degree of confidence (increasing or decreasing its value): in the previous example, any rule involving the cell size as a possible diagnostic indicator should be given a low confidence degree. The KP strategy merely reduces to a data-driven strategy.

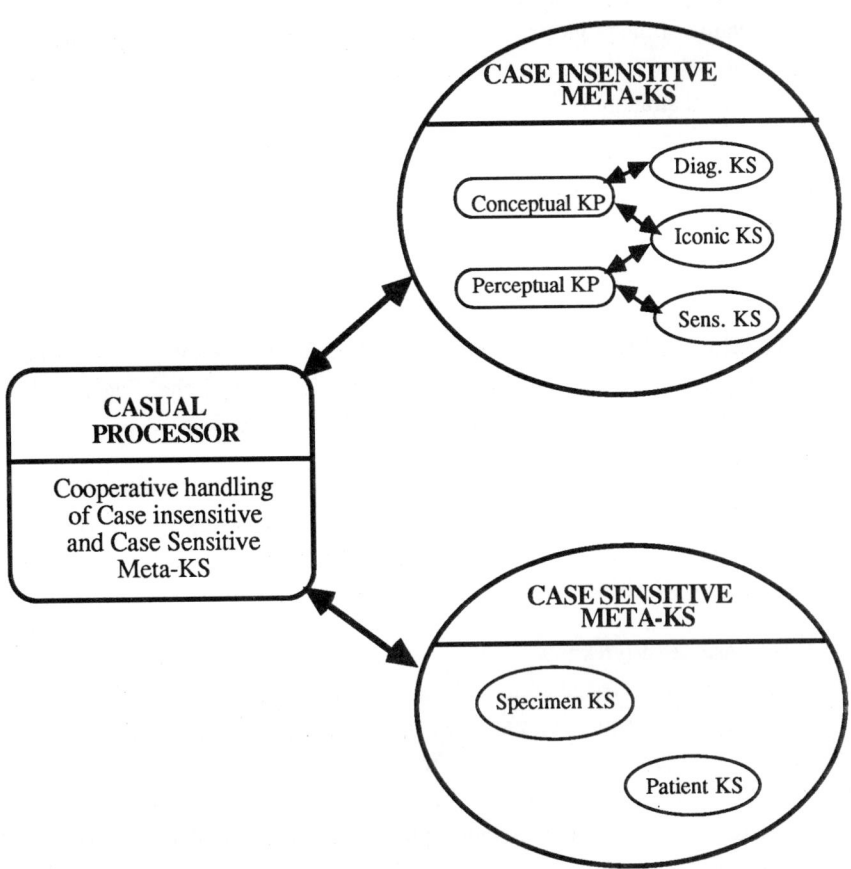

Figure 24.16. Modelling the case-insensitive and case-sensitive knowledge by means of meta-knowledge sources; a meta-knowledge processor is dedicated to the modelling of the overall coercive activities and is comprised of a set of knowledge processors.

24.4.3.3 Meta-knowledge sources and processors
The purpose is to propose a global modelling of the casual interactions: it implies representing the case-sensitive and the case-insensitive knowledge sources, as well as the

casual knowledge processors at a higher conceptual level, by considering them as playing the role of meta-knowledge sources and processors. Such notions are readily derived as a more abstract view of the previous ones. It provides a framework (Casual Meta-KP strategy) to express the expert analyzing strategy which is the higher level strategy that coordinates the overall system activities. Two main phases should be distinguished, which are the initialization phase and the completion phase:

- the initialization phase involves coercing the Case-insensitive Meta-KS according to specimen-specific circumstances, and thus transmitting to it the images to be analyzed; these early elements are used to progressively infer other elements (Meta-KS activities) until diagnostic hypotheses are obtained;

- the completion phase then involves verifying the coherence of the proposed diagnostic, regarding the patient-specific circumstances. The corresponding coercive activities are thus tentatively applied: in case of conflict, a feedback is requested to resume the analysis under constraint of the overall circumstances. Such strategy avoids focussing the system on any predefined conceptual space and thus appears as the correct solution to preserve the system diagnostic flexibility.

24.5. Conclusion

Our efforts have been concentrated on the modelling of the pathologist's expertise, as involved within the process of biomedical image interpretation. Two application fields have been considered, which are namely bladder cancer cytological diagnosis and breast cancer histological diagnosis.

Both experiments, as well as a careful investigation of human perceptual and cognitive behaviours, demonstrate the necessity to distinguish between static and dynamic problem representation (knowledge elements vs activities and strategies), i.e to describe the pathologist's knowledge but also the pathologist's know-how (Tsotsos, 1982). It furthermore appears that two fundamental capabilities are requested, which are the capability to memorize and the capability to process: these capabilities are addressed at very different conceptual levels, from early retinal information processing to diagnostic information processing.

Following such considerations, we proposed to distinguish between knowledge sources, considered as active memories, and knowledge processors, considered as active units. We furthermore introduced the notions of meta-knowledge sources and processors, as corresponding to a more abstract view of the previous ones. A powerful while flexible and recursive modelling of the overall image interpretation process may then be designed in the framework of a distributed architecture based on the modular networking of dedicated (meta-)knowledge sources and (meta-) knowledge processors (Shortliffe *et al.*, 1984).

References

Baak, J.P.A. (1982). Prognostic indicators in breast cancer-morphometric methods, Histopathology, **6**, 327-39.

Chauvet, J.M. & Rappaport, A.T. (1985). Traitement symbolique de la connaissance: une étude en médecine. Actes du Colloque Scientifique "De l'Intelligence Artificielle aux Biosciences", Centre d'Etude des Sciences et des Techniques Avancées,Paris,763-8.

Cordier, M.O. & Rousset, M.C. (1985). Le contrôle dans les moteurs d'inférences. Proc. of the Vth International Workshop on Expert Systems and their Applications, 227-59. Agence pour le Développement de l'Informatique, Paris.

Ferber, J. (1985). Les langages objets: de la programmation à la représentation des connaissances. Actes du Colloque Scientifique "De l'Intelligence Artificielle aux Biosciences", Centre d'Etude des Sciences et des Techniques Avancées,Paris, 40-8.

Garbay, C., Couderc, P. & Pesty, S. (1986). Expert system for histological diagnosis of breast cancer. Quantitative Image Analysis in Cancer Cytology and Histology, Elsevier Publishers B.V., 309-11.

Garbay, C. (1986). Images, stratégies perceptives et stratégies cognitives d'analyse. Thèse d'Etat, Université Scientifique, Technologique et Médicale et Institut National Polytechnique de Grenoble.

Granger, C. (1985). Reconnaissance d'objets par mise en correspondance en vision par ordinateur. Thèse de Doctorat, Université de Nice.

Gruber, T. & Cohen, P. (1987). Knowledge engineering tools at the architecture level. Proc. International Joint Conference on Artificial Intelligence, 100-3.

Pesty, S. & Garbay, C. (1987). Système d'interprétation d'images non naturelles. Application aux images de microscopie. Actes VIème Congrès "Reconnaissance des Formes et Intelligence Artificielle" (sous presse).

Rechenmann, F. (1985). Shirka: mécanismes d'inférences sur une base de connaissances centrée-objet. Actes Vème Congrès "Reconnaissance des Formes et Intelligence Artificielle" , AFCET / ADI / INRIA, 1243-54.

Shortliffe, E.H. & Clancey, W.J. (1984). Anticipating the second decade. Readings in Medical Artificial Intelligence, Addison-Wesley Publishing Company, 463-72.

Spoehr, K.T. & Lemkühle, S.W. (1982). Visual Information Processing. Freeman & Co.

Tsotsos, J.K. (1982). Knowledge of the visual process: content, form and use. Proc. of the IVth International Conference on Pattern Recognition. IEEE Computer Society Press, 654-69.

25 *V. Masson and R. Quiniou*

AN EXPERT SYSTEM IN APHASIA: DIAGNOSIS AND RE-EDUCATION

25.1 Introduction

Aphasia is a consequence of injuries in local regions of the brain. Aphasic patients who used to use language normally before, may be affected in the process of production or understanding of language. Two types of aphasia may be distinguished: Broca's and Wernicke's aphasia. These two manifestations correspond to distinct regions of injury. From a linguistic point of view (Guyard, 1985) aphasia is characterised by loosing some skills in language analysis. The aphasic patient still analyses language but this analysis is deficient. The preserved and impaired skills are different from one type of aphasia to the other. It is worth-noting that, in general, the patients' reasoning capabilities are not affected.

Generally neurolinguists are in charge of the re-education of aphasic patients. This re-education consists, firstly, to determine the patients' impaired skills and then to lead them to correct their errors themselves. The means used in typical re-education sessions is generally grammatical exercises. The role of these exercises is to trap the patient and to discover the way which systematically lead to errors. Then, the neurolinguist attempts to state the causality between the difficulty present in the test and the strategies used by the patient to solve the exercise.

However, for the re-education to be efficient, the number of re-education sessions must be numerous. Nowadays, a neurolinguist must be physically present during these sessions to analyse one patient's responses and then, from this analysis, to determine the nature of the next exercises. This limits drastically the number of sessions a patient may attend. Consequently, automating the re-education will, we think, lead to a better understanding of patients' troubles and also to better remission.

Automating the re-education of aphasic patients has further advantages. First of all, it may lead neurolinguists to improve their own understanding of language. With an automated re-education, we expect re-education sessions to be more complete because, during a traditional session, it is difficult for a neurolinguist to state all the possible hypotheses and to set up all the exercises which can confirm or infirm these hypotheses. Automating the re-education is expected to produce more complete and various sessions than traditional ones and of equal quality, that is, adapted to the patients' abilities.

Finally, a better knowledge of the patient's preserved and impaired skills is a first step towards a system that can assist the patient during the process of writing : here we think to a kind of linguistic prosthesis.

Our approach relies on the use of an expert system. The system automatically generates exercises, analyses the patient's reponses and then determines the sequence of exercises on the basis of this analysis.

A main feature of the system is the automatic generation of exercises. This satisfies the diversity requirement that a finite list of exercises obviously does not. The generation of exercises is based on different parameters defined by neurolinguists. Grammatical phenomena, types of exercises (to complete sentences, to build sentences from lists of words, etc.) or display mode are exemples of such parameters. An advantage of automatic generation is to allow the production of tests that presents a same difficulty under different presentations. A grammatical process may then appear clearer to the patient as the presentation of the test changes. Finally, the difficulty of a certain kind of exercise may vary along, for example, the vocabulary used.

A second feature of the system is to provide a qualitative analysis of the patient's responses. Our aim is not a quantitative evaluation of the patient's responses but to discover the strategies he uses to solve a difficulty. The analysis of the patient's responses is used to establish his portray, that is his actual state of rehabilitation and his linguistic troubles. In fact, the user model is an essential feature of the system that allows a personalised re-education for each patient. This is also an essential step towards a linguistic prosthesis.

In the next section we present, by means of two examples, the actual re-education sessions as they are managed by neurolinguists. We focus on the linguist's reasoning during the building of the next exercise he will propose to the patient. This reasoning is described in much details because this is the kind of reasoning we want for our system. Section 25.3 is devoted to the description of the different parts of the system : the exercise generator, the expert system and the patient model. In conclusion, we present the actual state of the implementation and the future work.

25.2 Actual diagnosis in re-education sessions

In this section, by means of examples, we describe the reasoning the neurolinguist makes during a session in order to diagnose the patient's troubles. The same reasoning is used during the re-education. The main differerence lies on the fact that different exercise presentations can be used in order to let the patient be aware of the problem he is faced to and let him elaborate strategies to overcome the difficulty. We hope to implement in the system that we are building the same kind of reasoning capabilities.

25.2.1 *Troubles diagnosis*

A re-education session always begins by the determination of the actual state of the patient. The diagnosis of the patient's linguistic troubles must be realised because this state is in constant evolution : the patient can progress inside his social environment as well as forget concepts that he seemed to have acquire before. On the basis of the patient's responses the neurolinguist builds hypotheses that he tries to confirm in the subsequent exercise he proposes to the patient. In fact, when he proposes a test he has already made presuppositions on the nature of the responses. When the patient gives unexpected responses, the neurolinguist builds new hypotheses, but without throwing away the old ones. A hypothesis confirmed by an exercise may well be infirmed by the next or conversely. Aphasia is characterised by the high potentiality of error and also the role played by such factors as inattention or chance may be important.

We now show, on examples, the kind of reasoning done by the neurolinguist during a diagnosis session. The first exemple we give concerns an aphasic patient of type Wernicke. The patient's responses are in italic.

un, une?

un	fort	From these results the neurolinguist formulates two hypotheses
une	forteresse	- either the patient has determined the gender of "grandeur" by
un	sport	opposition to the gender of "grande"
un	sportif	- either the patient has determined the gender on the basis of
une	grande	the word ending "eur"
un	grandeur	These two hypotheses are compatible with Wernicke's aphasia

Figure 25.1. The aim of the exercise is to determine the gender of the proposed words. The allowed responses are un (masculine) and une (feminine).

The neurolinguist takes the second hypothesis, i.e. that the word-ending "eur" has determined the gender (because there was no error in the pair *sport/sportif*). He then tries to confirm this hypothesis by proposing the next exercise.

The neurolinguist then tries to obtain another confirmation because he cannot rely on the results of a unique exercise. By proposing a list of pairs of words built on the same root, he wants to verify that the patient is not influenced by one of the members of the pair when he determines the gender of the other (this hypothesis is coherent with the linguistic troubles of Wernicke aphasics).

Finally the neurolinguist wants to verify that the patient cannot think of the gender feminine for a word ending by "eur" even though he is given a pair feminine/masculine built on the same root.

un, une?

un	tracteur	The given responses confirm the hypothesis.
un	voleur	
un	grandeur	
un	sapeur	
un	froideur	
un	sécateur	
un	longueur	

Figure 25.2. Determine the gender of the proposed words.

un, une?

un	froid	The responses are coherent for the patient has not determined
un	froideur	the gender of the words which end by "eur" on the basis of the
un	long	masculine adjectives
un	longueur	
un	grand	
un	grandeur	
un	haut	
un	hauteur	
un	blanc	
un	blancheur	

Figure 25.3. Determine the gender of the proposed words.

As expected, this test does not lead the patient to think that the femininine is a possible gender for words ending by "eur" as opposed to Wernicke aphasics who are sensible to partial identity on roots.

The second exemple is taken from a test by a patient from the opposite group of aphasic patients, that is Broca aphasics. Firstly, he is proposed the same exercise as in Figure 25.1.

This patient gives the same responses as the first patient. These responses surprise the neurolinguist because they are more compatible with Wernicke's aphasia than with Broca's. He then builds a new hypothesis : the gender of "grandeur" has been suggested by opposition to the gender of "grande". The neurolinguist then tries to confirm this hypothesis with an exercise containing no pair of words, the gender of which may be opposed by the patient.

un, une?

un	froid		
une	froide	*un*	froideur
un	long		
une	longue	*un*	longueur
un	grand		
une	grande	*un*	grandeur
un	haut		
une	haute	*un*	hauteur

Figure 25.4. Determine the gender of the proposed words.

un, une?

un	fort	The neurolinguist thinks to two hypotheses compatible with
une	forteresse	Broca's aphasia
un	sport	- either a random determination of the gender
un	sportif	- either the patient elaborates a rule from the first pair and
une	grande	which associates the masculine to the first member of the pair
un	grandeur	and the feminine to the second member. This rule is then
		applied to all the other pairs of the exercise

Figure 25.5. Determine the gender of the proposed words.

un, une?

un	tracteur	This confirms that the patient can think of the feminine for
un	voleur	words ending by "eur".
une	grandeur	The error concerning "sapeur" is forgotten, for the moment.
une	sapeur	
une	froideur	
un	sécateur	
une	longueur	

Figure 25.6. Determine the gender of the proposed words.

The next exercise tries to confirm that the gender was derived from the partial identity of the roots.

The neurolinguist has then to proposed another hypothesis for the error of the exercise shown in Figure 25.5. This can be a non significant error, for example.

un, une?

une	froide	The patient has not been trapped. This contradicts a hypothesis
une	froideur	that was judged incoherent with troubles of Broca's aphasia.
une	longue	
une	longueur	
une	grande	
une	grandeur	
une	douce	
une	douceur	

Figure 25.7. Determine the gender of the proposed words.

25.2.2 Re-education

The main principle of the re-education is to lead the patient to realise themselves that they are face to a difficulty that they do not solve correctly. Then the goal is to let them established new strategies that will solve this problem. The neurolinguist has several methods at his disposal to correct the patients. Some methods are adapted to one kind of aphasia and some to the other. The comparison principle is one of the principles used to associate methods to one or the other type of aphasia. This principle states that two contradictory responses are excluded.

Broca's aphasics still posess this principle. That's why neurolinguists used to simultaneously present them erroneous exercises and exercises where the patients answered correctly to similar questions. The patients are then able to correct their errors in the presence of correct responses. Another method used for Broca's aphasics is to augment the context inside an exercise. For example, if the patient has troubles in determining the gender of words ending by "eur", then the neurolinguist can propose a test such as Figure 25.8.

Wernicke's aphasics no longer posess the comparison principle. Exercises of the kind presented above cannot then be proposed to them. They are more sensible to the presentation of difficulties in the context of common sentences. Exercises of the kind below will surely give more results.

25.3 System description

The aim of the system is to provide aphasic patients with such re-education sessions as they used to have when managed by neurolinguists, that is, of the same kind as presented in the preceding section. In order to approach this goal, the system we have defined contains three main components :

- an inference engine which determines the features of the exercises that will be proposed to the patients

- an exercise generator which is able to create and display an exercise according to features determined by the inference engine
- a patient model wich will contain all the information relative to the patient.

Figure 25.10 gives a graphical representation of the system. The main components are described in more details in the remaining of the section.

un, une?

... liqueur forte	The patient can determine more easily the gender of
... profondeur importante	adjectives ("e" mark for the feminine) and he can then
... tracteur puissant	compare this gender with the the gender given by the
... vapeur chaude	word-ending "eur". This gives a real help because,
	for a Broca aphasic contradictory responses are
	excluded.

Figure 25.8. Determine the gender of the proposed words.

le, la?

je mesure ... hauteur de la table

j'examine ... blancheur de la page

Figure 25.9. Determine the gender of the proposed words.

25.3.1 *The inference engine*

The aim of the inference engine is to establish the sequence of exercises and the features of each of these exercises that will be generated and displayed by the exercise generator. The features of the next exercise that will be given to the patient are determined according to reasoning rules and rules for evaluating the patient's responses and also according to the patient model. Two main steps may be distinguished. During the first one, the actual linguistic difficulties of the patient are established. This corresponds to the neurolinguist's diagnosis. The features of the next test are then determined in order to improve the system knowledge of the patient's abilities (by refining and confirming hypotheses). The patient model is modified in accordance. The patient model must, indeed, represent the patient's deficient grammaticality the more faithfully as possible. When this modelisation (diagnosis) step is achieved, the second step or re-education step takes place. The goal of the system is now to make the patient improve himself, by focusing the exercises on a linguistic trouble discovered during the diagnosis step. The next test to be presented to the patient is determined according to the re-education strategies furnished by the neurolinguists and according also to the patient model (see subsection 25.3.3). For example, a strategy may be to let the patient discover his errors himself and let him, if possible, correct them himself. During the same session, several successive diagnosis and re-education steps may take place.

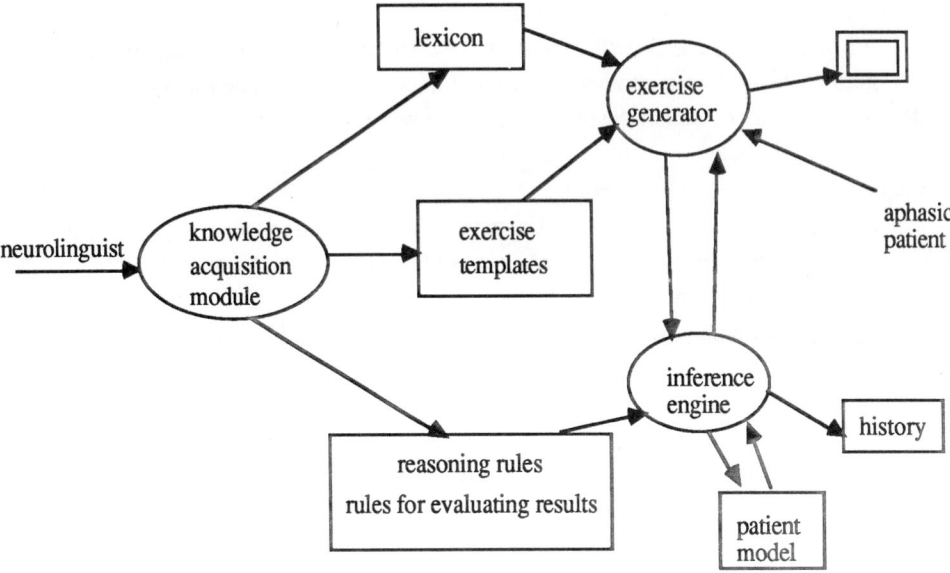

Figure 25.10 Synopsis of the system

When the features of the next test are determined they are given as input to the exercise generator which then creates the adequate exercise. The exercise generator displays it to the patient and collects his responses. It then transmits to the inference engine the text of the exercise, the patient responses and the way the patient has answered (the order of the responses, the corrections if any, etc.). On the basis of these information the inference engine is able to modify, if necessary, the patient model and then it determines the features of the next exercise.

The rules used for reasoning and evaluating the patient's responses are formalised as classical production rules which have a condition and an action part. Figure 25.11. gives an example of such a rule.

The application of such rules may be structured by use of metarules built on the same scheme. The strategy used by the inference engine is forward chaining because it is nearer to the neurolinguist's reasoning.

The knowledge acquisition module and the history will not be described in details here. They are tools to assist the neurolinguists. The aim of the first one is to provide facilities for modifying and augmenting the expert knowledge of the system (lexicon, reasoning rules, ...). It does not require knowledge in computer science from neurolinguists and will, in the future, provide natural language facilities to make this interaction easier. The history module has in charge to sum up the patients' evolution in order to let the neurolinguists analyse more easily the results given by the re-education sessions managed by the system.

> if   the patient is a Broca's aphasic
> and he has made an error in the determination of the gender of a word ending by "eur"
> and he has already confirmed such an error in a test
> and ...
> then try a second confirmation with an exercise of the same type and with an increased vocabulary difficulty

Figure 25.11 Example of reasoning rule.

It's worth noting that this system is very close to intelligent tutoring systems. However, it differs in at least one aspect : the explaining facilities that such system usually provide. Indeed, explaining linguistic errors to patients who have linguistic troubles is useless. This avoids the use of a complex natural language generator because the dialog between the patient and the system consists only of texts of exercises and patient's responses.

25.3.2 *The exercise generator*

The goal of the exercise generator is to create a test whose essential features have been determined by the inference engine. To achieved this goal, it uses two data structures given by the neurolinguist : exercise templates and a lexicon. The exercise which will be proposed to the patient is built after the exercise template by choosing the words in the lexicon and filling the "holes" of the chosen template. The exercise is then proposed to the patient and his responses are recorded together with informations concerning the patient's behaviour during the test. These informations are, for example, the order of the responses, the corrections if any, the response time, etc. Finally, the exercise generator transmits to the inference engine all the informations that may be useful for the responses analysis, that is the text of the exercise and the responses and also the behavioral informations.

In order to create the tests, the neurolinguists have defined some parameters that the system may alter during the generation of exercises. Several types of exercises are used for diagnosing and reeducating the aphasic patients, for example, to build sentences from a list of words given in disorder, to complete sentences, to determine the gender of words by giving the correct determiner or article, etc. The main features of the exercises concern :

    - how to display the exercise to the patient : list of words in rows, in columns, where to place the questions, above or below the text of the exercise, etc.

    - how to present the exercise : will the allowable responses be given to the patient or not, number of items, forbidden autocorrection or not, etc.

- which features must have the vocabulary used in the exercise : pairs of words having the same root, words with the same ending, category of the words (adjectives or/and nouns), semantic pairs such as fruit-tree/fruit (these words may not have the same root), etc.

These different parameters are organised in exercise templates. This avoids incoherent or useless tests. In the lexicon, each word is linked to his syntactical and semantical properties. For example, the word "chienne" (dog, feminine) is defined as a singular, feminine noun, with root "chien", word-ending "e" and is a member of the class "animal". The exercise chooses an exercise template which satisfies the constraints imposed by the inference engine (type of the exercise, display mode, vocabulary, etc.). The exercise is generated by extracting words from the lexicon for simple exercises. If the exercise consists in building sentences from lists of words, the exercise generator uses a simple analyser-generator of natural language. The same module is used to create the exercise and to analyse the patient's responses. This module is able to verify that the sentence produced by the patient is syntactically or semantically correct on the basis of the informations provided by the lexicon. The syntax of the proposed sentences is rather simple, so the analyser-generator is not very complex.

25.3.3 *The patient model*
Personalised re-education such as the one proposed by the neurolinguists themselves are highly desirable. That is, these sessions must be adapted to the actual state of the linguistic problems of each patient. The performances of such a system depends highly on the approximation of the actual state of the patient stored in the patient model. Therefore this is an essential part of the system.

The patient model contains some static facts such as the birthdate of the patient, the type of aphasia he suffers from, the associated handicaps, etc., but the most important ones are dynamic information. They represent either the general behaviour of the patient (ease of acquisition of new concepts, confusion in front of a new formulation of a concept, fatigue, etc.), or the linguistic problems of the patient. The last ones are determined from the text of the exercises, the patient's responses and the way the patient has answered. Our main interest lies in modelling the patient's knowledge and his linguistic troubles. This is very analogous to the notion of a student model in intelligent tutoring systems. We now discuss some user models being used in tutoring systems and finally present the solution we are exploring for representing aphasic patient models.

The most simple solution is to view the patient's linguistic knowledge as a subset of the grammatical processes as defined by the neurolinguists. This method know as the "overlay approach" and which is used in many tutoring systems (Clancey, 1982, Goldstein, 1982) to represent the student's knowledge does not meet our requirements. It can be used to represent the grammatical processes a patient ignores but not those he incorrectly applies. For example, the derivational process "pomme -> pommier" (apple -> apple-tree) when incorrectly applied to "raisin" (grapes) gives "raisinier" (grape-tree) instead of "vigne" (vine). In addition, the overlay approach cannot be used to represent incorrect processes (for example, a word-ending "eur" implies a masculine gender).

We want to be able to analyse the difference between the patient's actual responses and the responses he ought to have given according the established hypotheses. This kind of differential analysis is used in several tutoring systems (Coombs and Alty, 1984, Burton, 1982) and achieved on the basis of error or bug prototypes. The method known as the "bug approach" consists in determining the bug prototype that corresponds to the patient's responses. BUGGY and DEBUGGY, the systems of Brown and Burton seems rather interesting from this point of view. Each recorded bug corresponds to a hypothesis made on the alteration of a correct response to an erroneous one. The goal of the modelling (or diagnosing) step is to confirm and refine the discovered bugs (hypotheses). This method is then very close to the reasoning used by neurolinguists. However, the knowledge contained in the student model is tightly linked to the set of bugs defined in the system. The linguistic research concerning aphasia is constantly evolving and the expertise must often be modified. Then it is a main disavantage, for a system as ours, to use a model such that the information it contains may become useless as the expertise is modified from one session to another (this is to be opposed to Brown and Burton's system whose domain is the well-known simple arithmetic).

To face this difficulty, we have chosen to adapt an original method used by Kawai *et al.* (1986) for an intelligent tutoring system. Their method has the same representation power as Brown and Burton's one but it reduces drastically the importance of the expertise during the modelling step. The expertise is only used for interpreting the model during the re-education step.

The main idea of the method derived from Kawai et al.'s one is to synthesise a logic program from the proposed exercises and the obtained responses. This logic program is intended to represent the patient's knowledge. To discover the patient's problems corresponds to look for the bugs contained in this program according to a given specification (the correct responses to this exercise). The error types correspond to the three types of linguistic difficulties, mentioned above, that we are trying to modelise. As Kawai et al., we have experimented the Model Inference System (MIS) developed by Shapiro (1983) to build the patient model. MIS induces a Prolog program which satisfies all the facts describing the text of the exercise and the patient's responses. In order to orient the research of clauses for the program to be synthesised, MIS may interact with the user. Indeed, the system may need further informations to confirm or refine the hypotheses made upon the patient's behaviour. In our system, this kind of questions corresponds to submit the patient to new exercises. Then, this method corresponds exactly to the neurolinguist's one during the diagnostic step.

When the program synthesis is achieved, the patient's linguistic troubles are extracted from the model by a bug diagnosis system. Once again, as Kawai et al. we are experimenting the program diagnosis system also developed by Shapiro (1983). As it is used by Shapiro, this program is interactive. In our case it is not. Questions submitted to the user in the original system are here answered on the basis of the expertise. We consider that the expertise defines some kind of specification which can be used to tell what is a correct program. The diagnosis is then establish in view of the expertise. The patient's deficient grammaticality being determined along this line, the re-education step can begin.

25.4 Conclusion

The main originality of this project is that it is not based on a quantitative or statistical study of the patient's responses as are some connected works (Deloche, 1985). Our goal is to automatically propose re-education sessions as close as possible to those proposed by the neurolinguists who are actually in charge of this re-education. The two main features of the system is to be able to propose automatically a great number of various exercises and to make use of a precise modelling of all the patient's linguistic problems. A personalised re-education is a needed requirement in the view of our long-term goal which is the aphasic patient assistance during the process of writing, that is a system which will be able to automatically correct his errors.

The exercise generator has been implemented on a Macintosh Plus and has been evaluated by some aphasic patients. The functioning of the system on this machine which has graphic capabilities and a pointing device (the mouse) has been judged convincing. The prototype has only a small lexicon (about 100 words) and a reduced number of exercise templates (abut 10). However, it has been able to generate almost all the most common exercises. The inference engine is implemented in Prolog. The main difficulty concerns the formalisation of the expertise in production rules. As usual in expert system, the knowledge of the experts is rather intuitive and fuzzy. This is especially true for this domain, where expert are very far from such notions as algorithms. The algorithms of program synthesis have been implemented in Prolog on a SUN-3 workstation which is more powerful than the Macintosh Plus. The main difficulty we have met is also to formalise the patient's responses in a logic program and to compare it with the expertise.

The next step is to extend the system knowledge in every modules (lexicon, exercise templates, reasoning and evaluating rules) in order to come more closely to the classical sessions. Another extension concerns the use of the history. This history is to be used by the neurolinguists in order to improve the knowledge of aphasia they have and the kind of re-education adapted to each type of patient. In fine, the goal of such a tool is to assist them in elaborating a theory of language. To achieve this goal, we want to experiment techniques used in machine learning (Nicolas, 1986) in order to structure and model the patient's evolution during the re-education.

25.5 Acknowledgements

We truly thank H. Guyard (UER du langage, Université de Rennes II) for his collaboration in the project. He has given the expertise of the system and, has particularly, defined the succession of exercises of section 25.2.

References

Burton, R.R. (1982) Diagnosing bugs in a simple procedural skill. In: *Intelligent Tutoring Systems*, Academic Press

Clancey, W.J. (1982). Tutoring rules for guiding a case method dialog. In: *Intelligent Tutoring Systems*, Academic Press.

Coombs, M.J. & Alty J.L. (1984). Expert systems: An alternate paradigm., *International Journal of Man-Machine Studies*, **20**.

Deloche, G. (1985). Micro-informatique et rééducation des aphasiques., *Research Report Inserm U. 84*

Goldstein, I.P. (1982). The genetic graph: A representation for the evolution of procedural knowledge. In: *Intelligent Tutoring Systems*, Academic Press.

Guyard, H. (1985). Le test du test. Pour une linguistique expérimentale., *Tétralogiques 2*, Presse Universitaire de Rennes II.

Kawai, K., Mizogushi, R., Kausho, O. & Toyoda J. (1986). A framework for ICAI systems based on inductive inference and logique programming., *Proceeding of the Third Logic Programming Conference*, London

Nicolas, J. (1986). Learning as search : a logical approach., *Proceeding of CIIAM 86*, Hermes

Shapiro, E.Y., (1983). Algorithmic Programming Debugging, *MIT Press*

GIDE: A SYSTEM FOR INTELLIGENT HANDLING OF MEDICAL FILES OF EPILEPTICS

26.1 Introduction

Epilepsy is a chronic desease much more characterized by its clinical symptoms than by its real cause. The appreciation of the various cases is based on a history of records and on parameters which vary a great deal from one patient to another. As a result, the file of a patient is generaly characterized by:
- its thickness due to the chronic nature of the disease,
- the scatter of information owing to the difficulty in obtaining it.

The handling of such a file raises a number of problems and the aim of the system GIDE is to design an environment capable of permitting a quick and intelligent access to the files. The notion of rapidity used here is linked to the fact that the system does not wait on certain elements shown however in the files, and the intelligent aspect holds to the fact that the system itself determines whether an information presents enough interest to be given to the user in a given context. To cover its objectives the system must comprize the three types of elements below:
- tools enabling the representation of information contained in the files in their structural and static aspects,
- tools permitting the integration into these elements information of enabling the expression of their dynamics on the evaluation and visualization levels,
- tools allowing the incremental integration of non definitive and reviewable elements of expert evaluation.

In this article, after quickly covering the problems caused by the handling of the file, we shall show how one can, from a formalism of object centered representation (O.C.R.) organize the summary and the intelligent entry of the file on a patient. Moreover, beyond the specification of the functonalities of the system, we'll show that O.C.R. have the basic tools (pattern-matching and procedural attachements) enabling the expression of the dynamics of the system in various forms: production rule, predicate, procedure. This talk is illustrated with examples drawn from the model in the process of being developed using **Shirka**, an object centered representation system developed by INRIA.

26.2 GIDE application

In this paragraph we shall give a quick description of the problems usually encountred in the course of handling a patient's file, mentioning the solutions that the system could bring to the them.

26.2.1 *Problems posed by the handling of the file.*
The problems brought about by the handling of the medical file of an epileptic patient are related to the inadequacy of the information contained in the file and to the difficulty in having an exhaustive vision of them.

   In fact, most of the information contained in the files has its validity and even its relevance change with time and the acquisition of fresh information. Let us consider for instance the case of a less than 6 years old patient whom the doctor sees again after a year; even if his file contains indications about his weight, we cannot consider them as being valid, for it is likely that this weight has changed a great deal since the last consultation. This remark on the weight also applies to most of the information contained in the file. Moreover, as the patient is usually not conscious during his fits, the semiological description is made by his relatives or neighbours; this implies a great diversity of sources, and, as a result the acquisition of new information does not necessarily means that the information of same nature contained in the file have become false or useless. This situation prevents the doctor from having a good comprehension of the file.

26.2.2 *The aim of the system*
Each consultation usually starts with a preliminary phase which can sometimes be very long and during which the doctor synthesizes the file. In spite of the time spent on this synthesis, one cannot guarantee that all the significant elements in the file have been taken into account. To correct this situation, the system must indicate for instance, during the entry of the file, which elements are already known; if one already knows that the patient suffers from a functional epilepsy, it is not necessary to request a scan; similary if the patient is too young or a male, one must avoid worring about side effects or complications pertaining to pregnancy during the prescription of a treatment.

   The system must also enable the doctor to have an exhaustive view of the file without fully going through it; it must, for example, give a description of the semiology obtained by integrating the semiology observed in hospital into that observed by the family circle of the patient. One can sum up the role of the system in the handling of the file by saying that it enables during the entry, the suggestion of elements which could be interesting to record, and during the consultation, the realization of the synthesis and the summary of the file.

26.3 Choosing a formalism for the representation of knowledge in GIDE

The information used in GIDE must comprise two aspects:
- a desciptive aspect which enables the specification of the data or facts recorded in the file,
- a dynamic aspect which enables the handling of these data or facts either during the evaluation (or entry), or during the synthesis so that an expressive representation of it can be given.

The integration of these two aspects must be as large as possible to enable the consideration of the characteristics of the different types of information to be handled. Moreover, the collaboration with epileptologists has shown the necessity of being capable to express certain information in independent and non definitive granules, so that they can be revised or made up incrementally. Contrary to the needs expressed above, which seem to suggest a formalism based on the notion of object, this last aspect rather suggests the notion of production rules. In fact, for the realization of the program GIDE an O.C.R. formalism (Shirka) has been used and we shall show that it meets all the requirements mentionned above. This demonstration will be done in two stages:

Firstly, we shall explain why a system based on the notion of object is more suitable than a system made up of an inference engine and a set of production rules. Secondly, we shall show how the O.C.R. is better than O.O.L. (Object oriented language) for representing this kind of knowledge and especially for reproducing the effect of production rules from a combination of pattern-matching and procedural attachments.

26.3.1 *Production rules*

Historically, the notion of expert-system is linked to that of production rule. (this has been justify by the very simple size and the modularity of the latter). However, it seems today that a system composed only of production rules presents some disadvantages, the two most important among which are taken below:

In general, the operation of an intelligent system consists of identifying the objects of the real world, classifying them and trying to create new instances of those object from those which are known. But as shown in (Vignard 1984), in a system of production rules "the object-type does not exist; object are only described through characteristics disseminated in production rules".

With their modular nature, the production rules permit the expression of exact calculations, but they cannot by themselves integrate those calculation in a bigger context than the hypothetical part of the rules.The use of meta-rules and the **context-tree** in the MYCIN system (Shortliffe 1976) seems to be justified by the need of compensation for this handicap. In fact the notion of context used in MYCIN recalls a number of points in the notion of object. Moreover when epilepsy is concerned, many concepts are defined as specialisations of other concepts; for example, from the original concept of epilepsy one can define the concepts of primary, secondary, partial or generalized epilepsy; this suggests the notion of class and sub-class used in object oriented mechanisms.

26.3.2 *Object based knowledge representation*
The formalisms based on the notion of object are more and more used to represent knowledge. This is due to the fact that, in comparison with other formalisms, they offer tools which express better the declarative and structural knowledge; tools among which one can find the organisation of objects in classes, and the concept of heritage which enable(Kristine 1986):
>   - to factorize the knowledge to be represented,
>   - to realize the incremental conception from the general to the specialized,
>   - to take advantage of a high degree of polymorphism.

However one must distinguish between O.O.L (object oriented language) and O.C.R.(object centered representation); if the former offer by the notions of methods and message a dynamic aspect easy to apprehend and to use, they remain relatively limited since the attibutes of an object are only simple variables; their capacity to structure knowledge is hence very limited. In fact, the O.O.L are more like methods of programming than formalisms for knowledge representation. The O.C.R. are characterized by a semantic which is much more complex but also much richer. In the O.C.R. the attributes of an object are themselves structured objects, thus giving the O.C.R. great capacity to structure knowledge. Moreover, by combining the use of the procedural attachment and pattern-matching, one can reproduce the phase known as "evaluation phase" of production rules systems, and describe procedural attachments which have the same effect as production rules.

In the rest of this article, after a rapid presentation of Shirka, we shall show how the summary of the file is done in the program which is now being developped.

26.4 Presentation of Shirka

Shirka is a system of management of object centered knowledge which uses a model of representation inspired by FRAMES (Minsky, 1975). An entity in Shirka is called **schema**. A schema represents a class of objects or a particular object. The term "object" refers to a physical or conceptual entity semantically well-defined.

26.4.1 *The structure of a schema*
A schema is described by its name and the list of its attributes. each attribute is itself described by a name and a list of facets. These facets are chosen in a predefined set which cannot be extended by the user. If one decides for instance, to describe the schema DATE, one characrerizes it by the attributes DAY, MONTH, YEAR. Each attribute will then be described by facets which are primitives of Shirka. So DATE can be described as:

```
(def-sh '(DATE
        (sort-of    (= object))
        (DAY              ($un integer)
                    ($interval(1 31)))
        (MONTH    ($un sting)
                    ($range "january" "february"......"december"))
        (YEAR     ($un integer))))
```

Figure 26.1. the definition of the schema DATE

In this description, the facets used are $un, $interval, $range.
$un permits the introduction of the type of the attribute while precising it is single-valued; multi-valued attribute would have been introduced by $list-of.
$interval permits the specification of the interval in which the attribute has its values.
$range permits the introduction of the list of possible values of the attribute.
Shirka has more than thirty facets which can be distributed into the following groups:
> - the facets for type or type restriction,
> - the facets for determination of the values of the attributes,
> - the facets for response on event,
> - the facets for visualisation,
> - the facets for reading.

26.4.2 *The pattern matching*
The pattern matching is used to determine whether an instance belongs to a class, so that one should know if it can be given a value of a certain type, or wether one can apply some processing to it. It uses two parameters, one of which is the instance to be classified and the other the class (filter) in relation to which the instance must be situated. The filter is described by a schema of class whose name is that of the class to which the instances we are searching for (or we have) are related. Its structure is identical but each of its attributes can have additional restrictions compared to those represented on the schema of class.
Example (DATE
          (DAY   ($value 25)))
This example describes a filter which permits one to find the set of instances of the shema DATE whose component DAY has for value 25.

26.5 **The structuration of knowledge in GIDE**

26.5.1 *Description of a consultation*
The most complex entity of the system is the entity **consultation** whose diagram is shown below:

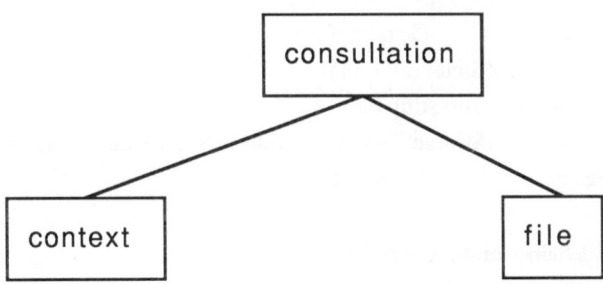

Figure 26.2

The attributs of the schema CONSULTATION are themselves complex schemas. A working session with GIDE consists in creating an instance of this schema. The component CONTEXT puts together the data which enable the system to make hypotheses on what the user may know (before the consultation) about the patient and his file. For example, it specifies whether the patient is present or not, wether the user wishes to re-make the diagnosis or the therapy, wether it is a routine consultation or not. The component CONTEXT is re-valued at each consultation through a set of question-answers with the user. The component FILE is a much more complex object and is represented in the figure below:

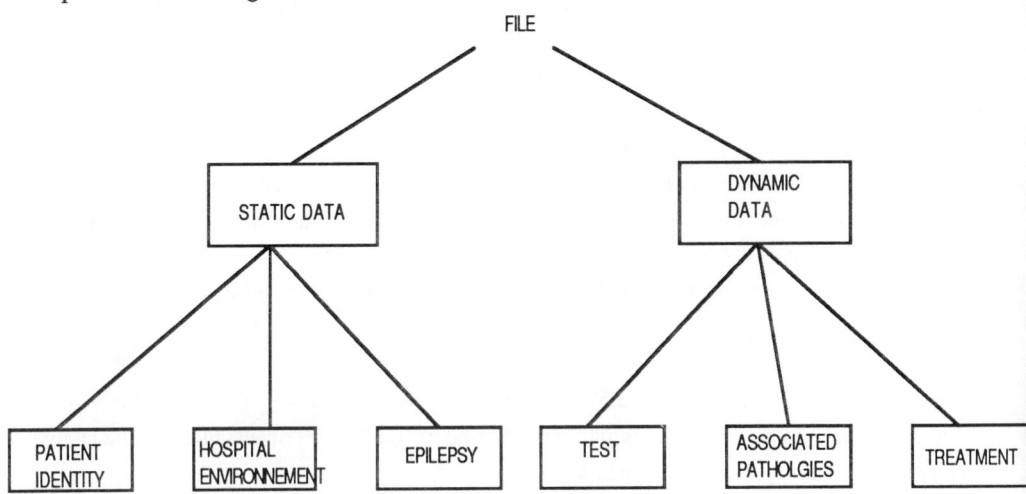

Figure 26.3. structure of the file

The data of static instantiation usually exist in only one copy in the file and can be modified, but cannot be erased nor duplicated. The data of dynamic instantiation can exist in several copies in the file; one can create some new ones at each consultation. For these data, arises the problem of the choice of copies to be used at a given time, and which answers best to the concern of the user. This problem is solved in the functionality "SUMMARY" as we shall show in paragraph 26.5.3.1

26.5.2 *Tools for inference*

Shirka offers a certain number of tools which are used in GIDE such as heritage, pattern-matching, default values and procedural attachment; moreover, one can reproduce the mechanism of reverse chaining (like in production rule systems) by combining several of these tools.

26.5.2.1 Heritage

Heritage is a mechanism common to all formalisms based on the notion of object (OOL and OCR). It can concern attributes or attribute values. So in addition to its specific attributes,which are sex, occupation, age, and birth-date the schema PERSON (figure 26.5) inherits from the schema IDENTITY (figure 26.4) the attributes name-forename address and telephone. Moreover, in the instantiation of the schema BOY (figure 26.6) for example, the value of the attribute occupation and sex will no longer be asked. They inherit respectively from the default value and from the value fixed by the definition in the schemas BOY and CHILD. The difference between a default value, and a value fixed by definition is that the default value can be modified; therefore one can find a boy having an occupation but his sex will always be "male".

```
(def-sh      '(IDENTITY
                (sort-of                  (= object))
                (NAME-FORENAME   ($un string))
                (PATIENT-ADDRESS ($un address))
                (TELEPHONE                                 ($un string))))
```

Figure 26.4. Definition of schema IDENTITY

26.4.2.2.Procedural attachments

Procedural attachments can have very different results according to facets which introduce them; they can be used:
- to determine the value of an attribute ($ sib-exec, $sib-filter, $sib-choice),
- to put a restraint on an attribute ($ check-first),
- to visualize the attribute ($ before-vi, $ for-vi),
- to read the attribute.

One can combine the possibilities of procedural attachments and the pattern-matching to obtain a more flexible performance of the system. Let us not forget that the pattern-matching is one of the main tools of inference used in Shirka.

```
(def-sh      '(PERSON
                (sort-of      (= identity))
                (SEX                          ($un sting)
                              ($range "male" "female"))
                (OCCUPATION        ($un string))
                (AGE               ($un integer)
                       .........   )
                (BIRTH-DATE        ............  )))
```

Figure 26.5. definition of the schema PERSON

```
(def-sh      (CHILD
                (Sort-of          (= person))
                (AGE                        ($internal 1 15))
                (OCCUPATION  ($ value "not in activity"))))

(def-sh      (BOY
                (Sort -of         (= child)
                (SEX                        ($ value "male"))
```

Figure26.6. Definition of the concepts CHILD and BOY

26.5.2.3 Production rules seen as a combination of pattern-matching and of the procedural attachments

In this paragraph, we shall show how one can obtain a result similar to that of production rules by adding several methods to one facet. Let us consider the following rule which can be used to describe the summary of a patient's identity:

> IF   the patient's age ranges from 16 to 120 and the patient's sex is "male"
> THEN (one can) sum up his identity using PROC1.

In MYCIN (Shortliffe, 1976), one would have said that this rule is linked to the context patient. Indeed, all premises of this rule revolve around the characteritics of the object PATIENT. As the object PATIENT exits in the system, one can create a sub-class of this class by specializing the attributes answering the characteristics mentioned in the rule. This sub-class can be described by the schema MAN below:

```
(def-sh (MAN
        (sort-of        (= person))
        (AGE                    ($Range (16 120))
        (SEX                    ($ check-first
                                (equality
                                    (value 1 <- sex))
                                    (value 2 < - "male")))))
```

Figure 26.7. The diagram MAN is a schema which gathers all the characteristics of the schema PERSON, but with additional restrictions.

The rule above can be represented by the following schema:
```
(def-sh (SUMMARY-MAN
        (sort-of    (= method))
        (patient            ($ un MAN))
        (name-fct ($ value PROC1))))
```

Figure 26.8. The PROC1 function will be activated only if the object PATIENT which is transmitted can be seen as part of the sub-class MAN and therefore confirming the additional restrictions on MAN opposed to PERSON.

In the same way, one can define rules of summary whose premises correspond to specialization of the object PERSON which are WOMAN,BOY, GIRL and whose name would be SUMMARY-WOMAN, SUMMARY-BOY,SUMMARY-GIRL respectively.

```
(def-sh (SUMMARY-WOMAN
        (sort-of    (method))
        (patient            ($ un WOMAN))
        (name -fct       ($ value PROC2)))
```

Figure 26.9. A schema equivalent to rule SUMMARY-WOMAN

The schema PERSON (figure 26.5) can be completed as shown below:

To visualize the schema PERSON (facet $ to-vi), the system will associate with the component "patient" of the schemas of processing(methods) mentioned above the instance of PERSON to be visualized (tagged"self"). With the pattern-matching and classification the system determines to which sub-class of the diagram PERSON the component "patient" of the proposed method of summary belongs. Depending on whether this object will be seen as part of the class MAN, WOMAN,..., the processings PROC1....PROC4 will be applied. The use of these schemas of processing is equivalent to that of the set of rules below:

1) IF   the patient's age ranges from 16 to 120 and the patient's sex is" male"
   THEN   sum up his identity using PROC1.

2) IF the patient's age ranges from 16 to 120 and the patient's sex is "female"
   THEN sum up her identity using PROC2.

3) IF the patient's age ranges from 0 to 15 and the patient's sex is "male"
   THEN sum up his identity using PROC3

4) IF the patient's age ranges from 0 to 15 and the patient's sex is "female"
   THEN sum up her identity using PROC4.

```
(def-sh (PERSON
        (sort-of   (=identity))
        (self

                ($ pour-vi
                   (SUMMARY-MAN (patient < -self))
                   (SUMMARY-FEMME (patient <-self))
                   (SUMMARY-BOY (patient <-self))
                -->no change in the rest<--
```

Figure 26.10.

26.5.3 *Expression of the functionalities of the system*

In (Noussi *et al* , 1986), the the structure of an object which could be used for the description of the entities of a patient's file is characterized by the following elements:

   a) description of the morphology of the object (class, sub-classes, attributes),
   b) description of the elements used for the instantiation of the object,
   c) description of method stating how the object responds to the calls of its environnement,
   d) description of *qualifications* used for the manipulation of the object without refering of the subjacent granules of informations.

The elements corresponding to points a) and b) are implicit in the primitives of Shirka. The element corresponding to points b) and c) are those which, in the present state of the system, make possible the realization of the functionalities "entry" (or evaluation) and "summary". They correspond to the definition of schemas which will be given as values to the facets $if-needed and $to-vi of the entities one wants to summarize or to register.

26.5.3.1 Specification of the functionality "SUMMARY"

The summary or the synthesis of of a file is obtained through the possibility of the system to create several visions of the same file, based on the choice of instances of schema used to represent it and the possibility of having several methods of visualization for the same concept in the file.

a) Obtaining several vision of the same file

The file is theorically made up of the set of intances of different schemas created during the consultation. Among those information, those termed information of dynamic instantiation evolve much more often and can exist in several copies in the file. From this file which we shall call **physical** file, the system creates a **vision** of a file made up of components chosen according to the present concerns. For example, if the doctor doesn't want to re-make the diagnosis, the only instances of fits selected will be the instance created the most recently; if the doctor wishes to change the therapy, the system will take as associated pathologies all the pathologies existing in the physical file, even those of which the patient is already treated. The element of the dynamic part are described by filters taking into account the element of the static part and the context. These filters permit the choice among the element actually in the file, those which are best adapted to the present situation. One can, in this way, obtain several visions of the same file according to the values of the context and the static elements in the file.

b) Using several methods of visualisation for the same object

On another level, the summary can be considered as a visualization for which the methods used (and for that matter the results) vary according to the specializations of the concepts involved in the context. The case described in paragraph 26.5.2.3 constitutes a form of summary since the procedure used varies depending on whether the instance involved can be seen as belonging to the sub-class MAN, WOMAN, or CHILD. Knowing the sub-class to which the instance to be summerize belongs, enables one to focus better on the information to be given as summary.

26.5.3.2 Specification of the functionality "entry"

The evaluation or the entry of an object is specified by the information given by the schema used as value for the facets $if-needed and $sib-filter. These schemas can introduce methods which, from the dialogue with the user create an instance of the object being evaluated. For the evaluation of the schema PERSON for example, the processing-schema used is the following:

```
(def-sh     '(INST-PERSON
                   (sort-of     (= method))
                   (result                      ($un PERSON))
                   (name-of-fct                 ($value ENTRY-PERSON)))
```
In this schema the function ENTRY-PERSON permits one to obtain the values of the atributes of the schema PERSON, which will be then assigned to *result*.

These schemas can also calculate the attributes of the schema to instantiated from other objects known, using a mechanism similar to that used in calculating the value of the attribute *age* of the schema PERSON as described below.

```
(def-sh     '(INST-AGE
                   (sort-of     (= method))
                   (DATA-ORIGINE      ($un date))
                   (DATE-TODAY        ($un date))
                   (AGE               ($un integer))
                   (NAME-FCT          ($value count-years))))
```

Figure 26.12. schema used for the evaluation of DATE

The schema above is use to calculate the patient's age using components representing the birth-date of the patient and and the date of the day through the function *count-year*. It is interesting to note that in this evaluation the system does not ask any question to the user, but deduce the wanted value from those which are already known. The use of this shema can be shown in the example below:

```
(def-sh     '(PERSON
                   (sort-of     (= identity))
                   ...........
                   ...........
                   (age          ($un integer)
                                 ($if-needed
                                        (inst-age
                                               (date-origine<- birth-date)
                                               (age1-> age))))
                   (birth-date   ($un date)
                                 ...........))))
```

Figure 26.13

If when trying to calculate the patient's age, his date of birth is not known, the system will automatically set the calculation the birth-date before come back to the calculation of the age.

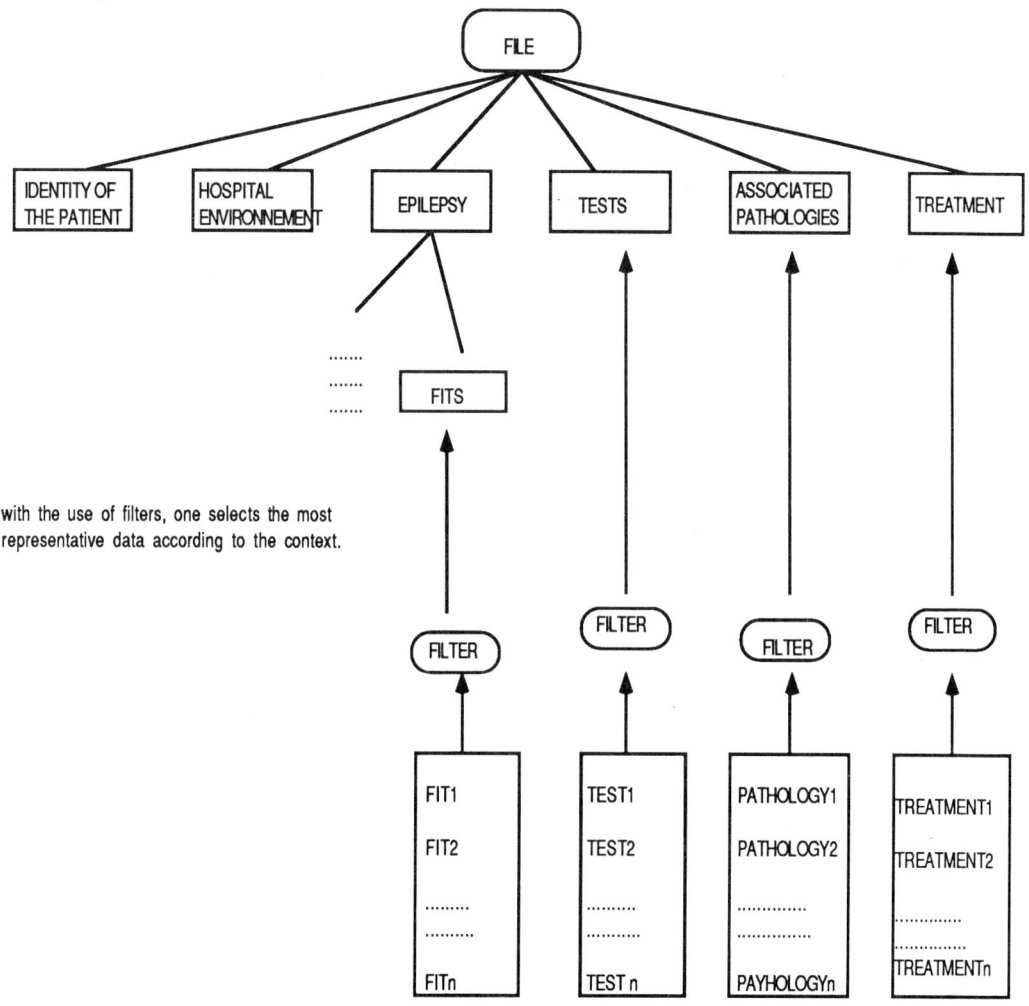

Figure 26.11 creation of a vision of the file

26.6 **Conclusion**

We have tried to show how an object centered approach could be used to synthesize the medical file of an epileptic patient. The importance of this kind of formalism in this work is that, besides the advantages it offers in the representation of declarative knowledge, it integrates procedural attachments which, combined with pattern-mathing enables the realization of processing similar to those done with production rules. One can however be confronted with the problem of memory size needed to implent such a system. In the case of GIDE, this problem is alleviated in sofar as in a work-session, the system handles only one file and not the whole set of files in the department. The problem of space used is therfore not very restricting in the first place. One can imagine a relational data base to store all the file of the department, using the system GIDE as an interface to handle the very file one wants a synthesis of.

References

Farreny, H. (1984). Les systèmes experts: principes et exemples. *Collection techniques avancées de l'informatique*, Cepadues edition.

Gardarin, G. & Viallet, F. (1987). Bases de donnée relationnelles Supra et cincom. Edition Eyrolles

Kristine, S. Th. (1986).Multiple inheritance, a structuring mechanism for data, process and procedure.

Minsky, M. (1975). A framework for representing knowledge, *MIT press*.

Noussi, R.,   Courant, M., & Robin, S. (1987). Formalisme de spécification des connaisances à base d'objet pour la synthèse des dossiers médicaux IRISA, *publication interne*, No 344

Rechenman, F. (1985).SHIRKA: mécanismes d'inférence sur une base de connaissances centrée objet, 5e congrès AFCET sur la reconnaissance des formes et l'intelligence artificielle, Grenoble nov. 1985.

Rechenman, F. Manuel d'utilisation de Shirka (*Document provisoire*; non publié)

Vignard, Ph. (1985). Un mécanisme d'exploitation à base de filtrage flou pour une représentation des connaissances centrée objet. *Thèse de 3è cycle IMAG*

Shortliffe, E. H.(1976). Computer-based medical consultation: MYCIN. American Elsevier.

DATA ANALYSIS AS AN AID TO LEARNING AND KNOWLEDGE BASE MAKING IN A MEDICAL FIELD

27.1 General presentation

At the moment, expert systems theory expects at least one human expert of a concerned domain. Nevertheless, there exist a few domains which are too vast, uncertain, incomplete and evolutive to be totaly mastered by any one specialist, and for which there do not exist experts able to construct a knowledge base usable as a knowledge engineering tool. However, it seems that assistance to reasoning and decision making is of paramount importance in such domains (particularly in the medical field).

We propose a knowledge extraction helping system with an application in medical genetics (Edwards & Buyse, 1986), (Veloso & Feijoo, 1986), (Rialle, 1985). This system aims at the production of inferential knowledge based on a pool of observed data such as syndromes, symptoms, frequencies, etc. On one hand, it offers the physician an assistance in his own approach to scientific research and, on the other hand, it constitutes a real automatic knowledge learning system. With this end in view, we propose a method and some tools for the exploration of the concerned domain descended from the Data Analysis (Benzecri *et al.*, 1981), (Macgibbon & Preus, 1979), (Gouvernet, 1979), (Preus & Ayme, 1983). In fact, the present work is situated at the cross-road of a number of scientific fields such as Medicine, Artificial Intelligence, Automatic Learning, Uncertain Reasoning, Mathematical modelling of decision problems, and Data Base theory.

One guiding idea of this work is that there is not a qualitative difference between knowledge which is elaborated and matured by any human expert and one which is stemmed from a mathematical analysis of experimental datas. Numerical methods of analysis such as Principal Coordinate Analysis, ROC-Analysis, etc., may give a point of view upon a question as relevant and useful as the expert one, and may safely and efficiently replace the latter when the domain is too vast. This point of view is reliable because of the explicit theories and experimental observations and verifications it is based on.

However, numerical analysis should not dissimulate the presence, and consequently the error source, of the expert who defines the variables to observe according to his proper experience.

27.2 Domain modelling

In the expert system point of view, Medical genetics is caraterized by: 1°) its vastness (several thousands of symptoms and syndromes), 2°) its uncertainty, 3°) its uncomplete state, 4°) the rapid increasing of knowledge. The domain modelling tries to keep in account these features and propose the following notions:

A - *Symptoms, symptomatical entities and scores*:

a - The symptom constitutes the basic element of the system from which the others will be elaboreted. In our application, symptoms are subdivided into four categories according to increasing levels of observation cost or observation difficulties. For this reason, every symptom is marked by a number comprised betweeen 1 and 4 with the following meanings:

1: *immediate clinic*: symptoms which are visible or identifiable without mediatory instruments (visual observation, by palping, etc.),

2: *extensive clinic*: identifiable symptoms by means of a mediatory instrument (mesure equipement, auscultation, etc.), in the place where the patient is observed,

3: *standard paraclinic*: symptoms which are revealed by a commonly used examination (like radiography) elsewhere than the place where the patient is observed,

4: *extensive paraclinic*: symptoms which are revealed by a long or expensive paraclinical examination (biopsy, scanner, NMR, etc.).

A symptom **s** corresponds to the occurrence of the event: "the symptomatical entitie **se** takes the value **v**": $s = \{ se \leftarrow v \}$.

b - a symptomatic entity (s.e.) is a spatio-temporal localization of symptoms. It often corresponds to an anatomical or functional localization where one expects to find symptoms or abnormalities corresponding to one or more illnesses. Symptomatic entities are arranged as a tree representing the human body . This s.e. tree induces a symptoms tree. In such a tree, the hierarchy corresponds to the imprecision level of the symptom descriptions (in the litterature, syndromes are often discribed with general or imprecise symptoms). The accurate symptoms are the leaves of the symptoms tree.

A symptomatical entity owns an oriented semantic axis (as shown on Figure 27.1) on which are distributed the various possibles values (ordinal values) of the symptoms. Thus, for each of the symptomatic entities, we may define a bijection between its semantical axis and the vectorial space **R**: to each ordinal value, we attribute an [**a priori**] chosen interval.The word **axis** points out a symptomatical entity's vectorial subspace.

c - a score (Robert *et al.*, 1986) is a grouping of a certain number of symptomatical entities corresponding to one of the following possibilities: a physiologic function, an anatomic localization, a similar abnormality in the body, etc.

Example: telorism

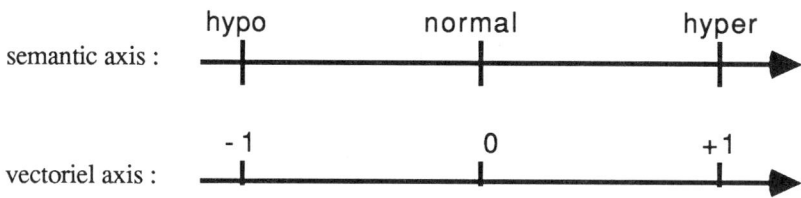

Each symptom will be represented by a vector:

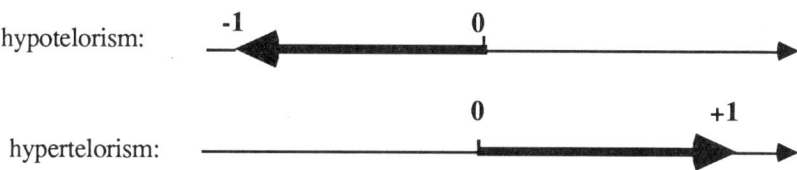

Figure 27.1.

The major interest of a score is that it allows one to strongly reduce the number of symptomatical entities and, consequently, it reduces the number of axes of the working space. A second interest is the possibility it offers to establish transversal links inside the s.e. tree. Indeed, in the pure s.e. tree, the links are only ascending or descending ones.Nevertheless, a number of s.e. may have a similar finality such as motionness, development, shape and so on.

B - *Syndromes*:

a - *Semiological representation*: this representation reflects the physician's vision of the patient, in which a syndrome is expressed as a more or less precise list of symptoms. If sd represents a syndrome and s_1 through s_n represent symptoms, we notice: sd = { s_1,..., s_n }.

b - *Vectorial representation*: this representation is adapted to a numerical analysis of sets of syndromes. It express the coordinates of a syndrome (called a syndrome-point) in a vectorial space whoses axes are constituted with symptomatical entities or scores.

Thus, if m represents the number of axes of the vectorial space, a syndrome will be represented as a m components vector in this space:

$$sd = \begin{pmatrix} x_1 \\ . \\ . \\ . \\ x_m \end{pmatrix} = x_1\,u_1 + ... + x_m\,u_m$$

The Descriptive Precision Coefficient (DPC) of a syndrome is calculated with the number **t** of terminal symptoms and the syndrome total number of symptoms:

$$DPC = \frac{t}{n} \qquad\qquad DPC \in [0, 1]$$

The DPC will take place in the choice of the syndromes which are possible causes in the patient symptomatic panel. This choice will have a consequential effect on the system's choice of the s.e. to propose for observation.

Finally, let us specify that a syndrome may have several DPC depending on which observation level or vectorial subspace the analysis is made. For exemple, a syndrome may be well defined at the first level (immediate clinic) of symptom observation (in this case the DPC of level 1 will be close to 1), at the very time when the same syndrome will be badly defined at level 3 (standard paraclinic) (in this case, the DPC of level 3 will be close to 0). This last precision reflects the fact that a syndrome may be better or les well described according to the level on which one observes it.

C - *working spaces : complete space and conjectural spaces*:

A working space is a multidimentional space (say m dimensions) constituted with the set of m s.e. and scores which are involved in the semiologic description of the syndromes. We distinguish two types of working spaces: the *complete space* (unique) and the *conjectural spaces*.

The complete space comprises the wholeness of the symptomatical entities and scores which are in the data base. This space will be essentially used by a static preparatory study of the complete domain (all syndromes in the space of all axes).

The conjectural spaces are the various subspaces involved in a particular diagnosis research. Each of them corresponds to the following couple of sets at a given time: (set of observations, candidate syndromes).

27.3 Preparatory static study

The preparatory static study consists of an exploration of the domain which is situated outside the dynamical learning process (that will be exposed in 27.4). This study intends to construct a part of the knowledge base which is directly deductible from the data base. It leads to a five step analysis, related to the five following spaces:

- <u>first step</u>: complete space,
- <u>second through fifth steps</u>: respectively the first through the fourth observation level subspaces.

For each of these steps, the process is:

1° Construction of the bidimentional matrix (syndromes x axes). This matrix comprises:
. in rows: every syndromes of the data base which has some not null components in the current level of observation,
. in columns: the coordinates of the syndromes in the current subspace.

2° Construction of the corresponding variance-covariance matrix and diagonalisation of this matrix.

3° Collection and analysis of the eigenvalues and eigenvectors of the matrix.

An eigenvector is expressed with the list of its components on the considered observation level. Let us define the word "contribution" as a synonym of "component value".

The analysis gives a list of the main normalized eigenvectors whose inertia is greater than 80 per cent of the whole cloud inertia and, for each of these eigenvectors, the sorted list of the axes which have the best contributions.

We extract from these lists the axes which appear the most frequently and with the strongest contributions. These axes are named *pertinent axes*.

Then, we propose to make an exploration of the syndrome cloud projected on plans determined by couples of pertinent axes. These various projections may be interpreted in a same way as a Principal Component Analysis, and may lead to various knowledges in the following examples:

> if score 60 > 9 then multiple pterygium syndrome
> if score 63 > 5 then Charlie syndrome
> if score 60 and score 63 are nul then palatal split (certainty 0.7)
> if score 62 = 0 then Apert syndrome or pterygium poplite

More generally, we may say that: 1°) a score allows us to pinpoint one or several isolated syndromes upon which it presents a maximum value; 2°) when two scores are nul, this allows us to discriminate in favour of a particular set of syndromes. Thus, such a couple induces a dichotomic approach which right away excludes half part of the syndromes set. The couples of selected scores are arranged in a decreasing order based on the discrimant power of the scores and s.e..The repetition of the dichotomic procedure on these sorted plans leads to a rapid decreasing of the remaining candidate syndromes set (Figure 27.2).

This preparatory static study has been applied to our data base and has induced the following results: the analysis of the 12 first eigenvectors given by the Jacobi algorithm revealed the 14 pertinent axes of prime importance from the 67 axes contained in the first observation level. Then we have successively analysed the projection on the entire syndrome set of the data base onto the 7 plans issued from the eigenvectors analyse. Each plan has permitted the separation of the syndromes into two significant groups: on one hand, those which had a projection on the origin of the axes, on the other hand, those whose projection were outside the origin. This analysis has resulted in the production of 7 dichotomic rules (notated: $DR_1,...,DR_7$) whose interest is to reinforce the patient observation process by prompting the physician to confirm or infirm the symptoms that belong to the pertinent axes. To know the absence or the occurrence of these symptoms will permit to rapidly select the subset which eventually contains the researched syndrome.

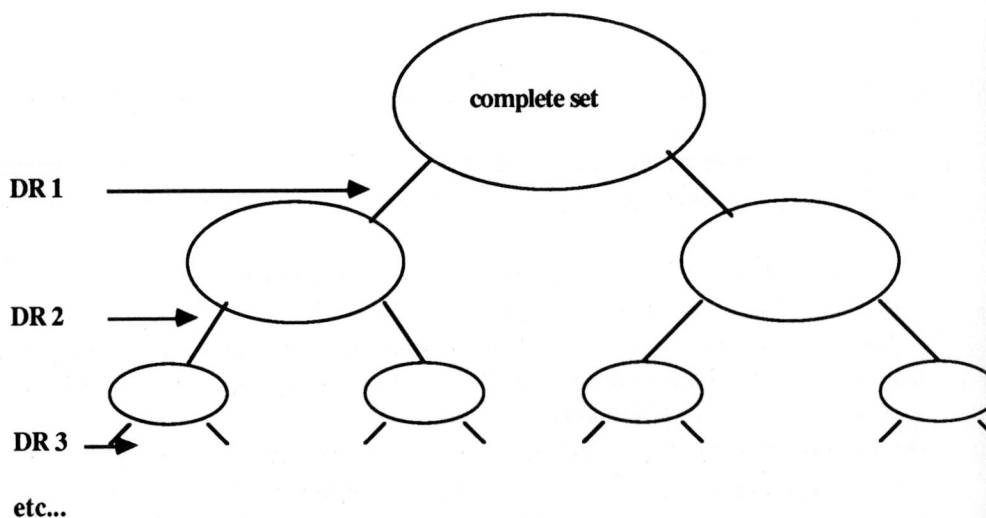

Figure 27.2.

27.4 Dynamic production of knowledge and learning

Dynamic production of knowledge (Walker & Blum, 1986) and learning (Michalsky, 1983), (Davis, 1979), (Politakis & Weiss, 1984) take place during a patient observation and diagnosis reseach. The system questionning and the answer analyse are made by phases squared with the various observation levels. At each phase, the system has to answer to this question : "is the Factual Base state (FBs) totally new, or has it been observed in the past ?". So, the meta-rule used as the basic postulate is:

IF   The actual state of the the Factual Base is known from the system

THEN   1° trigger a Data Analysis,
          2° memorise the couple (FBs, conclusion or question) deduced from
             the Data Analysis

ELSE   trigger the corresponding knowledge

Every time the system has produced an answer to the Factual Base state, by means of Data Analysis, this answer is stored in a Learning Base as a couple (FBs, consequence). The answer of the system is, more precisely, the second element of the couple (FBs, conclusion or question) and may be either a syndrome or syndrome set proposal, or an s.e. to propose the physician to observe.

The Learning Base is embedded in the Knowledge Base and exclusively gathers the Data Analysis obtained knowledges.

The Figure 27.3. shows the complete and ideal cycle covering the thorough study of a patient.

27.5 Prospective methodology

We are going to expose a methodology in a learning situation made of one to possibly four phases. This methodology is applicable under the hypothesis of a vast data base, made of the maximum number of symptoms and syndromes. The examples shown here are merely an illustration of the method. The latter include a procedural and a declarative aspect.

The analysis of the syndromes projection on the plans generated by the couples of pertinent axes of the first observation level (see the preparatory static study) has revealed the existence of two remarkable groups of syndromes on each of the 7 plans. These two remarkable groups are respectively composed of:
  - the syndromes that are situated at the origin of the axes (coordinate: 0,0),
  - the syndromes that have at least one non null coordinate.

Starting from this fact, we propose, as we will see in the first phase, a dichotomic approach of reduction of the candidate syndromes set. Here is the description of the first two phases.

First phase:

It comprises the generating process of the diagnosis hypothesis at observation level 1, and includes 3 steps:

- **step one**, data base initialising: The physician provides the system with the list of observed symptoms. The system complete this list with the symtoms that are situated over the observed symptoms in the symptoms hierarchy. This adding of less precise symptoms is necessary since many syndromes, in the litterature, are imprecisely defined with non terminal symtptoms (such as abnormal hands). These inexplicit symptoms are rarely those which are transmitted by the physician to the system. The observed symptoms such as precise congenital abnormalities may be seen as details, but nevertheless, they have to capture the syndromes referred to by less descriptive ones.

This step one of the first phase comprises a reinforcing process of the patient observation by mean of the level 1 pertinent axes. This process consists in the proposal of a series of complementary observations corresponding to the symptoms belonging to the pertinent axes and not belonging to the actual Factual Base. The confirmation or invalidation of these symptoms by the physician will speed up the the reduction of the candidate syndromes range since the corresponding axes are the most discriminant with regard to this range.

- **step two**, reduction of the candidate syndromes range by means of the dichotomic rules built up thanks to the preparatory static study. Theoretically, there may be an explosion of possible intersections (2^n intersections for n rules). In reality, this number has to be strongly decreased because of a number of empty intersections.

There are three types of ways from the root of the dichotomic tree to its leaves:
- the way leading to an intersection endowed with a lot of syndromes (more frequent type). This way causes the continuation of the process through the second phase.
- the way leading to a single syndrome or a restricted number of syndromes. This way causes the end of the analysing process and the proposal of this syndrome or range of syndromes for the physician's valuation.
- the way leading to an empty intersection. This case may square with the occurrence of a new syndrome.

The last two types result in the ending of the learning process, whereas the first one leads to a decreased range of syndromes which is offered to the second phase of the analysis.

- **step three**, fuller reseach of candidate syndromes by means of nearness analysis: this opreation is an analysis of nearness between the syndrome-points and the patient-point in the vectorial space. As a result of this analysis, we retain as as candidates the syndrome-points whose distance to the patient-point is lower than an experimentaly fixed threshold. This threshold is the radius of a sphere centered on the patient-point.

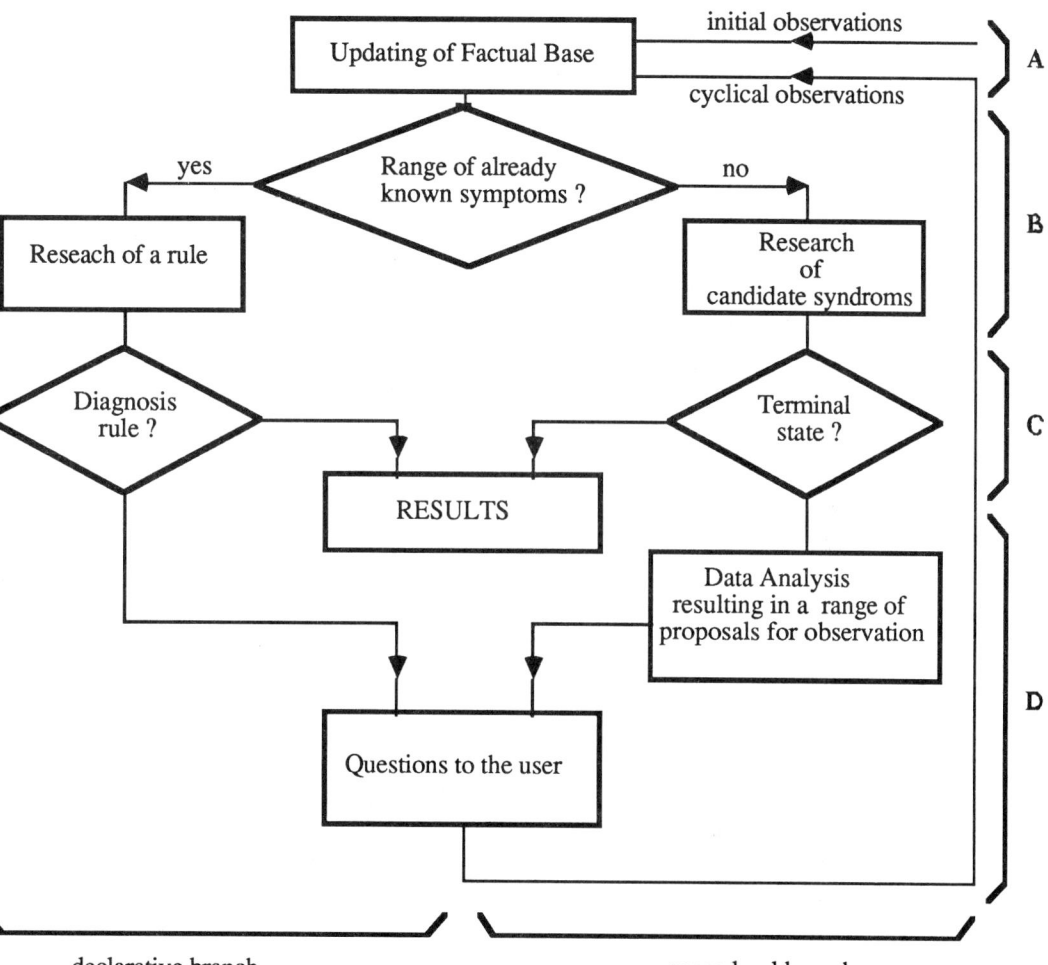

declarative branch   procedural branch

A : situation
B : action choice
C : test
D : actions

Figure 27.3.

The set A1 of the candidate syndromes constructed by nearness analysis may be completed by the set A2 of the syndromes that are directly selected by coincidence with the patient symptoms panel. If the set A2 - A1 is not empty, the system will fire a procedure to examine the axes which are very charged by the syndromes of this set.

The nearness research of candidate syndromes and the research by Factual Base coincidences are two methods that reinforce each other. Seemingly, it is possible to envisage the use of other methods. Equally, it is not out of the question that a complementary declarative process be used to strengthen the phase of generating hypothetical diagnosis.

At the end of this first phase, we obtein a complete selection of candidate syndromes. This selection may be empty or have only a few syndromes. In this case, the system proposes to the physician the results of its investigation. There is at this point the production of a new knowledge in so far as the observation panel has led to a terminal state of the enquiring process which is the failure of the system or the diagnosis proposal. After that, the physician has to decide if he retains or rejects this response in the Learning Base.

Second phase:

The second phase of this study intends to analyse the syndromes selection descended from the first phase. It consists of a Principal Components Analysis (PCA) of the projection of these candidate syndromes on the vectorial sbspace constituted from the second observation level axes.

The first two eigenvectors of the canonical PCA reveal the more discriminant axes. The reseach method of the pertinent axes lies in retaining the axes (number inferior to 4 or 5) that have the strongest contributions in the first eigenvector, then in the second one. This pertinent axes range allows the systems to make a request of complementary informations to the physician (as a confirmation or invalidation of the symptoms brought by these axes).

This action results in a new state of the Factual Base by the adding of new symptoms in their validated or invalidated aspect. As a consequence, this new state induces a reduction of the candidate syndromes set. Two ways are possible depending on the state of this revised syndrome set:

- either this set is empty, or has a single element, or is sufficiently restricted to be proposed as a result of the investigation. In the same manner as in the first phase, this possibility leads to the concluding of the process.

- or this set still contains a lot of syndromes. This case results in the activating of the third phase of the investigation which consists in the analysis of this set in the third observation level subspace, in exactly the same manner as in the second phase. The same actions may be repeated until the fourth level.

27.6 Conclusion

In this paper, we have dealt with a particular kind of scientific reseach field charactarized by the vastness of its knowledge object set, the rapid increasing of it, its uncertainty, and therefore its perpetual incompleteness. The Medical Genetics field is representative of such fields that in spite of their features need the production of a decision making knowledge.

As a response to this decision making knowledge production request, the use of the Data Analysis is justified because of the very nature and aims of this discipline. As a matter of fact Data Analysis concentrates a number of features able to bring solutions to the foreseen problem.   Namely :

- It is adapted to the processing of large data sets,
- it reveals empirical relations between variables,
- it furnishes a rigourous mathematical background to the data modelling,
- it may offer a spacial visualisation for complex situations or phenomena,
- therefore it produces valuable decision elements and counsels, capable of being admitted into a knowledge based system.

As a consequence, we may consider either the Data Analysis as an "expert entity" to whom we may propose observation datas to, and who gives back his conclusions, or as a rigourous and efficient tool, usable by a specialist to increase, reinforce or verify his personal knowledges.

Decision making as a goal is equally shared both by Data Analysis and by Expert Systems. So, it is not vain to associate the two in the domains where they are both efficient. This intention is all the more justified as if the expert were endowed of the capacity to mentally realise the data modelling, and construct the inertia matrix, he would obviously use such a capacity in his efforts to take a decision.

The integration of the Data Analysis in the expert system environment as a learning and knowledge base making tool does not go without some difficulties since this discipline is devoted to the treatment of numbers whereas expert systems are usually applied to the treatment of symbolic knowledges and variables. To this aspect of the problem, we have proposed a solution consisting to establish a bijection between the semantic and vactorial axes. It is obvious that the behaviour of the system depends on the art and the maner this bijection is realised. Nervertheless, the method has yet shown a certain number of results that augurs well of its pertinency and efficiency.

References

Benzecri, J.P. & all. (1981). Pratique de l'Analyse des Données. ed. Dunod, Paris, **1, 2, 3**.

Davis R. (1979). Interactive Transfert of Expertise: Acquisition of New Inference Rules. *Arificial Intelligence,* **12**, 121-57.

Edwards, C. N. & Buyse, M. L. (1986). Building a computerized international network for medical expertise: the birth defects information system. *Proceedings of IA-BIOMED 86 conference,* Centre de Recherche en Informatique Médicale, Montpellier (France), 115-9.

Gouvernet, J. (1979). Apport de Méthodes de Classification en Génétique Médicale, application aux maladies osseuses constitutionnelles. *Medical thesis,* Faculté de Médecine de Marseille (France).

Macgibbon, B. & Preus, M. (1979).The Distorded Shell Method of Clustering for Syndrome Classification. *American Journal of Human Genetics*, **31**, 498-507.

Michalsky, R.S. (1983). A theory and Methodology of Inductive Learning. *Arificial Intelligence,* 22, 111-61.

Politakis, P.G. & Weiss S.L. (1984). Using Empirical Analysis to Refine Expert System Knowledge Bases. *Arificial Intelligence,* **22**, 23-48.

Preus, M., Ayme, S. (1983). Formal Analysis of Dismorphism: objective methods of syndrome definition. *Clinical Genetics*, **23**, 1-16.

Rialle, V. (1985). Génération de Connaissances Expertes - Application à la Génétique Médicale. *Proceedings of the Ffth International Workshop on Expert Systems,* Avignon (France), **5**, 901-13.

Robert, C., Zarski, M. & Demongeot, J. (1986). Utilisation de la notion de score comme outil decisionnel en médecine, proposition pour la fabrication automatique de règles de production. *Proceedings of IA-BIOMED 86 conference,* Centre de Recherche en Informatique Médicale, Montpeliler (France), 234-44.

Veloso, M. & Feijoo, M.J. (1986). DYSMOR: Computer Based Differencial Diagnosis of Dysmorphic Syndromees.MEDINFO 86, *Elsevier SCientific Publishing,* North-Holland, 216-8.

Walker, M.G., Blum, R.L. (1986). Towrad Automated Discovery from Clinical Data Bases: the RADIX Projet. MEDINFO 86, *Elsevier SCientific Publishing,* North-Holland, 32-6.

USING CLINICAL DATAFILES IN BUILDING EXPERT SYSTEMS

Expert systems in medical decision making were up to now built with factual knowledge based on expert experience and in medical papers. We presently have at our disposal large clinical datafiles in the domains where expert systems may be anticipated; such files constitute the numerical expert-knowledge, complementary to the physician factual knowledge, and thereby we can't ignore it in building an expert system.

We propose, as a first use of such clinical data, to study how well some specific findings fit with the diagnoses we are interested in.

Clinical data will possibly at the same time provide us with few relevant unknown parameters (or variables, or scores) which summarises the information of many other parameters.

But rather than setting down high-sounding principles on the use of clinical datafiles in artificial intelligence, will review two cases illustrating extreme situations.

28.1 Building an expert system for coronary artery disease diagnosis.

When a patient has coronary disease, the first symptoms are, in most cases, chest pain or angina crisis whose semeiology has been famously described by Heberden in the London School Medicine. But among people suffering from such pains, 60 % of them only have a coronary disease. At the present time, to settle down a reliable diagnosis, physicians have to perform invasive examinations such as angiography or thallium scintigraphy. The clinical signs of pain are roughly used: risk factors have been determined (cf Diamond and Forester), according to age, sex and a three part classification of anginal pain: typical pain, atypical pain, nonanginal pain.

But what about using an computerized system to handle the numerous clinical signs of pain in the form of characteristic pain scores that have a good negative predicting power, to present patient without lesion undergoing angiography? In other words, does the detailed semeiology of pain constitute relevant findings for a coronary disease diagnosis expert system?

A 108 items questionnaire has been elaborated by cardiologists and 145 men answered to it: they all were infarct free and underwent an angiography in the same service during 1/10/84 → 30/5/85 period: 64 % of them had coronary artery disease.

As forecast, the univariate and bivariate analysis of the responses (means, standard deviations, correlations coefficients) were uninteresting for lesion diagnosis; but it pointed out that the group of 145 men of our population where analoguous to other groups mentioned in references.

We first focused on 59 workable binary questions and performed an unitary principal components analysis (unitary PCA). The first eigenvalue of the PCA explained 13.6 % of the total inertia of the 145 points-cloud in the hypercube of $\mathbb{R}^{59}$; it's not very good, though a unique variable represents at most 2.5 % of total inertia. In (1,2), (1,3), (1,4), (1,5) principal plans, the two sub-groups (people with lesions, people without lesion) mix in all part of the plan (cf Fig.28.1). Factorial discriminant analysis was also tried on these 59 variables, without any worth while results.

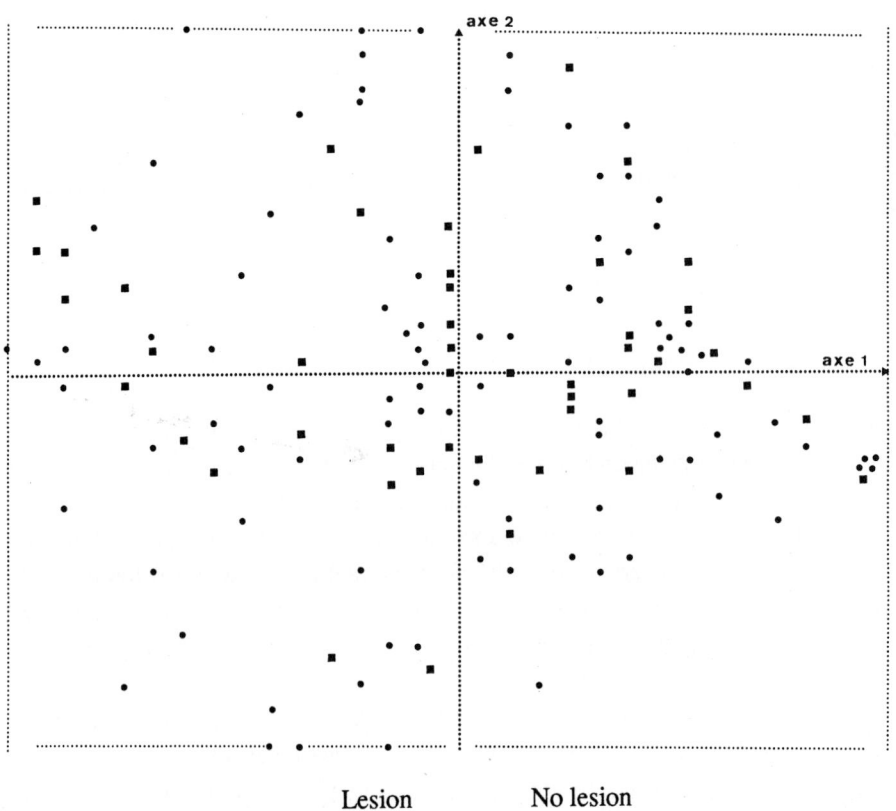

Figure 28.1. Canonical PCA with 59 variables: first principal plan representation.

So we tried analysis on subspaces of $\mathbb{R}^{59}$ defined by groups of questions; those were built by semantic association: center of pain, extension of pain, type of pain ...); all the provided bidimensionnal representation had the same structure (cf Fig.28.2): separately from some isolated points, one can see packs of points; looking in the datafile, it appeared that they had identical responses to all questions of the considered group of questions.The packs are different for each of the 8 performed PCA , but the percentage of disease is fairly 50 % in each pack: so it appears that the pain profiles emerging from these packs can't be of any help for diagnosing coronary lesion.

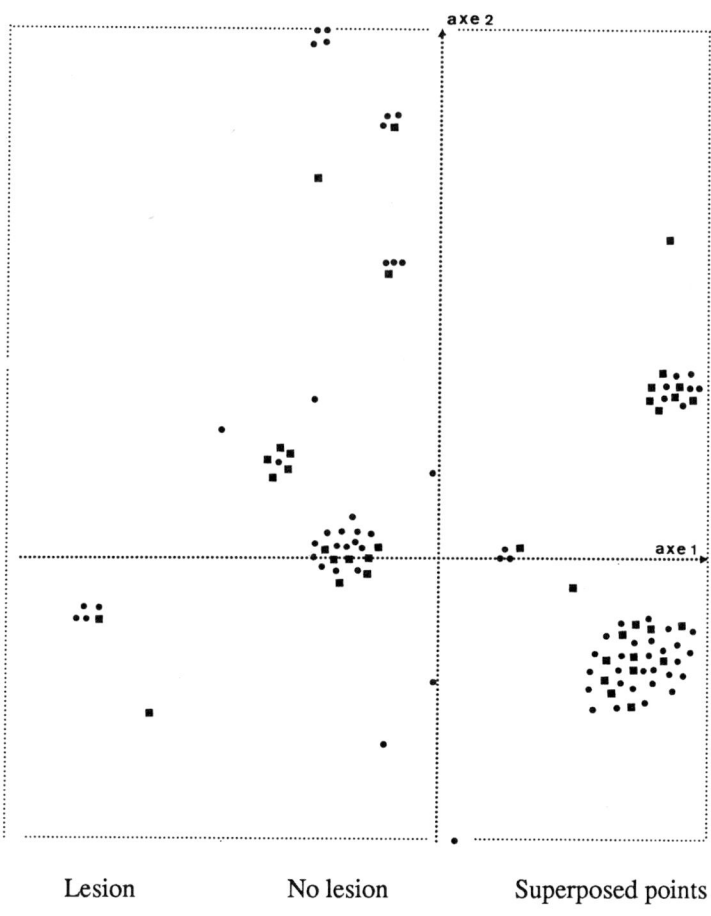

| Lesion | No lesion | Superposed points |

Figure 28.2. Chest pain

At this point, experts decided to give up building an expert system using such a detailed description of angina crisis: it appears that no combination of faint inference rules built with such signs would be reliable.

Coronary disease is a public health care problem; so it was worth trying the experiment constituted by analysing a clinical datafile (which was quite noninvasive for people who answered the questionnaire!), even if the chances of success were small.

28.2 Defining diagnosis of polyneuropathy

We now focus on a particular electromyographic examination on 8 nerves, providing 36 quantitative parameters, which is in favour of an expert system to manage them. Beside 'univariate rules', concerning single parameters, the electromyographists want to give a synthesis of these parameters and set a global three valued diagnosis: normality, moderate or severe polyneuropathy.

For this purpose, data have been collected in three groups of people: 30 of them form the check sample, 30 of them were chosen among people affected by chronical obstructive bronchopneumonia (BPCO group) and 30 of them affected by chronical respiratory deficiency (IRC group). The BPCO group was considered, before any electromyographic measurement, to be the moderate polyneuropathy one and in the same way, the IRC group was considered to be the severe polyneuropathy group.

We first wanted to check if, with respect to the electromyographic parameters, these three groups could effectively be separated. We had to consider the age as 37th parameter: age means are significantly different between groups and electromyographic parameters depend on the age of the patient; it could then occur that age is the main cause of the difference between the three groups.

A factorial discriminant analysis (FDA) was performed (see Fig.28.3) on the 37 variables and 90 individuals. It appears that by linear combination of the 37 parameters, groups are well separated; with the usual FDA reassignment using the neareast (for Mahalanobis distance) group center, 98 % of points are correctly classified. The BPCO groups appears clearly on Figure 28.3 as a middle group between the check sample and the IRC group. At this point, we consider that BPCO and IRC diseases provide us with a sample of polyneuropathy having varied intensity level. Furthermore, the discriminant functions are not highly correlated with age.

But the division into three groups (normal, moderate, severe) is artificial with regard to polyneuropathy continuous parameters, and the discriminant components are unstable and do not allow prevision (this frequently occurs when the qualitative parameter in the FDA is an ordinal one).

So we performed a normed PCA on the 37 parameters (cf Fig. 28.4 for individuals representation). The first principal component is the only one which is well correlated with the variable indicating normality, moderate or severe polyneuropathy; furthermore, this first principal component C_1 has the following properties:

- C_1 explains 33 % of total inertia, which is very good (a single parameter explains 2.7 % of inertia)
- classifying the 90 individuals according to decreasing values of C_1 has been

considered by electromyographists as a classification according to the severity of polyneuropathy.

- the importance of the age in C_1 cannot be disregarded but age is not an important part in C_1 values calculus.

- C_1 seems to be stable in the way that it provides a good classification for 'supplementary points'.

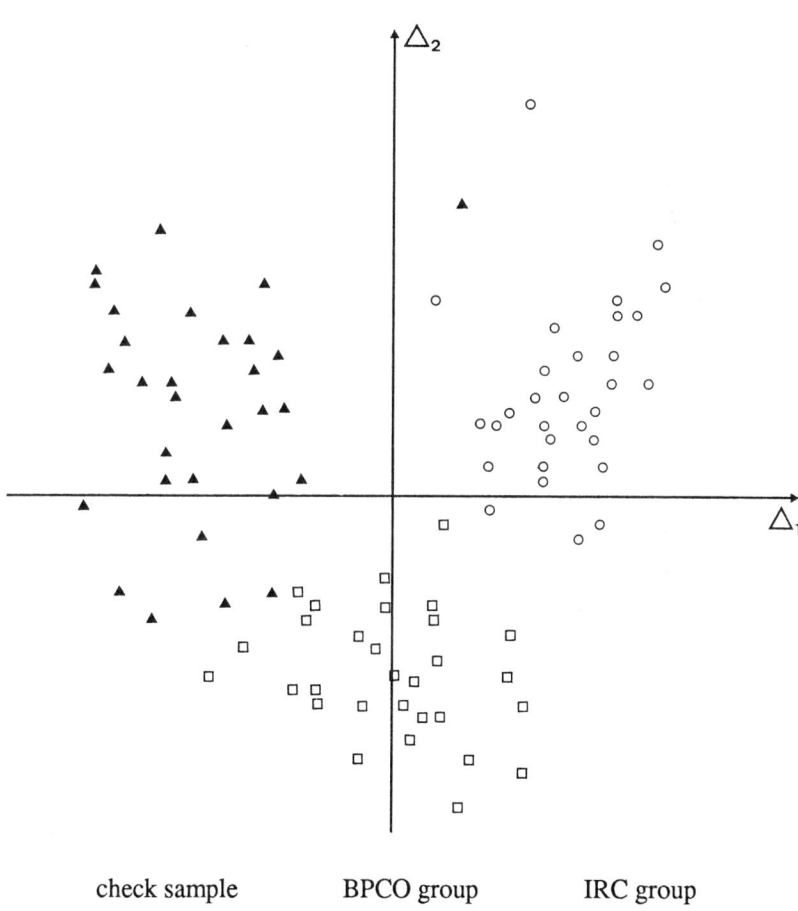

check sample   BPCO group   IRC group

Figure 28.3. FDA (37 variables, 90 individuals)

A three valued diagnosis, such as it was firstly specified, may have been reached with numerous rules of following type:

If $X_0 < \alpha_1$ and $X_{i1} \in I_1 , \dots , X_{ik} \in I_k$, then moderate polyneuropathy

If $X_0 > \alpha_1$ and $X_{i1} \in I_1' , \dots , X_{ik} \in I_k'$, then moderate polyneuropathy

If $X_0 < \alpha_0'$ and $X_{j1} \in I_1 , \dots , X_{jk} \in J_k$, then moderate polyneuropathy

.

.

.

etc

.

.

.

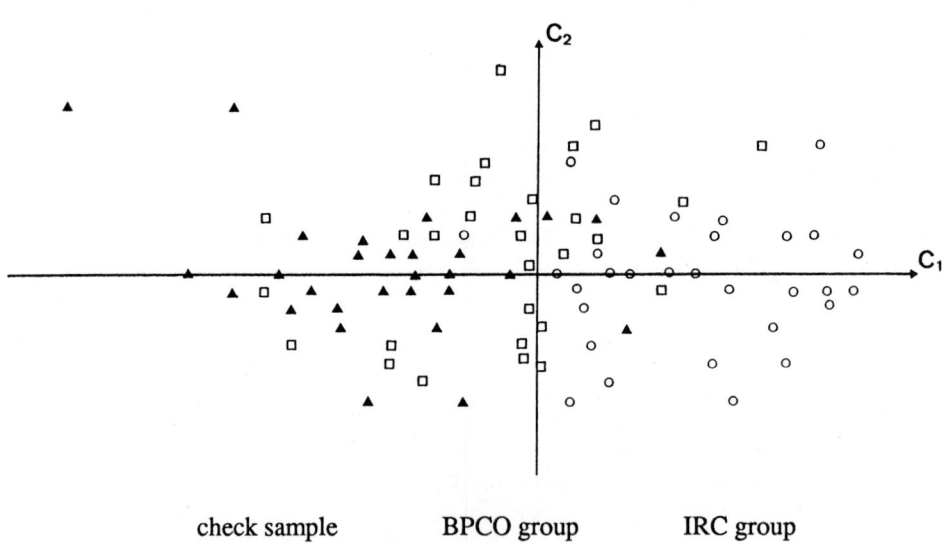

check sample   BPCO group   IRC group

Figure 28.4. Normed PCA (37 variables, 90 individuals)

All these rules are resumed by two or three rules on C_1 cut off's. Furthermore, the value of C_1 gives a more precise information than the three valued diagnosis (normality, moderate, severe)

Conclusion

Performing data multivariate analysis may avoid waste of time in managing irrelevant parameters. It may also allow to compact numerous rules and by the way avoid classical rules integration problems. Furthermore the analysis, providing new non-observable parameters (the PCA or FDA components) enlightens the diagnosis problems that automatic calculation have to face.

References

Diamond, G. & Forester, J. (1979). Analysis of probability as an aid in the clinical diagnosis of coronary artery disease. *The New England Journal of Medecine*, 1350-8.

Fouillet, P. & Reynes, J.F. (1986). Evaluation d'un protocole des polyneuropathies à partir de l'étude électrophysiologique de huit nerfs. *Mémoire*, Grenoble.

Greenberg, P. (1984). Comparison of the multivariate analysis and ladenza system for determination of the probability of coronary artery disease. *The American Journal of Cardiology*, **53**, 493-6.

Rialle, V. (1985). Génération de connaissances expertes. Application à la génétique médicale. *Proceeding V International workshop on expert systems and their applications*, Avignon, **II**,   901-15.

Robert, C., Zarsky, J.P., Demongeot, J. (1986). Utilisation de score comme outil décisionnel en médecine, *Proceedings A.I. Biomed 86*, Montpellier, 234-44.

Vignon, C. (1986). Intérêt d'un questionnaire dans l'évolution de la maladie coronarienne. *Thèse pour le doctorat en Médecine*, Lille.
Weintraub, W. (1985). A sequential approach to the diagnostic of coronary artery disease using multivariate analysis. *American Heart Journal*, 999-1005

AID FOR DIAGNOSIS OF ACUTE CRANIAL TRAUMA

29.1 Aim of this study

Starting with a blank expert system, we have tried to create an aid system to help the non-specialist practitioner to interpret the CT scan in the diagnosis of serious cranial trauma. The patients concerned arrive in emergency (often at night) as the result of accidents.

The speciality of the system resides in the considerable amount of information obtained from the CT scan images of the patient on the one hand, and from those stored in the mass memory and representative of standard cases on the other hand.

29.2 The problem

Cranio-cerebral traumatic lesions are very frequent. They often affect young people who must be seen very rapidly so that, they have the best possible hope of survival and socio-professional recovery.

They have been chosen as this study since they have the following advantages:

- a very wide range of CT scan pictures (CT scan proved to be the key exploration factor in cerebral traumatology).It is possible to compare the diagnosis with the report on any surgical operation later.

- the typical patient is taken to be one arriving in emergency at night suffering from recent cranio-cerebral trauma. Lesions of vital organs other than those caused by the cranial trauma, are considered as having been treated previously in order of seriousness. The information at our disposal comes from the medical file:

- civil status, medical history,the circumstances of the accident, the evolution of the consciousness of the patient

- the clinical examination : the depth of coma, the dilatation of pupil(s), reflexes, motility, cranial X-rays ...)

However this data does not lead to the localization and type of the cerebral lesions.

Using this data, the doctor can decide whether or not to carry out a CT scan as a night emergency. This examination is carried out as a pre-requisite for a emergency surgical operation.

29.3 Characteristics of the general expert system

The expert system (ES) is that of the Institute of Emergency Technology (IET) distributed by Control Data. ES is roughly patterned on the EMYCIN expert system. It does have strong backward chaining if / then rules,weaker forward chaining or data driven rules, and it allows certainty factors.

The major components of an ES rule file are:
- PARAMETERS, including GOALS which describe data values.
- RULES, including B-RULES, F-RULES, B-TABLES and F-TABLES, which prescribe the conditions needed to CONCLUDE a new value or action.
- MODULES which are groups of rules and parameters and functions..
- Optionally, you can also define your own LISP functions, using DE.

The options available with each ES component are briefly :
GOALS : the GOALS list shedules the overall process and should be listed first.ES processes each goal element sequentially.

Goals are either :
PARAMETER names which ES attempts to find values for or
LISP functions which are then executed.

PARAMETER : each data value whether an input value, an intermediate value or a goal value, needs to be defined. A parameter consists of a name and zero or more optional fields. When ES needs a value for a parameter, it examines the possible options in the following order until a value is found.
INITIAL-VALUE : a value for a function executed at file load time.
DO-BEFORE : LISP functions, eg.window-clearing - no value set
PROCEDURE : LISP functions - not commonly used - may set values
DEFAULT : LISP values or functions - always sets value
PROMPT : 1 or more lines of text or functions to show message
HELP : 1 or more lines to display if the user enter HELP
MULTIVALUED : indicates the parameter will accept multiple answers
MENU : numeric menu items presented
DO-AFTER : - at this point, the parameter already has a value.
                      - consists of 1 or more LISP functions,often window functions. No new
                      value is set unless via a CONCLUDE.

EXAMPLE :
(parameter ?recherche-s1)
(parameter s12 multivalued)

(translate "LOCALISATION SIGNS")
  (menu   ("unilateral dilatation of the pupil" mu)
            ("electroencephalographic signs" se)
            ("none of these signs" no))
 prompt "does the patient show one or more of these signs ?"))

MODULE : this is a special form of a parameter,but can also be called as the function (ES-module "rule-file" delete-option). It allows you to segment the rule files into groups which can then be invoked immediately by requesting a value for the module. This also allows :

   - ooping and repetition of groups of rules

   - dynamic loading into memory only if used and optionally deleting the rules from memory after execution if memory is limited. May need EXTERNAL-PARAMETER to identify parameters defined in other files.

B-RULE, F-RULE : these are the if / then structures in which the heuristics are actually specified in simple Lisp code format. Rules have these components : a name, IF, THEN, an optional TRANSLATE, and an optional Certainty or Attenuation Factor which defaults to 100.

  IF 1 or more LISP clauses which have an implicit AND relation

  THEN 1 or more LISP clauses - usually a CONCLUDE call.

  B-RULE or backchaining rules are examined by ES when it needs to find a value for a parameter.

    F-RULE or forward-chaining rules are executed whenever any value has been CONCLUDEd.

EXAMPLE :
```
(b-rule regle-d4
    (if (= i-1 'yes'
       (= vig 'clouded consciousness')
       (= s12 'no'))
    (then (conclude ?scanner 'oui )
          (tableau-clin )
    (ptb " CT SCAN SHOULD BE DONE SOON" )
    (cr)    (ptb "---->")
  (console-in )
    ( setq position-lesion 'nil) ))
```

B-TABLE, F-TABLE : when you need a series of rules, each of which represents a different combination of parameters and values - in effect a decision table - the table is a compact spreadsheet-like format specifying the rules. ES will convert these entries into the appropriate rule form.

FUNCTIONS : when you need additional features, you can easily define them in the usual Lisp method (using DE or DF). Functions are best used for routine procedures, such as reading or writing to a file or database.

29.4 Clinical parameters

The principal parameters chosen are:
- the neurological antecedents (signs of intracranial hypertension such as headaches and vomiting....) ; the presence of these signs may lead us to suspect the presence of a pre-existing cerebral lesion   (a tumor for example)
- the associated lesions other than the neurological ones : a patient suffering from a trauma (e.g. as a result of a road accident) often suffers from non-cranial lesions.In an emergency department,these lesions are of course treated according to their importance for survival.
- the state and evolution of wakefulness (which are of considerable importance since they enable the doctor to get an idea of the degree of suffering of the patient and its evolution). Four possible states can be listed : normal consciousness, clouded consciousness, stage 3 coma or
deep coma. The evolution of consciousness can be stable, improve or get worse.
- signs of localization : these signs indicate a lesion localized in one of the cerebral hemispheres. There may be homolateral signs (e.g unilateral dilatation of the pupil,localized electroencephalographic signs) which indicate a lesion on the side of the symptoms and controlateral signs which indicate a lesion on the opposite side (e.g. motility deficit, Babinski sign, focal epilepsy, displacement of the medial echo).

29.5 The method chosen

We have worked out a method in conformity with the human expert in three principal stages (which can be assimilated to three metarules).
1) We center the case studied.We admit the possibility of a wrong diagnosis if the patient has a neurological history.
2) We establish the urgency of the CT scan as a result of the data from the clinical examination (state of consciousness, signs of localization., worsening of the state of consciousness).
3) At this stage,we determine the type and localization of the traumatic lesions.
type of lesion: the user must follow the doctor's method:
- positioning of the density window level to search of blood collections,

- examination of hyperdensities as a result of the presence of blood from the periphery towards the interior of the cranium, control of density value

- simple semiological analysis (up against the cranium, inward concavity or convexity,).

- comparison of the results with the clinical data., analysis of medial structures displacement

- proposal of a reference image .

localization of the lesions : we suggest the following method :

- four schematized horizontal sections of the cranium are selected vertically.The user decides which of them tallies with the largest blood concentration.

- a schematized horizontal section divides the cranium up into ten zones.The user will have to choose the zone(s) occupied by the treated blood concentration.

If necessary, the system then starts over again for a secondary or tertiary haemorrhage lesion. At the end it proposes a diagnosis and prints a record of all the data obtained.

29.6 The material used

The system was put into an IBM XT computer with a 640 Kbytes central memory, a 320*200 graphic card, a high resolution colour monitor and a DGI1 numeration card. The numerization is carried out on 6 bits by pixel. The acquisition of an image is done in real-time and takes one video-image.

The graphic cards of the XT computer can only reproduce 16 levels of grey or false colours. The latter are not useable in radiography : the increase in contrast brought about by the sudden variation in shade is inacceptable and we are therefore obliged to reproduce the image in 16 shades of grey. There are two possibilities: the graphic card either gives a composite video signal (this is the case for the Tecmar Graphic Master card) or RGB signals in which case the TV monitor is connected to a peritel plug.

The images of 320*200 pixels on 16 levels of grey are somewhat mediocre,but this is nevertheless sufficient for the first stage of our study. Later we will go on to use 512*512 images on 8 bits (256 levels of grey) thanks to a card and a monitor which are independent of the computer.

29.7 The software

The diagnosis aid system comprises 77 parameters, 89 rules and 5 LISP functions. The ES inference engine works in a TLC-LISP environment. The data base is contained in a file of production rules noted as .RLS or .KB.

It is worth noting that these production rules have a certain number of qualities ; in particular they can call upon different functions in the .RLS file. These functions enable procedural actions to be started.

EXAMPLE :

```
(de attente ( )
   ( cr ) ( pb  "---->") ( console-in ))

(de affim  ( $im )
      ( screen-clear )
      ( cr )
      (prin2 "  PLEASE WAIT FOR NEXT  IMAGE")
      ( cr )
      (setq f ( open "nomim" 'update ))
      ( seek f 1 )
      (prin2 $im f )
      ( close f )
      (exec "c:\ dos\ mode co80" )
      ( exec "affim") (exec  "c: \ dos\ mode mono"))

(de fichier1 ( )
( setq sum2 ( reverse sum2 ))
(setq f ( open  "tabclin.txt" 'write ))
(prin3 sum2 f ) ( close f ))
```

It is also to be noted that the ES engine activates back-chaining rules (B-rules) just as well as forward chaining rules (F-rules). The latter are activated in priority every time the goal or sub-goal to be attained satisfies their conditions. When this possibility is added to the possibility of chaining dynamically, the list of goals to be attained, it is possible to influence the behaviour of the inference engine considerably. This means, in particular, that it is possible to create a non-monotonic behaviour mode for the engine. The first goal is to enable the user to back-step during the exploration of a case to permit one to rectify an mistake in a previous reply.

EXAMPLE :

```
( b-rule regle-a8
  ( if
      ( = hyperdensity 'yes)
      ( > blood density '85 )
      ( = localisation-periph  'yes)
      (< > density-form 'nil ))
  ( then  ( conclude ?recherche-localisation 'yes)
  ( cond (( = density-form 'blurred ) ( es-add-goals ?hypothese-les-p ))
        (( = density-form 'clean) ( es-add-goals  ?hypothese-les-p ))
        ( t ( es-add-goals ?hypothese-hed-hsd )))
```

29.8 Example of a medical case

A young man without any known medical history falls from a train at 7.30 pm. He is rushed to the nearest hospital suffering from an open fracture of the left ankle. He is conscious, his neurological examination is perfectly normal and the X-rays of the cranium do not show any fracture.

One hour after the accident, his state of consciousness deteriorates, he becomes comatose (P3) and an areactive right mydriasis appears. The local hospital requests his transfer to a specialized establishment and calls ahead to ask for an emergency cerebral scanner examination to be carried out.

If the expert system is consulted, it will first and check if an emergency CT scan examination is necessary :

"What is the patient's state of wakefulness ?"
Reply : Coma ≤ stage 3 ?

To obtain information on each stage of wakefulness, the practitioner can use the HELP function :

Conscious - clouded mentality : state of mental confusion, irresistible tendency towards sleep, responds to pain stimulae"

Coma less than or equal to stage 3 : abolition of consciousness, little reaction to pain stimulae.

Coma more than or equal to stage 4 : very serious state, consciousness and reflexes abolished, very serious anatomic problems.

"How has the patient's state of wakefulness evolved"?
Reply : Worsening

"Has there been a lucid interval" ?
Reply : Yes

"Does the patient present one or more of the following signs of localization :
1 . Unilateral mobility deficiency
2 . Unilateral Babinski sign
3 . Localized bout of epilepsies
4 . Deviation of the median echo
5 . None of these signs ?"
Reply : 5

"Does the patient show one or more of the following signs of localization :
1 . Unilateral mydriasis
2 . Localized electroencephalographic signals
3 . None of these signs ?"
Reply : 1

"On what side do they appear :
1 . Left
2 . Right ?"
Reply : 1

The expert system then examines all the symptoms shown by the patient and decides whether or not a scanner examination should be undertaken.

"The patient's clinical situation is as follows :
Comatose
Wakefulness worsening
Existence of a lucid interval
Signs indicating the presence of a controlateral lesion.

Emergency scanner examination is necessary."

The appointment for the emergency scanner examination is therefore accepted. The patient is transferred by ambulance and the scanner examination is carried out at 11.25 pm.

The expert system can now be used to help interpret the images.
"Are you in possession patient's CT scan :
1 : Yes
2 : No ?"
Reply 1

1 : Yes
2 : No ?"
Reply : 1

"Can you see one or more zones of pathological hyperdensity on your CT scan images
1 : Yes
2 : No
3 : Don't know ?"
Reply : 1

Measure density and indicate value = 71 UH

"Is this hyperdensity settled along the cranium ?
1 : Yes
2 : No ?"
Reply : 1

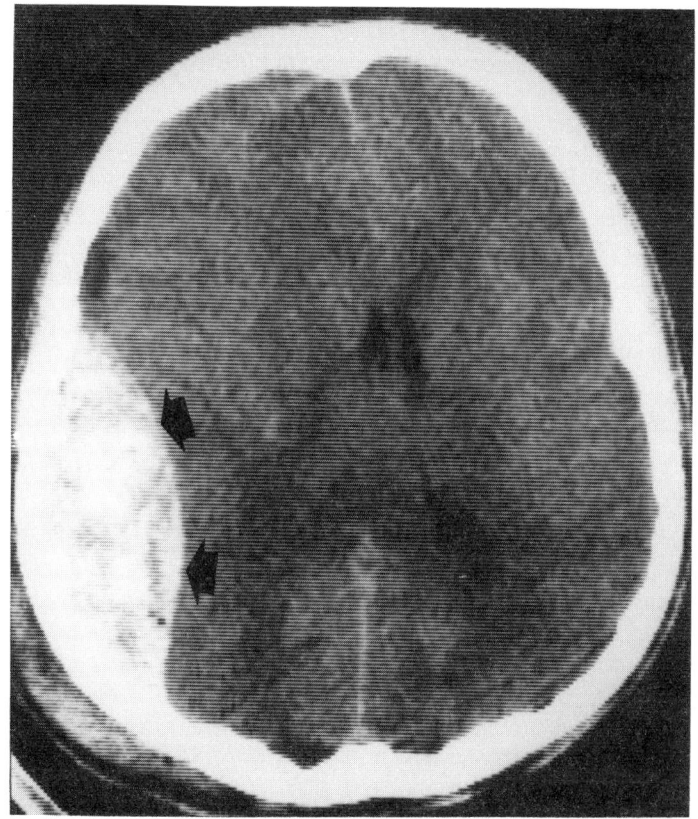

Figure 29.1. CT scan image for patient with cranial trauma : right hemisphere extra-dural hematoma

"Do you have CT scan images whose windows permit you to obtain the density of fresh blood ? (level from 20 to 100 UH)

"Is the observed hyperdensity :
1 : Convex inwards with clear edges and progressive settling against the cranium ?
2 : Concave inwards with clear edges and progressive settling against the cranium ?
3 : With blurred edges and non-progressive settling against the cranium ?
4 : With clear edges and/or non-progressive settling against the cranium ?
Reply : 1

"Which side is the observed hyperdensity localized on :
1 : Left
2 : Right ?"
Reply : 2

"Here is a standard image of an extra-dural hematoma. Its principal characteristics are as follows :
Opacity along the cranium, convex inwards, with clear edges and progressive settling along the cranium "

"Does the observed hyperdensity show the same characteristics ? "
Reply : Yes

"Can you see any displacement of the median structures or a decrease in the size of the ventricles ?
Reply : Median structures displaced."

"How are the median structures displaced :
1 : to the left
2 : to the right ?"
Reply 1

"Over how many contiguous sections does the hyperdensity show up ?"
Reply : 6

"The patient shows the following clinical picture :
- comatose
- Wakefulness worsening
- Existence of a lucid interval
- Signs indicating the presence of a contro-lateral lesion
Suggested diagnosis :
Patient suffers from a right-hemisphere extra-dural hematoma 6 cm high (given that the sections are 1 cm thick and contiguous)".

The patient then undergoes an emergency operation. Next day, the patient is doing well and CT scan is normalized.

29.9 Present development of the system

As a result of a first evaluation of the system in a hospital, several points have arisen :

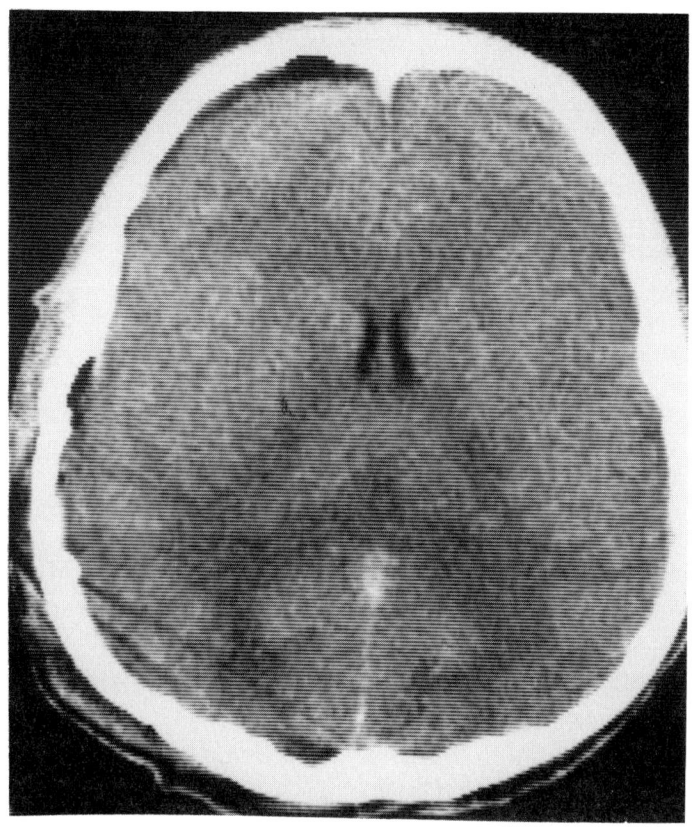

Figure 29.2. Post operatgive-CT scan : normalization of radiographic aspect.

1. Implementing of medical exploration:

the radiologist's role is to explore the X-rays as completely as possible. It is therefore unusual for him to diagnose haematomae and contusions without pointing to the possibility of cranial fractures. Special attention has to be given to the possible links between fractures and internal traumatic lesions e.g. the presence of air due to a depressed fracture of the skull or fracture of the sinus.

2. Improvement of dialogue possibilities:

This improvement can be made at several levels:

- the quality of the dialogue thanks to multiwindowing and synthesis-aid and filing.

- possibility of backstepping and correcting a mistaken reply.

- the coherency analyzer can be placed at the disposal of the cogniticien for the development of the data base (useless rule, rule contradictory with another one, rule requiring a choice by the expert).

- improvement brought about by an bank of images (> 1000): a document bank made up of a selection of file-images will surround the image with the clinical examination, case evolution, surgical report (if any), therapeutic indications and statistical information. This bank will be stored on a numerical optic disk (CD-WORM). Interactive software connected to the expert system will explore the bank.

3. Addition of pedagogical software:
This system can essentially be considered as a training tool. By having pedagogical software added to it, such as an automatic case generator and a reasoning analyzer, it can become a teaching tool.

All these improvements are presently in various states of development.

References

Bonnet, A. (1984). L'intelligence artificielle : Promesses et réalités, Inter-éditions, Paris.

Buchanan, E.H. & Shortliffe (1984). Rule based expert system. The Mycin experiments of the Stanford heuristic programming project, Ed. Addison-Wesley.

Clancey, W.J. (1983). The epistemology of a rule based expert system - a framework for explanation. *Artificial Intelligence*, **20**, 3, 215-55.

E.S., *manuel de références Control Data.*

Farreny, H. (1985). *Les systèmes experts, techniques avancées de l'informatique*, Cépadues éditions.

Gardeur, D. & Metzger, J. (1982). *TDM intracranienne*, livre IV, collection Ellipses, édition Marketing.

Laurière, J.L. (1986). *Intelligence artificielle: résolution de problèmes par l'homme et la machine*, Ed. Eyrolles.

Mc Carthy (1980). Circumscription - a form on non monotonic reasoning. *Artificial Intelligence*, **13**, 27-39.

More, R.C. (1985). Semantical consideration or non monotonic logic. *Artificial Intelligence*, **25**, 75-94.

Pitrat, J. (1985). *Textes ordinateurs et compréhension.* Ed. Eyrolles.

Voyer, R. (1987). *Moteurs de systèmes experts.* Ed. Eyrolles.

Winograd, T. (1982). *Language as a cognitive process.* I: syntax, Ed. Addison-Wesley.